ROTHMANS SNOOKER YEARBOOK 1986-87

Editor: Janice Hale

ROTHMANS
Queen Anne Press

A Queen Anne Press BOOK

First published in Great Britain in 1986 by
Queen Anne Press, a division of
Macdonald & Co (Publishers) Ltd,
Greater London House, Hampstead Road,
London NW1 7QX

A BPCC plc Company

Front cover photograph: Steve Davis (All Sport/Adrian Murrell)

Back cover photograph: Dennis Taylor congratulates Steve Davis on his Rothmans Grand Prix win (Rothmans UK Ltd)

All black and white photographs: Lancashire Picture Agency Ltd

British Library Cataloguing in Publication Data

Rothmans snooker yearbook.—1986–87–
1. Snooker—Periodicals
794.7'35'05 GV900.S6

ISBN 0-356-12362-6
ISBN 0-356-12363-4 Pbk

Typeset by Acorn Bookwork, Salisbury, Wiltshire

Printed and bound in Great Britain by Hazell, Watson & Viney Ltd,
Member of the BPCC Group, Aylesbury, Buckinghamshire

CONTENTS

ACKNOWLEDGEMENTS

The editor would like to thank the following for their assistance in compiling this book:
Clive Everton, editor of *Snooker Scene* magazine
Julie Kane, whose statistical research has been invaluable

FOREWORD
FROM ROTHMANS PUBLICATIONS LTD

When we introduced *Rothmans Snooker Yearbook* for the first time last year we could not have expected it to become a major success so quickly. The fact that it is now so popular is a great tribute to the editorial team, and in particular to the Editor Janice Hale.

Rothmans first became involved with snooker in 1984 through sponsorship of the Rothmans Grand Prix. That first event was won by Dennis Taylor and the 1985 tournament by Steve Davis. It is fitting that the quality of our champions on the table matches the quality of this publication, of which we are immensely proud.

We hope you continue to enjoy this most important of all snooker reference books.

FOREWORD FROM DAVID VINE

Twelve months ago when I wrote the foreword to launch the first edition of *Rothmans Snooker Yearbook* – the snooker world's newest and most comprehensive compendium – I talked about emotion, excitement and about the, at times, almost unbelievable stories the game produces for the fortunate few sitting in the theatre and the millions at home in their armchairs in front of the television set. To be honest, many of us thought we'd seen just about everything a snooker contest could provide. The last year has shown us how wrong we were.

We have watched the rise of Steve Davis to the point where he shares top billing with Britain's most famous sportsmen and beats them when it comes to sheer earning power; we have seen the tears of Dennis Taylor followed by the variety act which put fear into the hearts – and the wallets – of the 'professional' comedians; we will never forget the black-ball, world-final drama these two played out in front of a record-breaking television audience. Now we have something very different – snooker has done it again, it has given us Joe Johnson. What this pop-singing player will do in the season ahead is anyone's guess. It certainly won't be predictable.

This Yearbook will enable you to enjoy the game of snooker as much as those who play it for us, those who write about it for us – like Janice Hale, who has once again put so much care and detail into this second collector's item – and those, like me, who talk about it. In answer to some of your letters, hopefully we won't do too much of that in the coming season!

THE RANKING LIST

As both the number of professionals and the number of tournaments have increased, the game's governing body, the World Professional Billiards and Snooker Association, have had to devise some form of ranking list, not only to quantify the standings of the players but also to enable them to seed tournaments.

The ranking list is drawn up at the end of each season and, in a change from previous years, is based on performances over the past two seasons in events which are designated ranking tournaments.

To qualify for ranking status, a tournament must be open to all Snooker professionals. The tournaments that were taken into account in compiling the 1986 rankings were: The Goya Matchroom Trophy, Rothmans Grand Prix, Coral UK Open, Mercantile Credit Classic, Dulux British Open and, carrying more points, the Embassy World Professional Championship.

When seedings are decided for each tournament, the defending titleholder is automatically seeded one with the world champion, if he is not the defending titleholder, two. The remaining seeds are then taken, in order, from the ranking list.

To separate players who tie on ranking points, merit points, 'A' points and 'frames won' in the first round have also been introduced to the system which also favours performances in the immediate preceding season.

Players seeded 1–16 are exempt until the last 32 of the World Championship but in the other five events, players seeded 1–32 are exempt only until the last 64.

WORLD RANKING LIST 1986

	1984–85							
	Jameson	*Rothmans*	*Coral*	*Mercantile*	*Dulux*	*World*	*Ranking Points*	*Merit Points*
1 S. Davis	5R	½M 3R	5R	3R	½M 3R	8R	27	1
2 C. Thorburn	0	½M 4R	3R	4R	½M 1R	4R	16	1
3 Dennis Taylor	2R	½M 5R	1R	0	½M 2R	10R	20	1
4 T. Knowles	4R	½M 2R	2R	0	½M 1R	6R	15	1
5 J. White	2R	½M	2R	1R	½M	4R	9	1
6 A. Higgins	2R	½M	4R	1R	½M 3R	2R	12	1
7 W. Thorne	2R	½M 1R	2R	5R	½M	0	10	1
8 J. Johnson	½M 1R	½M	½M 1R	½M 3R	0	1M	5	3
9 K. Stevens	0	½M 2R	3R	1R	½M 4R	2R	12	1
10 T. Griffiths	1R	0	0	2R	½M	4R	7	½
11 T. Meo	1R	½M 1R	1R	0	½M 2R	2R	7	1
12 S. Francisco	½M 3R	½M 1R	½M	½M	½M 5R	1M	9	3½
13 N. Foulds	½M	½M 3R	0	0	½M	1M	3	2½
14 D. Mountjoy	0	½M 2R	1R	0	0	2R	5	½
15 R. Reardon	1R	½M 1R	2R	2R	½M	6R	12	1
16 R. Williams	½M	½M	½M 1R	½M 1R	0	1M	2	3
17 J. Parrott	0	½M	½M	0	½M	1M 4R	4	2½
18 J. Campbell	½M	½M	½M	0	0	1M	0	2½
19 J. Virgo	½M 1R	½M	0	½M 2R	½M	1M	3	3
20 E. Hughes	½M 3R	0	½M	½M 1R	½M 2R	1M	6	3
21 David Taylor	1R	½M 1R	1R	0	0	2R	5	½
22 M. Macleod	½M	½M	½M	½M 1R	½M 1R	1M	2	3½
23 C. Wilson	0	½M	½M 1R	½M 1R	0	0	2	1½
24 B. Werbeniuk	0	0	0	0	0	2R	2	0
25 E. Charlton	0	½M 1R	1R	0	0	2R	4	½

1985–86													
Goya	*Rothmans*	*Coral*	*Mercantile*	*Dulux*	*World*	*Ranking Points*	*Merit Points*	*A Points*	*Frames*	*Ranking Points*	*Merit Points*	*A Points*	*Frames*
3R	6R	6R	3R	6R	8R	32	0	0	0	59	1	0	0
6R	4R	2R	5R	2R	6R	25	0	0	0	41	1	0	0
4R	5R	4R	2R	1M	2M	15	3	0	0	35	4	0	0
1R	4R	3R	2R	1R	6R	17	0	0	0	32	1	0	0
5R	2R	4R	6R	1M	4R	21	1	0	0	30	2	0	0
2R	2R	2R	3R	4R	2R	15	0	0	0	27	1	0	0
2R	1M	5R	1M	5R	4R	16	2	0	0	26	3	0	0
3R	2R	1R	3R	1R	10R	20	0	0	0	25	3	0	0
1M	3R	3R	1M	2R	4R	12	2	0	0	24	3	0	0
2R	3R	3R	1M	3R	4R	15	1	0	0	22	1½	0	0
1M	3R	2R	1M	1R	2R	8	2	0	0	17	5½	0	0
1R	2R	2R	2R	3R	2M	10	2	0	0	17	3	0	0
4R	1R	2R	3R	1R	1R	12	0	0	0	15	2½	0	0
1R	1R	1R	4R	1M	2R	9	1	0	0	14	1½	0	0
1M	1M	1R	1M	1M	2M	1	6	0	0	13	7	0	0
1M	1R	2R	4R	2R	1R	10	1	0	0	12	4	0	0
3R	1M	1R	1M	2R	2R	8	2	0	0	12	4½	0	0
2R	2R	1R	2R	2R	2R	11	0	0	0	11	2½	0	0
1R	1M	1R	1R	4R	1R	8	1	0	0	11	4	0	0
1M	1R	1M	2R	1M	2R	5	3	0	0	11	6	0	0
2R	1R	2R	1M	1M	2M	5	4	0	0	10	4½	0	0
2R	1M	2R	1R	2R	2M	7	3	0	0	9	6½	0	0
2R	3R	1M	1M	1R	1R	7	2	0	0	9	3½	0	0
1R	1M	1M	2R	3R	1R	7	2	0	0	9	2	0	0
1M	1R	1M	1M	2R	2R	5	3	0	0	9	3½	0	0

	1984–85							
	Jameson	*Rothmans*	*Coral*	*Mercantile*	*Dulux*	*World*	*Ranking Points*	*Merit Points*
26 P. Francisco	0	½M	0	0	0	0	0	½
27 M. Hallett	0	½M 1R	½M	½M	½M	1M	1	3
28 D. Martin	0	½M	0	0	½M 1R	0	1	1
29 D. Reynolds	½M	½M 2R	0	0	½M	1M	2	2½
30 B. West	–	–	–	–	–	–	–	–
31 S. Longworth	0	0	0	½M 1R	½M	0	1	1
32 J. Wych	0	0	0	0	0	0	0	0
33 D. Fowler	½M	0	½M	0	½M	0	0	1½
34 J. Spencer	0	0	0	0	½M	0	0	½M
35 S. Duggan	0	0	0	0	0	0	0	0
36 P. Mans	0	0	0	0	0	0	0	0
37 T. Drago	–	–	–	–	–	–	–	–
38 M. Gauvreau	½M 1R	0	½M	½M	0	0	1	1½
39 D. O'Kane	½M	0	0	0	½M 2R	1M	2	2
40 S. Newbury	½M 1R	0	0	0	½M 1R	0	2	1
41 W. King	0	0	½M	½M 2R	0	0	2	1
42 P. Fagan	0	0	0	½M	0	1M 2R	2	1½
43 M. Wildman	0	½M	0	0	½M	0	0	1
44 G. Scott	0	0	0	½M	0	0	0	½
45 B. Harris	0	0	0	0	½M	0	0	½
46 R. Edmonds	0	0	0	0	0	1M	0	1
47 F. Davis	0	0	0	0	0	0	0	0
48 P. Browne	0	0	0	½M	0	0	0	½
49 T. Chappel	0	0	½M	0	0	0	0	½
50 G. Cripsey	0	0	0	0	0	0	0	0
51 S. Hendry	–	–	–	–	–	–	–	–
52 G. Miles	0	½M	0	0	½R 1M	0	½	1½
53 R. Chaperon	0	0	0	0	½M 1R	0	1	½
54 M. Bradley	0	0	0	0	½M 1R	0	1	½
55 T. Jones	0	½M	½M	0	0	1M	0	2
56 W. Jones	½M	0	0	0	½M	1M	0	2
57 T. Murphy	0	0	½M	0	0	0	0	½

1985–86													
Goya	*Rothmans*	*Coral*	*Mercantile*	*Dulux*	*World*	*Ranking Points*	*Merit Points*	*A Points*	*Frames*	*Ranking Points*	*Merit Points*	*A Points*	*Frames*
1A	2R	1R	2R	2R	2M	7	2	1		7	2½	1	
1M	1R	1R	1R	1R	2R	6	1			7	4		
1R	1R	1R	1R	1R	1R	6	0			7	1		
2R	1M	1R	1M	1R	1R	5	2			7	4½		
4F	1M	3R	1R	1M	2M	4	4	0	4	4	4	0	4
1M	2R	1M	1A	1R	2M	3	4	1		4	5	1	
1M	1A	1M	1M	3R	2M	3	5	1		3	5	1	
1M	1R	1R	1M	1R	1R	3	3	0	0	3	4½		
1R	1M	1R	1M	1M	1R	3	3	0	0	3	3½		
3R	1M	1A	1A	1M	1M	3	3	2	0	3	3	2	0
1M	1M	1M	1R	1R	1R	3	3			3	3		
2F	2R	1R	4F	1M	1A	3	1	1	6	3	1	1	6
1A	1A	1A	2R	1A	2M	2	2	4		3	3½	4	
1M	1M	1M	1R	1M	2M	1	6			3	8		
1M	1M	1M	1A	1R	2M	1	5	1		3	6	1	
1R	1A	1M	1M	1A	2M	1	4	2		3	5	2	
1M	1A	1M	1A	1R	1A	1	2	3		3	3½	3	
1M	1R	1M	1M	1R	2M	2	5			2	6		
1R	1R	1A	1A	1M	1M	2	2	2		2	2½	2	
1R	1R	1A	1M	1M	1A	2	2	2		2	2½	2	
1A	1R	1M	1A	1A	1R	2	1	3		2	2	3	
1A	1A	1R	1R	1M	1M	2	2	2		2	2	2	
1A	1A	1M	1R	1R	1A	2	1	3		2	1½	3	
1R	1M	1R	1A	1A	1A	2	1	3		2	1½	3	
1M	1F	1R	1R	1A	4F	2	1	1	5	2	1	1	5
1A	4F	2F	1R	1A	1R	2	0	2	6	2	0	2	6
1M	1R	1M	1A	1M	1M	1	4	1		2	5	1	
1R	1A	1A	1M	1M	1M	1	3	2		2	3½	2	
1R	1A	1M	1M	1M	1A	1	3	2		2	3½	2	
1M	1M	1M	1R	1M	1M	1	5			1	7		
1M	1R	1M	1A	1M	1M	1	4	1		1	6	1	
1R	1A	1M	1M	1A	2M	1	4	2		1	4½	2	

58 (60) P. Medati 1R-4½M-2A; 59 (80) J. Van Rensberg 1R-3M-3A; 60 (81) M. Gibson 1R-3M-2A; 61 (81) B. Mikkelsen 1R-3M-2A; 62 (67) John Rea 1R-2½M-3A; 63 (65) V. Harris 1R-2½M-3A; 64 (57) I. Black 1R-2M-3A; 65 (–) J. O'Boye 1R-2M-2A-8F; 66 (100) R. Bales 1R-2M-1A-9F; 67 (47) I. Williamson 1R-2½M-4A; 68 (53) L. Dodd 0R-5½M-2A; 69 (62) R. Foldvari 0R-4½M-3A; 70 (38) E. Sinclair 0R-4½M-2A; 71 (69) J. McLaughlin 0R-4½M-2A; 72 (–) D. Gilbert 0R-4M-1A-7F; 73 (46) J. Donnelly 0R-3M-3A; 74 (45) C. Roscoe 0R-3M-3A; 75 (43) M. Morra 0R-3M-3A; 76 (74) J. Fitzmaurice 0R-3M-3A; 77 (42) M. Watterson 0R-3M-2A; 78 (97) M. Darrington 0R-3M-1A-4F; 79 (48) G. Foulds 0R-2M-4A; 80 (–) S. Simngam 0R-2M-3A-2F; 81 (99) D. Sheehan 0R-2M-1A-5F; 82 (–) Jim Bear 0R-2M-1A-4F; 83 (64) J. Dunning 0R-1½M-1A; 84 (85) B. Oliver 0R-1M-5A; 85 (48) J. Meadowcroft 0R-1M-5A; 86 (77) G. Rigitano 0R-1M-5A; 87 (54) M. Fisher 0R-1M-5A; 88 (71) B. Kelly 0R-1M-5A; 89 (–) O. Agrawal 0R-1M-4A-4F; 90 (63) E. McLaughlin 0R-1M-4A; 91 (–) P. Houlihan 0R-1M-3A-9F; 92 (102) J. Hargreaves 0R-1M-2A-10F; 93 (88) D. Hughes 0R-1M-2A-10F; 94 (–) M. Smith 0R-1M-2A-7F; 95 (–) G. Jenkins 0R-1M-1A-4F; 96 (–) G. Watson 0R-1M-0A-8F; 97 (–) P. Thornley 0R-1M-0A; 98 (72) F. Jonik 0R-0M-6A; 99 (79) D. Chalmers 0R-0M-6A; 100 (73) C. Everton 0R-0M-6A; 101 (90) T. Kearney 0R-0M-4A-9F; 102 (–) G. Wilkinson 0R-0M-3A-10F; 103 (76) Jack Rea 0R-0M-3A-0F; 104 (86) P. Burke 0R-0M-2A-17F; 105 (87) J. Caggianello 0R-0M-2A-0F; 106 (93) P. Watchorn 0R-0M-1A-19F; 107 (96) D. Greaves 0R-0M-1A-15F; 108 (95) D. Mienie 0R-0M-1A-14F; 109 (92) B. Demarco 0R-0M-1A-13A; 110 (–) J. Rempe 0R-0M-1A-2F; 111 (75) P. Morgan 0R-0M-1A-0F; 112 (–) R. Grace 0R-0M-1A-0F; 113 (91) M. Parkin 0R-0M-0A-12F; 114 (94) B. Bennett 0R-0M-0A-11F; 115 M. Hines; 116 I. Anderson; 117 J. Giannaros; 118 L. Heywood

Steve Davis, who heads both the Ranking and the Money List

MONEY LIST

	Carlsberg	Langs	Goya	Rothmans	Canadian	Coral	Hofmeister
1 S. Davis	–	–	5,250	50,000	9,000	24,000	20,000
2 C. Thorburn	5,000	10,500	35,000	15,000	5,000	1,800	6,500
3 J. White	11,000	3,250	21,000	3,750	3,375	7,200	875
4 Dennis Taylor	–	1,750	10,500	30,000	15,000	7,200	6,500
5 J. Johnson	–	–	5,250	3,750	–	1,162	1,750
6 W. Thorne	–	6,500	2,625	1,093	–	14,400	6,500
7 T. Knowles	–	1,750	1,531	15,000	3,375	3,600	1,750
8 T. Griffiths	–	–	2,625	7,500	3,375	3,600	6,500
9 A. Higgins	7,500	1,750	2,625	3,750	–	1,800	875
10 T. Meo	–	–	1,531	3,750	–	1,800	20,000
11 K. Stevens	–	–	765	7,500	–	3,600	1,750
12 N. Foulds	–	–	10,500	2,421	–	1,800	3,250
13 R. Reardon	–	–	765	1,093	5,000	1,162	11,000
14 D. Mountjoy	–	–	1,531	2,421	–	1,162	3,250
15 E. Hughes	–	–	765	2,421	–	525	1,750
16 J. Virgo	–	–	1,531	1,093	–	1,162	1,750
17 E. Charlton	–	–	765	2,421	–	525	1,750
18 J. Campbell	–	–	2,625	3,750	–	1,162	3,250
19 S. Francisco	–	3,250	765	7,500	–	1,800	3,250
20 R. Williams	–	–	765	2,421	–	1,800	875
21 B. Werbeniuk	–	–	1,531	1,093	–	525	1,750
22 J. Parrott	5,000	–	5,250	1,093	3,375	1,162	3,250
23 M. Hallett	–	–	765	2,421	–	1,162	1,750
24 C. Wilson	–	–	2,625	7,500	–	525	1,750
25 M. Macleod	–	1,750	2,625	1,093	–	1,800	875
26 David Taylor	–	–	2,625	2,421	–	1,800	1,750
27 T. Jones	–	–	765	1,093	–	525	11,000
28 P. Francisco	–	–	–	3,750	–	1,162	3,250
29 D. Martin	–	–	1,531	2,421	–	1,162	875
30 D. Reynolds	–	–	2,625	1,093	–	1,162	875
31 P. Fagan	–	–	765	–	–	525	875
32 J. Spencer	–	–	1,531	1,093	–	1,162	1,750
33 P. Mans	–	–	765	1,093	–	525	3,250
34 J. Wych	–	–	765	–	–	525	–
35 B. West	–	–	–	1,093	–	3,600	1,750
36 M. Wildman	–	–	765	2,421	–	525	875
37 D. Fowler	–	–	765	2,421	–	1,162	1,750
38 S. Longworth	–	–	765	3,750	–	525	3,250
39 W. Jones	–	–	765	2,421	–	525	3,250
40 W. King	–	–	1,531	–	–	525	1,750
41 T. Murphy	–	–	1,531	–	–	525	875
42 S. Newbury	–	–	765	1,093	–	525	1,750
43 S. Duggan	–	–	5,250	1,093	–	–	875

44 S. Hendry £9,132; 45 F. Davis £8,873; 46 P. Browne £8,393; 47 R. Edmonds £8,274; 48 T. Drago £8,115; 49 P. Medati £8,095; 50 D. O'Kane £8,063; 51 G. Miles £7,743; 52 J. Donnelly £7,265; 53 John Rea £7,226; 54 G. Scott £7,109; 55 M. Gibson £6,812; 56 E. Sinclair £6,477; 57 R. Bales £6,148; 58 B. Harris £6,140; 59 M. Bradley £5,868; 60 G. Cripsey £5,732; 61 M. Gauvreau £5,671; 62 L. Dodd £5,664; 63 J. Van Rensberg £5,570; 64 J. McLaughlin £5,481; 65 I. Black £5,437; 66 T. Chappel £5,412; 67 R. Foldvari £5,140; 68 R. Chaperon £4,921; 69 C. Roscoe £4,796; 70 D. Gilbert £4,593; 71 B. Mikkelsen £4,563; 72 M. Watterson £4,156; 73 J. O'Boye £3,931; 74 V. Harris £3,798; 75 S. Simngam £3,768;

Kit Kat	*Mercantile*	*Belgian*	*Benson & Hedges*	*Dulux*	*World Cup*	*B & H Irish*	*National*	*World*	*Total £*
6,000	6,750	3,000	14,000	55,000	3,333	–	6,000	42,000	244,333
3,500	27,000	–	45,000	4,125	6,666	8,035	–	21,000	192,126
–	45,000	3,000	25,000	1,203	3,333	20,089	3,000	10,500	161,575
10,000	3,375	3,000	9,500	1,203	11,000	4,021	8,000	2,953	124,802
–	6,750	–	4,250	2,664	–	–	3,000	70,000	98,576
–	984	–	9,500	33,000	–	11,607	1,500	10,500	98,210
–	3,375	4,000	14,000	2,664	3,333	4,821	1,500	21,000	81,699
3,500	984	12,000	9,500	8,250	3,333	2,767	5,000	10,500	79,434
3,500	6,750	4,000	4,250	16,500	11,000	2,767	5,000	5,250	77,317
–	3,375	–	4,250	8,250	–	4,821	18,500	2,953	69,230
–	984	7,000	4,250	4,125	6,666	–	–	10,500	47,141
–	6,750	–	–	2,664	–	–	11,000	2,953	41,339
1,500	984	3,000	4,250	1,203	3,333	2,767	750	2,953	39,762
–	13,500	–	–	1,203	3,333	–	3,500	5,250	35,151
–	3,375	–	–	1,203	11,000	4,821	–	5,250	31,111
–	2,179	–	–	16,500	–	–	3,000	2,953	30,170
–	984	–	9,500	4,125	2,000	–	2,600	5,250	29,921
–	3,375	–	–	4,125	2,000	–	4,250	5,250	29,787
–	984	–	4,250	2,664	–	–	–	5,250	29,713
–	13,500	–	–	4,125	–	–	1,500	2,953	27,940
–	3,375	–	–	8,250	6,666	–	–	2,953	26,144
–	984	–	–	4,125	–	–	1,500	5,250	25,990
–	2,179	–	–	2,664	–	–	6,000	5,250	22,192
–	984	–	–	2,664	–	–	1,500	2,953	20,501
–	2,179	–	–	4,125	2,000	–	1,000	2,296	19,745
–	984	–	4,250	1,203	–	–	750	2,953	18,737
–	2,179	–	–	1,203	–	–	750	1,203	18,720
–	3,375	–	–	4,125	–	–	–	2,296	15,662
–	2,179	–	–	2,664	–	–	1,500	2,953	15,287
–	2,179	–	–	1,203	–	–	3,000	2,953	15,092
–	–	–	–	2,664	2,000	8,035	150	–	15,014
–	984	–	–	1,203	–	–	1,500	2,953	13,677
–	2,179	–	–	2,664	–	–	–	2,953	13,431
–	984	–	–	8,250	–	–	–	2,296	12,821
–	2,179	–	–	1,203	–	–	–	2,296	12,123
–	984	–	–	2,664	–	–	1,500	2,296	12,032
–	984	–	–	1,203	–	–	750	2,953	11,990
–	–	–	–	2,664	–	–	750	2,269	11,626
–	–	–	–	1,203	–	–	1,500	1,203	10,898
–	984	–	–	–	2,000	–	1,650	2,296	10,737
–	984	–	–	–	2,000	–	2,000	2,296	10,212
–	–	–	–	2,664	–	–	750	2,296	9,845
–	–	–	–	1,203	–	–	–	1,203	9,624

76 I. Williamson £3,593; 77 O. Agrawal £3,093; 78 J. Fitzmaurice £2,843; 79 G. Foulds £2,828; 80 M. Darrington £2,821; 81 M. Smith £2,734; 82 E. McLaughlin £2,640; 83 M. Morra £2,384; 84 Jim Bear £2,165; 85 B. Kelly £1,893; 86 D. Sheehan £1,870; 87 B. Oliver £1,843; 88 G. Wilkinson £1,750; 89 P. Houlihan £1,734; 90 P. Morgan £1,650; 91 D. Chalmers £1,625; 92 G. Jenkins £1,503; 93 J. Hargreaves £1,203; P. Thornley £1,203; 95 G. Watson £1,093; 96 B. Demarco £1,000; 97 M. Fisher £984; G. Rigitano £984; 99 I. Anderson £875; J. Giannaros £875; F. Jonik £875; 102 T. Kearney £800; P. Burke £800; 104 J. Dunning £765; D. Hughes £765; 106 L. Condo £625; L. Heywood £625; G. Robinson £625; 109 J. Meadowcroft £525; 110 Jack Rea £150; P. Watchorn £150.

THE PLAYERS

OMPRAKESH AGRAWAL (India)

Born 27.4.55
Turned professional 1985
World ranking 89

After winning the World Amateur Snooker title in 1984, Agrawal turned professional, the first Indian to do so, but achieved little of note in his first professional season.

1985	v Watchorn	5-2	1st round	Goya Matchroom Trophy
	v Fowler	2-5	2nd round	Goya Matchroom Trophy
	v Rempe	5-2	1st round	Rothmans Grand Prix
	v Dunning	2-5	2nd round	Rothmans Grand Prix
	v Hendry	9-2	1st round	Coral UK Open
	v Morra	8-9	2nd round	Coral UK Open
1986	v Demarco	4-5	1st round	Mercantile Credit Classic
	v Greaves	5-3	1st round	Dulux British Open
	v Miles	4-5	2nd round	Dulux British Open
	v D. Hughes	10-6	Qualifying	Embassy World Professional Championship
	v Newbury	5-10	Qualifying	Embassy World Professional Championship

IAN ANDERSON (Australia)

Born 2.4.46
Turned professional 1974
World ranking unranked (84)

For the first time since turning professional, Anderson did not compete on the British circuit last season. He was a member of the Australian team for the 1980 State Express World Team Classic.

1974	v Mans	1-8	1st round	World Professional Championship
1975	v Condo	15-8	1st round	World Professional Championship
	v Williams	4-15	2nd round	World Professional Championship
1976	v Jack Rea	5-8	Qualifying	Embassy World Professional Championship
1979	v S. Davis	1-9	Prelim	Embassy World Professional Championship
1981	v Martin	3-9	Qualifying	Embassy World Professional Championship
1982	v Houlihan	5-9	Qualifying	Embassy World Professional Championship
	v Sinclair	2-5	Qualifying	Jameson International
	v David Taylor	1-5	1st round	Professional Players Tournament
1983	v King	6-10	Qualifying	Embassy World Professional Championship
	v Oliver	9-1	Qualifying	Coral UK Championship
	v Dunning	2-9	Qualifying	Coral UK Championship

1984	v Watson	10-4	Qualifying	Embassy World Professional Championship
	v Donnelly	6-10	Qualifying	Embassy World Professional Championship
1985	v Kearney	10-8	Qualifying	Embassy World Professional Championship
	v Browne	5-10	Qualifying	Embassy World Professional Championship
	v King	2-8	Quarter-final	Australian Professional Championship

ROGER BALES (England)

Born 15.8.48
Turned professional 1984
World ranking 66 (100)

His second professional season brought Bales an encouraging nine wins with a victory over Dennis Taylor in the Dulux British Open giving him his first ranking point.

1984	v Sheehan	5-2	Qualifying	Jameson International
	v Murphy	5-4	Qualifying	Jameson International
	v Fisher	5-3	Qualifying	Jameson International
	v Reynolds	4-5	Qualifying	Jameson International
	v Higgins	1-5	1st round	Rothmans Grand Prix
	v Chalmers	9-2	Qualifying	Coral UK Open
	v E. McLaughlin	9-4	Qualifying	Coral UK Open
	v Gauvreau	8-9	Qualifying	Coral UK Open
1985	v Bennett	5-1	Qualifying	Mercantile Credit Classic
	v Kelly	5-3	Qualifying	Mercantile Credit Classic
	v Virgo	1-5	Qualifying	Mercantile Credit Classic
	v Dodd	3-9	Qualifying	Tolly Cobbold English Professional Championship
	v Black	6-4	Qualifying	Dulux British Open
	v Higgins	3-6	1st round	Dulux British Open
	v Chaperon	7-0	Qualifying	Embassy World Professional Championship
	v Drago	5-2	1st round	Goya Matchroom Trophy
	v Edmonds	5-0	2nd round	Goya Matchroom Trophy
	v S. Davis	2-5	3rd round	Goya Matchroom Trophy
	v Smith	5-1	1st round	Rothmans Grand Prix
	v Fisher	5-3	2nd round	Rothmans Grand Prix
	v Wilson	1-5	3rd round	Rothmans Grand Prix
	v Simngam	2-9	1st round	Coral UK Open
1986	v Parkin	5-0	1st round	Mercantile Credit Classic
	v Fowler	4-5	2nd round	Mercantile Credit Classic
	v V. Harris	9-7	2nd round	Tolly Cobbold English Professional Championship
	v Knowles	4-9	3rd round	Tolly Cobbold English Professional Championship
	v Parkin	5-1	1st round	Dulux British Open
	v Dunning	*wo*	2nd round	Dulux British Open
	v Dennis Taylor	5-4	3rd round	Dulux British Open
	v Williams	4-5	4th round	Dulux British Open
	v Gilbert	7-10	Qualifying	Embassy World Professional Championship

JIM BEAR (Canada)

Born 8.8.50
Turned professional 1983
World ranking 82

Bear turned professional after reaching the final of the 1982 World Amateur Championship in Calgary but let his membership lapse. He was reinstated as a professional in May 1985 and has therefore competed on the circuit for only one season.

1985	v Caggianello	4-5	1st round	Canadian Professional Championship
	v Houlihan	5-2	1st round	Goya Matchroom Trophy
	v Donnelly	5-2	2nd round	Goya Matchroom Trophy
	v Johnson	1-5	3rd round	Goya Matchroom Trophy
	v Kearney	3-5	1st round	Rothmans Grand Prix
	v Demarco	9-1	1st round	Coral UK Open
	v Watterson	9-0	2nd round	Coral UK Open
1986	v Kearney	0-5	1st round	Mercantile Credit Classic
	v O'Boye	1-5	1st round	Dulux British Open
	v Burke	10-8	Qualifying	Embassy World Professional Championship
	v Gauvreau	5-10	Qualifying	Embassy World Professional Championship

BERNARD BENNETT (England)

Born 31.8.31
Turned professional 1968
World ranking 114 (94)

Bennett is a Southampton businessman who owns three Snooker centres.

1969	v Williams	11-38	Quarter-final	World Professional Championship
1970	v David Taylor	8-11	1st round	World Professional Championship
1972	v Miles	6-15	Qualifying	World Professional Championship
1973	v Greaves	8-9	1st round	World Professional Championship
1974	v Simpson	8-2	1st round	World Professional Championship
	v Higgins	4-15	2nd round	World Professional Championship
1976	v Jack Rea	5-8	Qualifying	Embassy World Professional Championship
1977	v Thorne	4-11	Qualifying	Embassy World Professional Championship
	v Thorne	1-5	1st round	Super Crystalate Championship
1978	v Parkin	4-9	Prelim	World Professional Championship
	v Thorne	4-9	Qualifying	Coral UK Championship
1979	v Griffiths	2-9	Prelim	Embassy World Professional Championship
	v Jack Rea	8-9	1st round	Coral UK Championship
1980	v Hallett	4-9	Qualifying	Coral UK Championship
1981	v Wildman	3-9	Qualifying	John Courage English Professional Championship
	v Dunning	6-9	Qualifying	Embassy World Professional Championship
	v Fitzmaurice	1-5	Qualifying	Jameson International
	v Watterson	4-9	Qualifying	Coral UK Championship

1982	v French	3-9	Qualifying	Embassy World Professional Championship
	v M. Owen	5-2	Qualifying	Jameson International
	v Wych	0-5	Qualifying	Jameson International
	v Meadowcroft	4-5	1st round	Professional Players Tournament
	v Medati	1-9	Qualifying	Coral UK Championship
1983	v Meadowcroft	3-10	Qualifying	Embassy World Professional Championship
	v Donnelly	1-5	Qualifying	Jameson International
	v Demarco	5-4	Qualifying	Jameson International
	v Wilson	1-5	1st round	Professional Players Tournament
	v Macleod	0-9	Qualifying	Coral UK Championship
1984	v Watterson	5-10	Qualifying	Embassy World Professional Championship
	v Demarco	5-1	Qualifying	Jameson International
	v N. Foulds	0-5	Qualifying	Jameson International
	v Oliver	3-5	Qualifying	Rothmans Grand Prix
	v John Rea	5-9	Qualifying	Coral UK Open
1985	v Bales	1-5	Qualifying	Mercantile Credit Classic
	v Cripsey	0-9	Qualifying	Tolly Cobbold English Professional Championship
	v Martin	0-6	1st round	Dulux British Open
	v Medati	4-10	Qualifying	Embassy World Professional Championship
	v Cripsey	3-5	1st round	Goya Matchroom Trophy
	v D. Hughes	4-5	1st round	Rothmans Grand Prix
	v O'Boye	3-9	1st round	Coral UK Open
1986	v Houlihan	0-5	1st round	Mercantile Credit Classic
	v Scott	1-9	2nd round	Tolly Cobbold English Professional Championship
	v West	1-5	1st round	Dulux British Open
	v Sim-Ngam	0-10	Qualifying	Embassy World Professional Championship

IAN BLACK (Scotland)

Born 11.12.54
Turned professional 1981
World ranking 64 (57)

Black was Scottish professional champion in 1981 and runner-up the following year.

1981	v Macleod	5-4	Quarter-final	Scottish Professional Championship
	v E. McLaughlin	6-3	Semi-final	Scottish Professional Championship
	v Gibson	**11-7**	**Final**	**Scottish Professional Championship**
	v E. McLaughlin	5-3	Qualifying	Jameson International
	v Houlihan	4-9	Qualifying	Coral UK Championship
1982	v Parkin	9-6	Qualifying	Embassy World Professional Championship
	v Williams	2-9	Qualifying	Embassy World Professional Championship
	v Macleod	6-0	Quarter-final	Scottish Professional Championship
	v Ross	6-4	Semi-final	Scottish Professional Championship
	v Sinclair	7-11	Final	Scottish Professional Championship
	v Fitzmaurice	3-5	Qualifying	Jameson International

	v Virgo	2-5	1st round	Professional Players Tournament
	v Fisher	3-9	Qualifying	Coral UK Championship
1983	v Morra	10-9	Qualifying	Embassy World Professional Championship
	v Medati	10-4	Qualifying	Embassy World Professional Championship
	v Mans	3-10	1st round	Embassy World Professional Championship
	v E. McLaughlin	6-4	1st round	Scottish Professional Championship
	v Macleod	2-6	Semi-final	Scottish Professional Championship
	v King	3-5	Qualifying	Jameson International
	v Spencer	2-5	1st round	Professional Players Tournament
	v Williamson	9-6	Qualifying	Coral UK Championship
	v White	1-9	1st round	Coral UK Championship
1984	v Hines	5-10	Qualifying	Embassy World Professional Championship
	v Browne	5-4	Qualifying	Jameson International
	v Watterson	5-3	Qualifying	Jameson International
	v Macleod	3-5	Qualifying	Jameson International
	v P. Francisco	4-5	Qualifying	Rothmans Grand Prix
	v Chappel	3-9	Qualifying	Coral UK Open
1985	v J. McLaughlin	0-5	Qualifying	Mercantile Credit Classic
	v Bales	4-6	Qualifying	Dulux British Open
	v Chalmers	4-10	Qualifying	Embassy World Professional Championship
	v Rigitano	5-4	2nd round	Goya Matchroom Trophy
	v Mans	5-4	3rd round	Goya Matchroom Trophy
	v Duggan	1-5	4th round	Goya Matchroom Trophy
	v G. Foulds	3-5	2nd round	Rothmans Grand Prix
	v V. Harris	3-9	2nd round	Coral UK Open
1986	v G. Foulds	2-5	2nd round	Mercantile Credit Classic
	v Gibson	5-0	2nd round	Dulux British Open
	v S. Davis	2-5	3rd round	Dulux British Open
	v E. McLaughlin	6-4	Quarter-final	Canada Dry Scottish Professional Championship
	v Hendry	2-6	Semi-final	Canada Dry Scottish Professional Championship
	v B. Harris	10-8	Qualifying	Embassy World Professional Championship
	v Newbury	2-10	Qualifying	Embassy World Professional Championship

MALCOLM BRADLEY (England)

Born 8.7.48
Turned professional 1984
World ranking 54 (40)

In his second season as a professional, Bradley earned his first ranking point by reaching the last 32 of the Goya Matchroom Trophy with a win over Mike Hallett.

1984	v Darrington	5-3	Qualifying	Jameson International
	v Jack Rea	5-2	Qualifying	Jameson International
	v Morra	3-5	Qualifying	Jameson International
	v Jonik	5-1	Qualifying	Rothmans Grand Prix

	v Virgo	0-5	1st round	Rothmans Grand Prix
	v V. Harris	9-8	Qualifying	Coral UK Open
	v Kelly	9-6	Qualifying	Coral UK Open
	v Meadowcroft	9-7	Qualifying	Coral UK Open
	v Hallett	8-9	Qualifying	Coral UK Open
1985	v Browne	3-5	Qualifying	Mercantile Credit Classic
	v Williamson	9-8	Qualifying	Tolly Cobbold English Professional Championship
	v Knowles	8-9	Qualifying	Tolly Cobbold English Professional Championship
	v Morra	6-2	Qualifying	Dulux British Open
	v David Taylor	6-3	1st round	Dulux British Open
	v Fowler	5-4	2nd round	Dulux British Open
	v S. Davis	2-5	3rd round	Dulux British Open
	v Mienie	10-4	Qualifying	Embassy World Professional Championship
	v Mikkelsen	10-9	Qualifying	Embassy World Professional Championship
	v Wych	7-10	Qualifying	Embassy World Professional Championship
	v John Rea	5-1	2nd round	Goya Matchroom Trophy
	v Hallett	5-4	3rd round	Goya Matchroom Trophy
	v Johnson	2-5	4th round	Goya Matchroom Trophy
	v Gibson	4-5	2nd round	Rothmans Grand Prix
	v Jenkins	9-3	2nd round	Coral UK Open
	v White	4-9	1st round	Coral UK Open
1986	v Oliver	5-3	2nd round	Mercantile Credit Classic
	v N. Foulds	3-5	3rd round	Mercantile Credit Classic
	v Gilbert	9-5	2nd round	Tolly Cobbold English Professional Championship
	v S. Davis	3-9	3rd round	Tolly Cobbold English Professional Championship
	v Jack Rea	5-1	2nd round	Dulux British Open
	v Higgins	3-5	3rd round	Dulux British Open
	v Gilbert	7-10	Qualifying	Embassy World Professional Championship

PADDY BROWNE (Republic of Ireland)

Born 1.4.65
Turned professional 1983
World ranking 48 (61)

In his third season as a professional, Browne earned two ranking points by reaching the last 32 in both the Mercantile Credit Classic and Dulux British Open. He was Republic of Ireland amateur champion in 1982.

1983	v Murphy	2-5	Qualifying	Professional Players Tournament
1984	v Duggan	10-9	Qualifying	Embassy World Professional Championship
	v Roscoe	10-4	Qualifying	Embassy World Professional Championship
	v Sinclair	1-10	Qualifying	Embassy World Professional Championship
	v John Rea	5-2	Qualifying	Jameson International
	v Black	4-5	Qualifying	Jameson International

	v Duggan	2-5	Qualifying	Rothmans Grand Prix
	v G. Foulds	9-5	Qualifying	Coral UK Open
	v King	5-9	Qualifying	Coral UK Open
1985	v Bradley	5-3	Qualifying	Mercantile Credit Classic
	v Everton	5-0	Qualifying	Mercantile Credit Classic
	v Miles	5-3	Qualifying	Mercantile Credit Classic
	v White	2-5	1st round	Mercantile Credit Classic
	v Newbury	0-6	Qualifying	Dulux British Open
	v Murphy	3-6	Qualifying	Irish Professional Championship
	v Anderson	10-5	Qualifying	Embassy World Professional Championship
	v Morra	6-10	Qualifying	Embassy World Professional Championship
	v B. Harris	3-5	2nd round	Goya Matchroom Trophy
	v B. Harris	3-5	2nd round	Rothmans Grand Prix
	v Chalmers	9-4	2nd round	Coral UK Open
	v Thorne	6-9	3rd round	Coral UK Open
1986	v Everton	5-0	2nd round	Mercantile Credit Classic
	v Wilson	5-3	3rd round	Mercantile Credit Classic
	v Gauvreau	3-5	4th round	Mercantile Credit Classic
	v Hendry	5-0	2nd round	Dulux British Open
	v Spencer	5-0	3rd round	Dulux British Open
	v Charlton	1-5	4th round	Dulux British Open
	v Hendry	9-10	Qualifying	Embassy World Professional Championship
	v Burke	4-5	1st round	Strongbow Irish Professional Championship

PASCAL BURKE (Republic of Ireland)

Born 19.6.32
Turned professional 1982
World ranking 104 (86)

Burke was twice Republic of Ireland amateur champion and a world amateur semi-finalist in 1974.

1983	v E. Hughes	2-6	Quarter-final	Irish Professional Championship
	v Meo	0-5	1st round	Benson & Hedges Irish Masters
	v Morgan	9-10	Qualifying	Embassy World Professional Championship
	v G. Foulds	2-5	Qualifying	Jameson International
	v G. Foulds	5-4	Qualifying	Professional Players Tournament
	v Johnson	3-5	1st round	Professional Players Tournament
1984	v Kelly	10-7	Qualifying	Embassy World Professional Championship
	v B. Harris	10-4	Qualifying	Embassy World Professional Championship
	v Hallett	5-10	Qualifying	Embassy World Professional Championship
	v Kearney	5-4	Qualifying	Jameson International
	v Newbury	0-5	Qualifying	Jameson International
	v Darrington	5-3	Qualifying	Rothmans Grand Prix
	v Meo	1-5	1st round	Rothmans Grand Prix
	v Longworth	4-9	Qualifying	Coral UK Open
1985	v Newbury	1-5	Qualifying	Mercantile Credit Classic
	v Chalmers	5-6	Qualifying	Dulux British Open
	v Kearney	6-4	Qualifying	Irish Professional Championship
	v Higgins	0-6	Quarter-final	Irish Professional Championship

	v Newbury	3-10	Qualifying	Embassy World Professional Championship
	v Rempe	3-5	1st round	Goya Matchroom Trophy
	v Newbury	3-5	2nd round	Rothmans Grand Prix
	v Jenkins	5-9	1st round	Coral UK Open
1986	v D. Hughes	5-3	1st round	Mercantile Credit Classic
	v Chaperon	2-5	2nd round	Mercantile Credit Classic
	v Gilbert	1-5	1st round	Dulux British Open
	v Jim Bear	8-10	Qualifying	Embassy World Professional Championship
	v Browne	5-4	1st round	Strongbow Irish Professional Championship
	v E. Hughes	3-6	Quarter-final	Strongbow Irish Professional Championship

JOE CAGGIANELLO (Canada)

Born 16.5.55
Turned professional 1983
World ranking 105 (87)

1984	v Darrington	10-7	Qualifying	Embassy World Professional Championship
	v Oliver	7-10	Qualifying	Embassy World Professional Championship
1985	v Jim Bear	5-4	1st round	Canadian Professional Chamionship
	v Thorburn	2-6	Quarter-final	Canadian Professional Championship
	v Hargreaves	5-2	1st round	Goya Matchroom Trophy
	v King	0-5	2nd round	Goya Matchroom Trophy
	v Watterson	1-5	2nd round	Rothmans Grand Prix

JOHN CAMPBELL (Australia)

Born 10.4.53
Turned professional 1982
World ranking 18 (31)

After capturing the Australian Professional title for the first time, Campbell enjoyed his most successful season to date in 1985–86 reaching the last 16 of all six ranking tournaments.

In the summer, he also reached the final of the Winfield Australian Masters.

Campbell's consistency not only earned him a place in the top 20 but also made him the highest placed Australian in the world rankings.

1983	v Watterson	10-6	Qualifying	Embassy World Professional Championship
	v Donnelly	10-2	Qualifying	Embassy World Professional Championship
	v Thorburn	5-10	1st round	Embassy World Professional Championship
	v E. McLaughlin	2-5	Qualifying	Jameson International
	v Mountjoy	5-3	1st round	Professional Players Tournament
	v Miles	5-2	2nd round	Professional Players Tournament
	v Martin	5-0	3rd round	Professional Players Tournament
	v Knowles	3-5	Quarter-final	Professional Players Tournament
1984	v White	1-5	Qualifying	Lada Classic
	v Gauvreau	7-10	Qualifying	Embassy World Professional Championship
	v G. Foulds	5-3	Qualifying	Jameson International

John Campbell

	v S. Davis	1-5	1st round	Jameson International
	v W. Jones	5-4	1st round	Rothmans Grand Prix
	v Thorburn	1-5	2nd round	Rothmans Grand Prix
	v Donnelly	9-6	Qualifying	Coral UK Open
	v White	7-9	1st round	Coral UK Open
1985	v Scott	4-5	Qualifying	Mercantile Credit Classic
	v O'Kane	4-6	1st round	Dulux British Open
	v Morra	10-9	Qualifying	Embassy World Professional Championship
	v Charlton	3-10	1st round	Embassy World Professional Championship
	v Charlton	5-4	Quarter-final	Winfield Australian Masters
	v Parrott	6-4	Semi-finals	Winfield Australian Masters
	v Meo	2-7	Final	Winfield Australian Masters
	v Foldvari	8-5	Quarter-final	Australian Professional Championship
	v King	9-6	Semi-final	Australian Professional Championship
	v Charlton	**10-7**	**Final**	**Australian Professional Championship**
	v Morra	5-2	3rd round	Goya Matchroom Trophy
	v Mountjoy	5-1	4th round	Goya Matchroom Trophy
	v Thorburn	0-5	5th round	Goya Matchroom Trophy
	v Van Rensberg	5-4	3rd round	Rothmans Grand Prix
	v Mountjoy	5-2	4th round	Rothmans Grand Prix
	v Knowles	2-5	5th round	Rothmans Grand Prix
	v Medati	9-7	3rd round	Coral UK Open
	v David Taylor	4-9	4th round	Coral UK Open
1986	v Donnelly	5-2	3rd round	Mercantile Credit Classic
	v Mikkelsen	5-2	4th round	Mercantile Credit Classic
	v N. Foulds	1-5	5th round	Mercantile Credit Classic
	v West	5-4	3rd round	Dulux British Open
	v Medati	5-4	4th round	Dulux British Open
	v S. Davis	0-5	5th round	Dulux British Open
	v Van Rensberg	10-6	Qualifying	Embassy World Professional Championship
	v Reardon	10-8	1st round	Embassy World Professional Championship
	v Thorne	9-13	2nd round	Embassy World Professional Championship

DAVE CHALMERS (England)

Born 14.7.48
Turned professional 1984
World ranking 99 (79)

English amateur champion in 1982, Chalmers had a very disappointing 1985–86 season, winning only one match.

1984	Chalmers *wo* Condo *scr*		Qualifying	Jameson International
	v Oliver	5-4	Qualifying	Jameson International
	v Meadowcroft	1-5	Qualifying	Jameson International
	v Andrewartha	5-2	Qualifying	Rothmans Grand Prix
	v Williams	0-5	1st round	Rothmans Grand Prix
	v Bales	2-9	Qualifying	Coral UK Open

1985	v Mikkelsen	1-5	Prelim	Mercantile Credit Classic
	v Meadowcroft	9-3	Qualifying	Tolly Cobbold English Professional Championship
	v White	5-9	Qualifying	Tolly Cobbold English Professional Championship
	v Burke	6-5	Qualifying	Dulux British Open
	v Griffiths	0-6	1st round	Dulux British Open
	v Greaves	10-3	Qualifying	Embassy World Professional Championship
	v E. McLaughlin	10-9	Qualifying	Embassy World Professional Championship
	v Black	10-4	Qualifying	Embassy World Professional Championship
	v Hallett	1-10	Qualifying	Embassy World Professional Championship
	v Chaperon	2-5	2nd round	Goya Matchroom Trophy
	v Scott	2-5	2nd round	Rothmans Grand Prix
	v Browne	4-9	2nd round	Coral UK Open
1986	v Donnelly	0-5	2nd round	Mercantile Credit Classic
	v Fisher	9-2	2nd round	Tolly Cobbold English Professional Championship
	v Hallett	1-9	3rd round	Tolly Cobbold English Professional Championship
	v Scott	1-5	2nd round	Dulux British Open
	v F. Davis	6-10	Qualifying	Embassy World Professional Championship

ROBERT CHAPERON (Canada)

Born 10.5.58
Turned professional 1983
World ranking 53 (44)

Chaperon's best performance of the season was to beat Silvino Francisco 5-3 to reach the last 16 of the Goya Matchroom Trophy.

1984	v Fowler	0-5	Qualifying	Jameson International
	v Kearney	5-1	Qualifying	Rothmans Grand Prix
	v Gibson	5-4	Qualifying	Rothmans Grand Prix
	v Martin	4-5	Qualifying	Rothmans Grand Prix
	v T. Jones	1-9	Qualifying	Coral UK Open
1985	v G. Foulds	3-5	Qualifying	Mercantile Credit Classic
	v Fagan	6-5	Qualifying	Dulux British Open
	v Werbeniuk	6-1	1st round	Dulux British Open
	v W. Jones	5-2	2nd round	Dulux British Open
	v S. Francisco	2-5	3rd round	Dulux British Open
	v Bales	10-7	Qualifying	Embassy World Professional Championship
	v Heywood	10-1	Qualifying	Embassy World Professional Championship
	v Morgan	10-3	Qualifying	Embassy World Professional Championship
	v F. Davis	9-10	Qualifying	Embassy World Professional Championship
	v Thornley	5-1	1st round	Canadian Professional Championship
	v Stevens	6-4	Quarter-final	Canadian Professional Championship
	v Jonik	6-3	Semi-final	Canadian Professional Championship
	v Thorburn	4-6	Final	Canadian Professional Championship

	v Chalmers	5-2	2nd round	Goya Matchroom Trophy
	v S. Francisco	5-3	3rd round	Goya Matchroom Trophy
	v Macleod	4-5	4th round	Goya Matchroom Trophy
	v O'Boye	3-5	2nd round	Rothmans Grand Prix
	v J. McLaughlin	5-9	2nd round	Coral UK Open
1986	v Burke	5-2	2nd round	Mercantile Credit Classic
	v S. Davis	1-5	3rd round	Mercantile Credit Classic
	v V. Harris	5-0	2nd round	Dulux British Open
	v Wilson	3-5	3rd round	Dulux British Open
	v Jonik	10-8	Qualifying	Embassy World Professional Championship
	v Gauvreau	8-10	Qualifying	Embassy World Professional Championship

TONY CHAPPEL (Wales)

Born 28.5.60
Turned professional 1984
World ranking 49 (68)

A Terry Griffiths protégé, Chappel achieved his best performance in his second season when he beat Kirk Stevens 5-3 to reach the last 16 of the Goya Matchroom Trophy.

1984	v Mikkelsen	4-5	Qualifying	Jameson International
	v Scott	5-1	Qualifying	Rothmans Grand Prix
	v Stevens	3-5	1st round	Rothmans Grand Prix
	v Houlihan	9-3	Qualifying	Coral UK Open
	v Black	9-3	Qualifying	Coral UK Open
	v Reynolds	9-6	Qualifying	Coral UK Open
	v Stevens	7-9	1st round	Coral UK Open
	v Giannaros	2-5	Qualifying	Mercantile Credit Classic
	v Williamson	6-5	Qualifying	Dulux British Open
	v S. Davis	5-6	1st round	Dulux British Open
	v Hines	8-10	Qualifying	Embassy World Professional Championship
	v M. Owen	6-0	1st round	BCE Welsh Professional Championship
	v Griffiths	0-6	Quarter-final	BCE Welsh Professional Championship
1985	v Meadowcroft	5-2	2nd round	Goya Matchroom Trophy
	v Stevens	5-3	3rd round	Goya Matchroom Trophy
	v Wilson	0-5	4th round	Goya Matchroom Trophy
	v Dodd	5-2	2nd round	Rothmans Grand Prix
	v Mountjoy	1-5	3rd round	Rothmans Grand Prix
	v O'Kane	9-5	1st round	Coral UK Open
	v White	5-9	2nd round	Coral UK Open
1986	v Murphy	4-5	2nd round	Mercantile Credit Classic
	v Griffiths	4-6	Quarter-final	Zetters Welsh Professional Championship
	v Fowler	4-5	2nd round	Dulux British Open
	v Wych	6-10	Qualifying	Embassy World Professional Championship

EDDIE CHARLTON (Australia)

Born 31.10.29
Turned professional 1960
World ranking 25 (12)

Two disastrous seasons have seen the veteran Australian slip down the rankings so badly that, for the first time since they were instituted, he is now outside the top 16.

In his long professional career, Charlton has reached two world finals and six world semi-finals.

Although his steady, riskless style of play makes him a difficult player to beat, Charlton has never won a major international title.

1970	v Simpson	22-27	Semi-final	World Professional Championship
1972	v David Taylor	31-25	Quarter-final	World Professional Championship
	v Spencer	32-37	Semi-final	World Professional Championship
1973	v Mans	16-8	2nd round	World Professional Championship
	v Miles	16-6	Quarter-final	World Professional Championship
	v Higgins	23-9	Semi-final	World Professional Championship
	v Reardon	32-38	Final	World Professional Championship
	v Pulman	3-8	Semi-final	Norwich Union Open
1974	v Dunning	13-15	2nd round	World Professional Championship
1975	v F. Davis	5-3	Quarter-final	Benson & Hedges Masters
	v Spencer	2-5	Semi-final	Benson & Hedges Masters
	v Werbeniuk	15-11	2nd round	World Professional Championship
	v Thorburn	19-12	Quarter-final	World Professional Championship
	v Dennis Taylor	19-12	Semi-final	World Professional Championship
	v Reardon	30-31	Final	World Professional Championship
1976	v Williams	4-1	2nd round	Benson & Hedges Masters
	v Reardon	4-5	Semi-final	Benson & Hedges Masters
	v Pulman	15-9	1st round	Embassy World Professional Championship
	v F. Davis	15-13	Quarter-final	Embassy World Professional Championship
	v Higgins	18-20	Semi-final	Embassy World Professional Championship
1977	v David Taylor	13-5	1st round	Embassy World Professional Championship
	v Thorburn	12-13	Quarter-final	Embassy World Professional Championship
1978	v Thorne	13-12	1st round	Embassy World Professional Championship
	v Thorburn	13-12	Quarter-final	Embassy World Professional Championship
	v Reardon	14-18	Semi-final	Embassy World Professional Championship
1979	v Higgins	2-5	Quarter-final	Benson & Hedges Masters
	v Mountjoy	13-6	1st round	Embassy World Professional Championship
	v F. Davis	13-4	Quarter-final	Embassy World Professional Championship
	v Griffiths	17-19	Semi-final	Embassy World Professional Championship
1980	v Spencer	2-5	Quarter-final	Benson & Hedges Masters
	v Virgo	13-12	2nd round	Embassy World Professional Championship
	v Stevens	7-13	Quarter-final	Embassy World Professional Championship
1981	v Mountjoy	0-5	1st round	Benson & Hedges Masters
	v Mountjoy	7-13	2nd round	Embassy World Professional Championship
	v Martin	2-5	3rd round	Jameson International

1982	v White	5-4	1st round	Benson & Hedges Masters
	v Higgins	1-5	Quarter-final	Benson & Hedges Masters
	v Wilson	10-5	1st round	Embassy World Professional Championship
	v Werbeniuk	13-5	2nd round	Embassy World Professional Championship
	v Knowles	13-11	Quarter-final	Embassy World Professional Championship
	v Reardon	11-16	Semi-final	Embassy World Professional Championship
	v Virgo	4-5	1st round	Jameson International
	v D. Hughes	5-2	1st round	Professional Players Tournament
	v Williams	5-2	2nd round	Professional Players Tournament
	v Meo	5-3	3rd round	Professional Players Tournament
	v Reynolds	5-2	Quarter-final	Professional Players Tournament
	v Reardon	7-10	Semi-final	Professional Players Tournament
1983	v Virgo	5-2	1st round	Lada Classic
	v S. Davis	4-5	Quarter-final	Lada Classic
	v Meo	5-3	1st round	Benson & Hedges Masters
	v Werbeniuk	5-3	Quarter-final	Benson & Hedges Masters
	v Thorburn	5-6	Semi-final	Benson & Hedges Masters
	v David Taylor	5-4	1st round	Benson & Hedges Irish Masters
	v S. Davis	1-5	Quarter-final	Benson & Hedges Irish Masters
	v Dodd	10-7	1st round	Embassy World Professional Championship
	v Spencer	13-11	2nd round	Embassy World Professional Championship
	v S. Davis	5-13	Quarter-final	Embassy World Professional Championship
	v Johnson	5-2	1st round	Jameson International
	v Morra	5-3	2nd round	Jameson International
	v Thorne	5-0	Quarter-final	Jameson International
	v S. Davis	2-9	Semi-final	Jameson International
	v E. McLaughlin	5-0	1st round	Professional Players Tournament
	v Fisher	5-4	2nd round	Professional Players Tournament
	v Johnson	0-5	3rd round	Professional Players Tournament
1984	v Wilson	5-0	Qualifying	Lada Classic
	v White	5-3	1st round	Lada Classic
	v Wildman	4-5	Quarter-final	Lada Classic
	v White	2-5	1st round	Benson & Hedges Masters
	v Higgins	2-5	1st round	Benson & Hedges Irish Masters
	v Stevens	3-5	1st round	Tolly Cobbold Classic
	v Andrewartha	10-4	1st round	Embassy World Professional Championship
	v White	7-13	2nd round	Embassy World Professional Championship
	v David Taylor	5-4	Quarter-final	Winfield Australian Masters
	v Knowles	0-6	Semi-final	Winfield Australian Masters
	v Johnson	1-5	1st round	Jameson International
	v Everton	5-1	1st round	Rothmans Grand Prix
	v Parrott	5-1	2nd round	Rothmans Grand Prix
	v Mountjoy	4-5	3rd round	Rothmans Grand Prix
	v S. Francisco	9-4	1st round	Coral UK Open
	v Thorne	7-9	2nd round	Coral UK Open
1985	v Macleod	1-5	1st round	Mercantile Credit Classic
	v Spencer	3-5	1st round	Benson & Hedges Masters
	v B. Harris	3-6	1st round	Dulux British Open
	v Dennis Taylor	5-4	1st round	Benson & Hedges Irish Masters

	v Knowles	3-5	Quarter-final	Benson & Hedges Irish Masters
	v Campbell	10-3	1st round	Embassy World Professional Championship
	v Dennis Taylor	6-13	2nd round	Embassy World Professional Championship
	v Campbell	4-5	Quarter-final	Winfield Australian Masters
	v Wilkinson	8-2	Quarter-final	Australian Professional Championship
	v Morgan	9-3	Semi-final	Australian Professional Championship
	v Campbell	7-10	Final	Australian Professional Championship
	v Gibson	4-5	3rd round	Goya Matchroom Trophy
	v G. Foulds	5-1	3rd round	Rothmans Grand Prix
	v Drago	3-5	4th round	Rothmans Grand Prix
	v P. Francisco	5-9	3rd round	Coral UK Open
1986	v P. Francisco	1-5	3rd round	Mercantile Credit Classic
	v Stevens	5-4	1st round	Benson & Hedges Masters
	v Knowles	4-5	Quarter-final	Benson & Hedges Masters
	v Gilbert	5-2	3rd round	Dulux British Open
	v Browne	5-1	4th round	Dulux British Open
	v Virgo	4-5	5th round	Dulux British Open
	v Wilson	10-6	1st round	Embassy World Professional Championship
	v Stevens	12-13	2nd round	Embassy World Professional Championship

GRAHAM CRIPSEY (England)

Born 8.12.54
Turned professional 1982
World ranking 50 (89)

A former wall-of-death rider from Skegness, Cripsey reached the last 32 of two major tournaments, the Coral UK Open, by beating Cliff Wilson, and the Mercantile Credit Classic by beating John Spencer.

1982	v French	1-5	Qualifying	Jameson International
	v B. Harris	6-9	Qualifying	Coral UK Championship
1983	v D. Hughes	10-2	Qualifying	Embassy World Professional Championship
	v Meadowcroft	6-10	Qualifying	Embassy World Professional Championship
	v Ganim	4-5	Qualifying	Professional Players Tournament
	v Darrington	3-9	Qualifying	Coral UK Championship
1984	v Parkin	10-4	Qualifying	Embassy World Professional Championship
	v Gauvreau	1-10	Qualifying	Embassy World Professional Championship
	v Thornley	5-3	Qualifying	Jameson International
	v Dunning	3-5	Qualifying	Jameson International
	v Morra	3-5	Qualifying	Rothmans Grand Prix
	v Foldvari	9-7	Qualifying	Coral UK Open
	v Fitzmaurice	8-9	Qualifying	Coral UK Open
1985	v Medati	4-5	Qualifying	Mercantile Credit Classic
	v Bennett	9-0	Qualifying	Tolly Cobbold English Professional Championship
	v David Taylor	5-9	1st round	Tolly Cobbold English Professional Championship

	v O'Kane	4-6	Qualifying	Dulux British Open
	v Longworth	8-10	Qualifying	Embassy World Professional Championship
	v Bennett	5-3	1st round	Goya Matchroom Trophy
	v Medati	5-2	2nd round	Goya Matchroom Trophy
	v Dennis Taylor	1-5	3rd round	Goya Matchroom Trophy
	v Hargreaves	1-5	1st round	Rothmans Grand Prix
	v Greaves	9-4	1st round	Coral UK Open
	Cripsey *wo* Dunning *scr*		2nd round	Coral UK Open
	v Wilson	9-7	1st round	Coral UK Open
	v Dennis Taylor	2-9	2nd round	Coral UK Open
1986	v Drago	5-4	1st round	Mercantile Credit Classic
	v Newbury	5-4	2nd round	Mercantile Credit Classic
	v Spencer	5-1	3rd round	Mercantile Credit Classic
	v Higgins	2-5	4th round	Mercantile Credit Classic
	v Meadowcroft	9-1	2nd round	Tolly Cobbold English Professional Championship
	v Wildman	5-9	3rd round	Tolly Cobbold English Professional Championship
	v Darrington	5-4	1st round	Dulux British Open
	v Williamson	4-5	2nd round	Dulux British Open
	v Drago	4-10	Qualifying	Embassy World Professional Championship

MIKE DARRINGTON (England)

Born 13.9.31
Turned professional 1982
World ranking 78 (97)

1983	v Williams	0-10	Qualifying	Embassy World Professional Championship
	v Williamson	5-3	Qualifying	Jameson International
	v S. Francisco	2-5	Qualifying	Jameson International
	v Duggan	4-5	Qualifying	Professional Players Tournament
	v Cripsey	9-3	Qualifying	Coral UK Championship
	v Hallett	1-9	Qualifying	Coral UK Championship
1984	v Caggianello	7-10	Qualifying	Embassy World Professional Championship
	v Bradley	3-5	Qualifying	Jameson International
	v Burke	3-5	Qualifying	Rothmans Grand Prix
	v Longworth	5-9	Qualifying	Coral UK Open
1985	v Hargreaves	2-5	Qualifying	Mercantile Credit Classic
	v Virgo	0-9	1st round	Tolly Cobbold English Professional Championship
	v Scott	3-6	Qualifying	Dulux British Open
	v T. Jones	2-10	Qualifying	Embassy World Professional Championship
	v Gilbert	5-2	1st round	Goya Matchroom Trophy
	v Sinclair	0-5	2nd round	Goya Matchroom Trophy
	v Greaves	5-2	1st round	Rothmans Grand Prix

	v Foldvari	5-3	2nd round	Rothmans Grand Prix
	v N. Foulds	0-5	3rd round	Rothmans Grand Prix
	v Foldvari	9-6	2nd round	Coral UK Open
	v Martin	3-9	3rd round	Coral UK Open
1986	v O'Boye	0-5	1st round	Mercantile Credit Classic
	v Fowler	3-9	2nd round	Tolly Cobbold English Professional Championship
	v Cripsey	4-5	1st round	Dulux British Open
	v Meadowcroft	10-6	Qualifying	Embassy World Professional Championship
	v Edmonds	5-10	Qualifying	Embassy World Professional Championship

FRED DAVIS (England)

Born 14.8.13
Turned professional 1930
World ranking 47 (56)

Fred Davis is certainly professional snooker's oldest active player and is probably the oldest active professional sportsman in Britain. During the early part of his professional career he lived under the shadow of his elder brother, Joe, but then himself dominated the game in the late 1940s and 1950s, winning the world title eight times. When the game was revived in the late 1960s, Davis proved he was still a force to be reckoned with, reaching the 1969, 1974 and 1978 semi-finals.

In 1980, at the age of 67, Davis became only the second player – the first, of course, being Joe – to achieve the feat of winning both the World Professional Snooker and Billiards titles when he successfully challenged Rex Williams for the latter. He retained it when the event was staged later that same year in a tournament format and was runner-up to Rex Williams in 1983.

1969	v Reardon	25-24	Quarter-final	World Professional Championship
	v G. Owen	28-45	Semi-final	World Professional Championship
1970	v Reardon	26-31	Quarter-final	World Professional Championship
1972	v Spencer	21-31	Quarter-final	World Professional Championship
1973	v Greaves	16-1	2nd round	World Professional Championship
	v Higgins	14-16	Quarter-final	World Professional Championship
1974	v Werbeniuk	15-5	2nd round	World Professional Championship
	v Higgins	15-14	Quarter-final	World Professional Championship
	v Reardon	3-15	Semi-final	World Professional Championship
	v Thorburn	4-5	1st round	Norwich Union Open
1975	v Charlton	3-5	Quarter-final	Benson & Hedges Masters
	v Dennis Taylor	14-15	2nd round	World Professional Championship
1976	v Thorburn	4-2	1st round	Benson & Hedges Masters
	v Spencer	0-4	2nd round	Benson & Hedges Masters

	v Werbeniuk	15-12	1st round	Embassy World Professional Championship
	v Charlton	13-15	Quarter-final	Embassy World Professional Championship
1977	v Mountjoy	2-4	Quarter-final	Benson & Hedges Masters
	v Pulman	12-13	1st round	Embassy World Professional Championship
	v Fagan	0-5	2nd round	Super Crystalate UK Championship
1978	v Miles	3-4	1st round	Benson & Hedges Masters
	v Virgo	9-8	Qualifying	Embassy World Professional Championship
	v Dennis Taylor	13-9	1st round	Embassy World Professional Championship
	v Fagan	13-10	Quarter-final	Embassy World Professional Championship
	v Mans	16-18	Semi-final	Embassy World Professional Championship
	v Dunning	9-2	1st round	Coral UK Championship
	v Higgins	4-9	Quarter-final	Coral UK Championship
1979	v Mountjoy	2-5	1st round	Benson & Hedges Masters
	v Stevens	13-8	1st round	Embassy World Professional Championship
	v Charlton	4-13	Quarter-final	Embassy World Professional Championship
	v Edmonds	6-9	3rd round	Coral UK Championship
1980	v David Taylor	5-13	2nd round	Embassy World Professional Championship
	v Wildman	9-6	2nd round	Coral UK Championship
	v Higgins	6-9	Quarter-final	Coral UK Championship
1981	v Stevens	5-4	1st round	Benson & Hedges Masters
	v Griffiths	2-5	Quarter-final	Benson & Hedges Masters
	v Edmonds	6-9	1st round	John Courage English Professional
	v David Taylor	3-13	2nd round	Embassy World Professional Championship
	v Williams	0-5	2nd round	Jameson International
	v Knowles	6-9	2nd round	Coral UK Championship
1982	v Reynolds	7-10	1st round	Embassy World Professional Championship
	v Fisher	3-5	Qualifying	Jameson International
	v Sinclair	2-5	1st round	Professional Players Tournament
	v Hallett	7-9	1st round	Coral UK Open
1983	v Williams	1-10	Qualifying	Embassy World Professional Championship
	v Kelly	5-1	Qualifying	Jameson International
	v Morgan	3-5	Qualifying	Jameson International
	v Fisher	4-5	1st round	Professional Players Tournament
	v Watterson	6-9	Qualifying	Coral UK Championship
	v Donnelly	10-5	Qualifying	Embassy World Professional Championship
	v Werbeniuk	4-10	1st round	Embassy World Professional Championship
1984	v Dunning	5-4	Qualifying	Jameson International
	v Virgo	3-5	Qualifying	Jameson International
	v V. Harris	1-5	Qualifying	Rothmans Grand Prix
	v Fowler	4-9	Qualifying	Coral UK Open
1985	v E. McLaughlin	1-5	Qualifying	Mercantile Credit Classic
	v G. Foulds	2-9	Qualifying	Tolly Cobbold English Professional Championship
	v Longworth	1-6	Qualifying	Dulux British Open
	v Chaperon	10-9	Qualifying	Embassy World Professional Championship
	v Williams	6-10	Qualifying	Embassy World Professional Championship
	v Duggan	1-5	2nd round	Goya Matchroom Trophy
	v Simngam	2-5	2nd round	Rothmans Grand Prix
	v John Rea	9-8	2nd round	Coral UK Open
	v Werbeniuk	9-7	3rd round	Coral UK Open

	v Higgins	2-9	4th round	Coral UK Open
1986	v Kelly	5-3	2nd round	Mercantile Credit Classic
	v Stevens	5-2	3rd round	Mercantile Credit Classic
	v E. Hughes	3-5	4th round	Mercantile Credit Classic
	v D. Hughes	9-6	2nd round	Tolly Cobbold English Professional Championship
	v Martin	8-9	3rd round	Tolly Cobbold English Professional Championship
	v Kelly	5-4	2nd round	Dulux British Open
	v Macleod	4-5	3rd round	Dulux British Open
	v Chalmers	10-6	Qualifying	Embassy World Professional Championship
	v P. Francisco	1-10	Qualifying	Embassy World Professional Championship

STEVE DAVIS (England)

Born 22.8.57
Turned professional 1978
World ranking 1 (1)

Steve Davis turned professional in September 1978 with a good amateur record and in November 1980 captured the Coral UK Championship by beating Alex Higgins 16-6 in the final. From that point it seemed as if the Londoner would never stop winning, or at least reaching the finals of major tournaments. From then until the start of the 1984–85 season, he played 96 matches in major tournaments of the best of nine frames or more and lost only 11 of them.

Davis won two ranking tournaments in 1984–85 and three last season. He also reached the final of the Embassy World Championship in both years. In 1985 he led Dennis Taylor 8-0 only to lose 18-17 on the final black and last year was the odds-on favourite to beat the No. 16 seed, Joe Johnson, a 150-1 outsider at the start of the Championship.

But his fourth title eluded him again as Johnson ran out an 18-12 victor and Davis had to be content with remaining at No. 1 in the world rankings without being world champion.

1979	v Anderson	9-1	Prelim	Embassy World Professional Championship
	v Fagan	9-2	Qualifying	Embassy World Professional Championship
	v Dennis Taylor	11-13	1st round	Embassy World Professional Championship
	v Dunning	9-3	2nd round	Coral UK Championship
	v Mountjoy	9-5	3rd round	Coral UK Championship
	v Virgo	7-9	Quarter-final	Coral UK Championship
1980	v Morgan	9-0	Qualifying	Embassy World Professional Championship
	v Fagan	10-6	1st round	Embassy World Professional Championship
	v Griffiths	13-10	2nd round	Embassy World Professional Championship

Year	Opponent	Score	Round	Event
	v Higgins	9-13	Quarter-final	Embassy World Professional Championship
	v Hallett	9-1	1st round	Coral UK Championship
	v Werbeniuk	9-3	2nd round	Coral UK Championship
	v Meo	9-5	Quarter-final	Coral UK Championship
	v Griffiths	9-0	Semi-final	Coral UK Championship
	v Higgins	**16-6**	**Final**	**Coral UK Championship**
1981	v Mans	3-5	1st round	Benson & Hedges Masters
	v Dennis Taylor	5-2	Semi-final	Yamaha International Masters
	v David Taylor	**9-6**	**Final**	**Yamaha International Masters**
	v Meadowcroft	9-2	1st round	John Courage English Professional
	v Spencer	9-7	2nd round	John Courage English Professional
	v Edmonds	9-0	Semi-final	John Courage English Professional
	v Meo	**9-3**	**Final**	**John Courage English Professional**
	v White	10-8	1st round	Embassy World Professional Championship
	v Higgins	13-8	2nd round	Embassy World Professional Championship
	v Griffiths	13-9	Quarter-final	Embassy World Professional Championship
	v Thorburn	16-10	Semi-final	Embassy World Professional Championship
	v Mountjoy	**18-12**	**Final**	**Embassy World Professional Championship**
	v Mountjoy	5-0	Quarter-final	Langs Scottish Masters
	v White	5-6	Semi-final	Langs Scottish Masters
	v Mans	5-3	3rd round	Jameson International
	v David Taylor	5-1	Quarter-final	Jameson International
	v Higgins	9-8	Semi-final	Jameson International
	v Dennis Taylor	**9-0**	**Final**	**Jameson International**
	v Higgins	5-2	1st round	Northern Ireland Classic
	v Griffiths	9-6	Semi-final	Northern Ireland Classic
	v White	9-11	Final	Northern Ireland Classic
	v Thorne	9-2	3rd round	Coral UK Championship
	v Werbeniuk	9-5	Quarter-final	Coral UK Championship
	v White	9-0	Semi-final	Coral UK Championship
	v Griffiths	**16-3**	**Final**	**Coral UK Championship**
1982	v Spencer	5-2	1st round	Lada Classic
	v Reardon	5-4	Semi-final	Lada Classic
	v Griffiths	8-9	Final	Lada Classic
	v Mountjoy	5-2	Quarter-final	Benson & Hedges Masters
	v Meo	6-4	Semi-final	Benson & Hedges Masters
	v Griffiths	**9-5**	**Final**	**Benson & Hedges Masters**
	v Griffiths	**9-7**	**Final**	**Yamaha International Masters**
	v Miles	5-2	Semi-final	Tolly Cobbold Classic
	v Dennis Taylor	**8-3**	**Final**	**Tolly Cobbold Classic**
	v Mountjoy	5-2	Quarter-final	Benson & Hedges Irish Masters
	v Higgins	6-2	Semi-final	Benson & Hedges Irish Masters
	v Griffiths	5-9	Final	Benson & Hedges Irish Masters
	v Knowles	1-10	1st round	Embassy World Professional Championship
	v Knowles	5-4	1st round	Langs Scottish Masters
	v Dennis Taylor	6-1	Semi-final	Langs Scottish Masters
	v Higgins	**9-4**	**Final**	**Langs Scottish Masters**
	v Roscoe	5-0	1st round	Jameson International
	v Reynolds	5-0	2nd round	Jameson International
	v David Taylor	3-5	Quarter-final	Jameson International

	v Williams	9-6	1st round	Coral UK Open
	v Fagan	9-3	2nd round	Coral UK Open
	v Griffiths	6-9	Quarter-final	Coral UK Open
1983	v Dennis Taylor	5-2	1st round	Lada Classic
	v Charlton	5-4	Quarter-final	Lada Classic
	v Spencer	5-4	Semi-final	Lada Classic
	v Werbeniuk	**9-5**	**Final**	**Lada Classic**
	v Wildman	5-2	1st round	Benson & Hedges Masters
	v Mountjoy	4-5	Quarter-final	Benson & Hedges Masters
	v Dennis Taylor	5-1	Semi-final	Tolly Cobbold Classic
	v Griffiths	**7-5**	**Final**	**Tolly Cobbold Classic**
	v Charlton	5-1	Quarter-final	Benson & Hedges Irish Masters
	v Griffiths	6-2	Semi-final	Benson & Hedges Irish Masters
	v Reardon	**9-2**	**Final**	**Benson & Hedges Irish Masters**
	v Williams	10-4	1st round	Embassy World Professional Championship
	v Dennis Taylor	13-11	2nd round	Embassy World Professional Championship
	v Charlton	13-5	Quarter-final	Embassy World Professional Championship
	v Higgins	16-5	Semi-final	Embassy World Professional Championship
	v Thorburn	**18-6**	**Final**	**Embassy World Professional Championship**
	v Macleod	5-1	1st round	Langs Scottish Masters
	v Higgins	6-2	Semi-final	Langs Scottish Masters
	v Knowles	**9-6**	**Final**	**Langs Scottish Masters**
	v E. Hughes	5-1	1st round	Jameson International
	v Watterson	5-0	2nd round	Jameson International
	v S. Francisco	5-1	Quarter-final	Jameson International
	v Charlton	9-2	Semi-final	Jameson International
	v Thorburn	**9-4**	**Final**	**Jameson International**
	v Donnelly	5-1	1st round	Professional Players Tournament
	v Hallett	2-5	2nd round	Professional Players Tournament
	v G. Foulds	9-1	1st round	Coral UK Championship
	v Thorne	9-3	2nd round	Coral UK Championship
	v Meo	9-4	Quarter-final	Coral UK Championship
	v White	9-4	Semi-final	Coral UK Championship
	v Higgins	15-16	Final	Coral UK Championship
1984	v Spencer	5-2	1st round	Lada Classic
	v Griffiths	5-4	Quarter-final	Lada Classic
	v Parrott	5-4	Semi-final	Lada Classic
	v Meo	**9-8**	**Final**	**Lada Classic**
	v Meo	5-0	1st round	Benson & Hedges Masters
	v Stevens	3-5	Quarter-final	Benson & Hedges Masters
	v Meo	5-4	Quarter-final	Benson & Hedges Irish Masters
	v Higgins	6-4	Semi-final	Benson & Hedges Irish Masters
	v Griffiths	**9-1**	**Final**	**Benson & Hedges Irish Masters**
	v Thorne	5-2	1st round	Tolly Cobbold Classic
	v Stevens	5-4	Semi-final	Tolly Cobbold Classic
	v Knowles	**8-2**	**Final**	**Tolly Cobbold Classic**
	v King	10-3	1st round	Embassy World Professional Championship
	v Spencer	13-5	2nd round	Embassy World Professional Championship
	v Griffiths	13-10	Quarter-final	Embassy World Professional Championship
	v Dennis Taylor	16-9	Semi-final	Embassy World Professional Championship

	v White	**18-16**	**Final**	**Embassy World Professional Championship**
	v Thorburn	5-2	1st round	Langs Supreme Scottish Masters
	v Higgins	6-4	Semi-final	Langs Supreme Scottish Masters
	v White	**9-5**	**Final**	**Langs Supreme Scottish Masters**
	v Campbell	5-1	1st round	Jameson International
	v David Taylor	5-1	2nd round	Jameson International
	v Higgins	5-1	Quarter-final	Jameson International
	v E. Hughes	9-3	Semi-final	Jameson International
	v Knowles	**9-2**	**Final**	**Jameson International**
	v Morra	5-2	1st round	Rothmans Grand Prix
	v Miles	5-0	2nd round	Rothmans Grand Prix
	v David Taylor	5-1	3rd round	Rothmans Grand Prix
	v Reynolds	5-0	Quarter-final	Rothmans Grand Prix
	v Thorburn	7-9	Semi-final	Rothmans Grand Prix
	v Murphy	9-1	1st round	Coral UK Open
	v Meo	9-7	2nd round	Coral UK Open
	v White	9-4	Quarter-final	Coral UK Open
	v Stevens	9-2	Semi-final	Coral UK Open
	v Higgins	**16-8**	**Final**	**Coral UK Open**
1985	v S. Francisco	5-0	1st round	Mercantile Credit Classic
	v Higgins	5-2	2nd round	Mercantile Credit Classic
	v Reardon	5-1	Quarter-final	Mercantile Credit Classic
	v Thorne	8-9	Semi-final	Mercantile Credit Classic
	v Higgins	4-5	1st round	Benson & Hedges Masters
	v Fowler	9-3	1st round	Tolly Cobbold English Professional Championship
	v Williams	9-2	2nd round	Tolly Cobbold English Professional Championship
	v Virgo	9-2	Quarter-final	Tolly Cobbold English Professional Championship
	v Meo	9-8	Semi-final	Tolly Cobbold English Professional Championship
	v Knowles	**9-2**	**Final**	**Tolly Cobbold English Professional Championship**
	v Chappel	6-5	1st round	Dulux British Open
	v Virgo	5-2	2nd round	Dulux British Open
	v Bradley	5-2	3rd round	Dulux British Open
	v O'Kane	5-1	Quarter-final	Dulux British Open
	v Stevens	7-9	Semi-final	Dulux British Open
	v E. Hughes	5-4	Quarter-final	Benson & Hedges Irish Masters
	v Higgins	2-6	Semi-final	Benson & Hedges Irish Masters
	v N. Foulds	10-8	1st round	Embassy World Professional Championship
	v David Taylor	13-4	2nd round	Embassy World Professional Championship
	v Griffiths	13-6	Quarter-final	Embassy World Professional Championship
	v Reardon	16-5	Semi-final	Embassy World Professional Championship
	v Dennis Taylor	17-18	Final	Embassy World Professional Championship
	v Bales	5-2	3rd round	Goya Matchroom Trophy
	v Virgo	5-1	4th round	Goya Matchroom Trophy
	v Macleod	5-1	5th round	Goya Matchroom Trophy
	v White	3-5	Quarter-final	Goya Matchroom Trophy

	v Agrawal	5-0	3rd round	Rothmans Grand Prix
	v Fowler	5-1	4th round	Rothmans Grand Prix
	v Higgins	5-0	5th round	Rothmans Grand Prix
	v S. Francisco	5-2	Quarter-final	Rothmans Grand Prix
	v Thorburn	9-5	Semi-final	Rothmans Grand Prix
	v Dennis Taylor	**10-9**	**Final**	**Rothmans Grand Prix**
	v Griffiths	5-4	1st round	BCE Canadian Masters
	v Thorburn	8-1	Semi-final	BCE Canadian Masters
	v Dennis Taylor	5-9	Final	BCE Canadian Masters
	v Sheehan	9-1	3rd round	Coral UK Open
	v Drago	9-2	4th round	Coral UK Open
	v Meo	9-5	5th round	Coral UK Open
	v West	9-1	Quarter-final	Coral UK Open
	v White	9-5	Semi-final	Coral UK Open
	v Thorne	**16-14**	**Final**	**Coral UK Open**
	v Reardon	5-2	1st round	Kit Kat
	v Higgins	6-1	Semi-final	Kit Kat
	v Dennis Taylor	5-9	Final	Kit Kat
1986	v Chaperon	5-1	3rd round	Mercantile Credit Classic
	v Van Rensberg	5-1	4th round	Mercantile Credit Classic
	v P. Francisco	5-0	5th round	Mercantile Credit Classic
	v White	2-5	Quarter-final	Mercantile Credit Classic
	v Griffiths	2-5	1st round	BCE Belgian Classic
	v David Taylor	5-4	1st round	Benson & Hedges Masters
	v Thorne	5-4	Quarter-final	Benson & Hedges Masters
	v White	3-6	Semi-final	Benson & Hedges Masters
	v Bradley	9-3	3rd round	Tolly Cobbold English Professional Championship
	v Martin	9-4	4th round	Tolly Cobbold English Professional Championship
	v Virgo	9-2	Quarter-final	Tolly Cobbold English Professional Championship
	v Meo	7-9	Semi-final	Tolly Cobbold English Professional Championship
	v Black	5-2	3rd round	Dulux British Open
	v Martin	5-1	4th round	Dulux British Open
	v Campbell	5-0	5th round	Dulux British Open
	v Wych	5-2	Quarter-final	Dulux British Open
	v Higgins	9-3	Semi-final	Dulux British Open
	v Thorne	**12-7**	**Final**	**Dulux British Open**
	v Edmonds	10-4	1st round	Embassy World Professional Championship
	v Mountjoy	13-5	2nd round	Embassy World Professional Championship
	v White	13-5	Quarter-final	Embassy World Professional Championship
	v Thorburn	16-12	Semi-final	Embassy World Professional Championship
	v Johnson	12-18	Final	Embassy World Professional Championship

BERT DEMARCO (Scotland)

Born 9.6.24
Turned professional 1981
World ranking 109 (92)

Demarco won the Scottish Amateur Snooker Championship twice and the Scottish Billiards title once. He is now proprietor of snooker and squash clubs in Edinburgh.

1981	v D. Hughes	5-1	Qualifying	Jameson International
	v Hallett	4-5	Qualifying	Jameson International
	v Gibson	3-5	Quarter-final	Scottish Professional Championship
1982	v Watterson	6-9	Qualifying	Embassy World Professional Championship
	v Ross	5-6	Quarter-final	Scottish Professional Championship
	v Morra	2-5	Qualifying	Jameson International
	v Thorne	3-5	1st round	Professional Players Tournament
	v Hallett	1-9	Qualifying	Coral UK Championship
1983	v Kelly	4-10	Qualifying	Embassy World Professional Championship
	v Donnelly	4-6	1st round	Scottish Professional Championship
	v Watterson	3-5	Qualifying	Jameson International
	v Bennett	4-5	Qualifying	Professional Players Tournament
	v Murphy	4-9	Qualifying	Coral UK Open
1984	v Roscoe	7-10	Qualifying	Embassy World Professional Championship
	v Bennett	1-5	Qualifying	Jameson International
	v N. Foulds	2-5	1st round	Rothmans Grand Prix
	v Fowler	3-9	Qualifying	Coral UK Open
1985	v J. McLaughlin	1-5	Qualifying	Mercantile Credit Classic
	v Gibson	1-6	Qualifying	Dulux British Open
	v P. Francisco	4-10	Qualifying	Embassy World Professional Championship
	v Wilkinson	2-5	1st round	Goya Matchroom Trophy
	v West	2-5	1st round	Rothmans Grand Prix
	v Jim Bear	1-9	1st round	Coral UK Open
1986	v Agrawal	5-4	1st round	Mercantile Credit Classic
	v Wych	0-5	2nd round	Mercantile Credit Classic
	v Jenkins	1-5	1st round	Dulux British Open
	v Hendry	1-6	1st round	Canada Dry Scottish Professional Championship
	v Hendry	7-10	Qualifying	Embassy World Professional Championship

LES DODD (England)

Born 11.2.54
Turned professional 1982
World ranking 69 (53)

In his first professional season, Dodd qualified for the Crucible stage of the Embassy World Championship. Two last 32's were his best finishes in the 1985–86 season.

1982	v Macleod	5-1	Qualifying	Jameson International
	v Fitzmaurice	5-3	Qualifying	Jameson International
	v Mans	3-5	1st round	Jameson International
	v Williamson	9-1	Qualifying	Coral UK Championship
	v French	9-7	Qualifying	Coral UK Championship
	v David Taylor	7-9	1st round	Coral UK Championship
1983	v Williamson	10-9	Qualifying	Embassy World Professional Championship
	v Charlton	7-10	1st round	Embassy World Professional Championship
	v Gibson	1-5	Qualifying	Jameson International
	v Griffiths	3-5	1st round	Professional Players Tournament
	v G. Foulds	7-9	Qualifying	Coral UK Championship
1984	v Giannaros	10-1	Qualifying	Embassy World Professional Championship
	v N. Foulds	4-10	Qualifying	Embassy World Professional Championship
	v Foldvari	5-3	Qualifying	Jameson International
	v Wilson	5-1	Qualifying	Jameson International
	v Reardon	4-5	1st round	Jameson International
	v Medati	4-5	Qualifying	Rothmans Grand Prix
	v Newbury	9-6	Qualifying	Coral UK Open
	v Wilson	8-9	Qualifying	Coral UK Open
1985	v T. Jones	1-5	Qualifying	Mercantile Credit Classic
	v Bales	9-5	Qualifying	Tolly Cobbold English Professional Championship
	v Thorne	1-9	1st round	Tolly Cobbold English Professional Championship
	v V. Harris	1-6	Qualifying	Dulux British Open
	v O'Kane	7-10	Qualifying	Embassy World Professional Championship
	v Sim-Ngam	5-4	2nd round	Goya Matchroom Trophy
	v N. Foulds	3-5	3rd round	Goya Matchroom Trophy
	v Chappel	2-5	2nd round	Rothmans Grand Prix
	v Thorburn	4-9	3rd round	Coral UK Open
1986	v Rigitano	3-5	2nd round	Mercantile Credit Classic
	v Oliver	5-9	2nd round	Tolly Cobbold English Professional Championship
	v Jonik	5-4	2nd round	Dulux British Open
	v Thorne	2-5	3rd round	Dulux British Open
	v Fitzmaurice	10-6	Qualifying	Embassy World Professional Championship
	v Watterson	10-1	Qualifying	Embassy World Professional Championship
	v Mans	7-10	Qualifying	Embassy World Professional Championship

JIM DONNELLY (Scotland)

Born 13.6.46
Turned professional 1981
World ranking 73 (46)

Scottish amateur champion in 1978, Donnelly played for his country in the 1982 State Express World Team Classic, the 1985 Guinness World Cup and the 1986 Car Care Plan World Cup.

1981	v Johnson	4-5	Qualifying	Jameson International
	v Sinclair	5-0	Quarter-final	Scottish Professional Championship

	v Gibson	4-6	Semi-final	Scottish Professional Championship
	v Medati	7-9	Qualifying	Coral UK Championship
1982	v Gibson	9-8	Qualifying	Embassy World Professional Championship
	v Sinclair	9-8	Qualifying	Embassy World Professional Championship
	v Reardon	5-10	1st round	Embassy World Professional Championship
	v Macleod	5-6	1st round	Scottish Professional Championship
	v Williamson	3-5	Qualifying	Jameson International
	v Watterson	4-5	1st round	Professional Players Tournament
	v Ross	9-5	Qualifying	Coral UK Championship
	v Knowles	6-9	1st round	Coral UK Championship
1983	v Sheehan	10-6	Qualifying	Embassy World Professional Championship
	v Campbell	2-10	Qualifying	Embassy World Professional Championship
	v Demarco	6-4	1st round	Scottish Professional Championship
	v Sinclair	5-6	Semi-final	Scottish Professional Championship
	v Bennett	5-1	Qualifying	Jameson International
	v Wilson	5-1	Qualifying	Jameson International
	v David Taylor	5-3	1st round	Jameson International
	v S. Francisco	1-5	2nd round	Jameson International
	v S. Davis	1-5	1st round	Professional Players Tournament
	v Murphy	4-9	Qualifying	Coral UK Championship
1984	v Watchorn	10-7	Qualifying	Embassy World Professional Championship
	v Anderson	10-6	Qualifying	Embassy World Professional Championship
	v F. Davis	5-10	Qualifying	Embassy World Professional Championship
	v G. Foulds	3-5	Qualifying	Jameson International
	v Hargreaves	5-4	Qualifying	Rothmans Grand Prix
	v Wilson	2-5	1st round	Rothmans Grand Prix
	v Gibson	9-6	Qualifying	Coral UK Open
	v Campbell	6-9	Qualifying	Coral UK Open
1985	v Watchorn	5-1	Qualifying	Mercantile Credit Classic
	v Williams	3-5	Qualifying	Mercantile Credit Classic
	v W. Jones	1-6	Qualifying	Dulux British Open
	v Fowler	0-10	Qualifying	Embassy World Professional Championship
	v Jim Bear	2-5	2nd round	Goya Matchroom Trophy
	v Kelly	4-5	2nd round	Rothmans Grand Prix
	v Drago	8-9	1st round	Coral UK Open
1986	v Chalmers	5-0	2nd round	Mercantile Credit Classic
	v Campbell	2-5	3rd round	Mercantile Credit Classic
	v Wilkinson	5-4	2nd round	Dulux British Open
	v Meo	3-5	3rd round	Dulux British Open
	v John Rea	1-6	Quarter-final	Canada Dry Scottish Professional Championship
	v Smith	10-6	Qualifying	Embassy World Professional Championship
	v West	5-10	Qualifying	Embassy World Professional Championship

TONY DRAGO (Malta)

Born 22.9.65
Turned professional 1985
World ranking 37

In his first season as a professional, Drago recorded wins over Murdo Macleod and Eddie Charlton to reach the last 16 of the Rothmans Grand Prix and was a member of the Rest of the World team in the Car Care Plan World Cup. He is Malta's only professional.

1985	v Bales	2-5	1st round	Goya Matchroom Trophy
	v Watchorn	5-2	1st round	Rothmans Grand Prix
	v King	5-4	2nd round	Rothmans Grand Prix
	v Macleod	5-3	3rd round	Rothmans Grand Prix
	v Charlton	5-3	4th round	Rothmans Grand Prix
	v Wilson	2-5	5th round	Rothmans Grand Prix
	v Gilbert	9-5	1st round	Coral UK Open
	v Donnelly	9-8	2nd round	Coral UK Open
	v Wildman	9-5	3rd round	Coral UK Open
	v S. Davis	2-9	4th round	Coral UK Open
1986	v Cripsey	4-5	1st round	Mercantile Credit Classic
	v Gauvreau	5-3	2nd round	Dulux British Open
	v Williams	1-5	3rd round	Dulux British Open
	v Cripsey	10-4	Qualifying	Embassy World Professional Championship
	v P. Francisco	4-10	Qualifying	Embassy World Professional Championship

STEVE DUGGAN (England)

Born 10.4.58
Turned professional 1983
World ranking 35 (70)

Playing the professional circuit for the third time, Duggan had his most successful season beating Ray Reardon and Willie Thorne in reaching the quarter-finals of the Goya Matchroom Trophy.

1983	v Darrington	5-4	Qualifying	Professional Players Tournament
	v Dunning	5-2	1st round	Professional Players Tournament
	v Reardon	2-5	2nd round	Professional Players Tournament
	v G. Foulds	8-9	Qualifying	Coral UK Championship
1984	v Browne	9-10	Qualifying	Embassy World Professional Championship
	v T. Jones	5-2	Qualifying	Jameson International
	v Sinclair	0-5	Qualifying	Jameson International
	v Browne	5-2	Qualifying	Rothmans Grand Prix
	v S. Francisco	3-5	1st round	Rothmans Grand Prix
	v O'Kane	6-9	Qualifying	Coral UK Open
1985	v W. Jones	5-0	Qualifying	Mercantile Credit Classic
	v King	4-5	Qualifying	Mercantile Credit Classic
	v B. Harris	9-8	Qualifying	Tolly Cobbold English Professional Championship

	v Hallett	4-9	1st round	Tolly Cobbold English Professional Championship
	v Foldvari	4-6	Qualifying	Dulux British Open
	v T. Jones	8-10	Qualifying	Embassy World Professional Championship
	v F. Davis	5-1	2nd round	Goya Matchroom Trophy
	v Reardon	5-3	3rd round	Goya Matchroom Trophy
	v Black	5-1	4th round	Goya Matchroom Trophy
	v Thorne	5-4	5th round	Goya Matchroom Trophy
	v Thorburn	2-5	Quarter-final	Goya Matchroom Trophy
	v Gauvreau	5-4	2nd round	Rothmans Grand Prix
	v Wildman	4-5	3rd round	Rothmans Grand Prix
	v Wych	5-9	2nd round	Coral UK Open
1986	v King	2-5	2nd round	Mercantile Credit Classic
	v Longworth	4-9	2nd round	Tolly Cobbold English Professional Championship
	v Murphy	5-1	2nd round	Dulux British Open
	v Hallett	3-5	3rd round	Dulux British Open
	v Fisher	10-3	Qualifying	Embassy World Professional Championship
	v Wych	5-10	Qualifying	Embassy World Professional Championship

JOHN DUNNING (England)

Born 18.4.27
Turned professional 1970
World ranking 83 (64)

The best performance of Dunning's 16-year professional career was to reach the final group of the 1984 Yamaha International. During the qualifying section of the 1984 Rothmans Grand Prix, he suffered a heart-attack and a combination of his health and business commitments have subsequently restricted his playing commitments.

1972	v Houlihan	11-10	Qualifying	World Professional Championship
	v Miles	11-5	Qualifying	World Professional Championship
	v Pulman	7-19	1st round	World Professional Championship
1973	v David Taylor	4-9	1st round	World Professional Championship
1974	v David Taylor	8-6	1st round	World Professional Championship
	v Charlton	15-13	2nd round	World Professional Championship
	v Miles	13-15	Quarter-final	World Professional Championship
1975	v G. Owen	8-15	2nd round	World Professional Championship
1976	v Reardon	7-15	1st round	Embassy World Professional Championship
1977	v Virgo	6-11	Qualifying	Embassy World Professional Championship
	v Parkin	5-4	1st round	Super Crystalate UK Championship
	v Higgins	0-5	Quarter-final	Super Crystalate UK Championship
1978	v Fagan	5-9	Qualifying	Embassy World Professional Championship
	v Greaves	9-3	Qualifying	Coral UK Championship
	v F. Davis	2-9	1st round	Coral UK Championship
1979	v Jack Rea	9-5	Prelim	Embassy World Professional Championship
	v David Taylor	8-9	Qualifying	Embassy World Professional Championship

	v Greaves	9-8	1st round	Coral UK Championship
	v S. Davis	3-9	2nd round	Coral UK Championship
1980	v Johnson	6-9	Qualifying	Coral UK Championship
1981	v Greaves	9-4	Qualifying	John Courage English Professional
	v David Taylor	9-8	1st round	John Courage English Professional
	v Thorne	0-9	2nd round	John Courage English Professional
	v Bennett	9-6	Qualifying	Embassy World Professional Championship
	v Fagan	9-7	Qualifying	Embassy World Professional Championship
	v Stevens	4-10	1st round	Embassy World Professional Championship
	v Gibson	5-3	Qualifying	Jameson International
	v Martin	2-5	1st round	Jameson International
1982	v Macleod	9-4	Qualifying	Embassy World Professional Championship
	v Spencer	4-10	1st round	Embassy World Professional Championship
	v Roscoe	2-5	Qualifying	Jameson International
	v Wildman	4-5	1st round	Professional Players Tournament
	Houlihan *wo* Dunning *scr*		Qualifying	Coral UK Championship
1983	v B. Harris	3-5	Qualifying	Jameson International
	v Duggan	2-5	1st round	Professional Players Tournament
	v Andrewartha	9-2	Qualifying	Coral UK Championship
	v Spencer	7-9	1st round	Coral UK Championship
1984	v Oliver	3-10	Qualifying	Embassy World Professional Championship
	v Cripsey	5-3	Qualifying	Jameson International
	v F. Davis	4-5	Qualifying	Jameson International
	v D. Hughes	5-0	Qualifying	Rothmans Grand Prix
	v Mans	5-4	1st round	Rothmans Grand Prix
	v Knowles	1-5	2nd round	Rothmans Grand Prix
	v John Rea	3-9	Qualifying	Coral UK Open
1985	v W. Jones	6-10	Qualifying	Embassy World Professional Championship
	v Everton	5-2	2nd round	Goya Matchroom Trophy
	v Meo	0-5	3rd round	Goya Matchroom Trophy
	v Agrawal	0-5	2nd round	Rothmans Grand Prix
1986	v West	3-10	Qualifying	Embassy World Professional Championship

RAY EDMONDS (England)

Born 28.5.36
Turned professional 1978
World ranking 46 (51)

Twice World amateur champion, Edmonds only achieved a measure of this success as a professional snooker player but gained some consolation in March 1985 when he won the Eurotherm World Professional Billiards Championship by beating the defending titleholder Mark Wildman in the semi-finals and Norman Dagley in the final. He is a regular member of ITV's commentary team.

1978	v Virgo	4-9	Qualifying	Coral UK Championship
1979	v Meadowcroft	9-3	2nd round	Coral UK Championship
	v F. Davis	9-6	3rd round	Coral UK Championship
	v Werbeniuk	8-9	Quarter-final	Coral UK Championship
1980	v Hood	9-6	Qualifying	Embassy World Professional Championship
	v David Taylor	3-10	1st round	Embassy World Professional Championship
	v Hallett	8-9	Qualifying	Coral UK Championship
1981	v Hallett	9-3	Qualifying	John Courage English Professional
	v F. Davis	9-6	1st round	John Courage English Professional
	v Johnson	9-5	2nd round	John Courage English Professional
	v S. Davis	0-9	Semi-final	John Courage English Professional
	v Wildman	9-3	Qualifying	Embassy World Professional Championship
	v Williams	9-7	Qualifying	Embassy World Professional Championship
	v Spencer	9-10	1st round	Embassy World Professional Championship
	v E. Hughes	5-4	1st round	Jameson International
	v Spencer	3-5	2nd round	Jameson International
	v Thorne	4-9	2nd round	Coral UK Championship
1982	v Reynolds	6-9	Qualifying	Embassy World Professional Championship
	v D. Hughes	5-0	Qualifying	Jameson International
	v Miles	5-1	Qualifying	Jameson International
	v Spencer	2-5	1st round	Jameson International
	v Dennis Taylor	4-5	1st round	Professional Players Tournament
	v Fisher	8-9	Qualifying	Coral UK Championship
1983	v Jonik	10-4	Qualifying	Embassy World Professional Championship
	v Reynolds	6-10	Qualifying	Embassy World Professional Championship
	v Jack Rea	5-1	Qualifying	Jameson International
	v E. McLaughlin	5-1	Qualifying	Jameson International
	v Knowles	1-5	1st round	Jameson International
	v Stevens	1-5	1st round	Professional Players Tournament
	v Medati	7-9	Qualifying	Coral UK Championship
1984	v Greaves	10-0	Qualifying	Embassy World Professional Championship
	v Van Rensberg	9-10	Qualifying	Embassy World Professional Championship
	v Foldvari	1-5	Qualifying	Jameson International
	v Rigitano	3-5	Qualifying	Rothmans Grand Prix
	v John Rea	6-9	Qualifying	Coral UK Open
1985	v Hargreaves	5-2	Qualifying	Mercantile Credit Classic
	v Watterson	5-2	Qualifying	Mercantile Credit Classic
	v Johnson	4-5	Qualifying	Mercantile Credit Classic
	v Longworth	4-9	Qualifying	Tolly Cobbold English Professional Championship
	v Mienie	6-1	Qualifying	Dulux British Open
	v Miles	1-6	1st round	Dulux British Open
	v Foldvari	10-3	Qualifying	Embassy World Professional Championship
	v Wildman	10-7	Qualifying	Embassy World Professional Championship
	v Stevens	8-10	1st round	Embassy World Professional Championship
	v Bales	0-5	2nd round	Goya Matchroom Trophy
	v Kearney	5-2	2nd round	Rothmans Grand Prix
	v O'Kane	5-2	3rd round	Rothmans Grand Prix
	v Knowles	3-5	4th round	Rothmans Grand Prix
	v Van Rensberg	9-5	2nd round	Coral UK Open

	v Higgins	8-9	3rd round	Coral UK Open
1986	v Smith	2-5	2nd round	Mercantile Credit Classic
	v Smith	9-8	2nd round	Tolly Cobbold English Professional Championship
	v David Taylor	9-6	3rd round	Tolly Cobbold English Professional Championship
	v N. Foulds	4-9	4th round	Tolly Cobbold English Professional Championship
	v Hargreaves	3-5	2nd round	Dulux British Open
	v Kelly	10-0	Qualifying	Embassy World Professional Championship
	v Darrington	10-5	Qualifying	Embassy World Professional Championship
	v Wildman	10-9	Qualifying	Embassy World Professional Championship
	v S. Davis	4-10	1st round	Embassy World Professional Championship

FRANÇOIS ELLIS (South Africa)

Born –
Turned professional 1983
World ranking unranked

South African amateur champion in 1979, Ellis first turned professional in 1983, allowed his membership to the WPBSA to lapse and was reinstated in 1985. He has not yet played on the circuit.

CLIVE EVERTON (Wales)

Born 7.9.37
Turned professional 1981
World ranking 100 (73)

Everton's playing commitments now take second place to his media activities. Five times Welsh amateur billiards champion, he is snooker correspondent of the *Guardian* and *The Sunday Times*, the editor/proprietor of *Snooker Scene* magazine and a member of the BBC commentary team.

1981	v Kennerley	5-4	Qualifying	Jameson International
	v Watterson	4-5	Qualifying	Jameson International
	v Gibson	9-7	Qualifying	Coral UK Championship
	v White	4-9	Qualifying	Coral UK Championship
1982	v Reardon	1-6	1st round	Woodpecker Welsh Professional Championship
	v D. Hughes	4-9	Qualifying	Embassy World Professional Championship
	v Watterson	1-5	Qualifying	Jameson International
	v Fagan	5-2	1st round	Professional Players Tournament
	v Thorburn	2-5	2nd round	Professional Players Tournament
	v Murphy	4-9	Qualifying	Coral UK Championship

1983	v Griffiths	1-6	Quarter-final	Woodpecker Welsh Professional Championship
	v Wilson	1-10	Qualifying	Embassy World Professional Championship
	v Andrewartha	1-5	Qualifying	Jameson International
	v Thorne	1-5	1st round	Professional Players Tournament
	v Watterson	6-9	Qualifying	Coral UK Championship
1984	v Mountjoy	1-6	1st round	Strongbow Welsh Professional Championship
	v Parrott	2-10	Qualifying	Embassy World Professional Championship
	v Mikkelsen	0-5	Qualifying	Jameson International
	v Houlihan	5-3	Qualifying	Rothmans Grand Prix
	v Charlton	1-5	1st round	Rothmans Grand Prix
	v Watchorn	6-9	Qualifying	Coral UK Open
1985	v Browne	0-5	Qualifying	Mercantile Credit Classic
	v Fowler	1-6	Qualifying	Dulux British Open
	v G. Foulds	2-10	Qualifying	Embassy World Professional Championship
	v Reardon	2-6	Quarter-final	BCE Welsh Professional Championship
	v Dunning	2-5	2nd round	Goya Matchroom Trophy
	v P. Francisco	0-5	2nd round	Rothmans Grand Prix
	v Murphy	4-9	2nd round	Coral UK Open
1986	v Browne	0-5	2nd round	Mercantile Credit Classic
	v W. Jones	2-6	1st round	Zetters Welsh Professional Championship
	v Medati	1-5	2nd round	Dulux British Open
	v Miles	3-10	Qualifying	Embassy World Professional Championship

PATSY FAGAN (Republic of Ireland)

Born 15.1.51
Turned professional 1976
World ranking 42 (33)

After Fagan had won the inaugural United Kingdom Championship in 1977 and reached the quarter-finals of the Embassy World Championship the following spring, his form deteriorated as he suffered a mental block which made him unable to use the rest. Miraculously, however, the problem ceased to trouble him during the 1984–85 season and he reached the second round of the Embassy World Championship after a 10-6 victory over Willie Thorne.

Last season, his best performance was to beat Tony Knowles 5-4 in the quarter-finals of the Benson and Hedges Irish Masters.

1977	v Meadowcroft	11-9	Qualifying	Embassy World Professional Championship
	v Reardon	7-13	1st round	Embassy World Professional Championship
	v Jack Rea	5-1	1st round	Super Crystalate UK Championship
	v F. Davis	5-0	2nd round	Super Crystalate UK Championship
	v Meadowcroft	5-4	Quarter-final	Super Crystalate UK Championship
	v Virgo	9-8	Semi-final	Super Crystalate UK Championship
	v Mountjoy	**12-9**	**Final**	**Super Crystalate UK Championship**

1978	v Pulman	2-4	1st round	Benson & Hedges Masters
	v Dunning	9-5	Qualifying	Embassy World Professional Championship
	v Higgins	13-12	1st round	Embassy World Professional Championship
	v F. Davis	10-13	Quarter-final	Embassy World Professional Championship
	v David Taylor	7-9	1st round	Coral UK Championship
1979	v S. Davis	2-9	Qualifying	Embassy World Professional Championship
	v Hallett	9-4	2nd round	Coral UK Championship
	v Miles	9-5	3rd round	Coral UK Championship
	v Dennis Taylor	6-9	Quarter-final	Coral UK Championship
1980	v S. Davis	6-10	1st round	Embassy World Professional Championship
	v Johnson	9-4	1st round	Coral UK Championship
	v Griffiths	8-9	2nd round	Coral UK Championship
1981	v Dunning	7-9	Qualifying	Embassy World Professional Championship
	v Watterson	5-2	Qualifying	Jameson International
	v Higgins	3-5	2nd round	Jameson International
	v Hallett	5-9	Qualifying	Coral UK Championship
1982	v Murphy	2-6	Quarter-final	Irish Professional Championship
	v French	9-6	Qualifying	Embassy World Professional Championship
	v David Taylor	10-9	1st round	Embassy World Professional Championship
	v Stevens	7-13	2nd round	Embassy World Professional Championship
	v Watterson	1-5	Qualifying	Jameson International
	v Everton	2-5	1st round	Professional Players Tournament
	v B. Harris	9-6	1st round	Coral UK Championship
	v S. Davis	3-9	2nd round	Coral UK Championship
1983	v Murphy	6-4	Quarter-final	Irish Professional Championship
	v Dennis Taylor	1-6	Semi-final	Irish Professional Championship
	v Fisher	8-10	Qualifying	Embassy World Professional Championship
	v Martin	0-5	Qualifying	Jameson International
	v Parrott	2-5	1st round	Professional Players Tournament
1984	v Higgins	3-5	Qualifying	Lada Classic
	v Wych	3-10	Qualifying	Embassy World Professional Championship
	v Newbury	0-5	Qualifying	Jameson International
	v T. Jones	2-9	Qualifying	Coral UK Open
1985	v Williamson	5-1	Qualifying	Mercantile Credit Classic
	v Wildman	5-3	Qualifying	Mercantile Credit Classic
	v Griffiths	0-5	1st round	Mercantile Credit Classic
	v Murphy	6-2	Quarter-final	Irish Professional Championship
	v Higgins	3-6	Semi-final	Irish Professional Championship
	v Gibson	10-8	Qualifying	Embassy World Professional Championship
	v Wilson	10-9	Qualifying	Embassy World Professional Championship
	v Thorne	10-6	1st round	Embassy World Professional Championship
	v Reardon	9-13	2nd round	Embassy World Professional Championship
	v Mienie	5-4	2nd round	Goya Matchroom Trophy
	v White	2-5	3rd round	Goya Matchroom Trophy
	v Oliver	4-5	2nd round	Rothmans Grand Prix
	v B. Harris	9-2	2nd round	Coral UK Open
	v N. Foulds	5-9	3rd round	Coral UK Open
1986	v Fitzmaurice	3-5	2nd round	Mercantile Credit Classic
	v Fitzmaurice	5-4	2nd round	Dulux British Open
	v Mountjoy	5-1	3rd round	Dulux British Open

	v Parrott	0-5	4th round	Dulux British Open
	v Knowles	5-4	Quarter-final	Benson & Hedges Irish Masters
	v White	0-6	Semi-final	Benson & Hedges Irish Masters
	v Thornley	7-10	Qualifying	Embassy World Professional Championship
	v Kearney	0-5	1st round	Strongbow Irish Professional Championship

MICK FISHER (England)

Born 12.7.44
Turned professional 1982
World ranking 87 (54)

Fisher is the proprietor of the successful Greyfriars Snooker Centre in Bedford.

1982	v Murphy	5-1	Qualifying	Jameson International
	v F. Davis	5-3	Qualifying	Jameson International
	v David Taylor	1-5	1st round	Jameson International
	v Black	9-3	Qualifying	Coral UK Championship
	v Edmonds	9-8	Qualifying	Coral UK Championship
	v Reynolds	6-9	1st round	Coral UK Championship
1983	v Fagan	10-8	Qualifying	Embassy World Professional Championship
	v E. McLaughlin	10-9	Qualifying	Embassy World Professional Championship
	v Stevens	2-10	1st round	Embassy World Professional Championship
	v E. Hughes	4-5	Qualifying	Jameson International
	v F. Davis	5-4	1st round	Professional Players Tournament
	v Charlton	4-5	2nd round	Professional Players Tournament
	v Parrott	0-9	Qualifying	Coral UK Championship
1984	v Thornley	10-8	Qualifying	Embassy World Professional Championship
	v Gibson	7-10	Qualifying	Embassy World Professional Championship
	v Bales	3-5	Qualifying	Jameson International
	v Newbury	0-5	Qualifying	Rothmans Grand Prix
	v Watchorn	9-5	Qualifying	Coral UK Open
	v Williams	8-9	Qualifying	Coral UK Open
1985	v Longworth	1-5	Qualifying	Mercantile Credit Classic
	v French	9-8	Qualifying	Tolly Cobbold English Professional Championship
	v Meo	3-9	1st round	Tolly Cobbold English Professional Championship
	v John Rea	0-6	Qualifying	Dulux British Open
	v Rigitano	2-10	Qualifying	Embassy World Professional Championship
	v Mikkelsen	3-5	1st round	Goya Matchroom Trophy
	v Bales	3-5	2nd round	Rothmans Grand Prix
	v Simngam	4-9	2nd round	Coral UK Open
1986	v Jack Rea	5-3	2nd round	Mercantile Credit Classic
	v Higgins	0-5	3rd round	Mercantile Credit Classic
	v Chalmers	2-9	2nd round	Tolly Cobbold English Professional Championship
	v J. McLaughlin	3-5	2nd round	Dulux British Open
	v Duggan	3-10	Qualifying	Embassy World Professional Championship

JACK FITZMAURICE (England)

Born 25.4.28
Turned professional 1981
World ranking 76 (74)

Fitzmaurice won the All England CIU Championship in 1975 and was runner-up in the English Amateur Championship in 1958.

1981	v Bennett	5-1	Qualifying	Jameson International
	v E. Hughes	3-5	Qualifying	Jameson International
	v Gibson	6-9	Qualifying	Coral UK Championship
1982	v Morra	9-7	Qualifying	Embassy World Professional Championship
	v Stevens	4-10	1st round	Embassy World Professional Championship
	v Black	5-3	Qualifying	Jameson International
	v Dodd	3-5	Qualifying	Jameson International
	v Sheehan	5-1	1st round	Professional Players Tournament
	v Reynolds	0-5	2nd round	Professional Players Tournament
	v Kelly	0-8	Qualifying	Coral UK Championship
1983	v E. Hughes	7-10	Qualifying	Embassy World Professional Championship
	v Morgan	4-5	Qualifying	Jameson International
	v Martin	0-5	1st round	Professional Players Tournament
	v B. Harris	3-9	Qualifying	Coral UK Championship
1984	v Murphy	8-10	Qualifying	Embassy World Professional Championship
	v O'Kane	4-5	Qualifying	Jameson International
	v John Rea	2-5	Qualifying	Rothmans Grand Prix
	v Cripsey	9-8	Qualifying	Coral UK Open
	v Parrott	6-9	Qualifying	Coral UK Open
1985	v G. Foulds	1-5	Qualifying	Mercantile Credit Classic
	v Greaves	9-3	Qualifying	Tolly Cobbold English Professional Championship
	v Reynolds	2-9	1st round	Tolly Cobbold English Professional Championship
	v Watterson	1-6	Qualifying	Dulux British Open
	v T. Jones	4-10	Qualifying	Embassy World Professional Championship
	v Watterson	5-2	2nd round	Goya Matchroom Trophy
	v Macleod	1-5	3rd round	Goya Matchroom Trophy
	v Sinclair	5-3	2nd round	Rothmans Grand Prix
	v White	0-5	3rd round	Rothmans Grand Prix
	v W. Jones	3-9	2nd round	Coral UK Open
1986	v Fagan	5-3	2nd round	Mercantile Credit Classic
	v Dennis Taylor	1-5	3rd round	Mercantile Credit Classic
	v Miles	5-9	2nd round	Tolly Cobbold English Professional Championship
	v Fagan	4-5	2nd round	Dulux British Open
	v Dodd	6-10	Qualifying	Embassy World Professional Championship

ROBBIE FOLDVARI (Australia)

Born 2.6.60
Turned professional 1984
World ranking 69 (62)

A former Australian amateur billiards champion, Foldvari won the 1986 Monarflex World Professional Billiards title, only the second time he had competed in the event.

1984	v Rigitano	5-2	Qualifying	Jameson International
	v Edmonds	5-1	Qualifying	Jameson International
	v Dodd	3-5	Qualifying	Jameson International
	v Gauvreau	2-5	Qualifying	Rothmans Grand Prix
	v Greaves	9-5	Qualifying	Coral UK Open
	v Cripsey	7-9	Qualifying	Coral UK Open
1985	v Houlihan	5-1	Qualifying	Mercantile Credit Classic
	v Jack Rea	5-4	Qualifying	Mercantile Credit Classic
	v Martin	5-2	Qualifying	Mercantile Credit Classic
	v Thorne	2-5	1st round	Mercantile Credit Classic
	v Duggan	6-4	Qualifying	Dulux British Open
	v Meo	0-6	1st round	Dulux British Open
	v Oliver	10-3	Qualifying	Embassy World Professional Championship
	v Edmonds	3-10	Qualifying	Embassy World Professional Championship
	v Robinson	7-2	2nd round	Australian Professional Championship
	v Campbell	5-8	Quarter-final	Australian Professional Championship
	v V. Harris	5-4	2nd round	Goya Matchroom Trophy
	v Spencer	4-5	3rd round	Goya Matchroom Trophy
	v Darrington	3-5	2nd round	Rothmans Grand Prix
	v Darrington	6-9	2nd round	Coral UK Open
1986	v Houlihan	4-5	2nd round	Mercantile Credit Classic
	v Kearney	5-2	2nd round	Dulux British Open
	v Werbeniuk	4-5	3rd round	Dulux British Open
	v Rigitano	10-6	Qualifying	Embassy World Professional Championship
	v Miles	10-7	Qualifying	Embassy World Professional Championship
	v Parrott	6-10	Qualifying	Embassy World Professional Championship

GEOFF FOULDS (England)

Born 20.11.39
Turned professional 1981
World ranking 79 (78)

The senior of the London father-and-son combination, Foulds is resident professional at Ealing Snooker Club and has recently made a speciality of acting as technical adviser to film and television dramas with snooker backgrounds.

1981	v French	2-5	Qualifying	Jameson International
	v Kelly	9-7	Qualifying	Coral UK Championship
	v Knowles	1-9	Qualifying	Coral UK Championship

1982	v Wildman	8-9	Qualifying	Embassy World Professional Championship
	v Kelly	4-5	Qualifying	Jameson International
	v Spencer	1-5	1st round	Professional Players Tournament
	v Gibson	9-3	Qualifying	Coral UK Championship
	v Williams	7-9	Qualifying	Coral UK Championship
1983	v Gibson	10-6	Qualifying	Embassy World Professional Championship
	v Meo	4-10	Qualifying	Embassy World Professional Championship
	v Burke	5-2	Qualifying	Jameson International
	v E. Hughes	1-5	Qualifying	Jameson International
	v Burke	4-5	Qualifying	Professional Players Tournament
	v Duggan	9-8	Qualifying	Coral UK Championship
	v Dodd	9-7	Qualifying	Coral UK Championship
	v S. Davis	1-9	1st round	Coral UK Championship
1984	v Morra	2-10	Qualifying	Embassy World Professional Championship
	v P. Francisco	5-4	Qualifying	Jameson International
	v Williamson	5-4	Qualifying	Jameson International
	v Donnelly	5-3	Qualifying	Jameson International
	v Campbell	3-5	Qualifying	Jameson International
	v Murphy	1-5	Qualifying	Rothmans Grand Prix
	v D. Hughes	9-7	Qualifying	Coral UK Open
	v Browne	5-9	Qualifying	Coral UK Open
1985	v Chaperon	5-3	Qualifying	Mercantile Credit Classic
	v Jonik	5-2	Qualifying	Mercantile Credit Classic
	v Fitzmaurice	5-1	Qualifying	Mercantile Credit Classic
	v Hallett	4-5	Qualifying	Mercantile Credit Classic
	v F. Davis	9-2	Qualifying	Tolly Cobbold English Professional Championship
	v Parrott	4-9	1st round	Tolly Cobbold English Professional Championship
	v T. Jones	0-6	Qualifying	Dulux British Open
	v Parkin	10-6	Qualifying	Embassy World Professional Championship
	v Everton	10-2	Qualifying	Embassy World Professional Championship
	v Roscoe	10-7	Qualifying	Embassy World Professional Championship
	v Johnson	6-10	Qualifying	Embassy World Professional Championship
	v Roscoe	3-5	2nd round	Goya Matchroom Trophy
	v Black	5-3	2nd round	Rothmans Grand Prix
	v Charlton	1-5	3rd round	Rothmans Grand Prix
	v Sinclair	4-9	2nd round	Coral UK Open
1986	v Black	5-2	2nd round	Mercantile Credit Classic
	v Werbeniuk	3-5	3rd round	Mercantile Credit Classic
	v Watterson	9-1	2nd round	Tolly Cobbold English Professional Championship
	v N. Foulds	4-9	3rd round	Tolly Cobbold English Professional Championship
	v P. Francisco	2-5	2nd round	Dulux British Open
	v Roscoe	3-10	Qualifying	Embassy World Professional Championship

NEAL FOULDS (England)

Born 13.7.63
Turned professional 1983
World ranking 13 (23)

One semi-final, in the Goya Matchroom Trophy, and one quarter-final, in the Mercantile Credit Classic, have helped Foulds move up to 13th in the world rankings. He also reached the final of the Tolly Cobbold English Professional Championship where he lost 9-7 to Tony Meo.

1983	v French	2-5	Qualifying	Professional Players Tournament
	v Roscoe	9-2	Qualifying	Coral UK Championship
	v Meadowcroft	9-2	Qualifying	Coral UK Championship
	v David Taylor	4-9	1st round	Coral UK Championship
1984	v French	10-5	Qualifying	Embassy World Professional Championship
	v Dodd	10-4	Qualifying	Embassy World Professional Championship
	v Meadowcroft	10-2	Qualifying	Embassy World Professional Championship
	v Higgins	10-9	1st round	Embassy World Professional Championship
	v Mountjoy	6-13	2nd round	Embassy World Professional Championship
	v Bennett	5-0	Qualifying	Jameson International
	v Griffiths	3-5	1st round	Jameson International
	v Demarco	5-2	1st round	Rothmans Grand Prix
	v T. Jones	5-0	2nd round	Rothmans Grand Prix
	v Thorne	5-1	3rd round	Rothmans Grand Prix
	v Knowles	5-2	Quarter-final	Rothmans Grand Prix
	v Dennis Taylor	9-3	Semi-final	Rothmans Grand Prix
	v Fowler	6-9	Qualifying	Coral UK Open
1985	v Longworth	3-5	Qualifying	Mercantile Credit Classic
	v D. Hughes	9-3	1st round	Tolly Cobbold English Professional Championship
	v White	7-9	2nd round	Tolly Cobbold English Professional Championship
	v Hargreaves	6-1	1st round	Dulux British Open
	v Higgins	1-5	2nd round	Dulux British Open
	v Rigitano	10-8	Qualifying	Embassy World Professional Championship
	v S. Davis	8-10	1st round	Embassy World Professional Championship
	v Dodd	5-3	3rd round	Goya Matchroom Trophy
	v Knowles	5-3	4th round	Goya Matchroom Trophy
	v David Taylor	5-4	5th round	Goya Matchroom Trophy
	v Johnson	5-2	Quarter-final	Goya Matchroom Trophy
	v White	5-9	Semi-final	Goya Matchroom Trophy
	v Darrington	5-0	3rd round	Rothmans Grand Prix
	v Higgins	3-5	4th round	Rothmans Grand Prix
	v Fagan	9-5	3rd round	Coral UK Open
	v Johnson	9-8	4th round	Coral UK Open
	v Dennis Taylor	5-9	5th round	Coral UK Open
1986	v Bradley	5-3	3rd round	Mercantile Credit Classic
	v Hendry	5-4	4th round	Mercantile Credit Classic
	v Campbell	5-1	5th round	Mercantile Credit Classic
	v Mountjoy	3-5	Quarter-final	Mercantile Credit Classic

Neal Foulds

	v G. Foulds	9-4	3rd round	Tolly Cobbold English Professional Championship
	v Edmonds	9-4	4th round	Tolly Cobbold English Professional Championship
	v White	9-4	Quarter-final	Tolly Cobbold English Professional Championship
	v Hallett	9-8	Semi-final	Tolly Cobbold English Professional Championship
	v Meo	7-9	Final	Tolly Cobbold English Professional Championship
	v Hargreaves	5-4	3rd round	Dulux British Open
	v Griffiths	3-5	4th round	Dulux British Open
	v P. Francisco	10-9	Qualifying	Embassy World Professional Championship
	v Knowles	9-10	1st round	Embassy World Professional Championship

DANNY FOWLER (England)

Born 30.7.56
Turned professional 1984
World ranking 33 (55)

Having made a sound start to his professional career last season, Fowler qualified for the last 32 of the Embassy World Professional Championship in 1986.

1984	v Chaperon	5-0	Qualifying	Jameson International
	v Andrewartha	5-0	Qualifying	Jameson International
	v Martin	5-0	Qualifying	Jameson International
	v Dennis Taylor	0-5	1st round	Jameson International
	v Reynolds	2-5	1st round	Rothmans Grand Prix
	v Demarco	9-3	Qualifying	Coral UK Open
	v Oliver	9-3	Qualifying	Coral UK Open
	v F. Davis	9-4	Qualifying	Coral UK Open
	v N. Foulds	9-6	Qualifying	Coral UK Open
	v Reardon	2-9	1st round	Coral UK Open
1985	v Rigitano	5-0	Qualifying	Mercantile Credit Classic
	v Murphy	5-0	Qualifying	Mercantile Credit Classic
	v Meadowcroft	5-2	Qualifying	Mercantile Credit Classic
	v Wilson	4-5	Qualifying	Mercantile Credit Classic
	v Oliver	9-7	Qualifying	Tolly Cobbold English Professional Championship
	v S. Davis	3-9	1st round	Tolly Cobbold English Professional Championship
	v Everton	6-1	Qualifying	Dulux British Open
	v Williams	6-4	1st round	Dulux British Open
	v Bradley	4-5	2nd round	Dulux British Open
	v Hargreaves	10-0	Qualifying	Embassy World Professional Championship
	v Donnelly	10-0	Qualifying	Embassy World Professional Championship
	v Parrott	2-10	Qualifying	Embassy World Professional Championship
	v Agrawal	5-2	2nd round	Goya Matchroom Trophy

	v Thorne	1-5	3rd round	Goya Matchroom Trophy
	v Jonik	5-4	2nd round	Rothmans Grand Prix
	v Werbeniuk	5-1	3rd round	Rothmans Grand Prix
	v S. Davis	1-5	4th round	Rothmans Grand Prix
	v Wilkinson	9-6	2nd round	Coral UK Open
	v Mans	9-2	3rd round	Coral UK Open
	v Meo	2-9	4th round	Coral UK Open
1986	v Bales	5-4	2nd round	Mercantile Credit Classic
	v White	1-5	3rd round	Mercantile Credit Classic
	v Darrington	9-3	2nd round	Tolly Cobbold English Professional Championship
	v Johnson	7-9	3rd round	Tolly Cobbold English Professional Championship
	v Chappel	5-4	2nd round	Dulux British Open
	v Virgo	1-5	3rd round	Dulux British Open
	v Oliver	10-8	Qualifying	Embassy World Professional Championship
	v Scott	10-7	Qualifying	Embassy World Professional Championship
	v Macleod	10-6	Qualifying	Embassy World Professional Championship
	v Griffiths	2-10	1st round	Embassy World Professional Championship

PETER FRANCISCO (South Africa)

Born 14.2.62
Turned professional 1984
World ranking 26 (59)

Son of Mannie runner-up in World Amateur Championships at both games, and nephew of Silvino, Peter Francisco, with some consistent performances, entered the top 32 in the world rankings after only two seasons on the circuit. His best win of the season was over Jimmy White whom he beat 5-4 in the third round of the Dulux British Open.

1984	v G. Foulds	4-5	Qualifying	Jameson International
	v Black	5-4	Qualifying	Rothmans Grand Prix
	v Spencer	5-2	1st round	Rothmans Grand Prix
	v Reynolds	4-5	2nd round	Rothmans Grand Prix
	v Sheehan	9-5	Qualifying	Coral UK Open
	v Williamson	9-2	Qualifying	Coral UK Open
	v Sinclair	8-9	Qualifying	Coral UK Open
1985	v Longworth	4-5	Qualifying	Mercantile Credit Classic
	v Kelly	6-3	Qualifying	Dulux British Open
	v Virgo	2-6	1st round	Dulux British Open
	v Demarco	10-4	Qualifying	Embassy World Professional Championship
	v Murphy	10-4	Qualifying	Embassy World Professional Championship
	v Meadowcroft	10-5	Qualifying	Embassy World Professional Championship
	v Macleod	7-10	Qualifying	Embassy World Professional Championship
	v Gibson	4-5	2nd round	Goya Matchroom Trophy
	v Everton	5-0	2nd round	Rothmans Grand Prix
	v Virgo	5-4	3rd round	Rothmans Grand Prix
	v W. Jones	5-3	4th round	Rothmans Grand Prix

	v Griffiths	2-5	5th round	Rothmans Grand Prix
	v Charlton	9-5	3rd round	Coral UK Open
	v Williams	7-9	4th round	Coral UK Open
1986	v Jonik	5-2	2nd round	Mercantile Credit Classic
	v Charlton	5-1	3rd round	Mercantile Credit Classic
	v Martin	5-2	4th round	Mercantile Credit Classic
	v S. Davis	0-5	5th round	Mercantile Credit Classic
	v G. Foulds	5-2	2nd round	Dulux British Open
	v White	5-4	3rd round	Dulux British Open
	v Longworth	5-2	4th round	Dulux British Open
	v Higgins	2-5	5th round	Dulux British Open
	v Drago	10-4	Qualifying	Embassy World Professional Championship
	v F. Davis	10-1	Qualifying	Embassy World Professional Championship
	v N. Foulds	9-10	Qualifying	Embassy World Professional Championship

SILVINO FRANCISCO (South Africa)

Born 3.5.46
Turned professional 1978
World ranking 12 (13)

Last season, despite being involved in a dispute with the WPBSA, Francisco did well enough to climb from 13th to 12th in the rankings. The previous season, he won the Dulux British Open.

1982	v Ross	9-0	Qualifying	Embassy World Professional Championship
	v Morgan	9-1	Qualifying	Embassy World Professional Championship
	v Dennis Taylor	10-7	1st round	Embassy World Professional Championship
	v Reynolds	13-8	2nd round	Embassy World Professional Championship
	v Reardon	8-13	Quarter-final	Embassy World Professional Championship
1983	v Kelly	10-5	Qualifying	Embassy World Professional Championship
	v Dennis Taylor	9-10	1st round	Embassy World Professional Championship
	v Darrington	5-2	Qualifying	Jameson International
	v Donnelly	5-1	2nd round	Jameson International
	v S. Davis	1-5	Quarter-final	Jameson International
	v Morra	5-3	1st round	Professional Players Tournament
	v Scott	5-1	2nd round	Professional Players Tournament
	v Knowles	0-5	3rd round	Professional Players Tournament
1984	v Thorburn	5-1	Qualifying	Lada Classic
	v Wildman	1-5	1st round	Lada Classic
	v Van Rensberg	10-3	Qualifying	Embassy World Professional Championship
	v Meo	10-5	1st round	Embassy World Professional Championship
	v Reardon	8-13	2nd round	Embassy World Professional Championship
	v Kelly	5-3	Qualifying	Jameson International
	v Spencer	5-2	1st round	Jameson International
	v Virgo	5-2	2nd round	Jameson International
	v Knowles	6-9	Semi-final	Jameson International
	v Duggan	5-3	1st round	Rothmans Grand Prix
	v White	5-1	2nd round	Rothmans Grand Prix
	v Reynolds	1-5	3rd round	Rothmans Grand Prix

	v Sinclair	9-4	Qualifying	Coral UK Open
	v Charlton	4-9	1st round	Coral UK Open
1985	v T. Jones	5-1	Qualifying	Mercantile Credit Classic
	v S. Davis	0-5	1st round	Mercantile Credit Classic
	v Kearney	6-4	1st round	Dulux British Open
	v White	5-4	2nd round	Dulux British Open
	v Chaperon	5-2	3rd round	Dulux British Open
	v Meo	5-4	Quarter-final	Dulux British Open
	v Higgins	9-6	Semi-final	Dulux British Open
	v Stevens	**12-9**	**Final**	**Dulux British Open**
	v Medati	10-7	Qualifying	Embassy World Professional Championship
	v Dennis Taylor	2-10	1st round	Embassy World Professional Championship
	v Parrott	3-4	1st round	Winfield Australian Masters
	v Knowles	5-4	1st round	Langs Scottish Masters
	v Thorburn	0-6	Semi-final	Langs Scottish Masters
	v Chaperon	3-5	3rd round	Goya Matchroom Trophy
	v Kelly	5-2	3rd round	Rothmans Grand Prix
	v Martin	5-3	4th round	Rothmans Grand Prix

Silvino Francisco

	v White	5-4	5th round	Rothmans Grand Prix
	v S. Davis	2-5	Quarter-final	Rothmans Grand Prix
	v Wych	9-8	3rd round	Coral UK Open
	v Martin	9-6	4th round	Coral UK Open
	v Griffiths	5-9	5th round	Coral UK Open
1986	v Hendry	4-5	3rd round	Mercantile Credit Classic
	v Knowles	1-5	1st round	Benson & Hedges Masters
	v T. Jones	5-2	3rd round	Dulux British Open
	v Macleod	1-5	4th round	Dulux British Open
	v Williams	10-4	1st round	Embassy World Professional Championship
	v Knowles	10-13	2nd round	Embassy World Professional Championship

MARCEL GAUVREAU (Canada)

Born 9.1.55
Turned professional 1983
World ranking 38 (39)

A win over Kirk Stevens in the 1984 Jameson International remains Gauvreau's best performance although he did reach the last 16 of the 1986 Mercantile Credit Classic.

1983	v Miles	3-5	1st round	Professional Players Tournament
1984	v Campbell	10-7	Qualifying	Embassy World Professional Championship
	v Cripsey	10-1	Qualifying	Embassy World Professional Championship
	v Macleod	10-6	Qualifying	Embassy World Professional Championship
	v David Taylor	5-10	1st round	Embassy World Professional Championship
	v Jonik	5-1	Qualifying	Jameson International
	v Parrott	5-4	Qualifying	Jameson International
	v Stevens	5-1	1st round	Jameson International
	v Thorne	3-5	2nd round	Jameson International
	v Foldvari	5-2	Qualifying	Rothmans Grand Prix
	v Parrott	3-5	1st round	Rothmans Grand Prix
	v Bales	9-8	Qualifying	Coral UK Open
	v Mans	9-6	Qualifying	Coral UK Open
	v Knowles	5-9	1st round	Coral UK Open
1985	v Giannaros	5-3	Qualifying	Mercantile Credit Classic
	v Sinclair	5-1	Qualifying	Mercantile Credit Classic
	v Higgins	3-5	1st round	Mercantile Credit Classic
	v Greaves	6-3	Qualifying	Dulux British Open
	v Stevens	3-6	1st round	Dulux British Open
	v Van Rensberg	10-9	Qualifying	Embassy World Professional Championship
	v Reynolds	1-10	Qualifying	Embassy World Professional Championship
	v D. Hughes	4-5	2nd round	Goya Matchroom Trophy
	v Duggan	4-5	2nd round	Rothmans Grand Prix
	v O'Boye	5-9	2nd round	Coral UK Open
1986	v Simngam	5-1	2nd round	Mercantile Credit Classic
	v David Taylor	5-3	3rd round	Mercantile Credit Classic
	v Browne	5-3	4th round	Mercantile Credit Classic
	v White	2-5	5th round	Mercantile Credit Classic

	v Drago	3-5	2nd round	Dulux British Open
	v Jim Bear	10-5	Qualifying	Embassy World Professional Championship
	v Chaperon	10-8	Qualifying	Embassy World Professional Championship
	v Williams	3-10	Qualifying	Embassy World Professional Championship

JAMES GIANNAROS (Australia)

Born 25.7.52
Turned professional 1983
World ranking unranked (101)

Australian amateur champion in 1982, Giannaros did not compete on the circuit last season.

1984	v Dodd	1-10	Qualifying	Embassy World Professional Championship
1985	v Chappel	5-2	Qualifying	Mercantile Credit Classic
	v Gauvreau	3-5	Qualifying	Mercantile Credit Classic
	v Roscoe	6-1	Qualifying	Dulux British Open
	v Reynolds	3-6	1st round	Dulux British Open
	v Longworth	1-10	Qualifying	Embassy World Professional Championship
	v Condo	7-2	2nd round	Australian Professional Championship
	v Morgan	4-8	Quarter-final	Australian Professional Championship

MATT GIBSON (Scotland)

Born 7.5.53
Turned professional 1981
World ranking 60 (81)

Gibson reached the final of the Canada Dry Scottish Professional Championship last season and also had a 5-4 victory over Eddie Charlton in the third round of the Goya Matchroom Trophy.

1981	v Hood	5-3	Qualifying	Jameson International
	v Parkin	5-3	Qualifying	Jameson International
	v Dunning	3-5	Qualifying	Jameson International
	v Demarco	5-3	Quarter-final	Scottish Professional Championship
	v Donnelly	6-4	Semi-final	Scottish Professional Championship
	v Black	7-11	Final	Scottish Professional Championship
	v Fitzmaurice	9-6	Qualifying	Coral UK Championship
	v Everton	7-9	Qualifying	Coral UK Championship
1982	v Donnelly	8-9	Qualifying	Embassy World Professional Championship
	v E. McLaughlin	6-3	Quarter-final	Scottish Professional Championship
	v Sinclair	2-6	Semi-final	Scottish Professional Championship
	v Wildman	1-5	Qualifying	Jameson International
	v Martin	2-5	1st round	Professional Players Tournament
	v G. Foulds	3-9	Qualifying	Coral UK Championship
1983	v G. Foulds	6-10	Qualifying	Embassy World Professional Championship
	v Macleod	5-6	1st round	Scottish Professional Championship

	v Dodd	5-1	Qualifying	Jameson International
	v Scott	3-5	Qualifying	Jameson International
	v Morgan	4-5	Qualifying	Professional Players Tournament
	v Johnson	6-9	Qualifying	Coral UK Championship
1984	v Rigitano	10-7	Qualifying	Embassy World Professional Championship
	v Fisher	10-7	Qualifying	Embassy World Professional Championship
	v Johnson	3-10	Qualifying	Embassy World Professional Championship
	v Medati	5-3	Qualifying	Jameson International
	v W. Jones	2-5	Qualifying	Jameson International
	v Chaperon	4-5	Qualifying	Rothmans Grand Prix
	v Hargreaves	9-8	Qualifying	Coral UK Open
	v Donnelly	6-9	Qualifying	Coral UK Open
1985	v T. Jones	0-5	Qualifying	Mercantile Credit Classic
	v Demarco	6-1	Qualifying	Dulux British Open
	v Wildman	1-6	1st round	Dulux British Open
	v Hines	10-7	Qualifying	Embassy World Professional Championship
	v Fagan	8-10	Qualifying	Embassy World Professional Championship
	v P. Francisco	5-4	2nd round	Goya Matchroom Trophy
	v Charlton	5-4	3rd round	Goya Matchroom Trophy
	v Reynolds	0-5	4th round	Goya Matchroom Trophy
	v Bradley	5-4	2nd round	Rothmans Grand Prix
	v Knowles	1-5	3rd round	Rothmans Grand Prix
	v Longworth	2-9	2nd round	Coral UK Open
1986	v Virgo	3-5	3rd round	Mercantile Credit Classic
	v Black	0-5	2nd round	Dulux British Open
	v Sinclair	6-4	Quarter-final	Canada Dry Scottish Professional Championship
	v John Rea	6-0	Semi-final	Canada Dry Scottish Professional Championship
	v Hendry	5-10	Final	Canada Dry Scottish Professional Championship
	v Jenkins	10-4	Qualifying	Embassy World Professional Championship
	v Morra	10-9	Qualifying	Embassy World Professional Championship
	v Medati	6-10	Qualifying	Embassy World Professional Championship

DAVE GILBERT

Born 15.8.61
Turned professional 1985
World ranking 72

1985	v Darrington	2-5	1st round	Goya Matchroom Trophy
	v Wilkinson	5-4	1st round	Rothmans Grand Prix
	v Williamson	5-4	2nd round	Rothmans Grand Prix
	v Johnson	2-5	3rd round	Rothmans Grand Prix
	v Drago	5-9	1st round	Coral UK Open
1986	v Watson	5-4	1st round	Mercantile Credit Classic
	v T. Jones	3-5	2nd round	Mercantile Credit Classic
	v West	9-8	1st round	Tolly Cobbold English Professional Championship

	v Bradley	5-9	2nd round	Tolly Cobbold English Professional Championship
	v Burke	5-1	1st round	Dulux British Open
	v Morra	5-4	2nd round	Dulux British Open
	v Charlton	2-5	3rd round	Dulux British Open
	v Bales	10-7	Qualifying	Embassy World Professional Championship
	v Bradley	10-7	Qualifying	Embassy World Professional Championship
	v T. Jones	10-7	Qualifying	Embassy World Professional Championship
	v Martin	5-10	Qualifying	Embassy World Professional Championship

ROBBIE GRACE (South Africa)

Born –
Turned professional 1985
World ranking 112

1986	v Parkin	10-8	Qualifying	Embassy World Professional Championship
	v W. Jones	3-10	Qualifying	Embassy World Professional Championship

DAVID GREAVES (England)

Born 1.9.46
Turned professional 1973
World ranking 107 (96)

1973	v Bennett	9-8	1st round	World Professional Championship
	v F. Davis	1-16	2nd round	World Professional Championship
1975	v G. Owen	3-15	1st round	World Professional Championship
1976	v Charlton	8-5	Qualifying	Embassy World Professional Championship
	v David Taylor	1-8	Qualifying	Embassy World Professional Championship
1977	v David Taylor	0-11	Qualifying	Embassy World Professional Championship
	v David Taylor	4-5	1st round	Super Crystalate UK Championship
1978	v Barrie	3-9	Prelim	Embassy World Professional Championship
	v Dunning	3-9	Qualifying	Coral UK Championship
1979	v Williams	2-9	Prelim	Embassy World Professional Championship
	v Dunning	8-9	1st round	Coral UK Championship
1980	v Meadowcroft	1-9	Qualifying	Coral UK Championship
1981	v Dunning	4-9	Qualifying	John Courage English Professional
	v Parkin	9-5	Qualifying	Embassy World Professional Championship
	v Thorne	3-9	Qualifying	Embassy World Professional Championship
	v E. McLaughlin	1-5	Qualifying	Jameson International
1982	v Morgan	2-9	Qualifying	Embassy World Professional Championship
1983	v E. McLaughlin	7-10	Qualifying	Embassy World Professional Championship
	v Martin	1-5	Qualifying	Jameson International
	v Andrewartha	5-2	Qualifying	Professional Players Tournament
	v Reynolds	1-5	1st round	Professional Players Tournament
	v Wildman	5-9	Qualifying	Coral UK Championship
1984	v Edmonds	0-10	Qualifying	Embassy World Professional Championship
	v J. McLaughlin	3-5	Qualifying	Jameson International

	v King	0-5	Qualifying	Rothmans Grand Prix
	v Foldvari	5-9	Qualifying	Coral UK Open
1985	v T. Jones	2-5	Qualifying	Mercantile Credit Classic
	v Fitzmaurice	3-9	Qualifying	Tolly Cobbold English Professional Championship
	v Gauvreau	3-6	Qualifying	Dulux British Open
	v Chalmers	3-10	Qualifying	Embassy World Professional Championship
	v Simngam	2-5	1st round	Goya Matchroom Trophy
	v Darrington	2-5	1st round	Rothmans Grand Prix
	v Cripsey	4-9	1st round	Coral UK Open
1986	v Watchorn	5-4	1st round	Mercantile Credit Classic
	v Sinclair	1-5	2nd round	Mercantile Credit Classic
	v Medati	4-9	2nd round	Tolly Cobbold English Professional Championship
	v Agrawal	3-5	1st round	Dulux British Open
	v Smith	4-10	Qualifying	Embassy World Professional Championship

TERRY GRIFFITHS (Wales)

Born 16.10.47
Turned professional 1978
World ranking 10 (8)

Embassy world champion at his first attempt in 1979, Benson and Hedges winner in 1980, three times winner of the Benson and Hedges Irish Masters, 1982 Coral UK champion and winner of the 1982 Lada Classic, Griffiths has not in the last couple of seasons reproduced quite this level of excellence.

He has continued to play well in fits and starts and last season retained the Welsh Professional Championship and won the inaugural BCE Belgian Classic.

1978	v Williams	8-9	Qualifying	Coral UK Championship
1979	v Bennett	9-2	Prelim	Embassy World Professional Championship
	v Meadowcroft	9-6	Qualifying	Embassy World Professional Championship
	v Mans	13-8	1st round	Embassy World Professional Championship
	v Higgins	13-12	Quarter-final	Embassy World Professional Championship
	v Charlton	19-17	Semi-final	Embassy World Professional Championship
	v Dennis Taylor	**24-16**	**Final**	**Embassy World Professional Championship**
	v Wilson	9-4	3rd round	Coral UK Championship
	v Higgins	9-7	Quarter-final	Coral UK Championship
	v Werbeniuk	9-3	Semi-final	Coral UK Championship
	v Virgo	13-14	Final	Coral UK Championship
1980	v Thorburn	5-3	Quarter-final	Benson & Hedges Masters
	v Spencer	5-0	Semi-final	Benson & Hedges Masters
	v Higgins	**9-5**	**Final**	**Benson & Hedges Masters**
	v Mountjoy	**9-8**	**Final**	**Benson & Hedges Irish Masters**
	v S. Davis	10-13	2nd round	Embassy World Professional Championship
	v Fagan	9-8	2nd round	Coral UK Championship

	v Dennis Taylor	9-7	Quarter-final	Coral UK Championship
	v S. Davis	0-9	Semi-final	Coral UK Championship
1981	v F. Davis	5-2	Quarter-final	Benson & Hedges Masters
	v Spencer	6-5	Semi-final	Benson & Hedges Masters
	v Higgins	6-9	Final	Benson & Hedges Masters
	v Reardon	6-9	Semi-final	Woodpecker Welsh Professional Championship
	v Meo	13-6	2nd round	Embassy World Professional Championship
	v S. Davis	9-13	Quarter-final	Embassy World Professional Championship
	v Spencer	5-2	3rd round	Jameson International
	v Higgins	2-5	Quarter-final	Jameson International
	v Stevens	5-0	1st round	Northern Ireland Classic
	v S. Davis	6-9	Semi-final	Northern Ireland Classic
	v Miles	9-4	3rd round	Coral UK Championship
	v Knowles	9-5	Quarter-final	Coral UK Championship
	v Meo	9-3	Semi-final	Coral UK Championship
	v S. Davis	3-16	Final	Coral UK Championship
1982	v Thorburn	5-1	1st round	Lada Classic
	v Higgins	5-1	Semi-final	Lada Classic
	v S. Davis	**9-8**	**Final**	**Lada Classic**
	v Reardon	5-3	Quarter-final	Benson & Hedges Masters
	v Higgins	6-4	Semi-final	Benson & Hedges Masters
	v S. Davis	5-9	Final	Benson & Hedges Masters
	v S. Davis	7-9	Final	Yamaha International Masters
	v Roscoe	6-2	1st round	Woodpecker Welsh Professional Championship
	v Wilson	9-6	Semi-final	Woodpecker Welsh Professional Championship
	v Mountjoy	8-9	Final	Woodpecker Welsh Professional Championship
	v Meo	5-3	Quarter-final	Benson & Hedges Irish Masters
	v Reardon	6-3	Semi-final	Benson & Hedges Irish Masters
	v S. Davis	**9-5**	**Final**	**Benson & Hedges Irish Masters**
	v Thorne	6-10	1st round	Embassy World Professional Championship
	v Reardon	5-3	1st round	Langs Scottish Masters
	v Higgins	5-6	Semi-final	Langs Scottish Masters
	v Williams	5-2	1st round	Jameson International
	v Higgins	5-2	2nd round	Jameson International
	v Stevens	3-5	Quarter-final	Jameson International
	v Roscoe	5-1	1st round	Professional Players Tournament
	v Watterson	5-2	2nd round	Professional Players Tournament
	v Sinclair	5-3	3rd round	Professional Players Tournament
	v White	2-5	Quarter-final	Professional Players Tournament
	v Johnson	9-1	1st round	Coral UK Championship
	v Dennis Taylor	9-7	2nd round	Coral UK Championship
	v S. Davis	9-6	Quarter-final	Coral UK Championship
	v Meo	9-7	Semi-final	Coral UK Championship
	v Higgins	**16-15**	**Final**	**Coral UK Championship**
1983	v Mountjoy	1-5	1st round	Lada Classic
	v Stevens	5-3	1st round	Benson & Hedges Masters

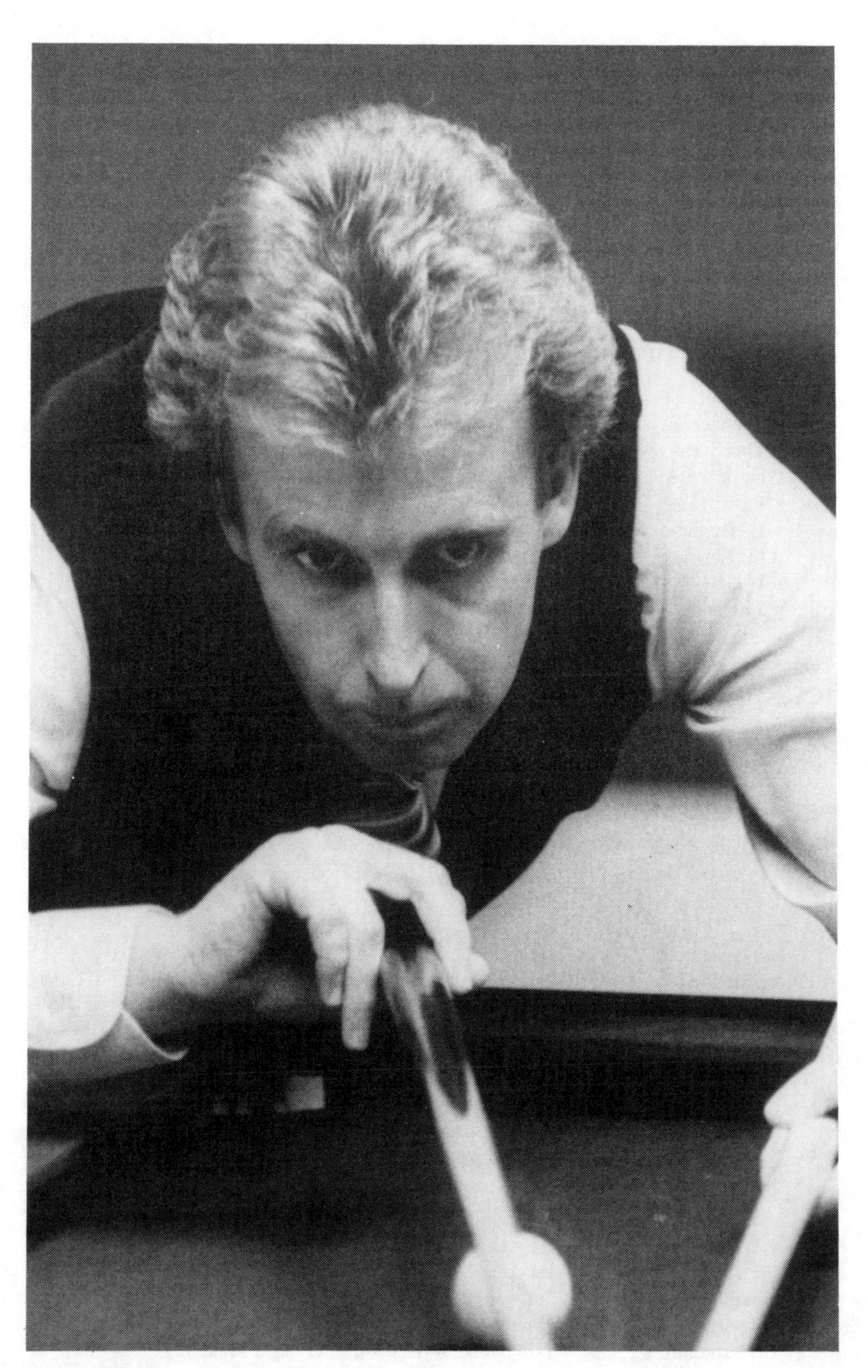

Terry Griffiths

	v Thorburn	3-5	Quarter-final	Benson & Hedges Masters
	v Everton	6-1	Quarter-final	Woodpecker Welsh Professional Championship
	v Reardon	4-9	Semi-final	Woodpecker Welsh Professional Championship
	v Werbeniuk	5-3	Semi-final	Tolly Cobbold Classic
	v S. Davis	5-7	Final	Tolly Cobbold Classic
	v Mountjoy	5-4	Quarter-final	Benson & Hedges Irish Masters
	v S. Davis	2-6	Semi-final	Benson & Hedges Irish Masters
	v Wildman	10-8	1st round	Embassy World Professional Championship
	v Thorburn	12-13	2nd round	Embassy World Professional Championship
	v Thorburn	1-5	1st round	Langs Scottish Masters
	v Miles	5-2	1st round	Jameson International
	v Scott	5-0	2nd round	Jameson International
	v Spencer	5-4	Quarter-final	Jameson International
	v Thorburn	8-9	Semi-final	Jameson International
	v Dodd	5-3	1st round	Professional Players Tournament
	v Parrott	5-1	2nd round	Professional Players Tournament
	v E. Hughes	2-5	3rd round	Professional Players Tournament
	v Martin	9-4	1st round	Coral UK Championship
	v Hallett	9-5	2nd round	Coral UK Championship
	v Johnson	9-2	Quarter-final	Coral UK Championship
	v Higgins	4-9	Semi-final	Coral UK Championship
1984	v Reynolds	5-2	Qualifying	Lada Classic
	v Roscoe	5-2	1st round	Lada Classic
	v S. Davis	4-5	Quarter-final	Lada Classic
	v Werbeniuk	5-1	1st round	Benson & Hedges Masters
	v Spencer	5-4	Quarter-final	Benson & Hedges Masters
	v Knowles	6-4	Semi-final	Benson & Hedges Masters
	v White	5-9	Final	Benson & Hedges Masters
	v Andrewartha	6-1	1st round	Strongbow Welsh Professional Championship
	v Mountjoy	5-9	Semi-final	Strongbow Welsh Professional Championship
	v Werbeniuk	5-2	1st round	Benson & Hedges Irish Masters
	v Knowles	5-0	Quarter-final	Benson & Hedges Irish Masters
	v Dennis Taylor	5-4	Semi-final	Benson & Hedges Irish Masters
	v S. Davis	1-9	Final	Benson & Hedges Irish Masters
	v Mifsud	10-2	1st round	Embassy World Professional Championship
	v Werbeniuk	10-5	2nd round	Embassy World Professional Championship
	v S. Davis	10-13	Quarter-final	Embassy World Professional Championship
	v Knowles	3-5	1st round	Langs Scottish Masters
	v N. Foulds	5-3	1st round	Jameson International
	v Higgins	4-5	2nd round	Jameson International
	v T. Jones	3-5	1st round	Rothmans Grand Prix
	v Wilson	6-9	1st round	Coral UK Open
1985	v Fagan	5-0	1st round	Mercantile Credit Classic
	v Williams	5-3	2nd round	Mercantile Credit Classic
	v Thorburn	4-5	Quarter-final	Mercantile Credit Classic
	v Werbeniuk	5-2	1st round	Benson & Hedges Masters

	v Higgins	5-1	Quarter-final	Benson & Hedges Masters
	v Mountjoy	2-6	Semi-final	Benson & Hedges Masters
	v Chalmers	6-0	1st round	Dulux British Open
	v Newbury	3-5	2nd round	Dulux British Open
	v Higgins	2-5	1st round	Benson & Hedges Irish Masters
	v Williams	10-3	1st round	Embassy World Professional Championship
	v Higgins	13-7	2nd round	Embassy World Professional Championship
	v S. Davis	6-13	Quarter-final	Embassy World Professional Championship
	v Chappel	6-0	Quarter-final	BCE Welsh Professional Championship
	v Reardon	9-3	Semi-final	BCE Welsh Professional Championship
	v Mountjoy	**9-4**	**Final**	**BCE Welsh Professional Championship**
	v Newbury	5-2	3rd round	Goya Matchroom Trophy
	v Spencer	5-1	4th round	Goya Matchroom Trophy
	v Parrott	1-5	5th round	Goya Matchroom Trophy
	v J. McLaughlin	5-4	3rd round	Rothmans Grand Prix
	v Harris	5-3	4th round	Rothmans Grand Prix
	v P. Francisco	5-2	5th round	Rothmans Grand Prix
	v Thorburn	1-5	Quarter-final	Rothmans Grand Prix
	v S. Davis	4-5	1st round	BCE Canadian Masters
	v T. Jones	9-5	3rd round	Coral UK Open
	v Reynolds	9-7	4th round	Coral UK Open
	v S. Francisco	9-5	5th round	Coral UK Open
	v Thorne	7-9	Quarter-final	Coral UK Open
	v Reardon	5-2	1st round	Kit Kat
	v Dennis Taylor	4-6	Semi-final	Kit Kat
1986	v V. Harris	3-5	3rd round	Mercantile Credit Classic
	v S. Davis	5-2	1st round	BCE Belgian Classic
	v Knowles	5-2	Semi-final	BCE Belgian Classic
	v Stevens	**9-7**	**Final**	**BCE Belgian Classic**
	v Higgins	5-4	1st round	Benson & Hedges Masters
	v Thorburn	2-5	Quarter-final	Benson & Hedges Masters
	v Chappel	6-4	Quarter-final	Zetters Welsh Professional Championship
	v Wilson	9-1	Semi-final	Zetters Welsh Professional Championship
	v Mountjoy	**9-3**	**Final**	**Zetters Welsh Professional Championship**
	v Scott	5-3	3rd round	Dulux British Open
	v N. Foulds	5-3	4th round	Dulux British Open
	v Macleod	5-2	5th round	Dulux British Open
	v Thorne	4-5	Quarter-final	Dulux British Open
	v Thorne	2-5	1st round	Benson & Hedges Irish Masters
	v Fowler	10-2	1st round	Embassy World Professional Championship
	v Higgins	13-12	2nd round	Embassy World Professional Championship
	v Johnson	12-13	Quarter-final	Embassy World Professional Championship

MIKE HALLETT (England)

Born 6.7.59
Turned professional 1979
World ranking 27 (28)

In his seven-year professional career, Hallett has scored some fine wins, notably in beating Dennis Taylor, the defending champion, in the first round of last season's Embassy World Championship. He has also recorded wins over Steve Davis in the 1983 Professional Players Tournament and Alex Higgins in the 1984 Rothmans Grand Prix. However, he has yet to knit a series of such wins together.

1979	v Parkin	9-1	1st round	Coral UK Championship
	v Fagan	4-9	2nd round	Coral UK Championship
1980	v Stevens	3-9	Qualifying	Embassy World Professional Championship
	v Bennett	9-4	Qualifying	Coral UK Championship
	v Edmonds	9-8	Qualifying	Coral UK Championship
	v S. Davis	1-9	1st round	Coral UK Championship
1981	v Edmonds	3-9	Qualifying	John Courage English Professional
	v Jonik	9-1	Qualifying	Embassy World Professional Championship
	v Meo	4-9	Qualifying	Embassy World Professional Championship
	v Demarco	5-4	Qualifying	Jameson International
	v Knowles	2-5	1st round	Jameson International
	v V. Harris	9-4	Qualifying	Coral UK Championship
	v D. Hughes	9-6	Qualifying	Coral UK Championship
	v Fagan	9-5	Qualifying	Coral UK Championship
	v Stevens	4-9	2nd round	Coral UK Championship
1982	v Johnson	9-8	Qualifying	Embassy World Professional Championship
	v Virgo	4-10	1st round	Embassy World Professional Championship
	v Jonik	5-2	Qualifying	Jameson International
	v Wildman	2-5	Qualifying	Jameson International
	v V. Harris	5-3	1st round	Professional Players Tournament
	v Virgo	2-5	2nd round	Professional Players Tournament
	v Demarco	9-1	Qualifying	Coral UK Championship
	v F. Davis	9-7	1st round	Coral UK Championship
	v Reardon	8-9	2nd round	Coral UK Championship
1983	v Andrewartha	10-7	Qualifying	Embassy World Professional Championship
	v King	10-6	Qualifying	Embassy World Professional Championship
	v Spencer	7-10	1st round	Embassy World Professional Championship
	v Roscoe	5-2	Qualifying	Jameson International
	v Morra	3-5	Qualifying	Jameson International
	v Kelly	5-0	1st round	Professional Players Tournament
	v S. Davis	5-2	2nd round	Professional Players Tournament
	v Meo	3-5	3rd round	Professional Players Tournament
	v Darrington	9-1	Qualifying	Coral UK Championship
	v Miles	9-4	1st round	Coral UK Championship
	v Griffiths	5-9	2nd round	Coral UK Championship
1984	v Dennis Taylor	5-4	Qualifying	Lada Classic
	v Knowles	3-5	1st round	Lada Classic

	v Burke	10-5	Qualifying	Embassy World Professional Championship
	v Mountjoy	4-10	1st round	Embassy World Professional Championship
	v O'Kane	4-5	Qualifying	Jameson International
	v Sheehan	5-1	1st round	Rothmans Grand Prix
	v Higgins	5-3	2nd round	Rothmans Grand Prix
	v Stevens	3-5	3rd round	Rothmans Grand Prix
	v Bradley	9-8	Qualifying	Coral UK Open
	v Mountjoy	2-9	1st round	Coral UK Open
1985	v G. Foulds	5-4	Qualifying	Mercantile Credit Classic
	v Reardon	3-5	1st round	Mercantile Credit Classic
	v Duggan	9-4	1st round	Tolly Cobbold English Professional Championship
	v Meo	4-9	2nd round	Tolly Cobbold English Professional Championship
	v Meo	4-5	2nd round	Dulux British Open
	v Chalmers	10-1	Qualifying	Embassy World Professional Championship
	v Thorburn	8-10	1st round	Embassy World Professional Championship
	v Bradley	4-5	3rd round	Goya Matchroom Trophy
	v Mikkelsen	5-3	3rd round	Rothmans Grand Prix
	v Johnson	4-5	4th round	Rothmans Grand Prix
	v Meadowcroft	9-1	3rd round	Coral UK Open
	v Stevens	5-9	4th round	Coral UK Open
1986	v John Rea	5-2	3rd round	Mercantile Credit Classic
	v Thorburn	3-5	4th round	Mercantile Credit Classic
	v Chalmers	9-1	3rd round	Tolly Cobbold English Professional Championship
	v Knowles	9-5	4th round	Tolly Cobbold English Professional Championship
	v Johnson	9-6	Quarter-final	Tolly Cobbold English Professional Championship
	v N. Foulds	8-9	Semi-final	Tolly Cobbold English Professional Championship
	v Duggan	5-3	3rd round	Dulux British Open
	v Higgins	1-5	4th round	Dulux British Open
	v Wych	10-7	Qualifying	Embassy World Professional Championship
	v Dennis Taylor	10-6	1st round	Embassy World Professional Championship
	v Johnson	6-13	2nd round	Embassy World Professional Championship

JOHN HARGREAVES (England)

Born 2.12.45
Turned professional 1983
World ranking 92 (102)

1983	v Morra	0-5	Qualifying	Professional Players Tournament
	v Williamson	4-9	Qualifying	Coral UK Championship
1984	v E. McLaughlin	5-10	Qualifying	Embassy World Professional Championship
	v Houlihan	5-2	Qualifying	Jameson International
	v Kelly	2-5	Qualifying	Jameson International

	v Donnelly	4-5	Qualifying	Rothmans Grand Prix
	v Medati	9-6	Qualifying	Coral UK Open
	v Gibson	8-9	Qualifying	Coral UK Open
1985	v Darrington	5-2	Qualifying	Mercantile Credit Classic
	v Edmonds	2-5	Qualifying	Mercantile Credit Classic
	v Medati	8-9	Qualifying	Tolly Cobbold English Professional Championship
	v N. Foulds	1-6	1st round	Dulux British Open
	v Fowler	0-10	Qualifying	Embassy World Professional Championship
	v Caggianello	2-5	1st round	Goya Matchroom Trophy
	v Cripsey	5-1	1st round	Rothmans Grand Prix
	v Longworth	2-5	2nd round	Rothmans Grand Prix
	v Mienie	9-7	1st round	Coral UK Open
	v Meadowcroft	8-9	2nd round	Coral UK Open
1986	v Cripsey	5-1	1st round	Mercantile Credit Classic
	v Longworth	2-5	2nd round	Mercantile Credit Classic
	v Houlihan	5-9	1st round	Tolly Cobbold English Professional Championship
	v Edmonds	5-3	2nd round	Dulux British Open
	v N. Foulds	4-5	3rd round	Dulux British Open
	v Mikkelsen	7-10	Qualifying	Embassy World Professional Championship

BOB HARRIS (England)

Born 12.3.56
Turned professional 1982
World ranking 45 (66)

1982	v Scott	4-5	Qualifying	Jameson International
	v Cripsey	9-6	Qualifying	Coral UK Championship
	v Watterson	9-3	Qualifying	Coral UK Championship
	v Fagan	6-9	1st round	Coral UK Championship
1983	v Wildman	7-10	Qualifying	Embassy World Professional Championship
	v Dunning	5-3	Qualifying	Jameson International
	v Wildman	2-5	Qualifying	Jameson International
	v King	3-5	Qualifying	Professional Players Tournament
	v E. McLaughlin	9-8	Qualifying	Coral UK Championship
	v Fitzmaurice	9-3	Qualifying	Coral UK Championship
	v Reardon	7-9	1st round	Coral UK Championship
1984	v Sheehan	10-3	Qualifying	Embassy World Professional Championship
	v Burke	4-10	Qualifying	Embassy World Professional Championship
	v Watchorn	7-9	Qualifying	Coral UK Open
1985	v Duggan	8-9	Qualifying	Tolly Cobbold English Professional Championship
	v Meadowcroft	6-1	Qualifying	Dulux British Open
	v Charlton	6-3	1st round	Dulux British Open
	v E. Hughes	4-5	2nd round	Dulux British Open
	v Rigitano	4-10	Qualifying	Embassy World Professional Championship
	v Browne	5-3	2nd round	Goya Matchroom Trophy
	v O'Kane	5-3	3rd round	Goya Matchroom Trophy

Year	Opponent	Score	Round	Tournament
	v Dennis Taylor	3-5	4th round	Goya Matchroom Trophy
	v Browne	5-3	2nd round	Rothmans Grand Prix
	v Spencer	5-2	3rd round	Rothmans Grand Prix
	v Griffiths	3-5	4th round	Rothmans Grand Prix
	v Fagan	2-9	2nd round	Coral UK Open
1986	v Morra	5-3	2nd round	Mercantile Credit Classic
	v Johnson	4-5	3rd round	Mercantile Credit Classic
	v T. Jones	5-9	2nd round	Tolly Cobbold English Professional Championship
	v Sinclair	5-3	2nd round	Dulux British Open
	v Martin	1-5	3rd round	Dulux British Open
	v Black	8-10	Qualifying	Embassy World Professional Championship

VIC HARRIS (England)

Born 16.8.45
Turned professional 1981
World ranking 63 (65)

English amateur champion in 1981, Harris has achieved two notable wins on the professional circuit, beating Terry Griffiths in the third round of the 1986 Mercantile Credit Classic and Doug Mountjoy 6-5 in the 1985 Dulux British Open.

Year	Opponent	Score	Round	Tournament
1981	v Sheehan	1-5	Qualifying	Jameson International
	v Higgins	3-5	Quarter-final	Langs Scottish Masters
	v Hallett	4-9	Qualifying	Coral UK Championship
	v Johnson	4-9	Qualifying	Embassy World Professional Championship
1982	v Hallett	3-5	1st round	Professional Players Tournament
	v M. Owen	9-4	Qualifying	Coral UK Championship
	v Johnson	8-9	Qualifying	Coral UK Championship
	v Sheehan	5-3	Qualifying	Jameson International
	v Virgo	2-5	Qualifying	Jameson International
1983	v Meo	0-10	Qualifying	Embassy World Professional Championship
	v Medati	0-5	Qualifying	Jameson International
	Harris *wo* Mifsud *scr*		Qualifying	Professional Players Tournament
	v Thorburn	1-5	1st round	Professional Players Tournament
	v Houlihan	9-6	Qualifying	Coral UK Championship
	v Williams	6-9	Qualifying	Coral UK Championship
1984	v Van Rensberg	7-10	Qualifying	Embassy World Professional Championship
	v Williamson	0-5	Qualifying	Jameson International
	v F. Davis	5-1	Qualifying	Rothmans Grand Prix
	v Knowles	1-5	1st round	Rothmans Grand Prix
	v Bradley	8-9	Qualifying	Coral UK Open
1985	v Newbury	3-5	Qualifying	Mercantile Credit Classic
	v Scott	7-9	Qualifying	Tolly Cobbold English Professional Championship
	v Dodd	6-1	Qualifying	Dulux British Open
	v Mountjoy	6-5	1st round	Dulux British Open

	v O'Kane	3-5	2nd round	Dulux British Open
	v O'Kane	5-10	Qualifying	Embassy World Professional Championship
	v Foldvari	4-5	2nd round	Goya Matchroom Trophy
	v Wych	5-3	2nd round	Rothmans Grand Prix
	v Higgins	1-5	3rd round	Rothmans Grand Prix
	v Black	9-3	2nd round	Coral UK Open
	v Spencer	5-9	3rd round	Coral UK Open
1986	v Roscoe	5-1	2nd round	Mercantile Credit Classic
	v Griffiths	5-3	3rd round	Mercantile Credit Classic
	v Williams	1-5	4th round	Mercantile Credit Classic
	v Bales	7-9	2nd round	Tolly Cobbold English Professional Championship
	v Chaperon	0-5	2nd round	Dulux British Open
	v T. Jones	7-10	Qualifying	Embassy World Professional Championship

STEPHEN HENDRY (Scotland)

Born 13.1.69
Turned professional 1985
World ranking 51

Having already become the youngest ever Scottish amateur champion, Hendry emulated this feat in the Scottish Championship. He was also the youngest ever competitor in the Embassy World Professional Championship in which he won four qualifying matches and put up a creditable display in losing 10-8 to Willie Thorne in the first round at the Crucible. His break of 141 in the qualifying competition was the highest of the Championship.

1985	v West	5-4	1st round	Goya Matchroom Trophy
	v E. McLaughlin	3-5	2nd round	Goya Matchroom Trophy
	v O'Boye	4-5	1st round	Rothmans Grand Prix
	v Agrawal	2-9	Qualifying	Coral UK Open
1986	v Sheehan	5-2	1st round	Mercantile Credit Classic
	v Miles	5-1	2nd round	Mercantile Credit Classic
	v S. Francisco	5-4	3rd round	Mercantile Credit Classic
	v N. Foulds	4-5	4th round	Mercantile Credit Classic
	v D. Hughes	5-1	1st round	Dulux British Open
	v Browne	0-5	2nd round	Dulux British Open
	v Demarco	6-1	1st round	Canada Dry Scottish Professional Championship
	v Macleod	6-5	Quarter-final	Canada Dry Scottish Professional Championship
	v Black	6-2	Semi-final	Canada Dry Scottish Professional Championship
	v Gibson	**10-5**	**Final**	**Canada Dry Scottish Professional Championship**
	v Demarco	10-7	Qualifying	Embassy World Professional Championship
	v Browne	10-9	Qualifying	Embassy World Professional Championship

	v W. Jones	10-8	Qualifying	Embassy World Professional Championship
	v O'Kane	10-9	Qualifying	Embassy World Professional Championship
	v Thorne	8-10	1st round	Embassy World Professional Championship

LEON HEYWOOD (Australia)

Born 26.5.52
Turned professional 1983
World ranking unranked (98)

1984	v Scott	7-10	Qualifying	Embassy World Professional Championship
1985	v Chaperon	1-10	Qualifying	Embassy World Professional Championship
	v Wilkinson	3-7	2nd round	Australian Professional Championship

ALEX HIGGINS (Northern Ireland)

Born 18.3.49
Turned professional 1971
World ranking 6 (9)

World champion in 1972 and 1982, Higgins has also won the Benson and Hedges Masters twice, in 1978 and 1981, as well as being runner-up in the two intervening years. He made an epic recovery from 0-7 to beat Steve Davis 16-15 in the 1983 Coral UK final and in the 1984–85 season won both the Hofmeister World Doubles with Jimmy White and the Guinness World Cup for Ireland with Dennis Taylor and Eugene Hughes, a title the Irish trio retained in 1986.

Higgins lost his Irish title to Dennis Taylor just before his fellow Ulsterman won the 1985 Embassy World Championship.

1972	v Gross	15-6	Qualifying	World Professional Championship
	v Parkin	11-3	Qualifying	World Professional Championship
	v Jack Rea	19-11	1st round	World Professional Championship
	v Pulman	31-23	Quarter-final	World Professional Championship
	v Williams	31-30	Semi-final	World Professional Championship
	v Spencer	**37-32**	**Final**	**World Professional Championship**
1973	v Houlihan	16-3	2nd round	World Professional Championship
	v Davis	16-14	Quarter-final	World Professional Championship
	v Charlton	9-23	Semi-final	World Professional Championship
	v Spencer	2-8	Semi-final	Norwich Union Open
1974	v Bennett	15-4	2nd round	World Professional Championship
	v F. Davis	14-15	Quarter-final	World Professional Championship
	v Dennis Taylor	5-1	1st round	Norwich Union Open
	v Werbeniuk	5-4	Quarter-final	Norwich Union Open
	v Reardon	8-9	Semi-final	Norwich Union Open
1975	v Werbeniuk	5-0	1st round	Benson & Hedges Masters
	v Williams	3-5	Quarter-final	Benson & Hedges Masters

	v David Taylor	15-2	2nd round	World Professional Championship
	v Williams	19-12	Quarter-final	World Professional Championship
	v Reardon	14-19	Semi-final	World Professional Championship
1976	v Miles	1-4	2nd round	Benson & Hedges Masters
	v Thorburn	15-14	1st round	Embassy World Professional Championship
	v Spencer	15-14	Quarter-final	Embassy World Professional Championship
	v Charlton	20-18	Semi-final	Embassy World Professional Championship
	v Reardon	16-27	Final	Embassy World Professional Championship
1977	v Mans	4-2	Quarter-final	Benson & Hedges Masters
	v Mountjoy	3-5	Semi-final	Benson & Hedges Masters
	v Mountjoy	12-13	1st round	Embassy World Professional Championship
	v David Taylor	5-4	2nd round	Super Crystalate UK Championship
	v Dunning	5-0	Quarter-final	Super Crystalate UK Championship
	v Mountjoy	2-9	Semi-final	Super Crystalate UK Championship
1978	v Dennis Taylor	4-3	Quarter-final	Benson & Hedges Masters
	v Reardon	5-1	Semi-final	Benson & Hedges Masters
	v Thorburn	**7-5**	**Final**	**Benson & Hedges Masters**
	v Fagan	12-13	1st round	Embassy World Professional Championship
	v Meadowcroft	9-6	1st round	Coral UK Championship
	v F. Davis	9-4	Quarter-final	Coral UK Championship
	v David Taylor	5-9	Semi-final	Coral UK Championship
1979	v Miles	3-6	Semi-final	Holsten Lager International
	v Charlton	5-2	Quarter-final	Benson & Hedges Masters
	v Mountjoy	5-1	Semi-final	Benson & Hedges Masters
	v Mans	4-8	Final	Benson & Hedges Masters
	v David Taylor	13-5	1st round	Embassy World Professional Championship
	v Griffiths	12-13	Quarter-final	Embassy World Professional Championship
	v Houlihan	9-3	3rd round	Coral UK Championship
	v Griffiths	7-9	Quarter-final	Coral UK Championship
1980	v F. Davis	5-1	1st round	Benson & Hedges Masters
	v Mans	5-1	Quarter-final	Benson & Hedges Masters
	v Reardon	5-2	Semi-final	Benson & Hedges Masters
	v Griffiths	5-9	Final	Benson & Hedges Masters
	v Reardon	**5-1**	**Final**	**British Gold Cup**
	v Meo	10-9	1st round	Embassy World Professional Championship
	v Mans	13-6	2nd round	Embassy World Professional Championship
	v S. Davis	13-9	Quarter-final	Embassy World Professional Championship
	v Stevens	16-13	Semi-final	Embassy World Professional Championship
	v Thorburn	16-18	Final	Embassy World Professional Championship
	v Thorne	9-7	2nd round	Coral UK Championship
	v F. Davis	9-6	Quarter-final	Coral UK Championship
	v Reardon	9-7	Semi-final	Coral UK Championship
	v S. Davis	6-16	Final	Coral UK Championship
1981	v Mountjoy	5-1	Quarter-final	Benson & Hedges Masters
	v Thorburn	6-5	Semi-final	Benson & Hedges Masters
	v Griffiths	**9-6**	**Final**	**Benson & Hedges Masters**
	v S. Davis	8-13	2nd round	Embassy World Professional Championship
	v V. Harris	5-3	Quarter-final	Langs Scottish Masters
	v Thorburn	2-6	Semi-final	Langs Scottish Masters
	v Fagan	5-3	2nd round	Jameson International

Alex Higgins

	v Mountjoy	5-1	3rd round	Jameson International
	v Griffiths	5-2	Quarter-final	Jameson International
	v S. Davis	8-9	Semi-final	Jameson International
	v S. Davis	2-5	1st round	Northern Ireland Classic
	v Martin	9-7	2nd round	Coral UK Championship
	v David Taylor	9-5	3rd round	Coral UK Championship
	v Meo	4-9	Quarter-final	Coral UK Championship
1982	v Dennis Taylor	5-1	1st round	Lada Classic
	v Griffiths	1-5	Semi-final	Lada Classic
	v Charlton	5-1	Quarter-final	Benson & Hedges Masters
	v Griffiths	4-6	Semi-final	Benson & Hedges Masters
	v D. Hughes	6-2	Semi-final	Irish Professional Championship
	v Dennis Taylor	13-16	Final	Irish Professional Championship
	v Wych	5-3	1st round	Benson & Hedges Irish Masters
	v Thorburn	5-4	Quarter-final	Benson & Hedges Irish Masters
	v S. Davis	2-6	Semi-final	Benson & Hedges Irish Masters
	v Meadowcroft	10-5	1st round	Embassy World Professional Championship
	v Mountjoy	13-12	2nd round	Embassy World Professional Championship
	v Thorne	13-10	Quarter-final	Embassy World Professional Championship
	v White	16-15	Semi-final	Embassy World Professional Championship
	v Reardon	**18-15**	**Final**	**Embassy World Professional Championship**
	v Sinclair	5-1	1st round	Langs Scottish Masters
	v Griffiths	6-5	Semi-final	Langs Scottish Masters
	v S. Davis	4-9	Final	Langs Scottish Masters
	v Kelly	5-3	1st round	Jameson International
	v Griffiths	2-5	2nd round	Jameson International
	v French	5-3	1st round	Professional Players Tournament
	v Reardon	2-5	2nd round	Professional Players Tournament
	v Martin	9-7	1st round	Coral UK Championship
	v Reynolds	9-8	2nd round	Coral UK Championship
	v Spencer	9-5	Quarter-final	Coral UK Championship
	v Reardon	9-6	Semi-final	Coral UK Championship
	v Griffiths	15-16	Final	Coral UK Championship
1983	v Werbeniuk	4-5	1st round	Lada Classic
	v Werbeniuk	4-5	1st round	Benson & Hedges Masters
	v Dennis Taylor	2-4	1st round	Tolly Cobbold Classic
	v Jack Rea	6-3	Quarter-final	Irish Professional Championship
	v E. Hughes	6-2	Semi-final	Irish Professional Championship
	v Dennis Taylor	**16-11**	**Final**	**Irish Professional Championship**
	v White	5-2	Quarter-final	Benson & Hedges Irish Masters
	v Reardon	3-6	Semi-final	Benson & Hedges Irish Masters
	v Reynolds	10-4	1st round	Embassy World Professional Championship
	v Thorne	13-8	2nd round	Embassy World Professional Championship
	v Werbeniuk	13-11	Quarter-final	Embassy World Professional Championship
	v S. Davis	5-16	Semi-final	Embassy World Professional Championship
	v White	5-3	1st round	Langs Supreme Scottish Masters
	v S. Davis	2-6	Semi-final	Langs Supreme Scottish Masters
	v Martin	2-5	1st round	Jameson International
	v Watterson	2-5	1st round	Professional Players Tournament
	v Macleod	9-6	1st round	Coral UK Championship

	v Medati	9-1	2nd round	Coral UK Championship
	v Knowles	9-5	Quarter-final	Coral UK Championship
	v Griffiths	9-4	Semi-final	Coral UK Championship
	v S. Davis	**16-15**	**Final**	**Coral UK Championship**
1984	v Fagan	5-3	Qualifying	Lada Classic
	v Parrott	2-5	1st round	Lada Classic
	v Mountjoy	5-2	1st round	Benson & Hedges Masters
	v Knowles	1-5	Quarter-final	Benson & Hedges Masters
	v Charlton	5-2	1st round	Benson & Hedges Irish Masters
	v Reardon	5-2	Quarter-final	Benson & Hedges Irish Masters
	v S. Davis	4-6	Semi-final	Benson & Hedges Irish Masters
	v N. Foulds	9-10	1st round	Embassy World Professional Championship
	v Stevens	5-2	1st round	Langs Supreme Scottish Masters
	v S. Davis	4-6	Semi-final	Langs Supreme Scottish Masters
	v Knowles	3-5	1st round	Carlsberg Challenge
	v Sinclair	5-1	1st round	Jameson International
	v Griffiths	5-4	2nd round	Jameson International
	v S. Davis	1-5	Quarter-final	Jameson International
	v Bales	5-1	1st round	Rothmans Grand Prix
	v Hallett	3-5	2nd round	Rothmans Grand Prix
	v T. Jones	9-7	1st round	Coral UK Open
	v Williams	9-7	2nd round	Coral UK Open
	v Thorne	9-5	Quarter-final	Coral UK Open
	v Thorburn	9-7	Semi-finals	Coral UK Open
	v S. Davis	8-16	Final	Coral UK Open
1985	v Gauvreau	5-3	1st round	Mercantile Credit Classic
	v S. Davis	2-5	2nd round	Mercantile Credit Classic
	v S. Davis	5-4	1st round	Benson & Hedges Masters
	v Griffiths	1-5	Quarter-final	Benson & Hedges Masters
	v Bales	6-3	1st round	Dulux British Open
	v N. Foulds	5-1	2nd round	Dulux British Open
	v Thorburn	5-2	3rd round	Dulux British Open
	v E. Hughes	5-2	Quarter-final	Dulux British Open
	v S. Francisco	6-9	Semi-final	Dulux British Open
	v Griffiths	5-2	1st round	Benson & Hedges Irish Masters
	v Stevens	5-3	Quarter-final	Benson & Hedges Irish Masters
	v S. Davis	6-2	Semi-final	Benson & Hedges Irish Masters
	v White	5-9	Final	Benson & Hedges Irish Masters
	v Burke	6-0	Quarter-final	Irish Professional Championship
	v Fagan	6-3	Semi-final	Irish Professional Championship
	v Dennis Taylor	5-10	Final	Irish Professional Championship
	v Reynolds	10-4	1st round	Embassy World Professional Championship
	v Griffiths	7-13	2nd round	Embassy World Professional Championship
	v Thorburn	5-4	Semi-final	Carlsberg Challenge
	v White	3-8	Final	Carlsberg Challenge
	v White	0-5	1st round	Langs Scottish Masters
	v D. Hughes	5-1	Third round	Goya Matchroom Trophy
	v Murphy	5-2	Fourth round	Goya Matchroom Trophy
	v Dennis Taylor	1-5	Fifth round	Goya Matchroom Trophy
	v V. Harris	5-1	3rd round	Rothmans Grand Prix

	v N. Foulds	5-3	4th round	Rothmans Grand Prix
	v S. Davis	0-5	5th round	Rothmans Grand Prix
	v Edmonds	9-8	3rd round	Coral UK Open
	v F. Davis	9-2	4th round	Coral UK Open
	v White	6-9	5th round	Coral UK Open
	v Thorburn	5-4	1st round	Kit Kat
	v S. Davis	6-1	Semi-final	Kit Kat
1986	v Fisher	5-0	3rd round	Mercantile Credit Classic
	v Cripsey	5-2	4th round	Mercantile Credit Classic
	v Dennis Taylor	5-4	5th round	Mercantile Credit Classic
	v Williams	2-5	Quarter-final	Mercantile Credit Classic
	v Dennis Taylor	5-1	1st round	BCE Belgian Classic
	v Stevens	4-5	Semi-final	BCE Belgian Classic
	v Griffiths	4-5	1st round	Benson & Hedges Masters
	v Bradley	5-3	3rd round	Dulux British Open
	v Hallett	5-1	4th round	Dulux British Open
	v P. Francisco	5-2	5th round	Dulux British Open
	v Werbeniuk	5-1	Quarter-final	Dulux British Open
	v S. Davis	3-9	Semi-final	Dulux British Open
	v Meo	4-5	1st round	Benson & Hedges Irish Masters
	v Spencer	10-7	1st round	Embassy World Professional Championship
	v Griffiths	12-13	2nd round	Embassy World Professional Championship
	v J. McLaughlin	6-2	Quarter-final	Strongbow Irish Professional Championship
	v E. Hughes	6-2	Semi-final	Strongbow Irish Professional Championship
	v Dennis Taylor	7-10	Final	Strongbow Irish Professional Championship

MIKE HINES (South Africa)

Born 21.3.45
Turned professional 1983
World ranking unranked (83)

1984	v Black	10-5	Qualifying	Embassy World Professional Championship
	v Williamson	6-10	Qualifying	Embassy World Professional Championship
1985	v Chappel	10-8	Qualifying	Embassy World Professional Championship
	v Watchorn	10-4	Qualifying	Embassy World Professional Championship
	v Gibson	7-10	Qualifying	Embassy World Professional Championship

PAT HOULIHAN (England)

Born 7.11.29
Turned professional 1969
World ranking 91 (unranked)

English amateur champion in 1965, Houlihan achieved his best performance in a professional event in the 1978 Embassy World Professional Championship when he qualified for the televised first round – his only television appearance to date.

1972	v Dunning	10-11	Qualifying	World Professional Championship
1973	v Jack Rea	9-2	1st round	World Professional Championship
	v Higgins	3-16	2nd round	World Professional Championship

1977	v Meadowcroft	1-5	1st round	Super Crystalate UK
1978	v Ross	9-1	Prelim	Embassy World Professional Championship
	v Meadowcroft	9-6	Qualifying	Embassy World Professional Championship
	v Thorburn	8-13	1st round	Embassy World Professional Championship
	v Andrewartha	3-9	Qualifying	Coral UK Championship
1979	v Barrie	9-5	Prelim	Embassy World Professional Championship
	v Mountjoy	6-9	Qualifying	Embassy World Professional Championship
	v Jack Rea	9-3	2nd round	Coral UK Championship
	v Higgins	3-9	3rd round	Coral UK Championship
1980	v Meo	1-9	Qualifying	Embassy World Professional Championship
	v Meo	1-9	1st round	Coral UK Championship
1981	v Spencer	1-9	1st round	John Courage English Professional
	v French	3-5	Qualifying	Jameson International
	v Kennerley	9-1	Qualifying	Coral UK Championship
	v Black	9-4	Qualifying	Coral UK Championship
	v Meadowcroft	9-4	Qualifying	Coral UK Championship
	v Miles	3-9	2nd round	Coral UK Championship
1982	v Anderson	9-5	Qualifying	Embassy World Professional Championship
	v Martin	3-9	Qualifying	Embassy World Professional Championship
	v E. McLaughlin	2-5	Qualifying	Jameson International
	v Knowles	4-5	1st round	Professional Players Tournament
	v Mountjoy	3-9	1st round	Coral UK Championship
1983	v Murphy	9-10	Qualifying	Embassy World Professional Championship
	v Scott	0-5	Qualifying	Jameson International
	v Sheehan	2-5	Qualifying	Professional Players Tournament
	v V. Harris	6-9	Qualifying	Coral UK Championship
1984	v Williamson	5-10	Qualifying	Embassy World Professional Championship
	v Hargreaves	2-5	Qualifying	Jameson International
	v Everton	3-5	Qualifying	Rothmans Grand Prix
	v Chappel	3-9	Qualifying	Coral UK Open
1985	v Foldvari	1-5	Qualifying	Mercantile Credit Classic
	v T. Jones	1-9	Qualifying	Tolly Cobbold English Professional Championship
	v Jim Bear	2-5	1st round	Goya Matchroom Trophy
	v Robinson	5-0	1st round	Rothmans Grand Prix
	v T. Jones	4-5	2nd round	Rothmans Grand Prix
	v Watson	9-4	1st round	Coral UK Open
	v Newbury	3-9	2nd round	Coral UK Open
1986	v Bennett	5-0	1st round	Mercantile Credit Classic
	v Foldvari	5-4	2nd round	Mercantile Credit Classic
	v Reynolds	1-5	3rd round	Mercantile Credit Classic
	v Hargreaves	9-5	1st round	Tolly Cobbold English Professional Championship
	v Dunning	*wo*	2nd round	Tolly Cobbold English Professional Championship
	v Spencer	5-9	3rd round	Tolly Cobbold English Professional Championship
	v Longworth	3-5	2nd round	Dulux British Open
	v Sheehan	7-10	Qualifying	Embassy World Professional Championship

DENNIS HUGHES (England)

Born 30.1.37
Turned professional 1981
World ranking 93 (88)

1981	v Jack Rea	5-4	Qualifying	Jameson International
	v Demarco	1-5	Qualifying	Jameson International
	v Hallett	6-9	Qualifying	Coral UK Championship
1982	v Higgins	2-6	Semi-final	Irish Professional Championship
	v Everton	9-4	Qualifying	Embassy World Professional Championship
	v Meo	4-9	Qualifying	Embassy World Professional Championship
	v Edmonds	0-5	Qualifying	Jameson International
	v Charlton	2-5	1st round	Professional Players Tournament
	v Meadowcroft	8-9	Qualifying	Coral UK Championship
1983	v Parkin	5-0	Qualifying	Jameson International
	v Johnson	1-5	Qualifying	Jameson International
	v Medati	1-5	Qualifying	Professional Players Tournament
	v Medati	2-9	Qualifying	Coral UK Championship
1984	v Parrott	3-10	Qualifying	Embassy World Professional Championship
	v Oliver	4-5	Qualifying	Jameson International
	v Dunning	0-5	Qualifying	Rothmans Grand Prix
	v G. Foulds	7-9	Qualifying	Coral UK Open
1985	v Watchorn	0-5	Prelim	Mercantile Credit Classic
	v Watterson	9-5	Qualifying	Tolly Cobbold English Professional Championship
	v N. Foulds	3-9	1st round	Tolly Cobbold English Professional Championship
	v Mikkelsen	0-6	Qualifying	Dulux British Open
	v French	10-5	Qualifying	Embassy World Professional Championship
	v Newbury	9-10	Qualifying	Embassy World Professional Championship
	v Kearney	5-1	1st round	Goya Matchroom Trophy
	v Gauvreau	5-4	2nd round	Goya Matchroom Trophy
	v Higgins	1-5	3rd round	Goya Matchroom Trophy
	v Bennett	5-4	1st round	Rothmans Grand Prix
	v Morra	2-5	2nd round	Rothmans Grand Prix
	v Kearney	9-8	1st round	Coral UK Open
	v King	0-9	2nd round	Coral UK Open
1986	v Burke	3-5	1st round	Mercantile Credit Classic
	v F. Davis	6-9	2nd round	Tolly Cobbold English Professional Championship
	v Hendry	1-5	1st round	Dulux British Open
	v Agrawal	6-10	Qualifying	Embassy World Professional Championship

EUGENE HUGHES (Republic of Ireland)

Born 4.11.55
Turned professional 1981
World ranking 20 (21)

After he had twice been Republic of Ireland champion at both billiards and snooker, Hughes's professional breakthrough came when he reached the semi-finals of the 1984 Jameson International. However, he had an indifferent season in 1985–86, his best performance being to reach the second round of the Embassy World Championship by beating David Taylor 10-7. He was a member of Ireland's winning World Cup team in both 1985 and 1986.

1981	v M. Owen	5-1	Qualifying	Jameson International
	v Fitzmaurice	5-3	Qualifying	Jameson International
	v Sinclair	5-2	Qualifying	Jameson International
	v Edmonds	4-5	1st round	Jameson International
1982	v Mountjoy	4-5	1st round	Benson & Hedges Irish Masters
	v Jack Rea	6-1	Quarter-final	Irish Professional Championship
	v Higgins	2-6	Semi-final	Irish Professional Championship
	v Knowles	7-9	Qualifying	Embassy World Professional Championship
	v Parkin	5-2	Qualifying	Jameson International
	v Martin	5-4	Qualifying	Jameson International
	v Reardon	3-5	1st round	Jameson International
	v Stevens	2-5	1st round	Professional Players Tournament
1983	v Burke	6-2	Quarter-final	Irish Professional Championship
	v Higgins	2-6	Semi-final	Irish Professional Championship
	v Fitzmaurice	10-7	Qualifying	Embassy World Professional Championship
	v Sinclair	10-8	Qualifying	Embassy World Professional Championship
	v Reardon	7-10	1st round	Embassy World Professional Championship
	v Fisher	5-4	Qualifying	Jameson International
	v G. Foulds	5-1	Qualifying	Jameson International
	v S. Davis	1-5	1st round	Jameson International
	v Sinclair	5-4	1st round	Professional Players Tournament
	v Werbeniuk	5-0	2nd round	Professional Players Tournament
	v Griffiths	5-2	3rd round	Professional Players Tournament
	v Thorne	1-5	Quarter-final	Professional Players Tournament
1984	v Knowles	1-5	Qualifying	Lada Classic
	v Dennis Taylor	1-5	1st round	Benson & Hedges Irish Masters
	v Mifsud	5-10	Qualifying	Embassy World Professional Championship
	v Roscoe	5-1	Qualifying	Jameson International
	v Mountjoy	5-1	1st round	Jameson International
	v Reardon	5-1	2nd round	Jameson International
	v Thorne	5-2	Quarter-final	Jameson International
	v S. Davis	3-9	Semi-final	Jameson International
	v John Rea	4-5	1st round	Rothmans Grand Prix
	v Morra	9-8	Qualifying	Coral UK Open
	v Meo	4-9	1st round	Coral UK Open
1985	v Newbury	5-3	Qualifying	Mercantile Credit Classic
	v Meo	5-4	1st round	Mercantile Credit Classic

Eugene Hughes

	v Reardon	1-5	2nd round	Mercantile Credit Classic
	v Watchorn	6-4	1st round	Dulux British Open
	v B. Harris	5-4	2nd round	Dulux British Open
	v Macleod	5-2	3rd round	Dulux British Open
	v Higgins	2-5	Quarter-final	Dulux British Open
	v Reardon	5-0	1st round	Benson & Hedges Irish Masters
	v S. Davis	4-5	Quarter-final	Benson & Hedges Irish Masters
	v Kelly	6-2	Quarter-final	Irish Professional Championship
	v Dennis Taylor	5-6	Semi-final	Irish Professional Championship
	v Newbury	10-6	Qualifying	Embassy World Professional Championship
	v Reardon	9-10	1st round	Embassy World Professional Championship
	v Murphy	3-5	3rd round	Goya Matchroom Trophy
	v Simngam	5-1	3rd round	Rothmans Grand Prix
	v Meo	3-5	4th round	Rothmans Grand Prix
	v West	3-9	3rd round	Coral UK Open
1986	v Wych	5-2	3rd round	Mercantile Credit Classic
	v F. Davis	5-3	4th round	Mercantile Credit Classic
	v Johnson	1-5	5th round	Mercantile Credit Classic
	v Longworth	4-5	3rd round	Dulux British Open
	v Reardon	5-2	1st round	Benson & Hedges Irish Masters
	v Thorburn	1-5	Quarter-final	Benson & Hedges Irish Masters
	v Murphy	10-7	Qualifying	Embassy World Professional Championship
	v David Taylor	10-7	1st round	Embassy World Professional Championship
	v Thorburn	6-13	2nd round	Embassy World Professional Championship
	v Sheehan	5-0	1st round	Strongbow Irish Professional Championship
	v Burke	6-3	Quarter-final	Strongbow Irish Professional Championship
	v Higgins	2-6	Semi-final	Strongbow Irish Professional Championship

GREG JENKINS (Australia)

Born –
Turned professional 1985
World ranking 95

1985	v Wilkinson	2-6	1st round	Australian Professional Championship
	v Burke	9-5	1st round	Coral UK Open
	v Bradley	3-9	2nd round	Coral UK Open
1986	v Watterson	2-5	2nd round	Mercantile Credit Classic
	v Demarco	5-1	1st round	Dulux British Open
	v Meadowcroft	5-2	2nd round	Dulux British Open
	v Wildman	4-5	3rd round	Dulux British Open
	v Gibson	4-10	Qualifying	Embassy World Professional Championship

JOE JOHNSON (England)

Born 29.7.52
Turned professional 1979
World ranking 8 (16)

Even steady progress up the ranking list, with one semi-final and two quarter-finals in ranking tournaments over the last two seasons, did not prepare the snooker world for Johnson's amazing capture of the Embassy World Professional title in May.

Runner-up to Cliff Wilson in the 1978 World Amateur Championship and, five years later, to Tony Knowles in the Professional Players Tournament, Johnson had always been regarded as a good player but not necessarily a potential winner of major titles.

However, with wins over Terry Griffiths in the quarter-finals and Tony Knowles in the semi-finals and through outplaying Steve Davis 18-12 in the final, Johnson won the record £70,000 first prize, and changed his status forever.

1979	v Werbeniuk	3-9	2nd round	Coral UK Championship
1980	v Dunning	9-6	Qualifying	Coral UK Championship
	v Fagan	4-9	1st round	Coral UK Championship
1981	v Knowles	9-2	Qualifying	John Courage English Professional
	Johnson *wo*		1st round	John Courage English Professional
	v Edmonds	5-9	2nd round	John Courage English Professional
	v Meo	8-9	Qualifying	Embassy World Professional Championship
	v Donnelly	5-4	Qualifying	Jameson International
	v Macleod	5-1	Qualifying	Jameson International
	v Wych	5-2	1st round	Jameson International
	v Miles	3-5	2nd round	Jameson International
	v Murphy	9-1	Qualifying	Coral UK Championship
	v Watterson	9-3	Qualifying	Coral UK Championship
	v Wilson	9-5	Qualifying	Coral UK Championship
	v Spencer	9-5	2nd round	Coral UK Championship
	v Reardon	7-9	3rd round	Coral UK Championship
1982	v Harris	9-4	Qualifying	Embassy World Professional Championship
	v Hallett	8-9	Qualifying	Embassy World Professional Championship
	v Wilson	4-5	Qualifying	Jameson International
	v Miles	5-1	1st round	Professional Players Tournament
	v Stevens	5-1	2nd round	Professional Players Tournament
	v Wildman	5-4	3rd round	Professional Players Tournament
	v Virgo	1-5	Quarter-final	Professional Players Tournament
	v V. Harris	9-8	Qualifying	Coral UK Championship
	v Griffiths	1-9	1st round	Coral UK Championship
	v W. Jones	5-6	1st round	Dulux British Open
	v G. Foulds	10-6	Qualifying	Embassy World Professional Championship
	v Werbeniuk	8-10	1st round	Embassy World Professional Championship
1983	v Thorburn	2-5	1st round	Benson & Hedges Masters
	v Watchorn	10-0	Qualifying	Embassy World Professional Championship
	v Wilson	8-10	Qualifying	Embassy World Professional Championship
	v D. Hughes	5-1	Qualifying	Jameson International
	v Charlton	2-5	1st round	Jameson International
	v Burke	5-3	1st round	Professional Players Tournament
	v White	5-3	2nd round	Professional Players Tournament
	v Charlton	5-0	3rd round	Professional Players Tournament
	v Thorburn	5-1	Quarter-final	Professional Players Tournament
	v Meo	9-6	Semi-final	Professional Players Tournament

Joe Johnson

	v Knowles	8-9	Final	Professional Players Tournament
	v Gibson	9-6	Qualifying	Coral UK Championship
	v Virgo	9-6	1st round	Coral UK Championship
	v David Taylor	9-3	2nd round	Coral UK Championship
	v Griffiths	2-9	Quarter-final	Coral UK Championship
1984	v Spencer	4-5	Qualifying	Lada Classic
	v Gibson	10-3	Qualifying	Embassy World Professional Championship
	v Dennis Taylor	1-10	1st round	Embassy World Professional Championship
	v Morra	5-0	Qualifying	Jameson International
	v Charlton	5-1	1st round	Jameson International
	v Dennis Taylor	2-5	2nd round	Jameson International
	v Medati	5-1	1st round	Rothmans Grand Prix
	v Williamson	4-5	2nd round	Rothmans Grand Prix
	v John Rea	9-6	Qualifying	Coral UK Open
	v Spencer	9-6	1st round	Coral UK Open
	v Stevens	2-9	2nd round	Coral UK Open
1985	v Edmonds	5-4	Qualifying	Mercantile Credit Classic
	v Knowles	5-1	1st round	Mercantile Credit Classic
	v Wilson	5-0	2nd round	Mercantile Credit Classic
	v King	5-3	Quarter-final	Mercantile Credit Classic
	v Thorburn	2-9	Semi-finals	Mercantile Credit Classic
	v Scott	9-1	1st round	Tolly Cobbold English Professional Championship
	v Virgo	4-9	2nd round	Tolly Cobbold English Professional Championship
	v White	4-5	Quarter-final	Winfield Australian Masters
	v Jim Bear	5-1	3rd round	Goya Matchroom Trophy
	v Bradley	5-2	4th round	Goya Matchroom Trophy
	v Wilson	5-1	5th round	Goya Matchroom Trophy
	v N. Foulds	2-5	Quarter-final	Goya Matchroom Trophy
	v Gilbert	5-2	3rd round	Rothmans Grand Prix
	v Hallett	5-4	4th round	Rothmans Grand Prix
	v Thorburn	1-5	5th round	Rothmans Grand Prix
	v Simngam	9-4	3rd round	Coral UK Open
	v N. Foulds	8-9	4th round	Coral UK Open
1986	v B. Harris	5-4	3rd round	Mercantile Credit Classic
	v Mans	5-2	4th round	Mercantile Credit Classic
	v E. Hughes	5-1	5th round	Mercantile Credit Classic
	v Thorburn	4-5	Quarter-final	Mercantile Credit Classic
	v Thorburn	3-5	1st round	Benson & Hedges Masters
	v Fowler	9-7	3rd round	Tolly Cobbold English Professional Championship
	v Spencer	9-7	4th round	Tolly Cobbold English Professional Championship
	v Hallett	6-9	Quarter-final	Tolly Cobbold English Professional Championship
	v J. McLaughlin	5-2	3rd round	Dulux British Open
	v Werbeniuk	3-5	4th round	Dulux British Open
	v Martin	10-3	1st round	Embassy World Professional Championship
	v Hallett	13-6	2nd round	Embassy World Professional Championship

v Griffiths	13-12	Quarter-final	Embassy World Professional Championship
v Knowles	16-8	Semi-final	Embassy World Professional Championship
v S. Davis	**18-12**	**Final**	**Embassy World Professional Championship**

TONY JONES (England)

Born 15.4.60
Turned professional 1983
World ranking 55 (50)

Jones, the 1983 English amateur champion, recorded the best win of his professional career when he beat Willie Thorne 5-3 to reach the last 32 of the Mercantile Credit Classic in January 1986.

1983	v Oliver	5-2	Qualifying	Professional Players Tournament
	v Werbeniuk	4-5	1st round	Professional Players Tournament
	v Sinclair	9-3	Qualifying	Coral UK Championship
	v Knowles	5-9	1st round	Coral UK Championship
1984	v King	9-10	Qualifying	Embassy World Professional Championship
	v French	5-1	Qualifying	Jameson International
	v Duggan	2-5	Qualifying	Jameson International
	v Sinclair	5-4	Qualifying	Rothmans Grand Prix
	v Griffiths	5-3	1st round	Rothmans Grand Prix
	v N. Foulds	0-5	2nd round	Rothmans Grand Prix
	v Chaperon	9-1	Qualifying	Coral UK Open
	v Fagan	9-2	Qualifying	Coral UK Open
	v Wildman	9-2	Qualifying	Coral UK Open
	v Higgins	7-9	1st round	Coral UK Open
1985	v Greaves	5-2	Qualifying	Mercantile Credit Classic
	v Gibson	5-0	Qualifying	Mercantile Credit Classic
	v Dodd	5-1	Qualifying	Mercantile Credit Classic
	v S. Francisco	1-5	Qualifying	Mercantile Credit Classic
	v Houlihan	9-1	Qualifying	Tolly Cobbold English Professional Championship
	v Williams	6-9	1st round	Tolly Cobbold English Professional Championship
	v G. Foulds	6-0	Qualifying	Dulux British Open
	v White	5-6	1st round	Dulux British Open
	v Darrington	10-2	Qualifying	Embassy World Professional Championship
	v Duggan	10-8	Qualifying	Embassy World Professional Championship
	v Fitzmaurice	10-4	Qualifying	Embassy World Professional Championship
	v Sinclair	10-2	Qualifying	Embassy World Professional Championship
	v Knowles	8-10	1st round	Embassy World Professional Championship
	v Kelly	5-3	2nd round	Goya Matchroom Trophy
	v David Taylor	4-5	3rd round	Goya Matchroom Trophy
	v Houlihan	5-4	2nd round	Rothmans Grand Prix
	v Meo	2-5	3rd round	Rothmans Grand Prix
	v Jonik	9-4	2nd round	Coral UK Open
	v Griffiths	5-9	3rd round	Coral UK Open

1986	v Gilbert	5-3	2nd round	Mercantile Credit Classic
	v Thorne	5-3	3rd round	Mercantile Credit Classic
	v Werbeniuk	3-5	4th round	Mercantile Credit Classic
	v. B. Harris	9-5	2nd round	Tolly Cobbold English Professional Championship
	v Virgo	7-9	3rd round	Tolly Cobbold English Professional Championship
	v O'Boye	5-2	2nd round	Dulux British Open
	v S. Francisco	2-5	3rd round	Dulux British Open
	v V. Harris	10-7	Qualifying	Embassy World Professional Championship
	v Gilbert	7-10	Qualifying	Embassy World Professional Championship

WAYNE JONES (Wales)

Born 24.12.59
Turned professional 1984
World ranking 56 (49)

Welsh amateur champion in 1983, Jones last season recorded wins over Willie Thorne in the third round of the Rothmans Grand Prix and Ray Reardon in reaching the semi-finals of the Zetters Welsh Professional Championship.

1984	v Watchorn	5-0	Qualifying	Jameson International
	v Gibson	5-2	Qualifying	Jameson International
	v Scott	5-0	Qualifying	Jameson International
	v Wildman	5-0	Qualifying	Jameson International
	v David Taylor	4-5	1st round	Jameson International
	v Watterson	5-3	Qualifying	Rothmans Grand Prix
	v Campbell	4-5	1st round	Rothmans Grand Prix
	v O'Kane	7-9	Qualifying	Coral UK Open
1985	v O'Kane	5-0	Qualifying	Mercantile Credit Classic
	v Duggan	0-5	Qualifying	Mercantile Credit Classic
	v Donnelly	6-1	Qualifying	Dulux British Open
	v Johnson	6-5	1st round	Dulux British Open
	v Chaperon	2-5	2nd round	Dulux British Open
	v Jack Rea	10-3	Qualifying	Embassy World Professional Championship
	v Dunning	10-6	Qualifying	Embassy World Professional Championship
	v Watterson	10-5	Qualifying	Embassy World Professional Championship
	v Miles	10-8	Qualifying	Embassy World Professional Championship
	v White	4-10	1st round	Embassy World Professional Championship
	v Newbury	2-6	1st round	BCE Welsh Professional Championship
	v Smith	5-3	2nd round	Goya Matchroom Trophy
	v Parrott	3-5	3rd round	Goya Matchroom Trophy
	v John Rea	5-0	2nd round	Rothmans Grand Prix
	v Thorne	5-0	3rd round	Rothmans Grand Prix
	v P. Francisco	3-5	4th round	Rothmans Grand Prix
	v Fitzmaurice	9-3	2nd round	Coral UK Open
	v Virgo	7-9	3rd round	Coral UK Open

1986	v Van Rensberg	4-5	2nd round	Mercantile Credit Classic
	v Everton	6-2	1st round	Zetters Welsh Professional Championship
	v Reardon	6-4	Quarter-final	Zetters Welsh Professional Championship
	v Mountjoy	7-9	Semi-final	Zetters Welsh Professional Championship
	v Rigitano	5-1	2nd round	Dulux British Open
	v Mans	2-5	3rd round	Dulux British Open
	v Grace	10-3	Qualifying	Embassy World Professional Championship
	v Hendry	8-10	Qualifying	Embassy World Professional Championship

FRANK JONIK (Canada)

Born 2.12.57
Turned professional 1979
World ranking 98 (72)

In his six-year professional career, Jonik's most notable win was beating Doug Mountjoy in the first round of the Professional Players Tournament in 1982.

1980	v Wildman	9-7	Qualifying	Embassy World Professional Championship
	v Wilson	6-9	Qualifying	Embassy World Professional Championship
1981	v Hallett	1-9	Qualifying	Embassy World Professional Championship
1982	v John Bear	4-9	Qualifying	Embassy World Professional Championship
	v Hallett	2-5	Qualifying	Jameson International
	v Mountjoy	5-3	1st round	Professional Players Tournament
	v Meo	0-5	2nd round	Professional Players Tournament
1983	v Edmonds	4-10	Qualifying	Embassy World Professional Championship
	v Wildman	4-5	1st round	Professional Players Tournament
1984	v Mikkelsen	9-10	Qualifying	Embassy World Professional Championship
	v J. McLaughlin	5-2	Qualifying	Jameson International
	v Gauvreau	1-5	Qualifying	Jameson International
	v Bradley	1-5	Qualifying	Rothmans Grand Prix
	v Newbury	3-9	Qualifying	Coral UK Open
1985	v G. Foulds	2-5	Qualifying	Mercantile Credit Classic
	v J. McLaughlin	6-2	Qualifying	Dulux British Open
	v Spencer	0-6	1st round	Dulux British Open
	v O'Kane	5-10	Qualifying	Embassy World Professional Championship
	v Mikkelsen	6-4	Quarter-final	Canadian Professional Championship
	v Chaperon	3-6	Semi-final	Canadian Professional Championship
	v Newbury	4-5	2nd round	Goya Matchroom Trophy
	v Fowler	4-5	2nd round	Rothmans Grand Prix
	v T. Jones	4-9	2nd round	Coral UK Open
1986	v P. Francisco	2-5	2nd round	Mercantile Credit Classic
	v Dodd	4-5	2nd round	Dulux British Open
	v Chaperon	8-10	Qualifying	Embassy World Professional Championship

TONY KEARNEY (Republic of Ireland)

Born 24.6.54
Turned professional 1984
World ranking 101 (90)

Kearney was Republic of Ireland amateur champion in 1980.

1984	v Burke	4-5	Qualifying	Jameson International
	v Chaperon	1-5	Qualifying	Rothmans Grand Prix
	v Murphy	2-9	Qualifying	Coral UK Open
1985	v French	5-1	Qualifying	Mercantile Credit Classic
	v Williamson	3-5	Qualifying	Mercantile Credit Classic
	v Watterson	6-4	Qualifying	Dulux British Open
	v S. Francisco	4-6	1st round	Dulux British Open
	v Burke	4-6	Qualifying	Irish Professional Championship
	v Anderson	8-10	Qualifying	Embassy World Professional Championship
	v D. Hughes	1-5	1st round	Goya Matchroom Trophy
	v Jim Bear	5-3	1st round	Rothmans Grand Prix
	v Edmonds	2-5	2nd round	Rothmans Grand Prix
	v D. Hughes	8-9	1st round	Coral UK Open
1986	v Jim Bear	5-0	1st round	Mercantile Credit Classic
	v Medati	2-5	2nd round	Mercantile Credit Classic
	v Smith	5-2	1st round	Dulux British Open
	v Foldvari	2-5	2nd round	Dulux British Open
	v Wilkinson	10-5	Qualifying	Embassy World Professional Championship
	v Scott	8-10	Qualifying	Embassy World Professional Championship
	v Fagan	5-0	1st round	Strongbow Irish Professional Championship
	v Murphy	2-6	Quarter-final	Strongbow Irish Professional Championship

BILLY KELLY (Republic of Ireland)

Born 1.5.45
Turned professional 1981
World ranking 88 (71)

1981	v Macleod	1-5	Qualifying	Jameson International
	v G. Foulds	7-9	Qualifying	Coral UK Championship
1982	v Sinclair	8-9	Qualifying	Embassy World Professional Championship
	v G. Foulds	5-4	Qualifying	Jameson International
	v Williamson	5-1	Qualifying	Jameson International
	v Higgins	3-5	1st round	Jameson International
	v Wych	0-5	1st round	Professional Players Tournament
	v Fitzmaurice (*retd*)	8-0	Qualifying	Coral UK Championship
	v Virgo	2-9	1st round	Coral UK Championship
1983	v Dennis Taylor	0-6	Quarter-final	Irish Professional Championship

	v Demarco	10-4	Qualifying	Embassy World Professional Championship
	v S. Francisco	5-10	Qualifying	Embassy World Professional Championship
	v F. Davis	1-5	Qualifying	Jameson International
	v Hallett	0-5	1st round	Professional Players Tournament
1984	v Burke	7-10	Qualifying	Embassy World Professional Championship
	v Hargreaves	5-2	Qualifying	Jameson International
	v King	5-4	Qualifying	Jameson International
	v S. Francisco	3-5	Qualifying	Jameson International
	v O'Kane	4-5	Qualifying	Rothmans Grand Prix
	v Bradley	6-9	Qualifying	Coral UK Open
	v Bales	3-5	Qualifying	Mercantile Credit Classic
	v P. Francisco	3-6	Qualifying	Dulux British Open
	v Watchorn	6-2	Qualifying	Irish Professional Championship
	v E. Hughes	2-6	Quarter-final	Irish Professional Championship
	v Rigitano	6-10	Qualifying	Embassy World Professional Championship
1985	v P. Francisco	3-6	Qualifying	Dulux British Open
	v Watchorn	6-2	Qualifying	Irish Professional Championship
	v E. Hughes	2-6	Quarter-final	Irish Professional Championship
	v Rigitano	6-10	Qualifying	Embassy World Professional Championship
	v T. Jones	3-5	2nd round	Goya Matchroom Trophy
	v Donnelly	5-4	2nd round	Rothmans Grand Prix
	v S. Francisco	2-5	3rd round	Rothmans Grand Prix
	v Medati	1-9	2nd round	Coral UK Open
1986	v F. Davis	3-5	2nd round	Mercantile Credit Classic
	v F. Davis	4-5	2nd round	Dulux British Open
	v Edmonds	0-10	Qualifying	Embassy World Professional Championship
	v Jack Rea	5-0	1st round	Strongbow Irish Professional Championship
	v Dennis Taylor	1-6	Quarter-final	Strongbow Irish Professional Championship

WARREN KING (Australia)

Born 1.4.55
Turned professional 1982
World ranking 41 (35)

Twice Australian amateur champion, King last season earned his one ranking point in the Goya Matchroom Trophy. He has three times been a member of Australia's World Cup team.

1983	v Anderson	10-6	Qualifying	Embassy World Professional Championship
	v Hallett	6-10	Qualifying	Embassy World Professional Championship
	v Black	5-3	Qualifying	Jameson International
	v Miles	3-5	Qualifying	Jameson International
	v B. Harris	5-3	Qualifying	Professional Players Tournament
	v Meo	2-5	1st round	Professional Players Tournament
1984	v Jones	10-9	Qualifying	Embassy World Professional Championship
	v Watterson	10-8	Qualifying	Embassy World Professional Championship
	v Martin	10-8	Qualifying	Embassy World Professional Championship
	v S. Davis	3-10	1st round	Embassy World Professional Championship

	v Kelly	4-5	Qualifying	Jameson International
	v Greaves	5-0	Qualifying	Rothmans Grand Prix
	v Macleod	4-5	1st round	Rothmans Grand Prix
	v Browne	9-5	Qualifying	Coral UK Open
	v Virgo	9-4	Qualifying	Coral UK Open
	v Dennis Taylor	5-9	1st round	Coral UK Open
1985	v Duggan	5-4	Qualifying	Mercantile Credit Classic
	v Reynolds	5-2	Qualifying	Mercantile Credit Classic
	v Spencer	5-2	1st round	Mercantile Credit Classic
	v White	5-2	2nd round	Mercantile Credit Classic
	v Johnson	3-5	Quarter-final	Mercantile Credit Classic
	v Medati	6-4	Qualifying	Dulux British Open
	v Reardon	5-6	1st round	Dulux British Open
	v Medati	9-10	Qualifying	Embassy World Professional Championship
	v Anderson	8-2	Quarter-final	Australian Professional Championship
	v Campbell	6-9	Semi-final	Australian Professional Championship
	v Caggianello	5-0	2nd round	Goya Matchroom Trophy
	v Williams	5-3	3rd round	Goya Matchroom Trophy
	v White	2-5	4th round	Goya Matchroom Trophy
	v Drago	4-5	2nd round	Rothmans Grand Prix
	v D. Hughes	9-0	2nd round	Coral UK Open
	v Williams	5-9	3rd round	Coral UK Open
1986	v Duggan	5-2	2nd round	Mercantile Credit Classic
	v Mountjoy	4-5	3rd round	Mercantile Credit Classic
	v John Rea	1-5	2nd round	Dulux British Open
	v Sheehan	10-4	Qualifying	Embassy World Professional Championship
	v Roscoe	10-5	Qualifying	Embassy World Professional Championship
	v Reynolds	7-10	Qualifying	Embassy World Professional Championship

TONY KNOWLES (England)

Born 13.6.55
Turned professional 1980
World ranking 4 (3)

Knowles held second place in the world rankings at the end of the 1983–84 season but slipped to 3rd in 1984–85. After mixed fortunes during 1985–86, he managed to hold onto 4th with a run to the semi-finals of the Embassy World Championship where he was beaten 16-8 by Joe Johnson.

1980	v Andrewartha	8-9	Qualifying	Coral UK Championship
1981	v Johnson	2-9	Qualifying	John Courage English Professional
	v Ross	7-0	Qualifying	Embassy World Professional Championship
	v Wych	9-3	Qualifying	Embassy World Professional Championship

	v Miles	8-10	1st round	Embassy World Professional Championship
	v Hallett	5-2	1st round	Jameson International
	v Virgo	2-5	2nd round	Jameson International
	v G. Foulds	9-1	Qualifying	Coral UK Championship
	v F. Davis	9-6	2nd round	Coral UK Championship
	v Mountjoy	9-6	3rd round	Coral UK Championship
	v Griffiths	5-9	Quarter-final	Coral UK Championship
1982	v Dennis Taylor	2-5	Semi-final	Tolly Cobbold Classic
	v E. Hughes	9-7	Qualifying	Embassy World Professional Championship
	v S. Davis	10-1	1st round	Embassy World Professional Championship
	v Miles	13-7	2nd round	Embassy World Professional Championship
	v Charlton	11-13	Quarter-final	Embassy World Professional Championship
	v S. Davis	4-5	1st round	Langs Scottish Masters
	v Sinclair	5-2	1st round	Jameson International
	v Reardon	5-2	2nd round	Jameson International
	v Wilson	5-4	Quarter-final	Jameson International
	v Stevens	9-8	Semi-final	Jameson International
	v David Taylor	**9-6**	**Final**	**Jameson International**
	v Houlihan	5-4	1st round	Professional Players Tournament
	v Wilson	4-5	2nd round	Professional Players Tournament
	v Donnelly	9-6	1st round	Coral UK Championship
	v Spencer	6-9	2nd round	Coral UK Championship
1983	v Stevens	0-5	1st round	Lada Classic
	v Mountjoy	1-5	1st round	Benson & Hedges Irish Masters
	v Miles	10-3	1st round	Embassy World Professional Championship
	v Reardon	13-12	2nd round	Embassy World Professional Championship
	v Meo	13-9	Quarter-final	Embassy World Professional Championship
	v Thorburn	15-16	Semi-final	Embassy World Professional Championship
	v Werbeniuk	0-5	Semi-final	Winfield Masters
	v Meo	5-4	1st round	Langs Scottish Masters
	v Thorburn	6-2	Semi-final	Langs Scottish Masters
	v S. Davis	6-9	Final	Langs Scottish Masters
	v Edmonds	5-1	1st round	Jameson International
	v Spencer	4-5	2nd round	Jameson International
	v Medati	5-1	1st round	Professional Players Tournament
	v Williams	5-4	2nd round	Professional Players Tournament
	v S. Francisco	5-0	3rd round	Professional Players Tournament
	v Campbell	5-3	Quarter-final	Professional Players Tournament
	v Thorne	9-7	Semi-final	Professional Players Tournament
	v Johnson	**9-8**	**Final**	**Professional Players Tournament**
	v T. Jones	9-5	1st round	Coral UK Championship
	v Mountjoy	9-5	2nd round	Coral UK Championship
	v Higgins	5-9	Quarter-final	Coral UK Championship
1984	v E. Hughes	5-1	Qualifying	Lada Classic
	v Hallett	5-3	1st round	Lada Classic
	v Parrott	1-5	Quarter-final	Lada Classic
	v Dennis Taylor	5-2	1st round	Benson & Hedges Masters
	v Higgins	5-1	Quarter-final	Benson & Hedges Masters
	v Griffiths	4-6	Semi-final	Benson & Hedges Masters
	v Griffiths	0-5	Quarter-final	Benson & Hedges Irish Masters

Tony Knowles

	v White	5-1	1st round	Tolly Cobbold Classic
	v Thorburn	5-3	Semi-final	Tolly Cobbold Classic
	v S. Davis	2-8	Final	Tolly Cobbold Classic
	v Parrott	7-10	1st round	Embassy World Professional Championship
	v White	5-3	Quarter-final	Winfield Australian Masters
	v Charlton	6-0	Semi-final	Winfield Australian Masters
	v Virgo	**7-3**	**Final**	**Winfield Australian Masters**
	v Griffiths	5-3	1st round	Langs Scottish Masters
	v White	5-6	Semi-final	Langs Scottish Masters
	v Higgins	5-3	1st round	Carlsberg Challenge
	v White	7-9	1st round	Carlsberg Challenge
	v Reynolds	5-1	1st round	Jameson International
	v Newbury	5-4	2nd round	Jameson International
	v White	5-4	Quarter-final	Jameson International
	v S. Francisco	9-6	Semi-final	Jameson International
	v S. Davis	2-9	Final	Jameson International
	v V. Harris	5-1	1st round	Rothmans Grand Prix
	v Dunning	5-1	2nd round	Rothmans Grand Prix
	v Williamson	5-2	3rd round	Rothmans Grand Prix
	v N. Foulds	2-5	Quarter-final	Rothmans Grand Prix
	v Gauvreau	9-5	1st round	Coral UK Open
	v Dennis Taylor	9-2	2nd round	Coral UK Open
	v Stevens	7-9	Quarter-final	Coral UK Open
1985	v Johnson	1-5	1st round	Mercantile Credit Classic
	v Mountjoy	3-5	1st round	Benson & Hedges Masters
	v Bradley	9-8	1st round	Tolly Cobbold English Professional Championship
	v Martin	9-3	2nd round	Tolly Cobbold English Professional Championship
	v David Taylor	9-2	Quarter-final	Tolly Cobbold English Professional Championship
	v Longworth	9-6	Semi-final	Tolly Cobbold English Professional Championship
	v S. Davis	2-9	Final	Tolly Cobbold English Professional Championship
	v French	6-2	1st round	Dulux British Open
	v Longworth	5-2	2nd round	Dulux British Open
	v Meo	2-5	3rd round	Dulux British Open
	v Charlton	5-3	Quarter-final	Benson & Hedges Irish Masters
	v White	4-6	Semi-final	Benson & Hedges Irish Masters
	v T. Jones	10-8	1st round	Embassy World Professional Championship
	v Mountjoy	13-6	2nd round	Embassy World Professional Championship
	v White	13-10	Quarter-final	Embassy World Professional Championship
	v Dennis Taylor	5-16	Semi-final	Embassy World Professional Championship
	v S. Francisco	4-5	1st round	Langs Scottish Masters
	v E. McLaughlin	5-1	3rd round	Goya Matchroom Trophy
	v N. Foulds	4-5	4th round	Goya Matchroom Trophy
	v Gibson	5-1	3rd round	Rothmans Grand Prix
	v Edmonds	5-3	4th round	Rothmans Grand Prix
	v Campbell	5-2	5th round	Rothmans Grand Prix

	v Stevens	5-4	Quarter-final	Rothmans Grand Prix
	v Dennis Taylor	6-9	Semi-final	Rothmans Grand Prix
	v Reardon	5-2	1st round	BCE Canadian Masters
	v O'Boye	9-5	3rd round	Coral UK Open
	v Spencer	9-7	4th round	Coral UK Open
	v David Taylor	9-7	5th round	Coral UK Open
	v White	4-9	Quarter-final	Coral UK Open
1986	v Rigitano	5-4	3rd round	Mercantile Credit Classic
	v Macleod	5-4	4th round	Mercantile Credit Classic
	v Williams	2-5	5th round	Mercantile Credit Classic
	v White	5-3	1st round	BCE Belgian Classic
	v Griffiths	2-5	Semi-final	BCE Belgian Classic
	v S. Francisco	5-1	1st round	Benson & Hedges Masters
	v Charlton	5-4	Quarter-final	Benson & Hedges Masters
	v Thorburn	4-6	Semi-final	Benson & Hedges Masters
	v Bales	9-4	3rd round	Tolly Cobbold English Professional Championship
	v Hallett	5-9	4th round	Tolly Cobbold English Professional Championship
	v Williamson	5-1	3rd round	Dulux British Open
	v Wych	4-5	4th round	Dulux British Open
	v Fagan	4-5	Quarter-final	Benson & Hedges Irish Masters
	v N. Foulds	10-9	1st round	Embassy World Professional Championship
	v S. Francisco	13-10	2nd round	Embassy World Professional Championship
	v Stevens	13-9	Quarter-final	Embassy World Professional Championship
	v Johnson	8-16	Semi-final	Embassy World Professional Championship

STEVE LONGWORTH (England)

Born 27.7.48
Turned professional 1984
World ranking 31 (37)

In just two seasons as a professional, Longworth, the 1984 English amateur champion, has earned a place in the top 32 by virtue of some solid, consistent performances, notably in beating John Parrott and David Taylor to reach the last 16 of the Rothmans Grand Prix.

1984	v Newbury	4-5	Qualifying	Jameson International
	v E. McLaughlin	2-5	Qualifying	Rothmans Grand Prix
	v Darrington	9-5	Qualifying	Coral UK Open
	v Burke	9-4	Qualifying	Coral UK Open
	v Morra	1-9	Qualifying	Coral UK Open
1985	v P. Francisco	5-4	Qualifying	Mercantile Credit Classic
	v Oliver	5-1	Qualifying	Mercantile Credit Classic
	v Fisher	5-1	Qualifying	Mercantile Credit Classic
	v N. Foulds	5-3	Qualifying	Mercantile Credit Classic
	v David Taylor	5-4	1st round	Mercantile Credit Classic
	v Cliff Thorburn	3-5	2nd round	Mercantile Credit Classic

	v Edmonds	9-4	Qualifying	Tolly Cobbold English Professional Championship
	v Wildman	9-3	1st round	Tolly Cobbold English Professional Championship
	v Medati	9-7	2nd round	Tolly Cobbold English Professional Championship
	v White	9-5	Quarter-final	Tolly Cobbold English Professional Championship
	v Knowles	6-9	Semi-final	Tolly Cobbold English Professional Championship
	v F. Davis	6-1	Qualifying	Dulux British Open
	v Wilson	6-3	1st round	Dulux British Open
	v Knowles	2-5	2nd round	Dulux British Open
	v Giannaros	10-1	Qualifying	Embassy World Professional Championship
	v Cripsey	10-8	Qualifying	Embassy World Professional Championship
	v Van Rensberg	7-10	Qualifying	Embassy World Professional Championship
	v Wilkinson	5-0	2nd round	Goya Matchroom Trophy
	v Thorburn	3-5	3rd round	Goya Matchroom Trophy
	v Hargreaves	5-2	2nd round	Rothmans Grand Prix
	v Parrott	5-2	3rd round	Rothmans Grand Prix
	v David Taylor	5-1	4th round	Rothmans Grand Prix
	v Stevens	3-5	5th round	Rothmans Grand Prix
	v Gibson	9-2	2nd round	Coral UK Open
	v Meo	5-9	3rd round	Coral UK Open
1986	v O'Boye	1-5	2nd round	Mercantile Credit Classic
	v Duggan	9-4	2nd round	Tolly Cobbold English Professional Championship
	v Reynolds	5-9	3rd round	Tolly Cobbold English Professional Championship
	v Houlihan	5-3	2nd round	Dulux British Open
	v E. Hughes	5-4	3rd round	Dulux British Open
	v P. Francisco	2-5	4th round	Dulux British Open
	v Watchorn	10-7	Qualifying	Embassy World Professional Championship
	v John Rea	10-4	Qualifying	Embassy World Professional Championship
	v Virgo	8-10	Qualifying	Embassy World Professional Championship

EDDIE McLAUGHLIN (Scotland)

Born 27.6.52
Turned professional 1981
World ranking 90 (63)

1981	v Black	5-3	Qualifying	Jameson International
	v Wildman	5-3	Qualifying	Jameson International
	v Greaves	5-1	Qualifying	Jameson International
	v Ross	5-3	Quarter-final	Scottish Professional Championship
	v Black	3-6	Semi-final	Scottish Professional Championship
	v Meo	2-5	1st round	Jameson International
	v Medati	5-9	Qualifying	Coral UK Championship

1982	v Macleod	8-9	Qualifying	Embassy World Professional Championship
	v Gibson	3-6	Quarter-final	Scottish Professional Championship
	v Houlihan	5-2	Qualifying	Jameson International
	v Williams	1-5	Qualifying	Jameson International
	v Mans	2-5	1st round	Professional Players Tournament
	v Wilson	6-9	Qualifying	Coral UK Championship
1983	v Greaves	10-7	Qualifying	Embassy World Professional Championship
	v Fisher	9-10	Qualifying	Embassy World Professional Championship
	v Black	4-6	1st round	Scottish Professional Championship
	v Campbell	5-2	Qualifying	Jameson International
	v Edmonds	1-5	Qualifying	Jameson International
	v Charlton	0-5	1st round	Professional Players Tournament
	v B. Harris	8-9	Qualifying	Coral UK Championship
1984	v Stevens	4-5	Qualifying	Lada Classic
	v Hargreaves	10-5	Qualifying	Embassy World Professional Championship
	v Andrewartha	8-10	Qualifying	Embassy World Professional Championship
	v O'Kane	1-5	Qualifying	Jameson International
	v Longworth	5-2	Qualifying	Rothmans Grand Prix
	v Mountjoy	4-5	1st round	Rothmans Grand Prix
	v Bales	4-9	Qualifying	Coral UK Open
1985	v Sheehan	5-2	Qualifying	Mercantile Credit Classic
	v F. Davis	5-1	Qualifying	Mercantile Credit Classic
	v Macleod	4-5	Qualifying	Mercantile Credit Classic
	v French	0-6	Qualifying	Dulux British Open
	v Chalmers	9-10	Qualifying	Embassy World Professional Championship
	v Hendry	5-3	2nd round	Goya Matchroom Trophy
	v Knowles	1-5	3rd round	Goya Matchroom Trophy
	v Van Rensberg	4-5	2nd round	Rothmans Grand Prix
1986	v J. McLaughlin	2-5	2nd round	Mercantile Credit Classic
	v West	3-5	2nd round	Dulux British Open
	v Black	4-6	Quarter-final	Canada Dry Scottish Professional Championship
	v John Rea	6-10	Qualifying	Embassy World Professional Championship

JACK McLAUGHLIN (Northern Ireland)

Born 29.1.59
Turned professional 1984
World ranking 71 (69)

McLaughlin won the Northern Ireland Amateur Championship in both 1983 and 1984.

1984	v Greaves	5-3	Qualifying	Jameson International
	v Jonik	2-5	Qualifying	Jameson International
	v Meadowcroft	5-1	Qualifying	Rothmans Grand Prix
	v Wildman	3-5	1st round	Rothmans Grand Prix
	v French	9-3	Qualifying	Coral UK Open
	v Roscoe	9-8	Qualifying	Coral UK Open

	v Miles	9-8	Qualifying	Coral UK Open
	v Thorburn	4-9	1st round	Coral UK Open
1985	v Demarco	5-1	Qualifying	Mercantile Credit Classic
	v Black	5-0	Qualifying	Mercantile Credit Classic
	v Scott	4-5	Qualifying	Mercantile Credit Classic
	v Jonik	2-6	Qualifying	Dulux British Open
	v Sheehan	6-3	Qualifying	Irish Professional Championship
	v Williamson	3-5	2nd round	Goya Matchroom Trophy
	v Medati	5-2	2nd round	Rothmans Grand Prix
	v Griffiths	4-5	3rd round	Rothmans Grand Prix
	v Chaperon	9-5	Qualifying	Coral UK Open
	v Reynolds	7-9	1st round	Coral UK Open
1986	v E. McLaughlin	5-2	2nd round	Mercantile Credit Classic
	v Thorburn	1-5	3rd round	Mercantile Credit Classic
	v Fisher	5-3	2nd round	Dulux British Open
	v Johnson	2-5	3rd round	Dulux British Open
	v Murphy	7-10	Qualifying	Embassy World Professional Championship
	v Watchorn	5-0	1st round	Strongbow Irish Professional Championship
	v Higgins	2-6	Quarter-final	Strongbow Irish Professional Championship

MURDO MACLEOD (Scotland)

Born 14.1.47
Turned professional 1981
World ranking 22 (26)

Twice Scottish professional champion, Macleod has acquired some notable scalps, including Willie Thorne (twice), David Taylor and Eddie Charlton, but he has never yet won a match in the televised phase of a competition.

1981	v Kelly	5-1	Qualifying	Jameson International
	v Johnson	1-5	Qualifying	Jameson International
	v Black	4-5	Quarter-final	Scottish Professional Championship
	v Roscoe	7-9	Qualifying	Coral UK Championship
1982	v E. McLaughlin	9-8	Qualifying	Embassy World Professional Championship
	v Dunning	4-9	Qualifying	Embassy World Professional Championship
	v Donnelly	6-5	1st round	Scottish Professional Championship
	v Black	0-6	Quarter-final	Scottish Professional Championship
	v Dodd	1-5	Qualifying	Jameson International
	v Thorne	5-2	2nd round	Professional Players Tournament
	v Reardon	2-5	3rd round	Professional Players Tournament
	v Martin	6-9	Qualifying	Coral UK Championship
1983	v M. Owen	10-5	Qualifying	Embassy World Professional Championship
	v Martin	7-10	Qualifying	Embassy World Professional Championship
	v Gibson	6-5	1st round	Scottish Professional Championship
	v Black	6-2	Semi-final	Scottish Professional Championship
	v Sinclair	**11-9**	**Final**	**Scottish Professional Championship**
	v S. Davis	1-5	1st round	Langs Supreme Scottish Masters
	v Medati	5-3	Qualifying	Jameson International
	v Reardon	2-5	1st round	Jameson International

	v Murphy	0-5	1st round	Professional Players Tournament
	v Bennett	9-0	Qualifying	Coral UK Championship
	v Higgins	6-9	1st round	Coral UK Championship
1984	v David Taylor	5-4	Qualifying	Lada Classic
	v Stevens	1-5	1st round	Lada Classic
	v Gauvreau	6-10	Qualifying	Embassy World Professional Championship
	v White	0-5	1st round	Langs Supreme Scottish Masters
	v Black	5-3	Qualifying	Jameson International
	v Meo	1-5	1st round	Jameson International
	v King	5-4	1st round	Rothmans Grand Prix
	v Thorne	3-5	2nd round	Rothmans Grand Prix
	v Scott	9-5	Qualifying	Coral UK Open
	v David Taylor	6-9	1st round	Coral UK Open
1985	v E. McLaughlin	5-4	Qualifying	Mercantile Credit Classic
	v Charlton	5-1	1st round	Mercantile Credit Classic
	v Virgo	0-5	2nd round	Mercantile Credit Classic
	v Murphy	6-5	1st round	Dulux British Open
	v Thorne	5-0	2nd round	Dulux British Open
	v E. Hughes	2-5	3rd round	Dulux British Open
	v P. Francisco	10-7	Qualifying	Embassy World Professional Championship
	v Mountjoy	5-10	1st round	Embassy World Professional Championship
	v Thorburn	1-5	1st round	Langs Scottish Masters
	v Fitzmaurice	5-1	3rd round	Goya Matchroom Trophy
	v Chaperon	5-4	4th round	Goya Matchroom Trophy
	v S. Davis	1-5	5th round	Goya Matchroom Trophy
	v Drago	3-5	3rd round	Rothmans Grand Prix
	v Murphy	9-7	3rd round	Coral UK Open
	v Reardon	9-5	4th round	Coral UK Open
	v West	4-9	5th round	Coral UK Open
1986	v Sinclair	5-3	3rd round	Mercantile Credit Classic
	v Knowles	4-5	4th round	Mercantile Credit Classic
	v F. Davis	5-4	3rd round	Dulux British Open
	v S. Francisco	5-1	4th round	Dulux British Open
	v Griffiths	2-5	5th round	Dulux British Open
	v Hendry	5-6	Quarter-final	Canada Dry Scottish Professional Championship
	v Fowler	6-10	Qualifying	Embassy World Professional Championship

PERRIE MANS (South Africa)

Born 14.10.40
Turned professional 1961
World ranking 36 (30)

Having reached the world final in 1978 and won the Benson and Hedges Masters the following year, Mans has slipped steadily down the rankings and is now outside the top 32 for the first time.

1973	v Gross	9-2	1st round	World Professional Championship
	v Charlton	8-16	2nd round	World Professional Championship

1974	v Anderson	8-1	1st round	World Professional Championship
	v Spencer	15-13	2nd round	World Professional Championship
	v Williams	4-15	Quarter-final	World Professional Championship
1975	v Dennis Taylor	12-15	1st round	World Professional Championship
1976	v Miles	15-10	1st round	Embassy World Professional Championship
	v Meadowcroft	15-8	Quarter-final	Embassy World Professional Championship
	v Reardon	10-20	Semi-final	Embassy World Professional Championship
1977	v Dennis Taylor	11-13	1st round	Embassy World Professional Championship
1978	v Barrie	9-6	Qualifying	Embassy World Professional Championship
	v Spencer	13-8	1st round	Embassy World Professional Championship
	v Miles	13-7	Quarter-final	Embassy World Professional Championship
	v F. Davis	18-16	Semi-final	Embassy World Professional Championship
	v Reardon	18-25	Final	Embassy World Professional Championship
1979	v Thorburn	5-4	Quarter-final	Benson & Hedges Masters
	v Reardon	5-3	Semi-final	Benson & Hedges Masters
	v Higgins	**8-4**	**Final**	**Benson & Hedges Masters**
	v Griffiths	8-13	1st round	Embassy World Professional Championship
1980	v Higgins	1-5	Quarter-final	Benson & Hedges Masters
	v Higgins	6-13	2nd round	Embassy World Professional Championship
1981	v S. Davis	5-3	1st round	Benson & Hedges Masters
	v Thorburn	4-5	Quarter-final	Benson & Hedges Masters
	v Werbeniuk	5-13	2nd round	Embassy World Professional Championship
	v Meo	5-3	2nd round	Jameson International
	v S. Davis	3-5	3rd round	Jameson International
1982	v Meo	10-8	1st round	Embassy World Professional Championship
	v White	6-13	2nd round	Embassy World Professional Championship
	v Dodd	5-3	1st round	Jameson International
	v Stevens	2-5	2nd round	Jameson International
	v E. McLaughlin	5-2	1st round	Professional Players Tournament
	v Wildman	4-5	2nd round	Professional Players Tournament
1983	v Black	10-3	1st round	Embassy World Professional Championship
	v Stevens	3-13	2nd round	Embassy World Professional Championship
	v Watterson	4-5	Qualifying	Jameson International
1984	v Parrott	0-10	Qualifying	Embassy World Professional Championship
	v Sinclair	2-5	Qualifying	Jameson International
	v Dunning	4-5	1st round	Rothmans Grand Prix
	v Gauvreau	6-9	Qualifying	Coral UK Open
1985	v Black	4-5	3rd round	Goya Matchroom Trophy
	v O'Boye	3-5	3rd round	Rothmans Grand Prix
	v Fowler	2-9	3rd round	Coral UK Open
1986	v Smith	5-4	3rd round	Mercantile Credit Classic
	v Johnson	2-5	4th round	Mercantile Credit Classic
	v W. Jones	5-2	3rd round	Dulux British Open
	v Stevens	1-5	4th round	Dulux British Open
	v Dodd	10-7	Qualifying	Embassy World Professional Championship
	v Mountjoy	3-10	1st round	Embassy World Professional Championship

DAVE MARTIN (England)

Born 9.5.48
Turned professional 1981
World ranking 28 (29)

Strangely, most of Martin's best performances have been achieved at Derby Assembly Rooms where he was a semi-finalist in the 1981 Jameson International, runner-up in the 1984 Yamaha International Masters and a winner over Ray Reardon in reaching the last 16 of the Dulux British Open in 1985.

In the preliminary rounds of that event last season, he made a break of 145 at Solihull Civic Centre.

1981	v Anderson	9-3	Qualifying	Embassy World Professional Championship
	v Pulman	9-2	Qualifying	Embassy World Professional Championship
	v Werbeniuk	4-10	1st round	Embassy World Professional Championship
	v Dunning	5-2	1st round	Jameson International
	v Werbeniuk	5-2	2nd round	Jameson International
	v Charlton	5-2	3rd round	Jameson International
	v Miles	5-1	Quarter-final	Jameson International
	v Dennis Taylor	1-9	Semi-final	Jameson International
	v Sinclair	9-7	Qualifying	Coral UK Championship
	v Higgins	7-9	2nd round	Coral UK Championship
1982	v Houlihan	9-3	Qualifying	Embassy World Professional Championship
	v Miles	5-10	Qualifying	Embassy World Professional Championship
	v E. Hughes	4-5	Qualifying	Jameson International
	v Gibson	5-2	1st round	Professional Players Tournament
	v Spencer	3-5	2nd round	Professional Players Tournament
	v Macleod	9-6	Qualifying	Coral UK Championship
	v Higgins	7-9	1st round	Coral UK Championship
1983	v Parkin	10-1	Qualifying	Embassy World Professional Championship
	v Macleod	10-7	Qualifying	Embassy World Professional Championship
	v Werbeniuk	4-10	Qualifying	Embassy World Professional Championship
	v Greaves	5-1	Qualifying	Jameson International
	v Fagan	5-0	Qualifying	Jameson International
	v Higgins	5-2	1st round	Jameson International
	v Mountjoy	0-5	2nd round	Jameson International
	v Fitzmaurice	5-0	1st round	Professional Players Tournament
	v Watterson	5-4	2nd round	Professional Players Tournament
	v Campbell	0-5	3rd round	Professional Players Tournament
	v French	9-3	Qualifying	Coral UK Championship
	v Griffiths	4-9	Qualifying	Coral UK Championship
1984	v King	8-10	Qualifying	Embassy World Professional Championship
	v Fowler	0-5	Qualifying	Jameson International
	v Chaperon	5-4	1st round	Rothmans Grand Prix
	v Meo	4-5	2nd round	Rothmans Grand Prix
	v Murphy	8-9	Qualifying	Coral UK Open
1985	v Foldvari	2-5	Qualifying	Mercantile Credit Classic
	v Miles	9-7	1st round	Tolly Cobbold English Professional Championship

	v Knowles	3-9	2nd round	Tolly Cobbold English Professional Championship
	v Bennett	6-0	1st round	Dulux British Open
	v Reardon	5-4	2nd round	Dulux British Open
	v O'Kane	4-5	3rd round	Dulux British Open
	v O'Kane	8-10	Qualifying	Embassy World Professional Championship
	v Sinclair	5-1	3rd round	Goya Matchroom Trophy
	v Thorburn	3-5	4th round	Goya Matchroom Trophy
	v Morra	5-2	3rd round	Rothmans Grand Prix
	v S. Francisco	3-5	4th round	Rothmans Grand Prix
	v Darrington	9-3	3rd round	Coral UK Open
	v S. Francisco	6-9	4th round	Coral UK Open
1986	v Murphy	5-3	3rd round	Mercantile Credit Classic
	v P. Francisco	2-5	4th round	Mercantile Credit Classic
	v F. Davis	9-8	3rd round	Tolly Cobbold English Professional Championship
	v S. Davis	4-9	4th round	Tolly Cobbold English Professional Championship
	v B. Harris	5-1	3rd round	Dulux British Open
	v S. Davis	1-5	4th round	Dulux British Open
	v Gilbert	10-5	Qualifying	Embassy World Professional Championship
	v Johnson	3-10	1st round	Embassy World Professional Championship

JIM MEADOWCROFT (England)

Born 15.12.46
Turned professional 1971
World ranking 85 (48)

A quarter-finalist in the 1976 Embassy World Championship, Jim Meadowcroft also reached the last eight of the UK Championship the following year with a win over Ray Reardon but his subsequent record has been marked by several honourable defeats against top-class players rather than by notable victories. In the last three years he has worked extensively as a summariser in the BBC's commentary team, as a coach and on the summer exhibition circuit of Butlins holiday camps.

1973	v Reardon	10-16	2nd round	World Professional Championship
1974	v Kennerley	8-5	1st round	World Professional Championship
	v Reardon	3-15	2nd round	World Professional Championship
1975	v Werbeniuk	9-15	1st round	World Professional Championship
1976	v Wheelwright	8-1	Qualifying	Embassy World Professional Championship
	v Gross	8-4	Qualifying	Embassy World Professional Championship
	v Thorne	8-5	Qualifying	Embassy World Professional Championship
	v Williams	15-7	1st round	Embassy World Professional Championship
	v Mans	8-15	Quarter-final	Embassy World Professional Championship
1977	v Fagan	9-11	Qualifying	Embassy World Professional Championship
	v Houlihan	5-1	1st round	Super Crystalate UK Championship
	v Reardon	5-4	2nd round	Super Crystalate UK Championship

	v Fagan	4-5	Quarter-final	Super Crystalate UK Championship
1978	v Houlihan	6-9	Qualifying	Embassy World Professional Championship
	v Jack Rea	9-5	Qualifying	Coral UK Championship
	v Higgins	6-9	1st round	Coral UK Championship
1979	v Van Rensberg	9-7	Prelim	Embassy World Professional Championship
	v Griffiths	6-9	Qualifying	Embassy World Professional Championship
	v Edmonds	3-9	2nd round	Coral UK Championship
1980	v Sinclair	9-1	Qualifying	Embassy World Professional Championship
	v Virgo	2-10	1st round	Embassy World Professional Championship
	v Greaves	9-1	Qualifying	Coral UK Championship
	v Thorne	1-9	1st round	Coral UK Championship
1981	v Barrie	9-3	Qualifying	John Courage English Professional
	v S. Davis	2-9	1st round	John Courage English Professional
	v White	8-9	Qualifying	Embassy World Professional Championship
	v Roscoe	5-4	Qualifying	Jameson International
	v Wilson	5-4	1st round	Jameson International
	v Stevens	1-5	2nd round	Jameson International
	v Houlihan	4-9	Qualifying	Coral UK Championship
1982	v Watterson	9-7	Qualifying	Embassy World Professional Championship
	v Higgins	5-10	1st round	Embassy World Professional Championship
	v Ross	5-0	Qualifying	Jameson International
	v White	1-5	1st round	Jameson International
	v Bennett	5-4	1st round	Professional Players Tournament
	v Sinclair	3-5	2nd round	Professional Players Tournament
	v D. Hughes	9-8	Qualifying	Coral UK Championship
	v Dennis Taylor	7-9	1st round	Coral UK Championship
1983	v Bennett	10-3	Qualifying	Embassy World Professional Championship
	v Cripsey	10-6	Qualifying	Embassy World Professional Championship
	v David Taylor	2-10	1st round	Embassy World Professional Championship
	v Roscoe	5-4	1st round	Professional Players Tournament
	v Thorburn	1-5	2nd round	Professional Players Tournament
	v N. Foulds	2-9	Qualifying	Coral UK Championship
1984	v Meo	1-5	Qualifying	Lada Classic
	v N. Foulds	2-10	Qualifying	Embassy World Professional Championship
	v Chalmers	5-1	Qualifying	Jameson International
	v Williams	4-5	Qualifying	Jameson International
	v J. McLaughlin	1-5	Qualifying	Rothmans Grand Prix
	v Bradley	7-9	Qualifying	Coral UK Open
1985	v Fowler	2-5	Qualifying	Mercantile Credit Classic
	v Chalmers	3-9	Qualifying	Tolly Cobbold English Professional Championship
	v B. Harris	1-6	Qualifying	Dulux British Open
	v P. Francisco	5-10	Qualifying	Embassy World Professional Championship
	v Chappel	2-5	2nd round	Goya Matchroom Trophy
	v West	2-5	2nd round	Rothmans Grand Prix
	v Hargreaves	9-8	2nd round	Coral UK Open
	v Hallett	1-9	3rd round	Coral UK Open
1986	v West	0-5	2nd round	Mercantile Credit Classic
	v Cripsey	1-9	2nd round	Tolly Cobbold English Professional Championship

	v Jenkins	2-5	2nd round	Dulux British Open
	v Darrington	6-10	Qualifying	Embassy World Professional Championship

PAUL MEDATI (England)

Born 14.11.44
Turned professional 1981
World ranking 58 (60)

1981	v Watterson	3-5	Qualifying	Jameson International
	v E. McLaughlin	9-5	Qualifying	Coral UK Championship
	v Donnelly	9-7	Qualifying	Coral UK Championship
	v Thorne	6-9	Qualifying	Coral UK Championship
1982	v Phillips	9-3	Qualifying	Embassy World Professional Championship
	v Wilson	5-9	Qualifying	Embassy World Professional Championship
	v Williams	3-5	Qualifying	Jameson International
	v Thorburn	1-5	1st round	Professional Players Tournament
	v Bennett	9-1	Qualifying	Coral UK Championship
	v White	7-9	1st round	Coral UK Championship
1983	v John Bear	10-7	Qualifying	Embassy World Professional Championship
	v Black	4-10	Qualifying	Embassy World Professional Championship
	v V. Harris	5-0	Qualifying	Jameson International
	v Macleod	3-5	Qualifying	Jameson International
	v D. Hughes	5-1	Qualifying	Professional Players Tournament
	v Knowles	1-5	1st round	Professional Players Tournament
	v D. Hughes	9-2	Qualifying	Coral UK Championship
	v Edmonds	9-7	Qualifying	Coral UK Championship
	v Reynolds	9-3	1st round	Coral UK Championship
	v Higgins	1-9	2nd round	Coral UK Championship
1984	v Mikkelsen	8-10	Qualifying	Embassy World Professional Championship
	v Gibson	3-5	Qualifying	Jameson International
	v Dodd	5-4	Qualifying	Rothmans Grand Prix
	v Johnson	1-5	1st round	Rothmans Grand Prix
	v Hargreaves	6-9	Qualifying	Coral UK Open
1985	v Cripsey	5-4	Qualifying	Mercantile Credit Classic
	v Roscoe	5-4	Qualifying	Mercantile Credit Classic
	v Parrott	5-3	Qualifying	Mercantile Credit Classic
	v Stevens	4-5	1st round	Mercantile Credit Classic
	v Hargreaves	9-8	Qualifying	Tolly Cobbold English Professional Championship
	v Spencer	9-4	1st round	Tolly Cobbold English Professional Championship
	v Longworth	7-9	2nd round	Tolly Cobbold English Professional Championship
	v King	4-6	Qualifying	Dulux British Open
	v Bennett	10-4	Qualifying	Embassy World Professional Championship
	v Williamson	10-8	Qualifying	Embassy World Professional Championship
	v King	10-9	Qualifying	Embassy World Professional Championship
	v S. Francisco	7-10	Qualifying	Embassy World Professional Championship
	v Cripsey	2-5	2nd round	Goya Matchroom Trophy

	v J. McLaughlin	2-5	2nd round	Rothmans Grand Prix
	v Kelly	9-1	2nd round	Coral UK Open
	v Campbell	7-9	3rd round	Coral UK Open
1986	v Kearney	5-2	2nd round	Mercantile Credit Classic
	v O'Kane	0-5	3rd round	Mercantile Credit Classic
	v Greaves	9-4	2nd round	Tolly Cobbold English Professional Championship
	v Thorne	2-9	3rd round	Tolly Cobbold English Professional Championship
	v Everton	5-1	2nd round	Dulux British Open
	v David Taylor	5-1	3rd round	Dulux British Open
	v Campbell	4-5	4th round	Dulux British Open
	v Simngam	10-9	Qualifying	Embassy World Professional Championship
	v Gibson	10-6	Qualifying	Embassy World Professional Championship
	v Wilson	6-10	Qualifying	Embassy World Professional Championship

TONY MEO (England)

Born 4.10.59
Turned professional 1979
World ranking 11 (10)

After being runner-up to Steve Davis in the 1984 Lada Classic and three times winning the Hofmeister World Doubles in partnership with Davis, Meo last season won his first major individual tournament in Britain, the Tolly Cobbold English Professional Championship.

He had previously won the Winfield Australian Masters, the longest established overseas event.

1979	v David Taylor	9-7	2nd round	Coral UK Championship
	v Virgo	6-9	3rd round	Coral UK Championship
1980	v Van Rensberg	9-1	Qualifying	Embassy World Professional Championship
	v Houlihan	9-1	Qualifying	Embassy World Professional Championship
	v Higgins	9-10	1st round	Embassy World Professional Championship
	v Hood	9-5	Qualifying	Coral UK Championship
	v Houlihan	9-1	1st round	Coral UK Championship
	v Virgo	9-1	2nd round	Coral UK Championship
	v S. Davis	5-9	Quarter-final	Coral UK Championship
1981	v Virgo	9-6	1st round	John Courage English Professional
	v Miles	9-7	2nd round	John Courage English Professional
	v Thorne	9-8	Semi-final	John Courage English Professional
	v S. Davis	3-9	Final	John Courage English Professional
	v Johnson	9-8	Qualifying	Embassy World Professional Championship
	v Hallett	9-4	Qualifying	Embassy World Professional Championship
	v Virgo	10-6	1st round	Embassy World Professional Championship
	v Griffiths	6-13	2nd round	Embassy World Professional Championship
	v E. McLaughlin	5-2	1st round	Jameson International
	v Mans	3-5	2nd round	Jameson International
	v Williams	9-8	2nd round	Coral UK Championship
	v Thorburn	9-6	3rd round	Coral UK Championship

Tony Meo

	v Higgins	9-4	Quarter-final	Coral UK Championship
	v Griffiths	3-9	Semi-final	Coral UK Championship
1982	v David Taylor	5-2	1st round	Benson & Hedges Masters
	v Thorburn	5-0	Quarter-final	Benson & Hedges Masters
	v S. Davis	4-6	Semi-final	Benson & Hedges Masters
	v Spencer	5-3	1st round	Benson & Hedges Irish Masters
	v Griffiths	3-5	Quarter-final	Benson & Hedges Irish Masters
	v D. Hughes	9-4	Qualifying	Embassy World Professional Championship
	v Mans	8-10	1st round	Embassy World Professional Championship
	v Sinclair	3-5	Qualifying	Jameson International
	v M. Owen	5-4	1st round	Professional Players Tournament
	v Jonik	5-0	2nd round	Professional Players Tournament
	v Charlton	3-5	3rd round	Professional Players Tournament
	v Scott	9-5	Qualifying	Coral UK Championship
	v Miles	9-4	1st round	Coral UK Championship
	v David Taylor	9-6	2nd round	Coral UK Championship
	v Virgo	9-6	Quarter-final	Coral UK Championship
	v Griffiths	7-9	Semi-final	Coral UK Championship
1983	v Charlton	3-5	1st round	Benson & Hedges Masters
	v Burke	5-0	1st round	Benson & Hedges Irish Masters
	v Reardon	4-5	Quarter-final	Benson & Hedges Irish Masters
	v V. Harris	10-0	Qualifying	Embassy World Professional Championship
	v G. Foulds	10-4	Qualifying	Embassy World Professional Championship
	v White	10-8	1st round	Embassy World Professional Championship
	v Mountjoy	13-11	2nd round	Embassy World Professional Championship
	v Knowles	9-13	Quarter-final	Embassy World Professional Championship
	v Knowles	4-5	1st round	Langs Supreme Scottish Masters
	v Watterson	3-5	1st round	Jameson International
	v King	5-2	1st round	Professional Players Tournament
	v Reynolds	5-0	2nd round	Professional Players Tournament
	v Hallett	5-3	3rd round	Professional Players Tournament
	v Stevens	5-3	Quarter-final	Professional Players Tournament
	v Johnson	6-9	Semi-final	Professional Players Tournament
	v Parrott	9-7	1st round	Coral UK Championship
	v Spencer	9-5	2nd round	Coral UK Championship
	v Davis	4-9	Quarter-final	Coral UK Championship
1984	v Meadowcroft	5-1	Qualifying	Lada Classic
	v Williams	5-3	1st round	Lada Classic
	v Stevens	5-2	Quarter-final	Lada Classic
	v Wildman	5-3	Semi-final	Lada Classic
	v S. Davis	8-9	Final	Lada Classic
	v S. Davis	0-5	1st round	Benson & Hedges Masters
	v White	5-4	1st round	Benson & Hedges Irish Masters
	v S. Davis	4-5	Quarter-final	Benson & Hedges Irish Masters
	v Thorburn	4-5	1st round	Tolly Cobbold Classic
	v S. Francisco	5-10	1st round	Embassy World Professional Championship
	v Stevens	5-1	Quarter-final	Winfield Australian Masters
	v Virgo	2-6	Semi-final	Winfield Australian Masters
	v Macleod	5-1	1st round	Jameson International
	v White	1-5	2nd round	Jameson International

	v Burke	5-1	1st round	Rothmans Grand Prix
	v Martin	5-4	2nd round	Rothmans Grand Prix
	v Thorburn	4-5	3rd round	Rothmans Grand Prix
	v E. Hughes	9-4	1st round	Coral UK Open
	v S. Davis	7-9	2nd round	Coral UK Open
1985	v E. Hughes	4-5	1st round	Mercantile Credit Classic
	v Fisher	9-3	1st round	Tolly Cobbold English Professional Championship
	v Hallett	9-4	2nd round	Tolly Cobbold English Professional Championship
	v Reynolds	9-4	Quarter-final	Tolly Cobbold English Professional Championship
	v S. Davis	8-9	Semi-final	Tolly Cobbold English Professional Championship
	v Foldvari	6-0	1st round	Dulux British Open
	v Hallett	5-4	2nd round	Dulux British Open
	v Knowles	5-2	3rd round	Dulux British Open
	v S. Francisco	4-5	Quarter-final	Dulux British Open
	v White	1-5	1st round	Benson & Hedges Irish Masters
	v Virgo	10-6	1st round	Embassy World Professional Championship
	v White	11-13	2nd round	Embassy World Professional Championship
	v Virgo	5-3	Quarter-final	Winfield Australian Masters
	v White	6-3	Semi-final	Winfield Australian Masters
	v Campbell	**7-2**	**Final**	**Winfield Australian Masters**
	v Dunning	5-0	3rd round	Goya Matchroom Trophy
	v Parrott	4-5	4th round	Goya Matchroom Trophy
	v T. Jones	5-2	3rd round	Rothmans Grand Prix
	v E. Hughes	5-3	4th round	Rothmans Grand Prix
	v Dennis Taylor	3-5	5th round	Rothmans Grand Prix
	v Longworth	9-5	3rd round	Coral UK Open
	v Fowler	9-2	4th round	Coral UK Open
	v S. Davis	5-9	5th round	Coral UK Open
1986	v O'Boye	5-3	3rd round	Mercantile Credit Classic
	v West	5-1	4th round	Mercantile Credit Classic
	v Thorburn	1-5	5th round	Mercantile Credit Classic
	v White	4-5	1st round	Benson & Hedges Masters
	v Scott	9-1	3rd round	Tolly Cobbold English Professional Championship
	v Wildman	9-3	4th round	Tolly Cobbold English Professional Championship
	v Reynolds	9-4	Quarter-final	Tolly Cobbold English Professional Championship
	v S. Davis	9-7	Semi-final	Tolly Cobbold English Professional Championship
	v N. Foulds	**9-7**	**Final**	**Tolly Cobbold English Professional Championship**
	v Donnelly	5-3	3rd round	Dulux British Open
	v Newbury	5-0	4th round	Dulux British Open
	v Thorburn	5-3	5th round	Dulux British Open
	v Virgo	3-5	Quarter-final	Dulux British Open

	v Higgins	5-4	1st round	Benson & Hedges Irish Masters
	v White	2-5	Quarter-final	Benson & Hedges Irish Masters
	v Parrott	6-10	1st round	Embassy World Professional Championship

DEREK MIENIE (South Africa)

Born –
Turned professional 1978
World ranking 108 (95)

Derek Mienie won the South African Professional Championship in 1979.

1979	v Mountjoy	1-9	Prelim	Embassy World Professional Championship
1985	v Edmonds	1-6	Qualifying	Dulux British Open
	v Bradley	4-10	Qualifying	Embassy World Professional Championship
1985	Mienie *wo* Watson *scr*		1st round	Goya Matchroom Trophy
	v Fagan	4-5	2nd round	Goya Matchroom Trophy
	v Simngam	3-5	1st round	Rothmans Grand Prix
	v Hargreaves	7-9	1st round	Coral UK Open
1986	v Smith	1-5	1st round	Mercantile Credit Classic
	v Thornley	3-10	Qualifying	Embassy World Professional Championship

BERNIE MIKKELSEN (Canada)

Born 11.4.50
Turned professional 1979
World ranking 61 (82)

Last season, Mikkelsen earned his first ranking point when he beat Ray Reardon 5-3 in the Mercantile Credit Classic.

1981	v White	4-9	Qualifying	Embassy World Professional Championship
1982	v Roscoe	6-9	Qualifying	Embassy World Professional Championship
1984	v Medati	10-8	Qualifying	Embassy World Professional Championship
	v Jonik	10-9	Qualifying	Embassy World Professional Championship
	v Thorne	3-10	Qualifying	Embassy World Professional Championship
	v Chappel	5-4	Qualifying	Jameson International
	v Everton	5-0	Qualifying	Jameson International
	v Roscoe	1-5	Qualifying	Jameson International
	v Sheehan	3-5	Qualifying	Rothmans Grand Prix
1985	v Chalmers	5-1	Prelim	Mercantile Credit Classic
	v Watchorn	1-5	Qualifying	Mercantile Credit Classic
	v D. Hughes	6-0	Qualifying	Dulux British Open
	v Bradley	9-10	Qualifying	Embassy World Professional Championship
	v Watson	5-3	1st round	Canadian Professional Championship
	v Jonik	4-6	Quarter-final	Canadian Professional Championship
	v Fisher	5-3	2nd round	Goya Matchroom Trophy

	v Reynolds	0-5	3rd round	Goya Matchroom Trophy
	v Murphy	5-4	2nd round	Rothmans Grand Prix
	v Hallett	3-5	3rd round	Rothmans Grand Prix
	v Williamson	9-3	2nd round	Coral UK Open
	v David Taylor	6-9	3rd round	Coral UK Open
1986	v Scott	5-1	2nd round	Mercantile Credit Classic
	v Reardon	5-3	3rd round	Mercantile Credit Classic
	v Campbell	2-5	4th round	Mercantile Credit Classic
	v Roscoe	4-5	2nd round	Dulux British Open
	v Hargreaves	10-7	Qualifying	Embassy World Professional Championship
	v Watterson	2-10	Qualifying	Embassy World Professional Championship

GRAHAM MILES (England)

Born 11.5.41
Turned professional 1969
World ranking 56 (32)

After he was runner-up in the 1974 Park Drive World Professional Championship and the 1976 Benson and Hedges Masters, the underlying trend in Miles's career was downwards. Among his successes were a place in the semi-finals of the 1978 Coral UK Championship, in which his break of 139 set a tournament record (later equalled by Tony Meo), and second prize in the 1979 Holsten Lager International.

1972	v Bennett	15-6	Qualifying	World Professional Championship
	v Dunning	5-11	Qualifying	World Professional Championship
1973	v Thompson	9-5	1st round	World Professional Championship
	v Pulman	16-10	2nd round	World Professional Championship
	v Charlton	6-16	Quarter-final	World Professional Championship
1974	v Morgan	15-7	2nd round	World Professional Championship
	v Dunning	15-13	Quarter-final	World Professional Championship
	v Williams	15-7	Semi-final	World Professional Championship
	v Reardon	12-22	Final	World Professional Championship
	v Sinclair	5-0	1st round	Norwich Union Open
	v Spencer	2-5	Quarter-final	Norwich Union Open
1975	v Reardon	3-5	Quarter-final	Benson & Hedges Masters
	v Thorburn	2-15	2nd round	World Professional Championship
1976	v Spencer	5-4	Semi-final	Benson & Hedges Masters
	v Reardon	3-7	Final	Benson & Hedges Masters
	v Mans	10-15	1st round	Embassy World Professional Championship
1977	v Reardon	2-5	Semi-final	Benson & Hedges Masters
	v Thorne	13-4	1st round	Embassy World Professional Championship
	v Pulman	10-13	Quarter-final	Embassy World Professional Championship
	v Ross	5-1	2nd round	Super Crystalate UK Championship
	v Virgo	2-5	Quarter-final	Super Crystalate UK Championship
1978	v David Taylor	13-10	1st round	Embassy World Professional Championship
	v Mans	7-13	Quarter-final	Embassy World Professional Championship
	v Williams	9-8	1st round	Coral UK Championship

	v Thorne	9-1	Quarter-final	Coral UK Championship
	v Mountjoy	1-9	Semi-final	Coral UK Championship
1979	v Higgins	6-3	Semi-final	Holsten Lager International
	v Spencer	7-11	Final	Holsten Lager International
	v Williams	9-5	Qualifying	Embassy World Professional Championship
	v Reardon	8-13	1st round	Embassy World Professional Championship
	v Fagan	5-9	3rd round	Coral UK Championship
1980	v Stevens	3-10	1st round	Embassy World Professional Championship
	v Sinclair	5-9	1st round	Coral UK Championship
1981	v Hood	9-1	1st round	John Courage English Professional
	v Meo	7-9	2nd round	John Courage English Professional
	v Knowles	10-8	1st round	Embassy World Professional Championship
	v Thorburn	2-13	2nd round	Embassy World Professional Championship
	v Johnson	5-3	2nd round	Jameson International
	v Thorburn	5-0	3rd round	Jameson International
	v Martin	1-5	Quarter-final	Jameson International
	v Houlihan	9-5	2nd round	Coral UK Championship
	v Griffiths	4-9	3rd round	Coral UK Championship
1982	v S. Davis	2-5	Semi-final	Tolly Cobbold Classic
	v Martin	10-5	1st round	Embassy World Professional Championship
	v Knowles	7-13	2nd round	Embassy World Professional Championship
	v Edmonds	1-5	Qualifying	Jameson International
	v Johnson	1-5	1st round	Professional Players Tournament
	v Meo	4-9	1st round	Coral UK Championship
1983	v Morgan	10-6	Qualifying	Embassy World Professional Championship
	v Knowles	3-10	1st round	Embassy World Professional Championship
	v King	5-3	Qualifying	Jameson International
	v Griffiths	2-5	1st round	Jameson International
	v Gauvreau	5-3	1st round	Professional Players Tournament
	v Campbell	2-5	2nd round	Professional Players Tournament
	v Hallett	4-9	1st round	Coral UK Championship
1984	v Williamson	10-6	Qualifying	Embassy World Professional Championship
	v Spencer	3-10	1st round	Embassy World Professional Championship
	v Newbury	1-5	Qualifying	Jameson International
	v Murphy	5-3	1st round	Rothmans Grand Prix
	v S. Davis	0-5	2nd round	Rothmans Grand Prix
	v J. McLaughlin	8-9	Qualifying	Coral UK Open
1985	v Browne	3-5	Qualifying	Mercantile Credit Classic
	v Martin	7-9	1st round	Tolly Cobbold English Professional Championship
	v Edmonds	6-1	1st round	Dulux British Open
	v Spencer	2-5	2nd round	Dulux British Open
	v Stevens	2-5	3rd round	Dulux British Open
	v W. Jones	8-10	Qualifying	Embassy World Professional Championship
	v O'Boye	5-2	2nd round	Goya Matchroom Trophy
	v Virgo	2-5	3rd round	Goya Matchroom Trophy
	v Rigitano	5-4	2nd round	Rothmans Grand Prix
	v Reynolds	5-3	3rd round	Rothmans Grand Prix
	v Stevens	2-5	4th round	Rothmans Grand Prix
	v Oliver	9-4	2nd round	Coral UK Open

	v Reardon	4-9	3rd round	Coral UK Open
1986	v Hendry	1-5	2nd round	Mercantile Credit Classic
	v Fitzmaurice	9-5	2nd round	Tolly Cobbold English Professional Championship
	v Williams	6-9	3rd round	Tolly Cobbold English Professional Championship
	v Agrawal	5-4	2nd round	Dulux British Open
	v Stevens	3-5	3rd round	Dulux British Open
	v Everton	10-3	Qualifying	Embassy World Professional Championship
	v Foldvari	7-10	Qualifying	Embassy World Professional Championship

PADDY MORGAN (Australia)

Born 7.1.43
Turned professional 1970
World ranking 111 (75)

Born in Belfast, Morgan later represented the Republic of Ireland and after living for a while in Coventry emigrated to Sydney. He was a member of the Australian trio in the first three World Cups.

1974	v Thorburn	8-4	1st round	World Professional Championship
	v Miles	7-15	2nd round	World Professional Championship
1975	v Thorburn	6-15	1st round	World Professional Championship
1978	v David Taylor	7-9	Qualifying	Embassy World Professional Championship
1980	v S. Davis	0-9	Qualifying	Embassy World Professional Championship
1981	v Sinclair	8-9	Qualifying	Embassy World Professional Championship
1982	v Greaves	9-2	Qualifying	Embassy World Professional Championship
	v S. Francisco	1-9	Qualifying	Embassy World Professional Championship
	v Werbeniuk	3-5	1st round	Professional Players Tournament
1983	v Burke	10-9	Qualifying	Embassy World Professional Championship
	v Miles	6-10	Qualifying	Embassy World Professional Championship
	v Fitzmaurice	5-4	Qualifying	Jameson International
	v F. Davis	5-3	Qualifying	Jameson International
	v Spencer	1-5	1st round	Jameson International
	v Gibson	5-4	Qualifying	Professional Players Tournament
	v David Taylor	3-5	1st round	Professional Players Tournament
1984	v Sanderson	8-10	Qualifying	Embassy World Professional Championship
1985	v Chaperon	3-10	Qualifying	Embassy World Professional Championship
	v Giannaros	8-4	Quarter-final	Australian Professional Championship
	v Charlton	3-9	Semi-final	Australian Professional Championship
1986	v Sinclair	8-10	Qualifying	Embassy World Professional Championship

MARIO MORRA (Canada)

Born 8.9.53
Turned professional 1979
World ranking 75 (43)

1981	v Thorne	5-9	Qualifying	Embassy World Professional Championship
	v Wildman	3-5	Qualifying	Jameson International
1982	v Murphy	9-5	Qualifying	Embassy World Professional Championship
	v Fitzmaurice	7-9	Qualifying	Embassy World Professional Championship
	v Demarco	5-2	Qualifying	Jameson International
	v Reynolds	1-5	Qualifying	Jameson International
	v Wilson	2-5	1st round	Professional Players Tournament
1983	v Black	9-10	Qualifying	Embassy World Professional Championship
	v Watchorn	5-3	Qualifying	Jameson International
	v Hallett	5-3	Qualifying	Jameson International
	v White	5-3	1st round	Jameson International
	v Charlton	3-5	2nd round	Jameson International
	v Hargreaves	5-0	Qualifying	Professional Players Tournament
	v S. Francisco	3-5	1st round	Professional Players Tournament
	v Burke	5-2	Qualifying	Lada Classic
	v Everton	5-0	Qualifying	Lada Classic
	v S. Francisco	1-5	Qualifying	Lada Classic
1984	v G. Foulds	10-2	Qualifying	Embassy World Professional Championship
	v Murphy	10-5	Qualifying	Embassy World Professional Championship
	v Reynolds	10-7	Qualifying	Embassy World Professional Championship
	v Thorburn	3-10	1st round	Embassy World Professional Championship
	v Bradley	5-3	Qualifying	Jameson International
	v Johnson	0-5	Qualifying	Jameson International
	v Cripsey	5-3	Qualifying	Rothmans Grand Prix
	v S. Davis	2-5	1st round	Rothmans Grand Prix
	v Longworth	9-1	Qualifying	Coral UK Open
	v E. Hughes	8-9	Qualifying	Coral UK Open
1985	v Newbury	2-5	Qualifying	Mercantile Credit Classic
	v Bradley	2-6	Qualifying	Dulux British Open
	v Browne	10-6	Qualifying	Embassy World Professional Championship
	v Campbell	9-10	Qualifying	Embassy World Professional Championship
	v John Bear	4-5	1st round	Canadian Professional Championship
	v Oliver	5-1	2nd round	Goya Matchroom Trophy
	v Campbell	2-5	3rd round	Goya Matchroom Trophy
	v D. Hughes	5-2	2nd round	Rothmans Grand Prix
	v Martin	2-5	3rd round	Rothmans Grand Prix
	v Agrawal	9-8	2nd round	Coral UK Open
	v Mountjoy	2-9	3rd round	Coral UK Open
1986	v B. Harris	3-5	2nd round	Mercantile Credit Classic
	v Gilbert	4-5	2nd round	Dulux British Open
	v Gibson	9-10	Qualifying	Embassy World Professional Championship

DOUG MOUNTJOY (Wales)

Born 8.6.42
Turned professional 1976
World ranking 14 (15)

After winning the 1976 World Amateur title, Mountjoy started his professional career by winning the 1977 Benson and Hedges Masters. He won the Coral UK Championship in 1978, was runner-up to Steve Davis for the world title in 1981 and has won the Welsh Professional title three times since 1980. His break of 145 in the 1981 Embassy World Championship stands second only to Cliff Thorburn's maximum as the highest break made in the event. After a steady 1984–85 season, in which he reached the final of the Benson and Hedges Masters, Mountjoy reached the semi-finals of the 1986 Mercantile Credit Classic before losing to Cliff Thorburn.

1977	v Higgins	5-3	Semi-final	Benson & Hedges Masters
	v Reardon	**7-6**	**Final**	**Benson & Hedges Masters**
	v Jack Rea	11-9	Qualifying	Embassy World Professional Championship
	v Higgins	13-12	1st round	Embassy World Professional Championship
	v Dennis Taylor	11-13	Quarter-final	Embassy World Professional Championship
	v Andrewartha	5-2	1st round	Super Crystalate UK Championship
	v Spencer	5-3	2nd round	Super Crystalate UK Championship
	v Thorne	5-4	Quarter-final	Super Crystalate UK Championship
	v Higgins	9-2	Semi-final	Super Crystalate UK Championship
	v Fagan	9-12	Final	Super Crystalate UK Championship
1978	v Spencer	3-5	Final	Benson & Hedges Irish Masters
	v Andrewartha	9-3	Qualifying	Embassy World Professional Championship
	v Reardon	9-13	1st round	Embassy World Professional Championship
	v Barrie	9-5	Qualifying	Coral UK Championship
	v Dennis Taylor	9-4	1st round	Coral UK Championship
	v Andrewartha	9-4	Quarter-final	Coral UK Championship
	v Miles	9-1	Semi-final	Coral UK Championship
	v David Taylor	**15-9**	**Final**	**Coral UK Championship**
1979	v F. Davis	5-2	1st round	Benson & Hedges Masters
	v Spencer	5-0	Quarter-final	Benson & Hedges Masters
	v Higgins	1-5	Semi-final	Benson & Hedges Masters
	v Reardon	**6-5**	**Final**	**Benson & Hedges Irish Masters**
	v Mienie	9-1	Prelim	Embassy World Professional Championship
	v Houlihan	9-6	Qualifying	Embassy World Professional Championship
	v Charlton	6-13	1st round	Embassy World Professional Championship
	v S. Davis	5-9	3rd round	Coral UK Championship
1980	v Griffiths	8-9	Final	Benson & Hedges Irish Masters
	v Wilson	10-6	1st round	Embassy World Professional Championship
	v Thorburn	10-13	2nd round	Embassy World Professional Championship

	v Williams	8-9	1st round	Coral UK Championship
1981	v Charlton	5-0	1st round	Benson & Hedges Masters
	v Higgins	1-5	Quarter-final	Benson & Hedges Masters
	v Wilson	6-9	Semi-final	Woodpecker Welsh Professional Championship
	v Thorne	10-6	1st round	Embassy World Professional Championship
	v Charlton	13-7	2nd round	Embassy World Professional Championship
	v Dennis Taylor	13-8	Quarter-final	Embassy World Professional Championship
	v Reardon	16-10	Semi-final	Embassy World Professional Championship
	v S. Davis	12-18	Final	Embassy World Professional Championship
	v S. Davis	0-5	Quarter-final	Langs Supreme Scottish Masters
	v Higgins	1-5	3rd round	Jameson International
	v Dennis Taylor	5-4	1st round	Northern Ireland Classic
	v White	8-9	Semi-final	Northern Ireland Classic
	v Knowles	6-9	3rd round	Coral UK Championship
1982	v Spencer	5-4	1st round	Benson & Hedges Masters
	v S. Davis	2-5	Quarter-final	Benson & Hedges Masters
	v Andrewartha	6-3	1st round	Welsh Professional Championship
	v Reardon	9-7	Semi-final	Welsh Professional Championship
	v Griffiths	**9-8**	**Final**	**Welsh Professional Championship**
	v E. Hughes	5-4	1st round	Benson & Hedges Irish Masters
	v S. Davis	2-5	Quarter-final	Benson & Hedges Irish Masters
	v Williams	10-3	1st round	Embassy World Professional Championship
	v Higgins	12-13	2nd round	Embassy World Professional Championship
	v Wilson	4-5	1st round	Jameson International
	v Jonik	3-5	1st round	Professional Players Tournament
	v Houlihan	9-3	1st round	Coral UK Championship
	v Virgo	5-9	2nd round	Coral UK Championship
1983	v Griffiths	5-1	1st round	Lada Classic
	v Werbeniuk	2-5	Quarter-final	Lada Classic
	v Virgo	5-1	1st round	Benson & Hedges Masters
	v S. Davis	5-4	Quarter-final	Benson & Hedges Masters
	v Reardon	3-6	Semi-final	Benson & Hedges Masters
	v M. Owen	6-0	Quarter-final	Woodpecker Welsh Professional Championship
	v Wilson	9-3	Semi-final	Woodpecker Welsh Professional Championship
	v Reardon	1-9	Final	Woodpecker Welsh Professional Championship
	v Knowles	5-1	1st round	Benson & Hedges Irish Masters
	v Griffiths	4-5	Quarter-final	Benson & Hedges Irish Masters
	v Wilson	10-2	1st round	Embassy World Professional Championship
	v Meo	11-13	2nd round	Embassy World Professional Championship
	v Wildman	5-4	1st round	Jameson International
	v Martin	5-0	2nd round	Jameson International
	v Thorburn	2-5	Quarter-final	Jameson International
	v Campbell	3-5	1st round	Professional Players Tournament
	v Watterson	9-2	1st round	Coral UK Championship
	v Knowles	5-9	2nd round	Coral UK Championship

Doug Mountjoy

1984	v Parrott	4-5	Qualifying	Lada Classic
	v Higgins	2-5	1st round	Benson & Hedges Masters
	v Everton	6-1	1st round	Strongbow Welsh Professional Championship
	v Griffiths	9-5	Semi-final	Strongbow Welsh Professional Championship
	v Wilson	**9-3**	**Final**	**Strongbow Welsh Professional Championship**
	v Hallett	10-4	1st round	Embassy World Professional Championship
	v N. Foulds	13-6	2nd round	Embassy World Professional Championship
	v Dennis Taylor	8-13	Quarter-final	Embassy World Professional Championship
	v E. Hughes	1-5	1st round	Jameson International
	v E. McLaughlin	5-4	1st round	Rothmans Grand Prix
	v Wildman	5-0	2nd round	Rothmans Grand Prix
	v Charlton	5-4	3rd round	Rothmans Grand Prix
	v Thorburn	3-5	Quarter-final	Rothmans Grand Prix
	v Hallett	9-2	1st round	Coral UK Open
	v White	2-9	2nd round	Coral UK Open
1985	v Wilson	4-5	1st round	Mercantile Credit Classic
	v Knowles	5-3	1st round	Benson & Hedges Masters
	v Meo	5-4	Quarter-final	Benson & Hedges Masters
	v Griffiths	6-2	Semi-final	Benson & Hedges Masters
	v Thorburn	6-9	Final	Benson & Hedges Masters
	v V. Harris	5-6	1st round	Dulux British Open
	v Macleod	10-5	1st round	Embassy World Professional Championship
	v Knowles	6-13	2nd round	Embassy World Professional Championship
	v Newbury	6-5	Quarter-final	BCE Welsh Professional Championship
	v Wilson	9-2	Semi-final	BCE Welsh Professional Championship
	v Griffiths	4-9	Final	BCE Welsh Professional Championship
	v Wych	5-1	3rd round	Goya Matchroom Trophy
	v Campbell	1-5	4th round	Goya Matchroom Trophy
	v Chappel	5-1	3rd round	Rothmans Grand Prix
	v Campbell	2-5	4th round	Rothmans Grand Prix
	v Morra	9-2	3rd round	Coral UK Open
	v West	4-9	4th round	Coral UK Open
1986	v King	5-4	3rd round	Mercantile Credit Classic
	v O'Kane	5-3	4th round	Mercantile Credit Classic
	v Werbeniuk	5-3	5th round	Mercantile Credit Classic
	v N. Foulds	5-3	Quarter-final	Mercantile Credit Classic
	v Thorburn	6-9	Semi-final	Mercantile Credit Classic
	v Dennis Taylor	2-5	1st round	Benson & Hedges Masters
	v Roscoe	6-4	Quarter-final	Zetters Welsh Professional Championship
	v W. Jones	9-7	Semi-final	Zetters Welsh Professional Championship
	v Griffiths	3-9	Final	Zetters Welsh Professional Championship
	v Fagan	1-5	3rd round	Dulux British Open
	v Mans	10-3	1st round	Embassy World Professional Championship
	v S. Davis	5-13	2nd round	Embassy World Professional Championship

TOMMY MURPHY (Northern Ireland)

Born 8.1.62
Turned professional 1981
World ranking 57 (56)

Northern Ireland amateur champion in 1981, Murphy had played three times for Northern Ireland in the World Cup before an All Ireland team was entered in 1985.

1981	v Johnson	1-9	Qualifying	Coral UK Championship
1982	v Fagan	6-2	Quarter-final	Irish Professional Championship
	v Dennis Taylor	0-6	Semi-final	Irish Professional Championship
	v Morra	5-9	Qualifying	Embassy World Professional Championship
	v Fisher	1-5	Qualifying	Jameson International
	v Reardon	0-5	1st round	Professional Players Tournament
	v Everton	9-4	Qualifying	Coral UK Championship
	v Sinclair	5-9	Qualifying	Coral UK Championship
1983	v Fagan	4-6	Quarter-final	Irish Professional Championship
	v Houlihan	10-9	Qualifying	Embassy World Professional Championship
	v Virgo	8-10	Qualifying	Embassy World Professional Championship
	v Sheehan	5-2	Qualifying	Jameson International
	v Thorne	2-5	Qualifying	Jameson International
	v Macleod	5-0	1st round	Professional Players Tournament
	v Stevens	1-5	2nd round	Professional Players Tournament
	v Demarco	9-4	Qualifying	Coral UK Championship
	v Donnelly	9-4	Qualifying	Coral UK Championship
	v Dennis Taylor	6-9	1st round	Coral UK Championship
1984	v Fitzmaurice	10-8	Qualifying	Embassy World Professional Championship
	v Morra	5-10	Qualifying	Embassy World Professional Championship
	v Bales	4-5	Qualifying	Jameson International
	v G. Foulds	5-1	Qualifying	Rothmans Grand Prix
	v Miles	3-5	1st round	Rothmans Grand Prix
	v Kearney	9-2	Qualifying	Coral UK Open
	v Watterson	9-4	Qualifying	Coral UK Open
	v Martin	9-8	Qualifying	Coral UK Open
	v S. Davis	1-9	1st round	Coral UK Open
1985	v Fowler	0-5	Qualifying	Mercantile Credit Classic
	v Sheehan	6-3	Qualifying	Dulux British Open
	v Macleod	5-6	1st round	Dulux British Open
	v Browne	6-3	Qualifying	Irish Professional Championship
	v Fagan	2-6	Quarter-final	Irish Professional Championship
	v P. Francisco	4-10	Qualifying	Embassy World Professional Championship
	v Jack Rea	5-1	2nd round	Goya Matchroom Trophy
	v E. Hughes	5-3	3rd round	Goya Matchroom Trophy
	v Higgins	2-5	4th round	Goya Matchroom Trophy
	v Mikkelsen	4-5	2nd round	Rothmans Grand Prix
	v Everton	9-4	2nd round	Coral UK Open
	v Macleod	7-9	3rd round	Coral UK Open
1986	v Chappel	5-4	2nd round	Mercantile Credit Classic
	v Martin	3-5	3rd round	Mercantile Credit Classic

	v Duggan	1-5	2nd round	Dulux British Open
	v J. McLaughlin	10-7	Qualifying	Embassy World Professional Championship
	v Thornley	10-3	Qualifying	Embassy World Professional Championship
	v E. Hughes	7-10	Qualifying	Embassy World Professional Championship
	v O'Boye	5-0	1st round	Strongbow Irish Professional Championship
	v Kearney	6-2	Quarter-final	Strongbow Irish Professional Championship
	v Dennis Taylor	3-6	Semi-final	Strongbow Irish Professional Championship

STEVE NEWBURY (Wales)

Born 21.4.56
Turned professional 1984
World ranking 40 (34)

Welsh amateur champion in 1980, Newbury achieved 34th place in the rankings after his first professional season mainly through reaching the last 16s of the Jameson International and the Dulux British Open but last season did slightly less well.

1984	v Longworth	5-4	Qualifying	Jameson International
	v Burke	5-0	Qualifying	Jameson International
	v Fagan	5-0	Qualifying	Jameson International
	v Miles	5-1	Qualifying	Jameson International
	v Werbeniuk	5-2	1st round	Jameson International
	v Knowles	4-5	2nd round	Jameson International
	v Fisher	5-0	Qualifying	Rothmans Grand Prix
	v Thorne	2-5	1st round	Rothmans Grand Prix
	v Rigitano	9-6	Qualifying	Coral UK Open
	v Jonik	9-3	Qualifying	Coral UK Open
	v Dodd	6-9	Qualifying	Coral UK Open
1985	v V. Harris	5-3	Qualifying	Mercantile Credit Classic
	v Burke	5-1	Qualifying	Mercantile Credit Classic
	v Morra	5-2	Qualifying	Mercantile Credit Classic
	v E. Hughes	3-5	Qualifying	Mercantile Credit Classic
	v Browne	6-0	Qualifying	Dulux British Open
	v Sinclair	6-3	1st round	Dulux British Open
	v Griffiths	5-3	2nd round	Dulux British Open
	v Dennis Taylor	3-5	3rd round	Dulux British Open
	v D. Hughes	10-9	Qualifying	Embassy World Professional Championship
	v Burke	10-3	Qualifying	Embassy World Professional Championship
	v Scott	10-2	Qualifying	Embassy World Professional Championship
	v E. Hughes	6-10	Qualifying	Embassy World Professional Championship
	v W. Jones	6-2	1st round	BCE Welsh Professional Championship
	v Mountjoy	5-6	Quarter-final	BCE Welsh Professional Championship
	v Jonik	5-4	2nd round	Goya Matchroom Trophy
	v Griffiths	2-5	3rd round	Goya Matchroom Trophy
	v Burke	5-3	2nd round	Rothmans Grand Prix
	v David Taylor	2-5	3rd round	Rothmans Grand Prix
	v Houlihan	9-3	2nd round	Coral UK Open
	v Stevens	7-9	3rd round	Coral UK Open
1986	v Cripsey	4-5	2nd round	Mercantile Credit Classic

	v Wilson	4-6	Quarter-final	Zetters Welsh Professional Championship
	v Oliver	5-2	2nd round	Dulux British Open
	v O'Kane	5-3	3rd round	Dulux British Open
	v Meo	0-5	4th round	Dulux British Open
	v Agrawal	10-5	Qualifying	Embassy World Professional Championship
	v Black	10-2	Qualifying	Embassy World Professional Championship
	v Spencer	7-10	Qualifying	Embassy World Professional Championship

JOE O'BOYE (Republic of Ireland)

Born 6.3.60
Turned professional 1985
World ranking 65

English amateur champion in 1980, O'Boye was three times refused professional status. He earned one ranking point in his first professional season by reaching the last 32 of the Rothmans Grand Prix.

1985	v Parkin	5-3	1st round	Goya Matchroom Trophy
	v Miles	2-5	2nd round	Goya Matchroom Trophy
	v Hendry	5-4	1st round	Rothmans Grand Prix
	v Chaperon	5-3	2nd round	Rothmans Grand Prix
	v Mans	5-3	3rd round	Rothmans Grand Prix
	v White	4-5	4th round	Rothmans Grand Prix
	v Bennett	9-3	1st round	Coral UK Open
	v Gauvreau	9-5	2nd round	Coral UK Open
	v Knowles	5-9	3rd round	Coral UK Open
1986	v Wilkinson	5-1	1st round	Mercantile Credit Classic
	v Longworth	5-1	2nd round	Mercantile Credit Classic
	v Meo	3-5	3rd round	Mercantile Credit Classic
	v Jim Bear	5-1	1st round	Dulux British Open
	v T. Jones	2-5	2nd round	Dulux British Open
	v Oliver	8-10	Qualifying	Embassy World Professional Championship
	v Murphy	0-5	1st round	Strongbow Irish Professional Championship

DENE O'KANE (New Zealand)

Born 24.2.63
Turned professional 1984
World ranking 39 (32)

New Zealand amateur champion at the age of 17 in 1980, O'Kane achieved a place in the top 32 after his first professional season but slipped down to the 33–64 category after his second.

1984	v Parkin	5-2	Qualifying	Jameson International
	v E. McLaughlin	5-1	Qualifying	Jameson International
	v Fitzmaurice	5-4	Qualifying	Jameson International
	v Hallett	5-4	Qualifying	Jameson International
	v Thorne	3-5	1st round	Jameson International
	v Kelly	5-4	Qualifying	Rothmans Grand Prix

	v David Taylor	1-5	1st round	Rothmans Grand Prix
	v W. Jones	9-7	Qualifying	Coral UK Open
	v Duggan	9-6	Qualifying	Coral UK Open
	v Scott	7-9	Qualifying	Coral UK Open
1985	v W. Jones	0-5	Qualifying	Mercantile Credit Classic
	v Cripsey	6-4	Qualifying	Dulux British Open
	v Campbell	6-4	1st round	Dulux British Open
	v V. Harris	5-3	2nd round	Dulux British Open
	v Martin	5-4	3rd round	Dulux British Open
	v S. Davis	1-5	Quarter-final	Dulux British Open
	O'Kane *wo* J. McLaughlin *scr*		Qualifying	Embassy World Professional Championship
	v V. Harris	10-5	Qualifying	Embassy World Professional Championship
	v Jonik	10-5	Qualifying	Embassy World Professional Championship
	v Dodd	10-7	Qualifying	Embassy World Professional Championship
	v Martin	10-8	Qualifying	Embassy World Professional Championship
	v David Taylor	4-10	1st round	Embassy World Professional Championship
	v B. Harris	3-5	3rd round	Goya Matchroom Trophy
	v Edmonds	2-5	3rd round	Rothmans Grand Prix
	v Chappel	5-9	3rd round	Coral UK Open
1986	v Medati	5-0	3rd round	Mercantile Credit Classic
	v Mountjoy	3-5	4th round	Mercantile Credit Classic
	v Newbury	3-5	3rd round	Dulux British Open
	v Hendry	9-10	Qualifying	Embassy World Professional Championship

BILL OLIVER (England)

Born 3.12.48
Turned professional 1983
World ranking 84 (85)

1983	v T. Jones	2-5	Qualifying	Professional Players Tournament
	v Andrewartha	1-9	Qualifying	Coral UK Championship
1984	v Dunning	10-3	Qualifying	Embassy World Professional Championship
	v Caggianello	10-7	Qualifying	Embassy World Professional Championship
	v Williams	8-10	Qualifying	Embassy World Professional Championship
	v D. Hughes	5-4	Qualifying	Jameson International
	v Chalmers	4-5	Qualifying	Jameson International
	v Bennett	5-3	Qualifying	Rothmans Grand Prix
	v White	1-5	1st round	Rothmans Grand Prix
	v Fowler	3-9	Qualifying	Coral UK Open
1985	v Longworth	1-5	Qualifying	Mercantile Credit Classic
	v Fowler	7-9	Qualifying	Tolly Cobbold English Professional Championship
	v Thorne	3-6	1st round	Dulux British Open
	v Foldvari	3-10	Qualifying	Embassy World Professional Championship
	v Morra	1-5	2nd round	Goya Matchroom Trophy

	v Fagan	5-4	2nd round	Rothmans Grand Prix
	v Thorburn	0-5	3rd round	Rothmans Grand Prix
	v Miles	4-9	2nd round	Coral UK Open
1986	v Bradley	3-5	2nd round	Mercantile Credit Classic
	v Dodd	9-5	2nd round	Tolly Cobbold English Professional Championship
	v Parrott	0-9	3rd round	Tolly Cobbold English Professional Championship
	v Newbury	2-5	2nd round	Dulux British Open
	v O'Boye	10-8	Qualifying	Embassy World Professional Championship
	v Fowler	8-10	Qualifying	Embassy World Professional Championship

MAURICE PARKIN (England)

Born –
Turned professional 1970
World ranking 113 (91)

Parkin won the English Amateur Championship in 1955 but has not played regularly on the professional circuit.

1972	v Thompson	11-10	Qualifying	World Professional Championship
	v Higgins	3-11	Qualifying	World Professional Championship
1973	v Simpson	3-9	1st round	World Professional Championship
1974	v M. Owen	5-8	1st round	World Professional Championship
1976	v Gross	5-8	Qualifying	Embassy World Professional Championship
1977	v Dunning	4-5	1st round	Super Crystalate UK Championship
1978	v Bennett	9-4	Prelim	Embassy World Professional Championship
	v Werbeniuk	2-9	Qualifying	Embassy World Professional Championship
	v David Taylor	2-9	Qualifying	Coral UK Championship
1979	v Virgo	0-9	Prelim	Embassy World Professional Championship
	v Hallett	1-9	1st round	Coral UK Championship
1981	v Gibson	3-5	Qualifying	Jameson International
	v Greaves	5-9	Qualifying	Embassy World Professional Championship
1982	v Black	6-9	Qualifying	Embassy World Professional Championship
	v E. Hughes	2-5	Qualifying	Jameson International
1983	v Martin	1-10	Qualifying	Embassy World Professional Championship
	v D. Hughes	0-5	Qualifying	Jameson International
1984	v Cripsey	4-10	Qualifying	Embassy World Professional Championship
	v O'Kane	2-5	Qualifying	Jameson International
1985	v G. Foulds	6-10	Qualifying	Embassy World Professional Championship
	v O'Boye	3-5	1st round	Goya Matchroom Trophy
1986	v Bales	0-5	1st round	Mercantile Credit Classic
	v Williamson	4-9	2nd round	Tolly Cobbold English Professional Championship
	v Bales	1-5	1st round	Dulux British Open
	v Grace	8-10	Qualifying	Embassy World Professional Championship

JOHN PARROTT (England)

Born 11.5.64
Turned professional 1983
World ranking 17 (18)

An exceptionally encouraging initial season in 1983–84 saw Parrott reach the semi-finals of the Lada Classic and the last 16 of the Embassy World Championship. He reached the World quarter-finals the following year but last season his only quarter-final was in the Goya Matchroom Trophy. He rose just one place in the ranking list, not the progress which many had predicted.

1983	v Watchorn	5-0	Qualifying	Professional Players Tournament
	v Fagan	5-2	1st round	Professional Players Tournament
	v Griffiths	1-5	2nd round	Professional Players Tournament
	v Scott	9-7	Qualifying	Coral UK Championship
	v Fisher	9-0	Qualifying	Coral UK Championship
	v Meo	7-9	1st round	Coral UK Championship
1984	v Mountjoy	5-4	Qualifying	Lada Classic
	v Higgins	5-2	1st round	Lada Classic
	v Knowles	5-1	Quarter-final	Lada Classic
	v S. Davis	4-5	Semi-final	Lada Classic
	v D. Hughes	10-3	Qualifying	Embassy World Professional Championship
	v Everton	10-2	Qualifying	Embassy World Professional Championship

John Parrott

	v Mans	10-0	Qualifying	Embassy World Professional Championship
	v Knowles	10-7	1st round	Embassy World Professional Championship
	v Dennis Taylor	11-13	2nd round	Embassy World Professional Championship
	v Gauvreau	4-5	Qualifying	Jameson International
	v Gauvreau	5-3	1st round	Rothmans Grand Prix
	v Charlton	1-5	2nd round	Rothmans Grand Prix
	v Fitzmaurice	9-6	Qualifying	Coral UK Open
	v Thorne	7-9	1st round	Coral UK Open
1985	v Medati	3-5	Qualifying	Mercantile Credit Classic
	v G. Foulds	9-4	1st round	Tolly Cobbold English Professional Championship
	v David Taylor	6-9	2nd round	Tolly Cobbold English Professional Championship
	v John Rea	6-4	1st round	Dulux British Open
	v Dennis Taylor	2-5	2nd round	Dulux British Open
	v Fowler	10-2	Qualifying	Embassy World Professional Championship
	v Spencer	10-3	1st round	Embassy World Professional Championship
	v Stevens	13-6	2nd round	Embassy World Professional Championship
	v Reardon	12-13	Quarter-final	Embassy World Professional Championship
	v Thorne	5-0	Quarter-final	Winfield Australian Masters
	v Campbell	4-6	Semi-final	Winfield Australian Masters
	v White	3-5	Semi-final	Carlsberg Trophy
	v W. Jones	5-3	3rd round	Goya Matchroom Trophy
	v Meo	5-4	4th round	Goya Matchroom Trophy
	v Griffiths	5-1	5th round	Goya Matchroom Trophy
	v Dennis Taylor	1-5	Quarter-final	Goya Matchroom Trophy
	v Longworth	2-5	3rd round	Rothmans Grand Prix
	v Dennis Taylor	1-5	1st round	BCE Canadian Masters
	v Sinclair	9-2	3rd round	Coral UK Open
	v Thorburn	6-9	4th round	Coral UK Open
1986	v Van Rensberg	3-5	3rd round	Mercantile Credit Classic
	v Oliver	9-0	3rd round	Tolly Cobbold English Professional Championship
	v Virgo	6-9	4th round	Tolly Cobbold English Professional Championship
	v Roscoe	5-2	3rd round	Dulux British Open
	v Fagan	5-0	4th round	Dulux British Open
	v Wych	4-5	5th round	Dulux British Open
	v Foldvari	10-6	Qualifying	Embassy World Professional Championship
	v Meo	10-4	1st round	Embassy World Professional Championship
	v White	8-13	2nd round	Embassy World Professional Championship

JACK REA (Northern Ireland)

Born –
Turned professional 1948
World ranking 103 (76)

For 20 years Irish professional champion until deposed by Alex Higgins in 1972, Rea made his name on the exhibition circuit with a unique mixture of jokes, patter, trick shots and straight snooker. His competitive appearances have been comparatively infrequent in recent years although it will always be on his record that he was runner-up for the world title in 1957.

1969	v G. Owen	17-25	Quarter-final	World Professional Championship
1970	v Spencer	15-31	Quarter-final	World Professional Championship
1972	v Higgins	11-19	1st round	World Professional Championship
1973	v Houlihan	2-9	1st round	World Professional Championship
1976	v Anderson	8-5	Qualifying	Embassy World Professional Championship
1977	v John Rea	9-11	Qualifying	Embassy World Professional Championship
	v Fagan	1-5	1st round	Super Crystalate UK Championship
1978	v Meadowcroft	5-9	Qualifying	Coral UK Championship
1979	v Dunning	5-9	Prelim	Embassy World Professional Championship
	v Bennett	9-8	1st round	Coral UK Championship
	v Houlihan	3-9	2nd round	Coral UK Championship
1980	v Thorne	1-9	Qualifying	Embassy World Professional Championship
1981	v D. Hughes	4-5	Qualifying	Jameson International
1982	v E. Hughes	1-6	Quarter-final	Irish Professional Championship
	v Bennett	8-5	Qualifying	Embassy World Professional Championship
	v Werbeniuk	2-5	2nd round	Professional Players Tournament
	v Roscoe	6-9	Qualifying	Coral UK Championship
1983	v Higgins	3-6	Quarter-final	Irish Professional Championship
	v David Taylor	7-8	Qualifying	Embassy World Professional Championship
	v Edmonds	1-5	Qualifying	Jameson International
	v French	5-9	Qualifying	Coral UK Championship
1984	v Bradley	2-5	Qualifying	Jameson International
1985	v Foldvari	4-5	Qualifying	Mercantile Credit Classic
	v Dennis Taylor	0-6	Quarter-final	Irish Professional Championship
	v Murphy	1-5	2nd round	Goya Matchroom Trophy
1986	v Fisher	3-5	2nd round	Mercantile Credit Classic
	v Bradley	1-5	2nd round	Dulux British Open
	v Kelly	0-5	1st round	Strongbow Irish Professional Championship

JOHN REA (Scotland)

Born 5.12.51
Turned professional 1984
World ranking 62 (67)

A victory over Ray Reardon in the 1986 Dulux British Open earned Rea his first ranking point in his two-year professional career.

1984	v Browne	2-5	Qualifying	Jameson International
	v Fitzmaurice	5-2	Qualifying	Rothmans Grand Prix
	v E. Hughes	5-4	1st round	Rothmans Grand Prix
	v David Taylor	1-5	2nd round	Rothmans Grand Prix
	v Bennett	9-5	Qualifying	Coral UK Open
	v Dunning	9-3	Qualifying	Coral UK Open
	v Edmonds	9-6	Qualifying	Coral UK Open
	v Johnson	6-9	Qualifying	Coral UK Open

1985	v Sheehan	2-5	Qualifying	Mercantile Credit Classic
	v Fisher	6-0	Qualifying	Dulux British Open
	v Parrott	4-6	1st round	Dulux British Open
	v W. Jones	3-10	Qualifying	Embassy World Professional Championship
	v Bradley	1-5	2nd round	Goya Matchroom Trophy
	v W. Jones	0-5	2nd round	Rothmans Grand Prix
	v F. Davis	8-9	2nd round	Coral UK Open
1986	v Williamson	5-4	2nd round	Mercantile Credit Classic
	v Hallett	2-5	3rd round	Mercantile Credit Classic
	v King	5-1	2nd round	Dulux British Open
	v Reardon	5-3	3rd round	Dulux British Open
	v Virgo	0-5	4th round	Dulux British Open
	v Donnelly	6-1	Quarter-final	Canada Dry Scottish Professional Championship
	v Gibson	0-6	Semi-final	Canada Dry Scottish Professional Championship
	v E. McLaughlin	10-6	Qualifying	Embassy World Professional Championship
	v Longworth	4-10	Qualifying	Embassy World Professional Championship

RAY REARDON (Wales)

Born 8.10.32
Turned professional 1967
World ranking 15 (6)

Welsh amateur champion six times in succession, the first of these when he was only 17, Reardon was professional snooker's dominant player in the 1970s, during which he won six world titles. The highlights of his recent career have been first prizes in the 1982 Professional Players Tournament and the 1983 Yamaha International Masters and two Welsh titles. His best performance in the 1984–85 season was to reach the world semi-finals but last season he won only two matches and for the first time in his career, at 15th, was not among the world's top eight.

1969	v F. Davis	24-25	Quarter-final	World Professional Championship
1970	v F. Davis	31-26	Quarter-final	World Professional Championship (Apr)
	v Spencer	37-33	Semi-final	World Professional Championship (Apr)
	v Pulman	**39-34**	**Final**	**World Professional Championship (Apr)**
	v Spencer	15-34	Semi-final	World Professional Championship (Nov)
1972	v Williams	23-25	Quarter-final	World Professional Championship
1973	v Meadowcroft	16-10	2nd round	World Professional Championship
	v G. Owen	16-6	Quarter-final	World Professional Championship
	v Spencer	23-22	Semi-final	World Professional Championship
	v Charlton	**38-32**	**Final**	**World Professional Championship**
1974	v Meadowcroft	15-3	2nd round	World Professional Championship
	v M. Owen	15-11	Quarter-final	World Professional Championship
	v F. Davis	15-3	Semi-final	World Professional Championship
	v Miles	**22-12**	**Final**	**World Professional Championship**

1974	v Burke	5-2	1st round	Norwich Union Open
–75	v Williams	5-2	Quarter-final	Norwich Union Open
	v Higgins	9-8	Semi-final	Norwich Union Open
	v Spencer	9-10	Final	Norwich Union Open
1975	v Miles	5-3	Quarter-final	Benson & Hedges Masters
	v Williams	5-4	Semi-final	Benson & Hedges Masters
	v Spencer	8-9	Final	Benson & Hedges Masters
	v Simpson	15-11	2nd round	World Professional Championship
	v Spencer	19-17	Quarter-final	World Professional Championship
	v Higgins	19-14	Semi-final	World Professional Championship
	v Charlton	**31-30**	**Final**	**World Professional Championship**
1976	v Charlton	5-4	Semi-final	Benson & Hedges Masters
	v Miles	**7-3**	**Final**	**Benson & Hedges Masters**
	v Dunning	15-7	1st round	Embassy World Professional Championship
	v Dennis Taylor	15-2	Quarter-final	Embassy World Professional Championship
	v Mans	20-10	Semi-final	Embassy World Professional Championship
	v Higgins	**27-16**	**Final**	**Embassy World Professional Championship**
1977	v Miles	5-2	Semi-final	Benson & Hedges Masters
	v Mountjoy	6-7	Final	Benson & Hedges Masters
	v Fagan	13-7	1st round	Embassy World Professional Championship
	v Spencer	6-13	Quarter-final	Embassy World Professional Championship
	v Meadowcroft	4-5	2nd round	Super Crystalate UK Championship
1978	v Higgins	1-5	Semi-final	Benson & Hedges Masters
	v Mountjoy	13-9	1st round	Embassy World Professional Championship
	v Werbeniuk	13-6	Quarter-final	Embassy World Professional Championship
	v Charlton	18-14	Semi-final	Embassy World Professional Championship
	v Mans	**25-18**	**Final**	**Embassy World Professional Championship**
	v Thorne	6-9	1st round	Coral UK Championship
1979	v David Taylor	5-2	Quarter-final	Benson & Hedges Masters
	v Mans	3-5	Semi-final	Benson & Hedges Masters
	v Mountjoy	5-6	Final	Benson & Hedges Irish Masters
	v Miles	13-8	1st round	Embassy World Professional Championship
	v Dennis Taylor	8-13	Quarter-final	Embassy World Professional Championship
1980	v Dennis Taylor	5-3	Quarter-final	Benson & Hedges Masters
	v Higgins	2-5	Semi-final	Benson & Hedges Masters
	v Higgins	1-5	Final	British Gold Cup
	v Werbeniuk	13-6	2nd round	Embassy World Professional Championship
	v David Taylor	11-13	Quarter-final	Embassy World Professional Championship
	v Andrewartha	9-3	2nd round	Coral UK Championship
	v Williams	9-4	Quarter-final	Coral UK Championship
	v Higgins	7-9	Semi-final	Coral UK Championship
1981	v Spencer	1-5	Quarter-final	Benson & Hedges Masters
	v Griffiths	9-6	Semi-final	Woodpecker Welsh Professional Championship
	v Wilson	**9-6**	**Final**	**Woodpecker Welsh Professional Championship**
	v Spencer	13-11	2nd round	Embassy World Professional Championship
	v Werbeniuk	13-10	Quarter-final	Embassy World Professional Championship
	v Mountjoy	10-16	Semi-final	Embassy World Professional Championship
	v White	4-5	Quarter-final	Langs Supreme Scottish Masters

Ray Reardon

	v Virgo	3-5	3rd round	Jameson International
	v Johnson	9-7	3rd round	Coral UK Championship
	v White	8-9	Quarter-final	Coral UK Championship
1982	v David Taylor	5-1	1st round	Lada Classic
	v S. Davis	4-5	Semi-final	Lada Classic
	v Dennis Taylor	5-3	1st round	Benson & Hedges Masters
	v Griffiths	3-5	Quarter-final	Benson & Hedges Masters
	v Everton	6-1	1st round	Welsh Professional Championship
	v Mountjoy	7-9	Semi-final	Welsh Professional Championship
	v Dennis Taylor	5-4	Quarter-final	Benson & Hedges Irish Masters
	v Griffiths	3-6	Semi-final	Benson & Hedges Irish Masters
	v Donnelly	10-5	1st round	Embassy World Professional Championship
	v Virgo	13-8	2nd round	Embassy World Professional Championship
	v S. Francisco	13-8	Quarter-final	Embassy World Professional Championship
	v Charlton	16-11	Semi-final	Embassy World Professional Championship
	v Higgins	15-18	Final	Embassy World Professional Championship
	v Griffiths	3-5	1st round	Langs Supreme Scottish Masters
	v E. Hughes	5-3	1st round	Jameson International
	v Knowles	2-5	2nd round	Jameson International
	v Murphy	5-0	1st round	Professional Players Tournament
	v Higgins	5-2	2nd round	Professional Players Tournament
	v Macleod	5-2	3rd round	Professional Players Tournament
	v Werbeniuk	5-3	Quarter-final	Professional Players Tournament
	v Charlton	10-7	Semi-final	Professional Players Tournament
	v White	**10-5**	**Final**	**Professional Players Tournament**
	v Wildman	9-5	1st round	Coral UK Championship
	v Hallett	9-8	2nd round	Coral UK Championship
	v White	9-8	Quarter-final	Coral UK Championship
	v Higgins	6-9	Semi-final	Coral UK Championship
1983	v Spencer	3-5	1st round	Lada Classic
	v Reynolds	5-1	1st round	Benson & Hedges Masters
	v White	5-2	Quarter-final	Benson & Hedges Masters
	v Mountjoy	6-3	Semi-final	Benson & Hedges Masters
	v Thorburn	7-9	Final	Benson & Hedges Masters
	v White	**9-6**	**Final**	**Yamaha International Masters**
	v Andrewartha	6-2	Quarter-final	Woodpecker Welsh Professional Championship
	v Griffiths	9-4	Semi-final	Woodpecker Welsh Professional Championship
	v Mountjoy	**9-1**	**Final**	**Woodpecker Welsh Professional Championship**
	v Meo	5-4	Quarter-final	Benson & Hedges Irish Masters
	v Higgins	6-3	Semi-final	Benson & Hedges Irish Masters
	v S. Davis	2-9	Final	Benson & Hedges Irish Masters
	v E. Hughes	10-7	1st round	Embassy World Professional Championship
	v Knowles	12-13	2nd round	Embassy World Professional Championship
	v Macleod	5-2	1st round	Jameson International
	v Thorne	0-5	2nd round	Jameson International
	v Ganim	5-4	1st round	Professional Players Tournament
	v Duggan	5-2	2nd round	Professional Players Tournament
	v Thorne	3-5	3rd round	Professional Players Tournament

	v B. Harris	9-7	1st round	Coral UK Championship
	v Wilson	9-4	2nd round	Coral UK Championship
	v White	4-9	Quarter-final	Coral UK Championship
1984	v Williams	4-5	Qualifying	Lada Classic
	v Virgo	5-3	1st round	Benson & Hedges Masters
	v White	3-5	Quarter-final	Benson & Hedges Masters
	v M. Owen	6-1	1st round	Strongbow Welsh Professional Championship
	v Wilson	4-9	Semi-final	Strongbow Welsh Professional Championship
	v Higgins	2-5	Quarter-final	Benson & Hedges Irish Masters
	v Wych	10-7	1st round	Embassy World Professional Championship
	v S. Francisco	13-8	2nd round	Embassy World Professional Championship
	v Stevens	2-13	Quarter-final	Embassy World Professional Championship
	v Dodd	5-4	1st round	Jameson International
	v E. Hughes	1-5	2nd round	Jameson International
	v Roscoe	5-1	1st round	Rothmans Grand Prix
	v Wilson	5-4	2nd round	Rothmans Grand Prix
	v Dennis Taylor	3-5	3rd round	Rothmans Grand Prix
	v Fowler	9-2	1st round	Coral UK Open
	v David Taylor	9-4	2nd round	Coral UK Open
	v Thorburn	8-9	Quarter-final	Coral UK Open
1985	v Hallett	5-3	1st round	Mercantile Credit Classic
	v E. Hughes	5-1	2nd round	Mercantile Credit Classic
	v S. Davis	1-5	Quarter-final	Mercantile Credit Classic
	v David Taylor	5-1	1st round	Benson & Hedges Masters
	v Thorburn	0-5	Quarter-final	Benson & Hedges Masters
	v King	6-5	1st round	Dulux British Open
	v Martin	4-5	2nd round	Dulux British Open
	v E. Hughes	0-5	1st round	Benson & Hedges Irish Masters
	v E. Hughes	10-9	1st round	Embassy World Professional Championship
	v Fagan	13-9	2nd round	Embassy World Professional Championship
	v Parrott	13-12	Quarter-final	Embassy World Professional Championship
	v S. Davis	5-16	Semi-final	Embassy World Professional Championship
	v Everton	6-2	Quarter-final	BCE Welsh Professional Championship
	v Griffiths	3-9	Semi-final	BCE Welsh Professional Championship
	v Duggan	3-5	3rd round	Goya Matchroom Trophy
	v Scott	4-5	3rd round	Rothmans Grand Prix
	v Knowles	5-2	1st round	BCE Canadian Masters
	v Dennis Taylor	3-8	Semi-final	BCE Canadian Masters
	v Miles	9-4	3rd round	Coral UK Open
	v Macleod	5-9	4th round	Coral UK Open
	v Griffiths	2-5	1st round	Kit Kat
1986	v Mikkelsen	3-5	3rd round	Mercantile Credit Classic
	v Stevens	1-5	1st round	BCE Belgian Classic
	v Thorne	4-5	1st round	Benson & Hedges Masters
	v W. Jones	4-6	Quarter-final	Zetters Welsh Professional Championship
	v John Rea	3-5	3rd round	Dulux British Open
	v E. Hughes	2-5	1st round	Benson & Hedges Irish Masters
	v Campbell	8-10	1st round	Embassy World Professional Championship

JIM REMPE (USA)

Born –
Turned professional 1980
World ranking 110 (unranked)

One of the all-time greats of the American pool circuit, Rempe has appeared in two World Cups as a member of the Rest of the World trio but has only competed in two authentic tournaments on the circuit.

1985	v Burke	5-3	1st round	Goya Matchroom Trophy
	v Wych	1-5	2nd round	Goya Matchroom Trophy
	v Agrawal	2-5	1st round	Rothmans Grand Prix

DEAN REYNOLDS (England)

Born 11.1.63
Turned professional 1981
World ranking 29 (24)

Only 19 when he reached the last 16 of the Embassy World Championship at his first attempt in 1982, Reynolds has comfortably maintained a place in the top 32 without challenging strongly for a place in the top 16. He has recorded wins over Silvino Francisco and Willie Thorne (three times).

1982	v Sheehan	9-5	Qualifying	Embassy World Professional Championship
	v Edmonds	9-6	Qualifying	Embassy World Professional Championship
	v F. Davis	10-7	1st round	Embassy World Professional Championship
	v S. Francisco	8-13	2nd round	Embassy World Professional Championship
	v Morra	5-1	Qualifying	Jameson International
	v Thorne	5-3	1st round	Jameson International
	v S. Davis	0-5	2nd round	Jameson International
	v Fitzmaurice	5-0	2nd round	Professional Players Tournament
	v Wilson	5-1	3rd round	Professional Players Tournament
	v Charlton	2-5	Quarter-final	Professional Players Tournament
	v Fisher	9-6	1st round	Coral UK Championship
	v Higgins	8-9	2nd round	Coral UK Championship
1983	v Reardon	1-5	1st round	Benson & Hedges Masters
	v Edmonds	10-6	Qualifying	Embassy World Professional Championship
	v Higgins	4-10	1st round	Embassy World Professional Championship
	v Williams	5-3	Qualifying	Jameson International
	v Dennis Taylor	3-5	1st round	Jameson International
	v Greaves	5-1	1st round	Professional Players Tournament
	v Meo	0-5	2nd round	Professional Players Tournament
	v Medati	3-9	1st round	Coral UK Championship
1984	v Griffiths	2-5	Qualifying	Lada Classic
	v Morra	7-10	Qualifying	Embassy World Professional Championship
	v Bales	5-4	Qualifying	Jameson International

	v Knowles	1-5	1st round	Jameson International
	v Fowler	5-2	1st round	Rothmans Grand Prix
	v P. Francisco	5-4	2nd round	Rothmans Grand Prix
	v S. Francisco	5-1	3rd round	Rothmans Grand Prix
	v S. Davis	0-5	Quarter-final	Rothmans Grand Prix
	v Chappel	6-9	Qualifying	Coral UK Open
1985	v King	2-5	Qualifying	Mercantile Credit Classic
	v Fitzmaurice	9-2	1st round	Tolly Cobbold English Professional Championship
	v Thorne	9-6	2nd round	Tolly Cobbold English Professional Championship
	v Meo	4-9	Quarter-final	Tolly Cobbold English Professional Championship
	v Giannaros	6-3	1st round	Dulux British Open
	v Thorburn	3-5	2nd round	Dulux British Open
	v Gauvreau	10-1	Qualifying	Embassy World Professional Championship
	v Higgins	4-10	1st round	Embassy World Professional Championship
	v Mikkelsen	5-0	3rd round	Goya Matchroom Trophy
	v Gibson	5-0	4th round	Goya Matchroom Trophy
	v White	1-5	5th round	Goya Matchroom Trophy
	v Miles	3-5	3rd round	Rothmans Grand Prix
	v J. McLaughlin	9-7	3rd round	Coral UK Open
	v Griffiths	7-9	4th round	Coral UK Open
1986	v Houlihan	5-1	3rd round	Mercantile Credit Classic
	v Dennis Taylor	4-5	4th round	Mercantile Credit Classic
	v Longworth	9-5	3rd round	Tolly Cobbold English Professional Championship
	v Thorne	9-8	4th round	Tolly Cobbold English Professional Championship
	v Meo	4-9	Quarter-final	Tolly Cobbold English Professional Championship
	v Wych	3-5	3rd round	Dulux British Open
	v Stevens	6-10	1st round	Embassy World Professional Championship

GINO RIGITANO (Canada)

Born 14.8.57
Turned professional 1983
World ranking 86 (77)

1984	v Gibson	7-10	Qualifying	Embassy World Professional Championship
	v Foldvari	2-5	Qualifying	Jameson International
	v Edmonds	5-3	Qualifying	Rothmans Grand Prix
	v Thorburn	4-5	1st round	Rothmans Grand Prix
	v Newbury	6-9	Qualifying	Coral UK Open
1985	v Fowler	0-5	Qualifying	Mercantile Credit Classic
	v Thorburn	3-6	1st round	Dulux British Open
	v Sheehan	10-9	Qualifying	Embassy World Professional Championship
	v B. Harris	10-4	Qualifying	Embassy World Professional Championship
	v Kelly	10-6	Qualifying	Embassy World Professional Championship

	v Fisher	10-2	Qualifying	Embassy World Professional Championship
	v N. Foulds	8-10	Qualifying	Embassy World Professional Championship
	v Black	4-5	2nd round	Goya Matchroom Trophy
	v Miles	4-5	2nd round	Rothmans Grand Prix
1986	v Dodd	5-3	2nd round	Mercantile Credit Classic
	v Knowles	4-5	3rd round	Mercantile Credit Classic
	v W. Jones	1-5	2nd round	Dulux British Open
	v Foldvari	6-10	Qualifying	Embassy World Professional Championship

COLIN ROSCOE (Wales)

Born 30.6.45
Turned professional 1981
World ranking 74 (45)

Welsh amateur champion in 1981, Roscoe reached the last 16 of the 1984 Lada Classic with a win over Bill Werbeniuk, his best performance on the circuit.

1981	v Macleod	9-7	Qualifying	Coral UK Championship
	v Williams	4-9	Qualifying	Coral UK Championship
	v Andrewartha	5-2	Qualifying	Jameson International
	v Sheehan	5-1	Qualifying	Jameson International
	v Meadowcroft	4-5	Qualifying	Jameson International
1982	v Griffiths	2-6	1st round	Welsh Professional Championship
	v Mikkelsen	9-6	Qualifying	Embassy World Professional Championship
	v Thorne	1-9	Qualifying	Embassy World Professional Championship
	v Dunning	5-2	Qualifying	Jameson International
	v French	5-2	Qualifying	Jameson International
	v S. Davis	0-5	1st round	Jameson International
	v Griffiths	1-5	1st round	Professional Players Tournament
	v Jack Rea	9-6	Qualifying	Coral UK Championship
	v Wildman	4-9	Qualifying	Coral UK Championship
1983	v Wilson	4-6	Quarter-final	Woodpecker Welsh Professional Championship
	v Sinclair	2-10	Qualifying	Embassy World Professional Championship
	v Hallett	2-5	Qualifying	Jameson International
	v Meadowcroft	4-5	1st round	Professional Players Tournament
	v N. Foulds	2-9	Qualifying	Coral UK Championship
1984	v Ganim	5-3	Qualifying	Lada Classic
	v Miles	5-2	Qualifying	Lada Classic
	v Werbeniuk	5-4	1st round	Lada Classic
	v Griffiths	2-5	2nd round	Lada Classic
	v Wilson	2-6	1st round	Strongbow Welsh Professional Championship
	v Demarco	10-7	Qualifying	Embassy World Professional Championship
	v Browne	4-10	Qualifying	Embassy World Professional Championship

	v Mikkelsen	5-1	Qualifying	Jameson International
	v French	5-0	Qualifying	Rothmans Grand Prix
	v Reardon	1-5	1st round	Rothmans Grand Prix
	v J. McLaughlin	8-9	Qualifying	Coral UK Open
1985	v Medati	4-5	Qualifying	Mercantile Credit Classic
	v Giannaros	1-6	Qualifying	Dulux British Open
	v G. Foulds	7-10	Qualifying	Embassy World Professional Championship
	v Wilson	3-6	Quarter-final	BCE Welsh Professional Championship
	v G. Foulds	5-3	2nd round	Goya Matchroom Trophy
	v Wilson	1-5	3rd round	Goya Matchroom Trophy
	v Watson	2-5	2nd round	Rothmans Grand Prix
	v West	5-9	2nd round	Coral UK Open
1986	v V. Harris	1-5	2nd round	Mercantile Credit Classic
	v Mountjoy	4-6	Quarter-final	Zetters Welsh Professional Championship
	v Mikkelsen	5-4	2nd round	Dulux British Open
	v Parrott	2-5	3rd round	Dulux British Open
	v G. Foulds	10-3	Qualifying	Embassy World Professional Championship
	v King	5-10	Qualifying	Embassy World Professional Championship

GEORGE SCOTT (England)

Born 16.9.29
Turned professional 1981
World ranking 44 (41)

Having turned professional at the age of 51 after being Liverpool's best amateur for as long as anyone could remember, Scott has recorded wins over Bill Werbeniuk, Dennis Taylor and Ray Reardon. He was one of the formative influences on the early career of John Parrott.

1982	v B. Harris	5-4	Qualifying	Jameson International
	v Thorburn	1-5	1st round	Jameson International
	v Meo	5-9	Qualifying	Coral UK Championship
1983	v Houlihan	5-0	Qualifying	Jameson International
	v Gibson	5-3	Qualifying	Jameson International
	v Werbeniuk	5-3	1st round	Jameson International
	v Griffiths	0-5	2nd round	Jameson International
	v Dennis Taylor	5-4	1st round	Professional Players Tournament
	v S. Francisco	1-5	2nd round	Professional Players Tournament
	v Parrott	7-9	Qualifying	Coral UK Championship
1984	v Heywood	10-7	Qualifying	Embassy World Professional Championship
	v Wych	6-10	Qualifying	Embassy World Professional Championship
	v W. Jones	0-5	Qualifying	Jameson International
	v Chappel	1-5	Qualifying	Rothmans Grand Prix
	v O'Kane	9-7	Qualifying	Coral UK Open
	v Macleod	5-9	Qualifying	Coral UK Open

1985	v J. McLaughlin	5-4	Qualifying	Mercantile Credit Classic
	v Campbell	5-4	Qualifying	Mercantile Credit Classic
	v Thorburn	1-5	1st round	Mercantile Credit Classic
	v V. Harris	9-7	Qualifying	Tolly Cobbold English Professional Championship
	v Johnson	1-9	1st round	Tolly Cobbold English Professional Championship
	v Darrington	6-3	Qualifying	Dulux British Open
	v Dennis Taylor	2-6	1st round	Dulux British Open
	v Newbury	2-10	Qualifying	Embassy World Professional Championship
	v Van Rensberg	5-4	2nd round	Goya Matchroom Trophy
	v Wildman	5-1	3rd round	Goya Matchroom Trophy
	v Thorne	1-5	4th round	Goya Matchroom Trophy
	v Chalmers	5-2	2nd round	Rothmans Grand Prix
	v Reardon	5-4	3rd round	Rothmans Grand Prix
	v Wilson	3-5	4th round	Rothmans Grand Prix
	v Sheehan	6-9	2nd round	Coral UK Open
1986	v Mikkelsen	1-5	2nd round	Mercantile Credit Classic
	v Bennett	9-1	2nd round	Tolly Cobbold English Professional Championship
	v Meo	1-9	3rd round	Tolly Cobbold English Professional Championship
	v Chalmers	5-1	2nd round	Dulux British Open
	v Griffiths	3-5	3rd round	Dulux British Open
	v Kearney	10-8	Qualifying	Embassy World Professional Championship
	v Fowler	7-10	Qualifying	Embassy World Professional Championship

DESSIE SHEEHAN (Republic of Ireland)

Born 3.9.49
Turned professional 1981
World ranking 81 (99)

1981	v V. Harris	5-1	Qualifying	Jameson International
	v Roscoe	1-5	Qualifying	Jameson International
1982	v E. Hughes	1-6	1st round	Irish Professional Championship
	v V. Harris	3-5	Qualifying	Jameson International
	v Dennis Taylor	3-5	1st round	Benson & Hedges Irish Masters
	v Reynolds	5-9	Qualifying	Embassy World Professional Championship
	v Fitzmaurice	1-5	1st round	Professional Players Tournament
1983	v Donnelly	6-10	Qualifying	Embassy World Professional Championship
	v Murphy	2-5	Qualifying	Jameson International
	v Houlihan	5-2	Qualifying	Professional Players Tournament
	v Williams	1-5	1st round	Professional Players Tournament
1984	v B. Harris	3-10	Qualifying	Embassy World Professional Championship
	v Bales	2-5	Qualifying	Jameson International

	v Mikkelsen	5-3	Qualifying	Rothmans Grand Prix
	v Hallett	1-5	1st round	Rothmans Grand Prix
	v P. Francisco	5-9	Qualifying	Coral UK Open
1985	v John Rea	5-2	Qualifying	Mercantile Credit Classic
	v E. McLaughlin	2-5	Qualifying	Mercantile Credit Classic
	v Murphy	3-6	Qualifying	Dulux British Open
	v J. McLaughlin	3-6	Qualifying	Irish Professional Championship
	v Rigitano	9-10	Qualifying	Embassy World Professional Championship
	v Smith	2-5	1st round	Goya Matchroom Trophy
	v Watson	1-5	1st round	Rothmans Grand Prix
	v Watchorn	9-7	1st round	Coral UK Open
	v Scott	9-6	2nd round	Coral UK Open
	v S. Davis	1-9	3rd round	Coral UK Open
1986	v Hendry	2-5	1st round	Mercantile Credit Classic
	v Simngam	5-2	1st round	Dulux British Open
	v Watterson	*wo*	2nd round	Dulux British Open
	v Thorburn	0-5	3rd round	Dulux British Open
	v Houlihan	10-7	Qualifying	Embassy World Professional Championship
	v King	4-10	Qualifying	Embassy World Professional Championship
	v E. Hughes	0-5	1st round	Strongbow Irish Professional Championship

SAKCHAIR SIMNGAM (Thailand)

Born 12.6.52
Turned professional 1985
World ranking 80

Simngam, the first Thai to become a professional, was a member of the Rest of the World side in the Car Care Plan World Cup.

1985	v Greaves	5-2	1st round	Goya Matchroom Trophy
	v Dodd	4-5	2nd round	Goya Matchroom Trophy
	v Mienie	5-3	1st round	Rothmans Grand Prix
	v F. Davis	5-2	2nd round	Rothmans Grand Prix
	v E. Hughes	1-5	3rd round	Rothmans Grand Prix
	v Bales	9-2	1st round	Coral UK Open
	v Fisher	9-4	2nd round	Coral UK Open
	v Johnson	4-9	3rd round	Coral UK Open
1986	v Hargreaves	5-1	1st round	Mercantile Credit Classic
	v Gauvreau	1-5	2nd round	Mercantile Credit Classic
	v Sheehan	2-5	1st round	Dulux British Open
	v Bennett	10-0	Qualifying	Embassy World Professional Championship
	v Medati	9-10	Qualifying	Embassy World Professional Championship

EDDIE SINCLAIR (Scotland)

Born 5.5.37
Turned professional 1979
World ranking 70 (38)

Seven times Scottish amateur champion and twice Scottish professional champion, Sinclair has been an ever-present member of Scotland's World Cup team.

Year	Opponent	Score	Round	Event
1980	v Meadowcroft	1-9	Qualifying	Embassy World Professional Championship
	v Kennerley	9-1	Qualifying	Coral UK Championship
	v Miles	9-5	1st round	Coral UK Championship
	v Dennis Taylor	6-9	2nd round	Coral UK Championship
1981	v Donnelly	0-5	Quarter-final	Scottish Professional Championship
	v Morgan	9-8	Qualifying	Embassy World Professional Championship
	v Wilson	4-9	Qualifying	Embassy World Professional Championship
	v E. Hughes	2-5	Qualifying	Jameson International
	v Wildman	9-8	Qualifying	Coral UK Championship
	v Hood	9-0	Qualifying	Coral UK Championship
	v Martin	7-9	Qualifying	Coral UK Championship
1982	v Kelly	9-8	Qualifying	Embassy World Professional Championship
	v Donnelly	8-9	Qualifying	Embassy World Professional Championship
	v Phillips	6-3	Quarter-final	Scottish Professional Championship
	v Gibson	6-2	Semi-final	Scottish Professional Championship
	v Black	**11-7**	**Final**	**Scottish Professional Championship**
	v Higgins	1-5	1st round	Langs Supreme Scottish Masters
	v Anderson	5-2	Qualifying	Jameson International
	v Meo	5-3	Qualifying	Jameson International
	v Knowles	2-5	1st round	Jameson International
	v F. Davis	5-2	1st round	Professional Players Tournament
	v Meadowcroft	5-3	2nd round	Professional Players Tournament
	v Griffiths	3-5	3rd round	Professional Players Tournament
	v Murphy	9-5	Qualifying	Coral UK Championship
	v Spencer	8-9	1st round	Coral UK Championship
1983	v Roscoe	10-2	Qualifying	Embassy World Professional Championship
	v E. Hughes	8-10	Qualifying	Embassy World Professional Championship
	v Donnelly	6-5	Semi-final	Scottish Professional Championship
	v Macleod	9-11	Final	Scottish Professional Championship
	v Andrewartha	5-4	Qualifying	Jameson International
	v Thorburn	0-5	1st round	Jameson International
	v E. Hughes	4-5	1st round	Professional Players Tournament
	v T. Jones	3-9	Qualifying	Coral UK Championship
1984	v S. Davis	2-5	Qualifying	Lada Classic
	v Browne	10-1	Qualifying	Embassy World Professional Championship
	v Stevens	1-10	1st round	Embassy World Professional Championship
	v Duggan	5-0	Qualifying	Jameson International
	v Mans	5-2	Qualifying	Jameson International
	v Higgins	1-5	1st round	Jameson International
	v T. Jones	4-5	Qualifying	Rothmans Grand Prix
	v P. Francisco	9-8	Qualifying	Coral UK Open

	v S. Francisco	4-9	Qualifying	Coral UK Open
1985	v Newbury	3-6	1st round	Dulux British Open
	v T. Jones	2-10	Qualifying	Embassy World Professional Championship
	v Darrington	5-0	2nd round	Goya Matchroom Trophy
	v Martin	1-5	3rd round	Goya Matchroom Trophy
	v Fitzmaurice	3-5	2nd round	Rothmans Grand Prix
	v G. Foulds	9-4	2nd round	Coral UK Open
	v Parrott	2-9	3rd round	Coral UK Open
1986	v Greaves	5-1	2nd round	Mercantile Credit Classic
	v Macleod	2-5	3rd round	Mercantile Credit Classic
	v B. Harris	3-5	2nd round	Dulux British Open
	v Gibson	4-6	Quarter-final	Canada Dry Scottish Professional Championship
	v Morgan	10-8	Qualifying	Embassy World Professional Championship
	v Van Rensberg	2-10	Qualifying	Embassy World Professional Championship

MARTIN SMITH (England)

Born –
Turned professional 1985
World ranking 94

1985	v Sheehan	5-2	1st round	Goya Matchroom Trophy
	v W. Jones	3-5	2nd round	Goya Matchroom Trophy
	v Bales	1-5	1st round	Rothmans Grand Prix
	v Wilkinson	9-4	1st round	Coral UK Open
1986	v Mienie	5-1	1st round	Mercantile Credit Classic
	v Edmonds	5-2	2nd round	Mercantile Credit Classic
	v Mans	4-5	3rd round	Mercantile Credit Classic
	v Edmonds	8-9	2nd round	Tolly Cobbold English Professional Championship
	v Kearney	2-5	1st round	Dulux British Open
	v Greaves	10-4	Qualifying	Embassy World Professional Championship
	v Donnelly	6-10	Qualifying	Embassy World Professional Championship

JOHN SPENCER (England)

Born 18.9.35
Turned professional 1967
World ranking 34 (20)

English amateur champion in 1966, Spencer won the first of his three world professional titles three years later and with Ray Reardon, and to a slightly lesser extent, Alex Higgins, dominated the early 1970s. He won several first prizes in tournaments now defunct including the 1979 Holsten Lager International at Slough, in which his 147 was the first maximum in a televised event. Unfortunately, this was before the days when every frame was recorded and the television crew were on a meal break when history was made.

He slipped steadily down the rankings after his third world title in 1977 and in the summer of 1984 even the continuance of his career was threatened by persistent double vision which is now controlled only by a daily intake of steroids.

1969	v Pulman	30-19	Quarter-final	World Professional Championship
	v Williams	55-18	Semi-final	World Professional Championship
	v G. Owen	46-27	Final	World Professional Championship
1970	v Jack Rea	31-15	Quarter-final	World Professional Championship (Apr)
	v Reardon	33-37	Semi-final	World Professional Championship (Apr)
	v Reardon	34-15	Semi-final	World Professional Championship (Nov)
	v Simpson	**42-31**	**Final**	**World Professional Championship (Nov)**
1972	v F. Davis	31-21	Quarter-final	World Professional Championship
	v Charlton	37-32	Semi-final	World Professional Championship
	v Higgins	32-37	Final	World Professional Championship
1973	v David Taylor	16-5	2nd round	World Professional Championship
	v Williams	16-7	Quarter-final	World Professional Championship
	v Reardon	22-23	Semi-final	World Professional Championship
	v Higgins	8-2	Semi-final	Norwich Union Open
	v Pulman	**8-7**	**Final**	**Norwich Union Open**
1974	v Mans	13-15	2nd round	World Professional Championship
	v Edmonds	5-0	1st round	Norwich Union Open
	v Miles	5-2	Quarter-final	Norwich Union Open
	v Thorburn	9-7	Semi-final	Norwich Union Open
	v Reardon	**10-9**	**Final**	**Norwich Union Open**
1975	v Pulman	5-3	Quarter-final	Benson & Hedges Masters
	v Charlton	5-2	Semi-final	Benson & Hedges Masters
	v Reardon	**9-8**	**Final**	**Benson & Hedges Masters**
	v Pulman	15-10	2nd round	World Professional Championship
	v Reardon	17-19	Quarter-final	World Professional Championship
1976	v Miles	4-5	Semi-final	Benson & Hedges Masters
	v David Taylor	15-5	1st round	Embassy World Professional Championship
	v Higgins	14-15	Quarter-final	Embassy World Professional Championship
1977	v Virgo	13-9	1st round	Embassy World Professional Championship
	v Reardon	13-6	Quarter-final	Embassy World Professional Championship
	v Pulman	18-16	Semi-final	Embassy World Professional Championship
	v Thorburn	**25-21**	**Final**	**Embassy World Professional Championship**
	v Mountjoy	3-5	2nd round	Super Crystalate UK Championship
1978	v Thorburn	3-5	Semi-final	Benson & Hedges Masters
	v Mountjoy	**5-3**	**Final**	**Benson & Hedges Irish Masters**
	v Mans	8-13	1st round	Embassy World Professional Championship
	v Andrewartha	8-9	1st round	Coral UK Championship
1979	v Williams	6-2	Semi-final	Holsten Lager International
	v Miles	**11-7**	**Final**	**Holsten Lager International**
	v Mountjoy	0-5	Quarter-final	Benson & Hedges Masters
	v Werbeniuk	11-13	1st round	Embassy World Professional Championship
	v Werbeniuk	8-9	3rd round	Coral UK Championship

1980	v Charlton	5-2	Quarter-final	Benson & Hedges Masters
	v Griffiths	0-5	Semi-final	Benson & Hedges Masters
	v Stevens	8-13	2nd round	Embassy World Professional Championship
	v Wildman	7-9	1st round	Coral UK Championship
1981	v Dennis Taylor	5-2	1st round	Benson & Hedges Masters
	v Reardon	5-1	Quarter-final	Benson & Hedges Masters
	v Griffiths	5-6	Semi-final	Benson & Hedges Masters
	v Houlihan	9-1	1st round	John Courage English Professional
	v S. Davis	7-9	2nd round	John Courage English Professional
	v Edmonds	10-9	1st round	Embassy World Professional Championship
	v Reardon	11-13	2nd round	Embassy World Professional Championship
	v Edmonds	5-3	2nd round	Jameson International
	v Griffiths	2-5	3rd round	Jameson International
	v Johnson	5-9	2nd round	Coral UK Championship
1982	v S. Davis	2-5	1st round	Lada Classic
	v Mountjoy	4-5	1st round	Benson & Hedges Masters
	v Meo	3-5	1st round	Benson & Hedges Irish Masters
	v Dunning	10-4	1st round	Embassy World Professional Championship
	v Thorne	5-13	2nd round	Embassy World Professional Championship
	v Edmonds	5-2	1st round	Jameson International
	v Virgo	4-5	2nd round	Jameson International
	v G. Foulds	5-1	1st round	Professional Players Tournament
	v Martin	5-3	2nd round	Professional Players Tournament
	v Virgo	1-5	3rd round	Professional Players Tournament
	v Sinclair	9-8	1st round	Coral UK Championship
	v Knowles	9-6	2nd round	Coral UK Championship
	v Higgins	5-9	Quarter-final	Coral UK Championship
1983	v Reardon	5-3	1st round	Lada Classic
	v David Taylor	5-2	Quarter-final	Lada Classic
	v S. Davis	4-5	Semi-final	Lada Classic
	v Hallett	10-7	1st round	Embassy World Professional Championship
	v Charlton	11-13	2nd round	Embassy World Professional Championship
	v Higgins	2-3	1st round	Winfield Masters
	v Morgan	5-1	1st round	Jameson International
	v Knowles	5-4	2nd round	Jameson International
	v Griffiths	4-5	Quarter-final	Jameson International
	v Black	5-2	1st round	Professional Players Tournament
	v Thorne	1-5	2nd round	Professional Players Tournament
	v Dunning	9-7	1st round	Coral UK Championship
	v Meo	5-9	2nd round	Coral UK Championship
1984	v Johnson	5-4	Qualifying	Lada Classic
	v S. Davis	1-5	1st round	Lada Classic
	v Thorburn	5-4	1st round	Benson & Hedges Masters
	v Griffiths	4-5	Quarter-final	Benson & Hedges Masters
	v Miles	10-3	1st round	Embassy World Professional Championship
	v S. Davis	5-13	2nd round	Embassy World Professional Championship
	v S. Francisco	2-5	1st round	Jameson International
	v P. Francisco	2-5	1st round	Rothmans Grand Prix
	v Johnson	6-9	1st round	Coral UK Open
1985	v King	2-5	1st round	Mercantile Credit Classic

	v Charlton	5-3	1st round	Benson & Hedges Masters
	v White	2-5	Quarter-final	Benson & Hedges Masters
	v Medati	4-9	1st round	Tolly Cobbold English Professional Championship
	v Jonik	6-0	1st round	Dulux British Open
	v Miles	3-5	2nd round	Dulux British Open
	v Parrott	3-10	1st round	Embassy World Professional Championship
	v Foldvari	5-4	3rd round	Goya Matchroom Trophy
	v Griffiths	1-5	4th round	Goya Matchroom Trophy
	v B. Harris	2-5	3rd round	Rothmans Grand Prix
	v V. Harris	9-5	3rd round	Coral UK Open
	v Knowles	7-9	4th round	Coral UK Open
	v S. Davis	2-5	1st round	Kit Kat
1986	v Cripsey	1-5	3rd round	Mercantile Credit Classic
	v Houlihan	9-5	3rd round	Tolly Cobbold English Professional Championship
	v Johnson	7-9	4th round	Tolly Cobbold English Professional Championship
	v Browne	0-5	3rd round	Dulux British Open
	v Higgins	7-10	1st round	Embassy World Professional Championship

KIRK STEVENS (Canada)

Born 17.8.58
Turned professional 1978
World ranking 9 (5)

At the end of the 1983–84 season, Stevens was ranked No. 4 but dropped one place in 1984–85 despite reaching the final of the Dulux British Open. Last season he dropped still further to ninth as he struggled to cope with much publicised personal problems including the aftermath of the drug addiction for which he was effectively treated in a Toronto clinic in the summer of 1985. His best performance was to reach the quarter-finals of the Embassy World Championship.

1979	v Amdor	9-1	Prelim	Embassy World Professional Championship
	v Pulman	9-0	Qualifying	Embassy World Professional Championship
	v F. Davis	8-13	1st round	Embassy World Professional Championship
1980	v Hallett	9-3	Qualifying	Embassy World Professional Championship
	v Miles	10-3	1st round	Embassy World Professional Championship
	v Spencer	13-8	2nd round	Embassy World Professional Championship
	v Charlton	13-7	Quarter-final	Embassy World Professional Championship
	v Higgins	13-16	Semi-final	Embassy World Professional Championship
1981	v F. Davis	4-5	1st round	Benson & Hedges Masters
	v David Taylor	3-5	Semi-final	Yamaha International Masters
	v Dunning	10-4	1st round	Embassy World Professional Championship
	v Dennis Taylor	11-13	2nd round	Embassy World Professional Championship
	v Thorburn	1-5	Quarter-final	Langs Supreme Scottish Masters

Kirk Stevens

	v Meadowcroft	5-1	2nd round	Jameson International
	v David Taylor	0-5	3rd round	Jameson International
	v Griffiths	0-5	1st round	Northern Ireland Classic
	v Hallett	9-4	2nd round	Coral UK Championship
	v Werbeniuk	7-9	3rd round	Coral UK Championship
1982	v Fitzmaurice	10-4	1st round	Embassy World Professional Championship
	v Fagan	13-7	2nd round	Embassy World Professional Championship
	v White	9-13	Quarter-final	Embassy World Professional Championship
	v Watterson	5-3	1st round	Jameson International
	v Mans	5-2	2nd round	Jameson International
	v Griffiths	5-3	Quarter-final	Jameson International
	v Knowles	3-9	Semi-final	Jameson International
	v E. Hughes	5-2	1st round	Professional Players Tournament
	v Johnson	1-5	2nd round	Professional Players Tournament
1983	v Knowles	5-0	1st round	Lada Classic
	v Thorburn	5-3	Quarter-final	Lada Classic
	v Werbeniuk	2-5	Semi-final	Lada Classic
	v Griffiths	3-5	1st round	Benson & Hedges Masters
	v Fisher	10-2	1st round	Embassy World Professional Championship
	v Mans	13-3	2nd round	Embassy World Professional Championship
	v Thorburn	12-13	Quarter-final	Embassy World Professional Championship
	v Thorburn	2-5	Semi-final	Winfield Masters
	v Edmonds	5-1	1st round	Professional Players Tournament
	v Murphy	5-1	2nd round	Professional Players Tournament
	v Wildman	5-0	3rd round	Professional Players Tournament
	v Meo	3-5	Quarter-final	Professional Players Tournament
1984	v E. McLaughlin	5-4	Qualifying	Lada Classic
	v Macleod	5-1	1st round	Lada Classic
	v Meo	2-5	Quarter-final	Lada Classic
	v David Taylor	5-1	1st round	Benson & Hedges Masters
	v S. Davis	5-3	Quarter-final	Benson & Hedges Masters
	v White	4-6	Semi-final	Benson & Hedges Masters
	v Charlton	5-3	1st round	Tolly Cobbold Classic
	v S. Davis	4-5	Semi-final	Tolly Cobbold Classic
	v Sinclair	10-1	1st round	Embassy World Professional Championship
	v David Taylor	13-10	2nd round	Embassy World Professional Championship
	v Reardon	13-2	Quarter-final	Embassy World Professional Championship
	v White	14-16	Semi-final	Embassy World Professional Championship
	v Meo	1-5	Quarter-final	Winfield Australian Masters
	v Higgins	2-5	1st round	Langs Supreme Scottish Masters
	v White	0-5	1st round	Carlsberg Challenge
	v Gauvreau	1-5	1st round	Jameson International
	v Chappel	5-3	1st round	Rothmans Grand Prix
	v Williams	5-3	2nd round	Rothmans Grand Prix
	v Hallett	5-3	3rd round	Rothmans Grand Prix
	v Dennis Taylor	2-5	Quarter-final	Rothmans Grand Prix
	v Chappel	9-7	1st round	Coral UK Open
	v Johnson	9-2	2nd round	Coral UK Open
	v Knowles	9-7	Quarter-final	Coral UK Open
	v S. Davis	2-9	Semi-final	Coral UK Open

1985	v Medati	5-4	1st round	Mercantile Credit Classic
	v Thorne	1-5	2nd round	Mercantile Credit Classic
	v Meo	2-5	1st round	Benson & Hedges Masters
	v Gauvreau	6-3	1st round	Dulux British Open
	v Wildman	5-2	2nd round	Dulux British Open
	v Miles	5-2	3rd round	Dulux British Open
	v Dennis Taylor	5-2	Quarter-final	Dulux British Open
	v S. Davis	9-7	Semi-final	Dulux British Open
	v S. Francisco	9-12	Final	Dulux British Open
	v Higgins	3-5	Quarter-final	Benson & Hedges Irish Masters
	v Edmonds	10-8	1st round	Embassy World Professional Championship
	v Parrott	6-13	2nd round	Embassy World Professional Championship
	v Chaperon	4-6	Quarter-final	Canadian Professional Championship
	v Chappel	3-5	3rd round	Goya Matchroom Trophy
	v Watson	5-0	3rd round	Rothmans Grand Prix
	v Miles	5-2	4th round	Rothmans Grand Prix
	v Longworth	5-3	5th round	Rothmans Grand Prix
	v Knowles	4-5	Quarter-final	Rothmans Grand Prix
	v Newbury	9-7	3rd round	Coral UK Open
	v Hallett	9-5	4th round	Coral UK Open
	v Williams	9-7	5th round	Coral UK Open
	v Dennis Taylor	1-9	Quarter-final	Coral UK Open
1986	v F. Davis	2-5	3rd round	Mercantile Credit Classic
	v Reardon	5-1	1st round	BCE Belgian Classic
	v Higgins	5-4	Semi-final	BCE Belgian Classic
	v Griffiths	7-9	Final	BCE Belgian Classic
	v Charlton	4-5	1st round	Benson & Hedges Masters
	v Miles	5-3	3rd round	Dulux British Open
	v Wilson	5-0	4th round	Dulux British Open
	v Thorne	4-5	5th round	Dulux British Open
	v Reynolds	10-6	1st round	Embassy World Professional Championship
	v Charlton	13-12	2nd round	Embassy World Professional Championship
	v Knowles	9-13	Quarter-final	Embassy World Professional Championship

DAVID TAYLOR (England)

Born 29.7.43
Turned professional 1968
World ranking 21 (14)

English and world amateur champion in 1968, Taylor took ten years to make a significant impact on the professional game by reaching the final of the 1978 Coral UK Championship. He has appeared in two other major finals, the 1981 Yamaha International Masters and the 1982 Jameson International, in which he beat Steve Davis in the quarter-finals, and was a world semi-finalist in 1980.

After two seasons when he did just enough to maintain his place in the top 16, Taylor last season dropped to 21st after only once reaching the last 16 of a ranking tournament.

1970	v Bennett	11-8	1st round	World Professional Championship
	v Pulman	22-39	Quarter-final	World Professional Championship
1972	v Charlton	25-31	Quarter-final	World Professional Championship
1973	v Dunning	9-4	1st round	World Professional Championship
	v Spencer	5-16	2nd round	World Professional Championship
1974	v Dunning	6-8	1st round	World Professional Championship
1975	v King	15-8	1st round	World Professional Championship
	v Higgins	2-15	2nd round	World Professional Championship
1976	v Greaves	8-1	Qualifying	Embassy World Professional Championship
	v Jack Rea	8-7	Qualifying	Embassy World Professional Championship
	v Spencer	5-15	1st round	Embassy World Professional Championship
1977	v Greaves	11-0	Qualifying	Embassy World Professional Championship
	v Charlton	5-13	1st round	Embassy World Professional Championship
	v Greaves	5-4	1st round	Super Crystalate UK Championship
	v Higgins	4-5	2nd round	Super Crystalate UK Championship
1978	v Morgan	9-7	Qualifying	Embassy World Professional Championship
	v Miles	10-13	1st round	Embassy World Professional Championship
	v Parkin	9-2	Qualifying	Coral UK Championship
	v Fagan	9-7	1st round	Coral UK Championship
	v Virgo	9-2	Quarter-final	Coral UK Championship
	v Higgins	9-5	Semi-final	Coral UK Championship
	v Mountjoy	9-15	Final	Coral UK Championship
1979	v Fagan	5-4	1st round	Benson & Hedges Masters
	v Reardon	2-5	Quarter-final	Benson & Hedges Masters
	v Dunning	9-8	Qualifying	Embassy World Professional Championship
	v Higgins	5-13	1st round	Embassy World Professional Championship
	v Meo	7-9	2nd round	Coral UK Championship
1980	v Edmonds	10-3	1st round	Embassy World Professional Championship
	v F. Davis	13-5	2nd round	Embassy World Professional Championship
	v Reardon	13-11	Quarter-final	Embassy World Professional Championship
	v Thorburn	7-16	Semi-final	Embassy World Professional Championship
	v Williams	7-9	2nd round	Coral UK Championship
1981	v Stevens	5-3	Semi-final	Yamaha International Masters
	v S. Davis	6-9	Final	Yamaha International Masters
	v Dunning	8-9	1st round	John Courage English Professional
	v Wilson	10-6	1st round	Embassy World Professional Championship
	v F. Davis	13-3	2nd round	Embassy World Professional Championship
	v Thorburn	6-13	Quarter-final	Embassy World Professional Championship
	v Stevens	5-0	3rd round	Jameson International
	v S. Davis	1-5	Quarter-final	Jameson International
	v Higgins	5-9	3rd round	Coral UK Championship
1982	v Reardon	1-5	1st round	Lada Classic
	v Meo	2-5	1st round	Benson & Hedges Masters
	v Fagan	9-10	1st round	Embassy World Professional Championship
	v Fisher	5-1	1st round	Jameson International
	v Werbeniuk	5-2	2nd round	Jameson International
	v S. Davis	5-3	Quarter-final	Jameson International
	v Virgo	9-5	Semi-final	Jameson International
	v Knowles	6-9	Final	Jameson International
	v Anderson	5-1	1st round	Professional Players Tournament

Year	Opponent	Score	Round	Tournament
	v Dennis Taylor	1-5	2nd round	Professional Players Tournament
	v Dodd	9-7	1st round	Coral UK Championship
	v Meo	6-9	2nd round	Coral UK Championship
1983	v White	5-3	1st round	Lada Classic
	v Spencer	2-5	Quarter-final	Lada Classic
	v White	2-5	1st round	Benson & Hedges Masters
	v Charlton	4-5	1st round	Benson & Hedges Irish Masters
	v Meadowcroft	10-2	1st round	Embassy World Professional Championship
	v Werbeniuk	10-13	2nd round	Embassy World Professional Championship
	v Donnelly	3-5	1st round	Jameson International
	v Morgan	5-3	1st round	Professional Players Tournament
	v Wildman	3-5	2nd round	Professional Players Tournament
	v N. Foulds	9-4	1st round	Coral UK Championship
	v Johnson	3-9	2nd round	Coral UK Championship
1984	v Macleod	4-5	Qualifying	Lada Classic
	v Stevens	1-5	1st round	Benson & Hedges Masters
	v Gauvreau	10-5	1st round	Embassy World Professional Championship
	v Stevens	10-13	2nd round	Embassy World Professional Championship
	v Charlton	4-5	Quarter-final	Winfield Australian Masters
	v W. Jones	5-4	1st round	Jameson International
	v S. Davis	1-5	2nd round	Jameson International
	v O'Kane	5-1	1st round	Rothmans Grand Prix
	v John Rea	5-1	2nd round	Rothmans Grand Prix
	v S. Davis	1-5	3rd round	Rothmans Grand Prix
	v Macleod	9-6	1st round	Coral UK Open
	v Reardon	4-9	2nd round	Coral UK Open
1985	v Longworth	4-5	1st round	Mercantile Credit Classic
	v Reardon	1-5	1st round	Benson & Hedges Masters
	v Cripsey	9-5	1st round	Tolly Cobbold English Professional Championship
	v Parrott	9-6	2nd round	Tolly Cobbold English Professional Championship
	v Knowles	2-9	Quarter-final	Tolly Cobbold English Professional Championship
	v Bradley	3-6	1st round	Dulux British Open
	v O'Kane	10-4	1st round	Embassy World Professional Championship
	v S. Davis	4-13	2nd round	Embassy World Professional Championship
	v White	0-4	1st round	Winfield Australian Masters
	v T. Jones	5-4	3rd round	Goya Matchroom Trophy
	v Werbeniuk	5-4	4th round	Goya Matchroom Trophy
	v N. Foulds	4-5	5th round	Goya Matchroom Trophy
	v Newbury	5-2	3rd round	Rothmans Grand Prix
	v Longworth	1-5	4th round	Rothmans Grand Prix
	v Mikkelsen	9-6	3rd round	Coral UK Open
	v Campbell	9-4	4th round	Coral UK Open
	v Knowles	7-9	5th round	Coral UK Open
1986	v Gauvreau	3-5	3rd round	Mercantile Credit Classic
	v S. Davis	4-5	1st round	Benson & Hedges Masters
	v Edmonds	6-9	3rd round	Tolly Cobbold English Professional Championship

	v Medati	1-5	3rd round	Dulux British Open
	v E. Hughes	7-10	1st round	Embassy World Professional Championship

DENNIS TAYLOR (Northern Ireland)

Born 19.1.49
Turned professional 1971
World ranking 3 (4)

Although Taylor has always been regarded as a good player, it was not until the 1985–86 season – his 13th as a professional – that he proved himself a winner. It took a traumatic bereavement to give this transformation impetus. The sudden death of his mother in Coalisland, Co Tyrone, caused Taylor to withdraw from the quarter-finals of the Jameson International and it was only through family pressure that he competed in the next event on the circuit, the Rothmans Grand Prix. Carried by an emotional wave, he won that event by beating Cliff Thorburn 10-2 in the final and succeeded in uniting his family in joy and alleviating their grief.

As often happens after a first major victory, Taylor's form deteriorated for a while but, just prior to the Embassy World Championship, he regained the Irish Professional Championship and then proceeded steadily towards the world final without a close match. Once there, he lost the first eight frames to Steve Davis but pulled up to trail only 7-9 overnight and on the second day levelled the match at 15-15 before going two down with three to play at 15-17. He forced the match to a deciding frame, providing an unforgettable climax to one of the greatest matches ever seen. A record 18.5 million viewers watched on BBC2 as, well past midnight, Taylor needed the last four colours to win and Davis only one. Eventually, Taylor potted them all to take the world title at his twelfth attempt.

Last season, Taylor started well enough, reaching the semi-finals of the first three ranking tournaments and winning both the Kit Kat and BCE Canadian Masters but after Christmas won only one match. He was beaten 10-6 by Mike Hallett in his first match in defence of his world title.

1973	v Thorburn	8-9	1st round	World Professional Championship
1974	v Higgins	1-5	1st round	Norwich Union Open
1975	v Mans	15-12	1st round	World Professional Championship
	v F. Davis	15-14	2nd round	World Professional Championship
	v G. Owen	19-9	Quarter-final	World Professional Championship
	v Charlton	12-19	Semi-final	World Professional Championship
1976	v G. Owen	15-9	1st round	Embassy World Professional Championship
	v Reardon	2-15	Quarter-final	Embassy World Professional Championship
1977	v Karnehm	11-0	Qualifying	Embassy World Professional Championship
	v Mans	13-11	1st round	Embassy World Professional Championship

	v Mountjoy	13-11	Quarter-final	Embassy World Professional Championship
	v Thorburn	16-18	Semi-final	Embassy World Professional Championship
1978	v F. Davis	9-13	1st round	Embassy World Professional Championship
	v Mountjoy	4-9	1st round	Coral UK Championship
1979	v S. Davis	13-11	1st round	Embassy World Professional Championship
	v Reardon	13-8	Quarter-final	Embassy World Professional Championship
	v Virgo	19-12	Semi-final	Embassy World Professional Championship
	v Griffiths	16-24	Final	Embassy World Professional Championship
	v Thorne	9-8	3rd round	Coral UK Championship
	v Fagan	9-6	Quarter-final	Coral UK Championship
	v Virgo	4-9	Semi-final	Coral UK Championship
1980	v Reardon	3-5	Quarter-final	Benson & Hedges Masters
	v Wych	10-13	2nd round	Embassy World Professional Championship
	v Sinclair	9-6	2nd round	Coral UK Championship
	v Griffiths	2-9	Quarter-final	Coral UK Championship
1981	v Spencer	2-5	1st round	Benson & Hedges Masters
	v S. Davis	2-5	Semi-final	Yamaha International Masters
	v Stevens	13-11	2nd round	Embassy World Professional Championship
	v Mountjoy	8-13	Quarter-final	Embassy World Professional Championship
	v Williams	5-1	3rd round	Jameson International
	v Virgo	5-2	Quarter-final	Jameson International
	v Martin	9-1	Semi-final	Jameson International
	v S. Davis	0-9	Final	Jameson International
	v Mountjoy	4-5	1st round	Northern Ireland Classic
	v White	5-9	3rd round	Coral UK Championship
1982	v Higgins	1-5	1st round	Lada Classic
	v Reardon	3-5	1st round	Benson & Hedges Masters
	v Knowles	5-2	Semi-final	Tolly Cobbold Classic
	v S. Davis	3-8	Final	Tolly Cobbold Classic
	v Murphy	6-0	Semi-final	Irish Professional Championship
	v Higgins	**16-13**	**Final**	**Irish Professional Championship**
	v Sheehan	5-3	1st round	Benson & Hedges Irish Masters
	v Reardon	4-5	Quarter-final	Benson & Hedges Irish Masters
	v S. Francisco	7-10	1st round	Embassy World Professional Championship
	v White	5-4	1st round	Langs Supreme Scottish Masters
	v S. Davis	1-6	Semi-final	Langs Supreme Scottish Masters
	v Wildman	5-2	1st round	Jameson International
	v Thorburn	5-2	2nd round	Jameson International
	v Virgo	3-5	Quarter-final	Jameson International
	v Edmonds	5-4	1st round	Professional Players Tournament
	v David Taylor	5-1	2nd round	Professional Players Tournament
	v White	3-5	3rd round	Professional Players Tournament
	v Meadowcroft	9-7	1st round	Coral UK Championship
	v Griffiths	7-9	2nd round	Coral UK Championship
1983	v S. Davis	2-5	1st round	Lada Classic
	v S. Davis	1-5	Semi-final	Tolly Cobbold Classic
	v Kelly	6-0	Quarter-final	Irish Professional Championship
	v Fagan	6-1	Semi-final	Irish Professional Championship
	v Higgins	11-16	Final	Irish Professional Championship
	v White	4-5	1st round	Benson & Hedges Irish Masters

Dennis Taylor

	v S. Francisco	10-9	1st round	Embassy World Professional Championship
	v S. Davis	11-13	2nd round	Embassy World Professional Championship
	v Reynolds	5-3	1st round	Jameson International
	v Thorburn	3-5	2nd round	Jameson International
	v Scott	4-5	1st round	Professional Players Tournament
	v Murphy	9-6	1st round	Coral UK Championship
	v White	4-9	2nd round	Coral UK Championship
1984	v Hallett	4-5	Qualifying	Lada Classic
	v Knowles	2-5	1st round	Benson & Hedges Masters
	v E. Hughes	5-1	1st round	Benson & Hedges Irish Masters
	v Thorburn	5-2	Quarter-final	Benson & Hedges Irish Masters
	v Griffiths	4-5	Semi-final	Benson & Hedges Irish Masters
	v Johnson	10-1	1st round	Embassy World Professional Championship
	v Parrott	13-11	2nd round	Embassy World Professional Championship
	v Mountjoy	13-8	Quarter-final	Embassy World Professional Championship
	v S. Davis	9-16	Semi-final	Embassy World Professional Championship
	v Fowler	5-0	1st round	Jameson International
	v Watchorn	5-1	1st round	Rothmans Grand Prix
	v Virgo	5-3	2nd round	Rothmans Grand Prix
	v Reardon	5-3	3rd round	Rothmans Grand Prix
	v Stevens	5-2	Quarter-final	Rothmans Grand Prix
	v N. Foulds	9-3	Semi-final	Rothmans Grand Prix
	v Thorburn	**10-2**	**Final**	**Rothmans Grand Prix**
	v King	9-5	1st round	Coral UK Open
	v Knowles	2-9	2nd round	Coral UK Open
1985	v Williams	3-5	1st round	Mercantile Credit Classic
	v Thorburn	3-5	1st round	Benson & Hedges Masters
	v Scott	6-2	1st round	Dulux British Open
	v Parrott	5-2	2nd round	Dulux British Open
	v Newbury	5-3	3rd round	Dulux British Open
	v Stevens	2-5	Quarter-final	Dulux British Open
	v Charlton	4-5	1st round	Benson & Hedges Irish Masters
	v Jack Rea	6-0	Quarter-final	Irish Professional Championship
	v E. Hughes	6-5	Semi-final	Irish Professional Championship
	v Higgins	**10-5**	**Final**	**Irish Professional Championship**
	v S. Francisco	10-2	1st round	Embassy World Professional Championship
	v Charlton	13-6	2nd round	Embassy World Professional Championship
	v Thorburn	13-5	Quarter-final	Embassy World Professional Championship
	v Knowles	16-5	Semi-final	Embassy World Professional Championship
	v S. Davis	**18-17**	**Final**	**Embassy World Professional Championship**
	v Thorne	3-5	1st round	Langs Scottish Masters
	v Cripsey	5-1	3rd round	Goya Matchroom Trophy
	v B. Harris	5-3	4th round	Goya Matchroom Trophy
	v Higgins	5-1	5th round	Goya Matchroom Trophy
	v Parrott	5-1	Quarter-final	Goya Matchroom Trophy
	v Thorburn	5-9	Semi-final	Goya Matchroom Trophy
	v West	5-1	3rd round	Rothmans Grand Prix
	v Williams	5-2	4th round	Rothmans Grand Prix
	v Meo	5-3	5th round	Rothmans Grand Prix
	v Wilson	5-2	Quarter-final	Rothmans Grand Prix
	v Knowles	9-6	Semi-final	Rothmans Grand Prix

	v S. Davis	9-10	Final	Rothmans Grand Prix
	v Parrott	5-1	1st round	BCE Canadian Masters
	v Reardon	8-3	Semi-final	BCE Canadian Masters
	v S. Davis	**9-5**	**Final**	**BCE Canadian Masters**
	v Jim Bear	9-3	3rd round	Coral UK Open
	v Cripsey	9-2	4th round	Coral UK Open
	v N. Foulds	9-5	5th round	Coral UK Open
	v Stevens	9-1	Quarter-final	Coral UK Open
	v Thorne	7-9	Semi-final	Coral UK Open
	v F. Davis	5-0	1st round	Kit Kat
	v Griffiths	6-4	Semi-final	Kit Kat
	v S. Davis	**9-5**	**Final**	**Kit Kat**
1986	v Fitzmaurice	5-1	3rd round	Mercantile Credit Classic
	v Reynolds	5-4	4th round	Mercantile Credit Classic
	v Higgins	4-5	5th round	Mercantile Credit Classic
	v Higgins	1-5	1st round	BCE Belgian Classic
	v Mountjoy	5-2	1st round	Benson & Hedges Masters
	v White	3-5	Quarter-final	Benson & Hedges Masters
	v Bales	4-5	3rd round	Dulux British Open
	v Thorne	2-5	Quarter-final	Benson & Hedges Irish Masters
	v Hallett	6-10	1st round	Embassy World Professional Championship
	v Kelly	6-1	Quarter-final	Strongbow Irish Professional Championship
	v Murphy	6-3	Semi-final	Strongbow Irish Professional Championship
	v Higgins	**10-7**	**Final**	**Strongbow Irish Professional Championship**

CLIFF THORBURN (Canada)

Born 16.1.48
Turned professional 1973
World ranking 2 (2)

Winner of the Benson and Hedges Masters for the third time in four years, Thorburn also won the Langs Scottish Masters and the Goya Matchroom Trophy and reached the final of the Mercantile Credit Classic in confirming his status as No. 2 in the world.

The first Canadian to win the world title, in 1980, and still the only overseas player to do so, Thorburn also reached the 1977 and 1983 world finals, the latter by winning a series of epic battles which reveal his great virtues of concentration, patience and mental stamina at their best. It was also during this event that he became the first player to make a 147 maximum in the World Championship.

1973	v Dennis Taylor	9-8	1st round	World Professional Championship
	v Williams	15-16	2nd round	World Professional Championship
1974	v Morgan	4-8	1st round	World Professional Championship
	v F. Davis	5-4	1st round	Norwich Union Open
	v Pulman	5-3	Quarter-final	Norwich Union Open
	v Spencer	7-9	Semi-final	Norwich Union Open
1975	v Pulman	3-5	1st round	Benson & Hedges Masters
	v Morgan	15-6	1st round	World Professional Championship

Year	Opponent	Score	Round	Event
	v Miles	15-2	2nd round	World Professional Championship
	v Charlton	12-19	Quarter-final	World Professional Championship
1976	v Higgins	14-15	1st round	Embassy World Professional Championship
1977	v Ross	11-0	Qualifying	Embassy World Professional Championship
	v Williams	13-6	1st round	Embassy World Professional Championship
	v Charlton	13-12	Quarter-final	Embassy World Professional Championship
	v Dennis Taylor	18-16	Semi-final	Embassy World Professional Championship
	v Spencer	21-25	Final	Embassy World Professional Championship
1978	v Mountjoy	4-2	Quarter-final	Benson & Hedges Masters
	v Spencer	5-3	Semi-final	Benson & Hedges Masters
	v Higgins	5-7	Final	Benson & Hedges Masters
	v Houlihan	13-8	1st round	Embassy World Professional Championship
	v Charlton	12-13	Quarter-final	Embassy World Professional Championship
1979	v Mans	4-5	Quarter-final	Benson & Hedges Masters
	v Virgo	10-13	1st round	Embassy World Professional Championship
1980	v Virgo	5-3	1st round	Benson & Hedges Masters
	v Griffiths	3-5	Quarter-final	Benson & Hedges Masters
	v Mountjoy	13-10	2nd round	Embassy World Professional Championship
	v Wych	13-6	Quarter-final	Embassy World Professional Championship
	v David Taylor	16-7	Semi-final	Embassy World Professional Championship
	v Higgins	**18-16**	**Final**	**Embassy World Professional Championship**
1981	v Mans	5-4	Quarter-final	Benson & Hedges Masters
	v Higgins	5-6	Semi-final	Benson & Hedges Masters
	v Miles	13-2	2nd round	Embassy World Professional Championship
	v David Taylor	13-6	Quarter-final	Embassy World Professional Championship
	v S. Davis	10-16	Semi-final	Embassy World Professional Championship
	v Stevens	5-1	Quarter-final	Langs Supreme Scottish Masters
	v Higgins	6-2	Semi-final	Langs Supreme Scottish Masters
	v White	4-9	Final	Langs Supreme Scottish Masters
	v Miles	0-5	3rd round	Jameson International
	v White	2-5	1st round	Northern Ireland Classic
	v Meo	6-9	3rd round	Coral UK Championship
1982	v Griffiths	1-5	1st round	Lada Classic
	v Meo	0-5	Quarter-final	Benson & Hedges Masters
	v Higgins	4-5	Quarter-final	Benson & Hedges Irish Masters
	v White	4-10	1st round	Embassy World Professional Championship
	v Scott	5-1	1st round	Jameson International
	v Dennis Taylor	2-5	2nd round	Jameson International
	v Medati	5-1	1st round	Professional Players Tournament
	v Everton	5-2	2nd round	Professional Players Tournament
	v Werbeniuk	2-5	3rd round	Professional Players Tournament
1983	v Wilson	5-3	1st round	Lada Classic
	v Stevens	3-5	Quarter-final	Lada Classic
	v Johnson	5-2	1st round	Benson & Hedges Masters
	v Griffiths	5-3	Quarter-final	Benson & Hedges Masters
	v Charlton	6-5	Semi-final	Benson & Hedges Masters
	v Reardon	**9-7**	**Final**	**Benson & Hedges Masters**
	v Campbell	10-5	1st round	Embassy World Professional Championship
	v Griffiths	13-12	2nd round	Embassy World Professional Championship
	v Stevens	13-12	Quarter-final	Embassy World Professional Championship
	v Knowles	16-15	Semi-final	Embassy World Professional Championship

	v S. Davis	6-18	Final	Embassy World Professional Championship
	v Stevens	5-2	Semi-final	Winfield Masters
	v Werbeniuk	**7-3**	**Final**	**Winfield Masters**
	v Griffiths	5-1	1st round	Langs Supreme Scottish Masters
	v Knowles	2-6	Semi-final	Langs Supreme Scottish Masters
	v Sinclair	5-0	1st round	Jameson International
	v Dennis Taylor	5-3	2nd round	Jameson International
	v Mountjoy	5-2	Quarter-final	Jameson International
	v Griffiths	9-8	Semi-final	Jameson International
	v S. Davis	4-9	Final	Jameson International
	v V. Harris	5-1	1st round	Professional Players Tournament
	v Meadowcroft	5-1	2nd round	Professional Players Tournament
	v Wilson	5-3	3rd round	Professional Players Tournament
	v Johnson	1-5	Quarter-final	Professional Players Tournament
1984	v S. Francisco	1-5	Qualifying	Lada Classic
	v Spencer	4-5	1st round	Benson & Hedges Masters
	v Dennis Taylor	2-5	Quarter-final	Benson & Hedges Irish Masters
	v Meo	5-4	1st round	Tolly Cobbold Classic
	v Knowles	3-5	Semi-final	Tolly Cobbold Classic
	v Morra	10-3	1st round	Embassy World Professional Championship
	v Thorne	13-11	2nd round	Embassy World Professional Championship
	v White	8-13	Quarter-final	Embassy World Professional Championship
	v S. Davis	2-5	1st round	Langs Supreme Scottish Masters
	v Virgo	0-5	1st round	Jameson International
	v Rigitano	5-4	1st round	Rothmans Grand Prix
	v Campbell	5-1	2nd round	Rothmans Grand Prix
	v Meo	5-4	3rd round	Rothmans Grand Prix
	v Mountjoy	5-3	Quarter-final	Rothmans Grand Prix
	v S. Davis	9-7	Semi-final	Rothmans Grand Prix
	v Dennis Taylor	2-10	Final	Rothmans Grand Prix
	v J. McLaughlin	9-4	1st round	Coral UK Open
	v Wilson	9-3	2nd round	Coral UK Open
	v Reardon	9-8	Quarter-final	Coral UK Open
	v Higgins	7-9	Semi-final	Coral UK Open
1985	v Scott	5-1	1st round	Mercantile Credit Classic
	v Longworth	5-3	2nd round	Mercantile Credit Classic
	v Griffiths	5-4	Quarter-final	Mercantile Credit Classic
	v Johnson	9-2	Semi-final	Mercantile Credit Classic
	v Thorne	8-13	Final	Mercantile Credit Classic
	v Dennis Taylor	5-3	1st round	Benson & Hedges Masters
	v Reardon	5-0	Quarter-final	Benson & Hedges Masters
	v White	6-4	Semi-final	Benson & Hedges Masters
	v Mountjoy	**9-6**	**Final**	**Benson & Hedges Masters**
	v Rigitano	6-3	1st round	Dulux British Open
	v Reynolds	5-3	2nd round	Dulux British Open
	v Higgins	2-5	3rd round	Dulux British Open
	v White	3-5	Quarter-final	Benson & Hedges Irish Masters
	v Hallett	10-8	1st round	Embassy World Professional Championship
	v Werbeniuk	13-3	2nd round	Embassy World Professional Championship
	v Dennis Taylor	5-13	Quarter-final	Embassy World Professional Championship

Cliff Thorburn

	v Caggianello	6-2	Quarter-final	Canadian Professional Championship
	v Wych	6-5	Semi-final	Canadian Professional Championship
	v Chaperon	**6-4**	**Final**	**Canadian Professional Championship**
	v Higgins	4-5	Semi-final	Carlsberg Trophy
	v Macleod	5-1	1st round	Langs Scottish Masters
	v S. Francisco	6-0	Semi-final	Langs Scottish Masters
	v Thorne	**9-7**	**Final**	**Langs Scottish Masters**
	v Longworth	5-3	3rd round	Goya Matchroom Trophy
	v Martin	5-3	4th round	Goya Matchroom Trophy
	v Campbell	5-0	5th round	Goya Matchroom Trophy
	v Duggan	5-2	Quarter-final	Goya Matchroom Trophy
	v Dennis Taylor	9-5	Semi-final	Goya Matchroom Trophy
	v White	**12-10**	**Final**	**Goya Matchroom Trophy**
	v Oliver	5-0	3rd round	Rothmans Grand Prix
	v Wildman	5-2	4th round	Rothmans Grand Prix
	v Johnson	5-1	5th round	Rothmans Grand Prix
	v Griffiths	5-1	Quarter-final	Rothmans Grand Prix
	v S. Davis	5-9	Semi-final	Rothmans Grand Prix
	v White	5-3	1st round	BCE Canadian Masters
	v S. Davis	1-8	Semi-final	BCE Canadian Masters
	v Dodd	9-4	3rd round	Coral UK Open
	v Parrott	9-6	4th round	Coral UK Open
	v Thorne	7-9	5th round	Coral UK Open
	v Higgins	4-5	1st round	Kit Kat
1986	v J. McLaughlin	5-1	3rd round	Mercantile Credit Classic
	v Hallett	5-3	4th round	Mercantile Credit Classic
	v Meo	5-1	5th round	Mercantile Credit Classic
	v Johnson	5-4	Quarter-final	Mercantile Credit Classic
	v Mountjoy	9-6	Semi-final	Mercantile Credit Classic
	v White	12-13	Final	Mercantile Credit Classic
	v Johnson	5-3	1st round	Benson & Hedges Masters
	v Griffiths	5-2	Quarter-final	Benson & Hedges Masters
	v Knowles	6-4	Semi-final	Benson & Hedges Masters
	v White	**9-5**	**Final**	**Benson & Hedges Masters**
	v Sheehan	5-0	3rd round	Dulux British Open
	v Wildman	5-1	4th round	Dulux British Open
	v Meo	3-5	5th round	Dulux British Open
	v E. Hughes	5-1	Quarter-final	Benson & Hedges Irish Masters
	v Thorne	4-6	Semi-final	Benson & Hedges Irish Masters
	v Werbeniuk	10-5	1st round	Embassy World Professional Championship
	v E. Hughes	13-6	2nd round	Embassy World Professional Championship
	v Thorne	13-6	Quarter-final	Embassy World Professional Championship
	v S. Davis	12-16	Semi-final	Embassy World Professional Championship

WILLIE THORNE (England)

Born 4.3.54
Turned professional 1975
World ranking 7 (11)

The 1984–85 season brought Thorne his first major title, the Mercantile Credit Classic, but also a series of defeats by players ranked beneath him, which partly explains why he rose only one place in the rankings. With Cliff Thorburn, he reached the final of the Hofmeister World Doubles Championship. They were beaten by Alex Higgins and Jimmy White.

Last season, Thorne reached the finals of two ranking events, the Coral UK Open and Dulux British Open but on both occasions lost to Steve Davis. However, he did rise from 11th to 7th in the rankings.

1976	v Condo	8-3	Qualifying	Embassy World Professional Championship
	v Meadowcroft	5-8	Qualifying	Embassy World Professional Championship
1977	v Bennett	11-4	Qualifying	Embassy World Professional Championship
	v Miles	4-13	1st round	Embassy World Professional Championship
	v Bennett	5-1	1st round	Super Crystalate UK Championship
	v Williams	5-4	2nd round	Super Crystalate UK Championship
	v Mountjoy	4-5	Quarter-final	Super Crystalate UK Championship
1978	v Williams	9-3	Qualifying	Embassy World Professional Championship
	v Charlton	12-13	1st round	Embassy World Professional Championship
	v Bennett	9-4	Qualifying	Coral UK Championship
	v Reardon	9-6	1st round	Coral UK Championship
	v Miles	1-9	Quarter-final	Coral UK Championship
1979	v Jim Charlton	9-3	Prelim	Embassy World Professional Championship
	v Virgo	8-9	Qualifying	Embassy World Professional Championship
	v Andrewartha	9-4	2nd round	Coral UK Championship
	v Dennis Taylor	8-9	3rd round	Coral UK Championship
1980	v Jack Rea	9-1	Qualifying	Embassy World Professional Championship
	v Werbeniuk	9-10	1st round	Embassy World Professional Championship
	v Meadowcroft	9-1	1st round	Coral UK Championship
	v Higgins	7-9	2nd round	Coral UK Championship
1981	v Wildman	9-2	1st round	John Courage English Professional
	v Dunning	9-0	2nd round	John Courage English Professional
	v Meo	8-9	Semi-final	John Courage English Professional
	v Morra	9-5	Qualifying	Embassy World Professional Championship
	v Greaves	9-3	Qualifying	Embassy World Professional Championship
	v Mountjoy	6-10	1st round	Embassy World Professional Championship
	v Medati	9-6	Qualifying	Coral UK Championship
	v Edmonds	9-4	2nd round	Coral UK Championship
	v S. Davis	2-9	3rd round	Coral UK Championship
1982	v Roscoe	9-1	Qualifying	Embassy World Professional Championship
	v Griffiths	10-6	1st round	Embassy World Professional Championship
	v Spencer	13-5	2nd round	Embassy World Professional Championship
	v Higgins	10-13	Quarter-final	Embassy World Professional Championship
	v Reynolds	3-5	1st round	Jameson International

	v Demarco	5-3	1st round	Professional Players Tournament
	v Macleod	4-5	2nd round	Professional Players Tournament
	v Wilson	7-9	1st round	Coral UK Championship
	v Virgo	10-3	1st round	Embassy World Professional Championship
	v Higgins	8-13	2nd round	Embassy World Professional Championship
1983	v Murphy	5-2	Qualifying	Jameson International
	v Virgo	5-2	1st round	Jameson International
	v Reardon	5-0	2nd round	Jameson International
	v Charlton	0-5	Quarter-final	Jameson International
	v Everton	5-1	1st round	Professional Players Tournament
	v Spencer	5-1	2nd round	Professional Players Tournament
	v Reardon	5-3	3rd round	Professional Players Tournament
	v E. Hughes	5-1	Quarter-final	Professional Players Tournament
	v Knowles	7-9	Semi-final	Professional Players Tournament
	v Wildman	9-5	1st round	Coral UK Championship
	v S. Davis	3-9	2nd round	Coral UK Championship
1984	v S. Davis	2-5	1st round	Tolly Cobbold Classic
	v Mikkelsen	10-3	Qualifying	Embassy World Professional Championship
	v Virgo	10-9	1st round	Embassy World Professional Championship
	v Thorburn	11-13	2nd round	Embassy World Professional Championship
	v Virgo	3-5	Quarter-final	Winfield Australian Masters
	v O'Kane	5-3	1st round	Jameson International
	v Gauvreau	5-3	2nd round	Jameson International
	v E. Hughes	2-5	Quarter-final	Jameson International
	v Newbury	5-2	1st round	Rothmans Grand Prix
	v Macleod	5-3	2nd round	Rothmans Grand Prix
	v N. Foulds	1-5	3rd round	Rothmans Grand Prix
	v Parrott	9-7	1st round	Coral UK Open
	v Charlton	9-7	2nd round	Coral UK Open
	v Higgins	5-9	Quarter-final	Coral UK Open
1985	v Foldvari	5-2	1st round	Mercantile Credit Classic
	v Stevens	5-1	2nd round	Mercantile Credit Classic
	v Virgo	5-1	Quarter-final	Mercantile Credit Classic
	v S. Davis	9-8	Semi-final	Mercantile Credit Classic
	v Thorburn	**13-8**	**Final**	**Mercantile Credit Classic**
	v White	2-5	1st round	Benson & Hedges Masters
	v Dodd	9-1	1st round	Tolly Cobbold English Professional Championship
	v Reynolds	6-9	2nd round	Tolly Cobbold English Professional Championship
	v Oliver	6-3	1st round	Dulux British Open
	v Macleod	0-5	2nd round	Dulux British Open
	v Fagan	6-10	1st round	Embassy World Professional Championship
	v Parrott	0-5	Quarter-final	Winfield Australian Masters
	v Dennis Taylor	5-3	1st round	Langs Scottish Masters
	v White	6-2	Semi-final	Langs Scottish Masters
	v Thorburn	7-9	Final	Langs Scottish Masters
	v Fowler	5-1	3rd round	Goya Matchroom Trophy
	v Scott	5-1	4th round	Goya Matchroom Trophy
	v Duggan	4-5	5th round	Goya Matchroom Trophy

Willie Thorne

	v W. Jones	0-5	3rd round	Rothmans Grand Prix
	v Browne	9-6	3rd round	Coral UK Open
	v Virgo	9-8	4th round	Coral UK Open
	v Thorburn	9-7	5th round	Coral UK Open
	v Griffiths	9-7	Quarter-final	Coral UK Open
	v Dennis Taylor	9-7	Semi-final	Coral UK Open
	v S. Davis	14-16	Final	Coral UK Open
1986	v T. Jones	3-5	3rd round	Mercantile Credit Classic
	v Reardon	5-4	1st round	Benson & Hedges Masters
	v S. Davis	4-5	Quarter-final	Benson & Hedges Masters
	v Medati	9-2	3rd round	Tolly Cobbold English Professional Championship
	v Reynolds	8-9	4th round	Tolly Cobbold English Professional Championship
	v Dodd	5-2	3rd round	Dulux British Open
	v Mans	5-1	4th round	Dulux British Open
	v Stevens	5-4	5th round	Dulux British Open
	v Griffiths	5-4	Quarter-final	Dulux British Open
	v Virgo	9-4	Semi-final	Dulux British Open
	v S. Davis	7-12	Final	Dulux British Open
	v Griffiths	5-2	1st round	Benson & Hedges Irish Masters
	v Dennis Taylor	5-2	Quarter-final	Benson & Hedges Irish Masters
	v Thorburn	6-4	Semi-final	Benson & Hedges Irish Masters
	v White	5-9	Final	Benson & Hedges Irish Masters
	v Hendry	10-8	1st round	Embassy World Professional Championship
	v Campbell	13-9	2nd round	Embassy World Professional Championship
	v Thorburn	6-13	Quarter-final	Embassy World Professional Championship

PAUL THORNLEY (Canada)

Born –
Turned professional 1979
World ranking 97 (unranked)

1984	v Fisher	8-10	Qualifying	Embassy World Professional Championship
	v Cripsey	3-5	Qualifying	Jameson International
	v Williamson	2-5	Qualifying	Rothmans Grand Prix
1985	v Chaperon	1-5	1st round	Canadian Professional Championship
	v Mienie	10-3	Qualifying	Embassy World Professional Championship
	v Fagan	10-7	Qualifying	Embassy World Professional Championship
	v Murphy	3-10	Qualifying	Embassy World Professional Championship

JIMMY VAN RENSBERG (South Africa)

Born 24.10.31
Turned professional 1978
World ranking 59 (80)

Van Rensberg was 11 times South African amateur champion.

1979	v Meadowcroft	7-9	Prelim	Embassy World Professional Championship
1980	v Meo	1-9	Qualifying	Embassy World Professional Championship
1984	v V. Harris	10-7	Qualifying	Embassy World Professional Championship
	v Edmonds	10-9	Qualifying	Embassy World Professional Championship
	v S. Francisco	3-10	Qualifying	Embassy World Professional Championship
1985	v Longworth	10-7	Qualifying	Embassy World Professional Championship
	v Gauvreau	9-10	Qualifying	Embassy World Professional Championship
	v Scott	4-5	2nd round	Goya Matchroom Trophy
	v E. McLaughlin	5-4	2nd round	Rothmans Grand Prix
	v Campbell	4-5	3rd round	Rothmans Grand Prix
	v Edmonds	5-9	2nd round	Coral UK Open
1986	v W. Jones	5-4	2nd round	Mercantile Credit Classic
	v Parrott	5-3	3rd round	Mercantile Credit Classic
	v S. Davis	1-5	4th round	Mercantile Credit Classic
	v Wych	0-5	2nd round	Dulux British Open
	v Williamson	10-9	Qualifying	Embassy World Professional Championship
	v Sinclair	10-2	Qualifying	Embassy World Professional Championship
	v Campbell	6-10	Qualifying	Embassy World Professional Championship

JOHN VIRGO (England)

Born 3.4.46
Turned professional 1976
World ranking 19 (19)

Coral UK champion in 1979, a few months after reaching the world semi-finals, Virgo has never quite sustained what this promised. Even with the keen sense of humour which is revealed in the impressions of his fellow players with which he entertains exhibition crowds, he might find it difficult to appreciate that in the two tournaments in which he did shine, the Champion of Champions in 1980 in which he was runner-up and the Professional Snooker League in 1984 which he won, were both financial failures of sufficient magnitude to leave him without any prize-money.

1977	v Andrewartha	11-1	Prelim	Embassy World Professional Championship
	v Dunning	11-6	Qualifying	Embassy World Professional Championship
	v Spencer	9-13	1st round	Embassy World Professional Championship
	v Dennis Taylor	5-2	2nd round	Super Crystalate UK Championship
	v Miles	5-2	Quarter-final	Super Crystalate UK Championship
	v Fagan	8-9	Semi-final	Super Crystalate UK Championship
1978	v F. Davis	8-9	Qualifying	Embassy World Professional Championship
	v Edmonds	9-4	Qualifying	Coral UK Championship
	v Pulman	9-3	1st round	Coral UK Championship
	v David Taylor	2-9	Quarter-final	Coral UK Championship
1979	v Parkin	9-0	Prelim	Embassy World Professional Championship
	v Thorne	9-8	Qualifying	Embassy World Professional Championship
	v Thorburn	13-10	1st round	Embassy World Professional Championship
	v Werbeniuk	13-9	Quarter-final	Embassy World Professional Championship

	v Dennis Taylor	12-19	Semi-final	Embassy World Professional Championship
	v Meo	9-6	3rd round	Coral UK Championship
	v S. Davis	9-7	Quarter-final	Coral UK Championship
	v Dennis Taylor	9-4	Semi-final	Coral UK Championship
	v Griffiths	**14-13**	**Final**	**Coral UK Championship**
1980	v Thorburn	3-5	1st round	Benson & Hedges Masters
	v Meadowcroft	10-2	1st round	Embassy World Professional Championship
	v Charlton	12-13	2nd round	Embassy World Professional Championship
	v Meo	1-9	2nd round	Coral UK Championship
1981	v Meo	6-9	1st round	John Courage English Professional
	v Meo	6-10	1st round	Embassy World Professional Championship
	v Knowles	5-2	2nd round	Jameson International
	v Reardon	5-3	3rd round	Jameson International
	v Dennis Taylor	2-5	Quarter-final	Jameson International
	v White	6-9	2nd round	Coral UK Championship
1982	v Hallett	10-4	1st round	Embassy World Professional Championship
	v Reardon	8-13	2nd round	Embassy World Professional Championship
	v V. Harris	5-2	Qualifying	Jameson International
	v Charlton	5-4	1st round	Jameson International
	v Spencer	5-4	2nd round	Jameson International
	v Dennis Taylor	5-4	Quarter-final	Jameson International
	v David Taylor	5-9	Semi-final	Jameson International
	v Black	5-2	1st round	Professional Players Tournament
	v Hallett	5-2	2nd round	Professional Players Tournament
	v Spencer	5-1	3rd round	Professional Players Tournament
	v Johnson	5-1	Quarter-final	Professional Players Tournament
	v White	4-10	Semi-final	Professional Players Tournament
	v Kelly	9-2	1st round	Coral UK Championship
	v Mountjoy	9-5	2nd round	Coral UK Championship
	v Meo	6-9	Quarter-final	Coral UK Championship
1983	v Charlton	2-5	1st round	Lada Classic
	v Mountjoy	1-5	1st round	Benson & Hedges Masters
	v Murphy	10-8	Qualifying	Embassy World Professional Championship
	v Thorne	3-10	1st round	Embassy World Professional Championship
	v Thorne	2-5	1st round	Jameson International
	v French	5-4	1st round	Professional Players Tournament
	v Wilson	2-5	2nd round	Professional Players Tournament
	v Johnson	6-9	1st round	Coral UK Championship
1984	v Wildman	2-5	Qualifying	Lada Classic
	v Reardon	3-5	1st round	Benson & Hedges Masters
	v Thorburn	9-10	1st round	Embassy World Professional Championship
	v Thorne	5-3	Quarter-final	Winfield Australian Masters
	v Meo	6-2	Semi-final	Winfield Australian Masters
	v Knowles	3-7	Final	Winfield Australian Masters
	v F. Davis	5-3	Qualifying	Jameson International
	v Thorburn	5-0	1st round	Jameson International
	v S. Francisco	2-5	2nd round	Jameson International
	v Bradley	5-0	1st round	Rothmans Grand Prix
	v Dennis Taylor	3-5	2nd round	Rothmans Grand Prix
	v King	4-9	Qualifying	Coral UK Open

John Virgo

1985	v Bales	5-1	Qualifying	Mercantile Credit Classic
	v Werbeniuk	5-2	1st round	Mercantile Credit Classic
	v Macleod	5-0	2nd round	Mercantile Credit Classic
	v Thorne	1-5	Quarter-final	Mercantile Credit Classic
	v Darrington	9-0	1st round	Tolly Cobbold English Professional Championship
	v Johnson	9-4	2nd round	Tolly Cobbold English Professional Championship
	v S. Davis	2-9	Quarter-final	Tolly Cobbold English Professional Championship
	v P. Francisco	6-2	1st round	Dulux British Open
	v S. Davis	2-5	2nd round	Dulux British Open
	v Wych	10-4	Qualifying	Embassy World Professional Championship
	v Meo	6-10	1st round	Embassy World Professional Championship
	v Meo	3-5	Quarter-final	Winfield Australian Masters
	v Miles	5-2	3rd round	Goya Matchroom Trophy
	v S. Davis	1-5	4th round	Goya Matchroom Trophy
	v P. Francisco	4-5	3rd round	Rothmans Grand Prix
	v W. Jones	9-7	3rd round	Coral UK Open
	v Thorne	8-9	4th round	Coral UK Open
1986	v Gibson	5-3	3rd round	Mercantile Credit Classic
	v White	2-5	4th round	Mercantile Credit Classic
	v T. Jones	9-7	3rd round	Tolly Cobbold English Professional Championship
	v Parrott	9-6	4th round	Tolly Cobbold English Professional Championship
	v S. Davis	2-9	Quarter-final	Tolly Cobbold English Professional Championship
	v Fowler	5-1	3rd round	Dulux British Open
	v John Rea	5-0	4th round	Dulux British Open
	v Charlton	5-4	5th round	Dulux British Open
	v Meo	5-3	Quarter-final	Dulux British Open
	v Thorne	4-9	Semi-final	Dulux British Open
	v White	7-10	1st round	Embassy World Professional Championship

PAUL WATCHORN (Republic of Ireland)

Born 19.7.58
Turned professional 1982
World ranking 106 (93)

1983	v Johnson	0-10	Qualifying	Embassy World Professional Championship
	v Morra	3-5	Qualifying	Jameson International
	v Parrott	0-5	Qualifying	Professional Players Tournament
1984	v Donnelly	7-10	Qualifying	Embassy World Professional Championship
	v W. Jones	0-5	Qualifying	Jameson International
	v Dennis Taylor	1-5	1st round	Rothmans Grand Prix
	v B. Harris	9-7	Qualifying	Coral UK Open
	v Everton	9-6	Qualifying	Coral UK Open

	v Fisher	5-9	Qualifying	Coral UK Open
1985	v D. Hughes	5-0	Prelim	Mercantile Credit Classic
	v Mikkelsen	5-1	Qualifying	Mercantile Credit Classic
	v Donnelly	1-5	Qualifying	Mercantile Credit Classic
	v Fitzmaurice	6-1	Qualifying	Dulux British Open
	v E. Hughes	4-6	1st round	Dulux British Open
	v Kelly	2-6	Qualifying	Irish Professional Championship
	v Hines	4-10	Qualifying	Embassy World Professional Championship
	v Agrawal	2-5	1st round	Goya Matchroom Trophy
	v Drago	2-5	1st round	Rothmans Grand Prix
	v Sheehan	9-7	1st round	Coral UK Open
1986	v Greaves	4-5	1st round	Mercantile Credit Classic
	v Wilkinson	4-5	1st round	Dulux British Open
	v Longworth	7-10	Qualifying	Embassy World Professional Championship
	v J. McLaughlin	0-5	1st round	Strongbow Irish Professional Championship

GERRY WATSON (Canada)

Born 28.9.49
Turned professional 1983
World ranking (unranked)

1984	v Anderson	4-10	Qualifying	Embassy World Professional Championship
	v Mikkelsen	3-5	1st round	Canadian Professional Championship
	v Sheehan	5-1	1st round	Rothmans Grand Prix
	v Roscoe	5-2	2nd round	Rothmans Grand Prix
	v Stevens	0-5	3rd round	Rothmans Grand Prix
	v Houlihan	4-9	1st round	Coral UK Open
1986	v Gilbert	4-5	1st round	Mercantile Credit Classic

MIKE WATTERSON (England)

Born 26.8.42
Turned professional 1981
World ranking 47 (42)

Although he is a good enough player to have recorded wins over Tony Meo and Alex Higgins, Watterson's niche in snooker history will be his innovative role as a promoter. It was he who took the Embassy World Championship to the Crucible Theatre in 1977, a success which led to his instigating and promoting other events, notably the Coral UK Championship, the Jameson International, the Yamaha International Masters and the State Express (now Car Care Plan) World Cup.

1981	v Medati	5-3	Qualifying	Jameson International
	v Everton	5-4	Qualifying	Jameson International
	v Fagan	2-5	Qualifying	Jameson International
	v Bennett	9-4	Qualifying	Coral UK Championship
	v Johnson	3-9	Qualifying	Coral UK Championship

1982	v Demarco	9-6	Qualifying	Embassy World Professional Championship
	v Meadowcroft	7-9	Qualifying	Embassy World Professional Championship
	v Everton	5-1	Qualifying	Jameson International
	v Fagan	5-1	Qualifying	Jameson International
	v Stevens	3-5	1st round	Jameson International
	v Donnelly	5-4	1st round	Professional Players Tournament
	v Griffiths	2-5	2nd round	Professional Players Tournament
	v B. Harris	3-9	Qualifying	Coral UK Championship
1983	v Campbell	6-10	Qualifying	Embassy World Professional Championship
	v Demarco	5-3	Qualifying	Jameson International
	v Mans	5-4	Qualifying	Jameson International
	v Meo	5-3	1st round	Jameson International
	v S. Davis	0-5	2nd round	Jameson International
	v Higgins	5-2	1st round	Professional Players Tournament
	v Martin	4-5	2nd round	Professional Players Tournament
	v Everton	9-6	Qualifying	Coral UK Championship
	v F. Davis	9-6	Qualifying	Coral UK Championship
	v Mountjoy	2-9	1st round	Coral UK Championship
1984	v Bennett	10-5	Qualifying	Embassy World Professional Championship
	v King	8-10	Qualifying	Embassy World Professional Championship
	v Black	3-5	Qualifying	Jameson International
	v W. Jones	3-5	Qualifying	Rothmans Grand Prix
	v Murphy	4-9	Qualifying	Coral UK Open
1985	v Edmonds	2-5	Qualifying	Mercantile Credit Classic
	v Kearney	4-6	Qualifying	Dulux British Open
	v W. Jones	5-10	Qualifying	Embassy World Professional Championship
	v Fitzmaurice	2-5	2nd round	Goya Matchroom Trophy
	v Caggianello	5-1	2nd round	Rothmans Grand Prix
	v Williams	2-5	3rd round	Rothmans Grand Prix
	v Jim Bear	0-9	2nd round	Coral UK Open
1986	v Jenkins	5-2	2nd round	Mercantile Credit Classic
	v Williams	0-5	3rd round	Mercantile Credit Classic
	v G. Foulds	1-9	2nd round	Tolly Cobbold English Professional Championship
	v Mikkelsen	10-2	Qualifying	Embassy World Professional Championship
	v Dodd	1-10	Qualifying	Embassy World Professional Championship

BILL WERBENIUK (Canada)

Born 14.1.47
Turned professional 1973
World ranking 24 (17)

In three seasons, Werbeniuk has fallen from 8th to 24th in the world rankings. He won only one match in the 1984–85 season but did better last season in reaching the last 16 of the Mercantile Credit Classic and the quarter-finals of the Dulux British Open.

His massive girth is attributable in part to the huge amount of lager he uses as a medication to control a hereditary nervous disorder which causes his cue arm to tremble. In the 1985 Embassy World Championship he made a break of 143, the joint third-highest in the 58-year history of the event.

1974	v Thompson	8-3	1st round	World Professional Championship
	v F. Davis	5-15	2nd round	World Professional Championship
	v Dunning	5-1	1st round	Norwich Union Open
	v Higgins	4-5	Quarter-final	Norwich Union Open
1975	v Higgins	0-5	1st round	Benson & Hedges Masters
	v Meadowcroft	15-9	1st round	Embassy World Professional Championship
	v Charlton	11-15	2nd round	Embassy World Professional Championship
1976	v F. Davis	12-15	1st round	Embassy World Professional Championship
1978	v Parkin	9-2	Qualifying	Embassy World Professional Championship
	v Pulman	13-4	1st round	World Professional Championship
	v Reardon	6-13	Quarter-final	World Professional Championship
1979	v Andrewartha	9-2	Qualifying	Embassy World Professional Championship
	v Spencer	13-11	1st round	Embassy World Professional Championship
	v Virgo	9-13	Quarter-final	Embassy World Professional Championship
	v Johnson	9-3	2nd round	Coral UK Championship
	v Spencer	9-8	3rd round	Coral UK Championship
	v Edmonds	9-8	Quarter-final	Coral UK Championship
	v Griffiths	3-9	Semi-final	Coral UK Championship
1980	v Thorne	10-9	1st round	Embassy World Professional Championship
	v Reardon	6-13	2nd round	Embassy World Professional Championship
	v S. Davis	3-9	2nd round	Coral UK Championship
1981	v Martin	10-4	1st round	Embassy World Professional Championship
	v Mans	13-5	2nd round	Embassy World Professional Championship
	v Reardon	10-13	Quarter-final	Embassy World Professional Championship
	v Martin	2-5	2nd round	Jameson International
	v Stevens	9-7	3rd round	Coral UK Championship
	v S. Davis	5-9	Quarter-final	Coral UK Championship
1982	v John Bear	10-7	1st round	Embassy World Professional Championship
	v Charlton	5-13	2nd round	Embassy World Professional Championship
	v Wych	5-3	1st round	Jameson International
	v David Taylor	2-5	2nd round	Jameson International
	v Morgan	5-3	1st round	Professional Players Tournament
	v Jack Rea	5-2	2nd round	Professional Players Tournament
	v Thorburn	5-2	3rd round	Professional Players Tournament
	v Reardon	3-5	Quarter-final	Professional Players Tournament
1983	v Higgins	5-4	1st round	Lada Classic
	v Mountjoy	5-2	Quarter-final	Lada Classic
	v Stevens	5-2	Semi-final	Lada Classic
	v S. Davis	5-9	Final	Lada Classic
	v Higgins	5-4	1st round	Benson & Hedges Masters
	v Charlton	3-5	Quarter-final	Benson & Hedges Masters
	v Griffiths	3-5	Semi-final	Tolly Cobbold Classic
	v Martin	10-4	1st round	Embassy World Professional Championship
	v David Taylor	13-10	2nd round	Embassy World Professional Championship
	v Higgins	11-13	Quarter-final	Embassy World Professional Championship
	v Knowles	5-0	Semi-final	Winfield Masters

	v Thorburn	3-7	Final	Winfield Masters
	v Scott	3-5	1st round	Jameson International
	v T. Jones	5-4	1st round	Professional Players Tournament
	v E. Hughes	0-5	2nd round	Professional Players Tournament
1984	v Roscoe	4-5	Qualifying	Lada Classic
	v Griffiths	1-5	1st round	Benson & Hedges Masters
	v Griffiths	2-5	1st round	Benson & Hedges Irish Masters
	v F. Davis	10-4	1st round	Embassy World Professional Championship
	v Griffiths	5-10	2nd round	Embassy World Professional Championship
	v Williamson	2-5	1st round	Rothmans Grand Prix
	v Williams	1-9	1st round	Coral UK Open
1985	v Virgo	2-5	1st round	Mercantile Credit Classic
	v Griffiths	2-5	1st round	Benson & Hedges Masters
	v Chaperon	1-6	1st round	Dulux British Open
	v Johnson	10-8	1st round	Embassy World Professional Championship
	v Thorburn	3-13	2nd round	Embassy World Professional Championship
	v Williamson	5-2	3rd round	Goya Matchroom Trophy
	v David Taylor	4-5	4th round	Goya Matchroom Trophy
	v Fowler	1-5	3rd round	Rothmans Grand Prix
	v F. Davis	7-9	3rd round	Coral UK Open
1986	v G. Foulds	5-3	3rd round	Mercantile Credit Classic
	v T. Jones	5-3	4th round	Mercantile Credit Classic
	v Mountjoy	3-5	5th round	Mercantile Credit Classic
	v Foldvari	5-4	3rd round	Dulux British Open
	v Johnson	5-3	4th round	Dulux British Open
	v Williams	5-3	5th round	Dulux British Open
	v Higgins	1-5	Quarter-final	Dulux British Open
	v Thorburn	5-10	1st round	Embassy World Professional Championship

BARRY WEST (England)

Born 24.10.58
Turned professional 1985
World ranking 30

Reaching the quarter-finals of the Coral UK helped West become the highest ranked of the batch of professionals who played on the circuit for the first time last season.

His position, at 30, excuses him from the first two rounds of the first five ranking tournaments and until the fourth round of the World Championship.

1985	v Hendry	4-5	1st round	Goya Matchroom Trophy
	v Meadowcroft	5-2	2nd round	Rothmans Grand Prix
	v Dennis Taylor	1-5	3rd round	Rothmans Grand Prix
	v Roscoe	9-5	2nd round	Coral UK Open
	v E. Hughes	9-3	3rd round	Coral UK Open
	v Mountjoy	9-4	4th round	Coral UK Open
	v Macleod	9-4	5th round	Coral UK Open
	v S. Davis	1-9	Quarter-final	Coral UK Open

1986	v Darrington	5-0	1st round	Mercantile Credit Classic
	v Meadowcroft	5-0	2nd round	Mercantile Credit Classic
	v Wildman	5-2	3rd round	Mercantile Credit Classic
	v Meo	1-5	4th round	Mercantile Credit Classic
	v Gilbert	8-9	1st round	Tolly Cobbold English Professional Championship
	v Bennett	5-1	1st round	Dulux British Open
	v E. McLaughlin	5-3	2nd round	Dulux British Open
	v Campbell	4-5	3rd round	Dulux British Open
	v Dunning	10-3	Qualifying	Embassy World Professional Championship
	v Donnelly	10-5	Qualifying	Embassy World Professional Championship
	v Werbeniuk	8-10	Qualifying	Embassy World Professional Championship

JIMMY WHITE (England)

Born 2.5.62
Turned professional 1980
World ranking 5 (7)

The youngest-ever English amateur champion at the age of 16, the youngest-ever world amateur champion at 18 and the youngest-ever winner of a professional tournament, the Langs Scottish Masters, at 19, White came within two frames of becoming the youngest-ever world professional champion a few days after his 22nd birthday. Down 12-4 to Steve Davis overnight in the 1984 Embassy World Championship final, White lost only 18-16 after demonstrating yet again the greatest flair and natural talent the game has ever seen.

After losing to Cliff Thorburn in the final of the Goya Matchroom Trophy at the start of the season, White beat the Canadian in the final of the Mercantile Credit Classic after needing a snooker in the deciding frame. He also retained the Benson and Hedges Irish Masters and reached the final of the Benson and Hedges Masters, a title he had won in 1984.

1981	v Mikkelsen	9-4	Qualifying	Embassy World Professional Championship
	v Meadowcroft	9-8	Qualifying	Embassy World Professional Championship
	v S. Davis	8-10	1st round	Embassy World Professional Championship
	v Reardon	5-4	Quarter-final	Langs Supreme Scottish Masters
	v S. Davis	6-5	Semi-final	Langs Supreme Scottish Masters
	v Thorburn	**9-4**	**Final**	**Langs Supreme Scottish Masters**
	v Williams	1-5	1st round	Jameson International
	v Thorburn	5-2	1st round	Northern Ireland Classic
	v Mountjoy	9-8	Semi-final	Northern Ireland Classic
	v S. Davis	**11-9**	**Final**	**Northern Ireland Classic**
	v Everton	9-4	Qualifying	Coral UK Championship
	v Virgo	9-6	2nd round	Coral UK Championship
	v Dennis Taylor	9-5	3rd round	Coral UK Championship
	v Reardon	9-8	Quarter-final	Coral UK Championship
	v S. Davis	0-9	Semi-final	Coral UK Championship

1982	v Charlton	4-5	1st round	Benson & Hedges Masters
	v Wildman	9-4	Qualifying	Embassy World Professional Championship
	v Thorburn	10-4	1st round	Embassy World Professional Championship
	v Mans	13-6	2nd round	Embassy World Professional Championship
	v Stevens	13-9	Quarter-final	Embassy World Professional Championship
	v Higgins	15-16	Semi-final	Embassy World Professional Championship
	v Dennis Taylor	4-5	1st round	Langs Supreme Scottish Masters
	v Meadowcroft	5-1	1st round	Jameson International
	v Wilson	2-5	2nd round	Jameson International
	v Wych	5-0	2nd round	Professional Players Tournament
	v Dennis Taylor	5-3	3rd round	Professional Players Tournament
	v Griffiths	5-2	Quarter-final	Professional Players Tournament
	v Virgo	10-4	Semi-final	Professional Players Tournament
	v Reardon	5-10	Final	Professional Players Tournament
	v Medati	9-7	1st round	Coral UK Championship
	v Wilson	9-5	2nd round	Coral UK Championship
	v Reardon	8-9	Quarter-final	Coral UK Championship
1983	v David Taylor	3-5	1st round	Lada Classic
	v David Taylor	5-2	1st round	Benson & Hedges Masters
	v Reardon	2-5	Quarter-final	Benson & Hedges Masters
	v Reardon	6-9	Final	Yamaha International Masters
	v Dennis Taylor	5-4	1st round	Benson & Hedges Irish Masters
	v Higgins	2-5	Quarter-final	Benson & Hedges Irish Masters
	v Meo	8-10	1st round	Embassy World Professional Championship
	v Higgins	3-5	1st round	Langs Supreme Scottish Masters
	v Morra	3-5	1st round	Jameson International
	v Williamson	5-2	1st round	Professional Players Tournament
	v Johnson	3-5	2nd round	Professional Players Tournament
	v Black	9-1	1st round	Coral UK Championship
	v Dennis Taylor	9-4	2nd round	Coral UK Championship
	v Reardon	9-4	Quarter-final	Coral UK Championship
	v S. Davis	4-9	Semi-final	Coral UK Championship
1984	v Campbell	5-1	Qualifying	Lada Classic
	v Charlton	3-5	1st round	Lada Classic
	v Charlton	5-2	1st round	Benson & Hedges Masters
	v Reardon	5-3	Quarter-final	Benson & Hedges Masters
	v Stevens	6-4	Semi-final	Benson & Hedges Masters
	v Griffiths	**9-5**	**Final**	**Benson & Hedges Masters**
	v Meo	4-5	1st round	Benson & Hedges Irish Masters
	v Knowles	1-5	1st round	Tolly Cobbold Classic
	v Williams	10-6	1st round	Embassy World Professional Championship
	v Charlton	13-7	2nd round	Embassy World Professional Championship
	v Thorburn	13-8	Quarter-final	Embassy World Professional Championship
	v Stevens	16-14	Semi-final	Embassy World Professional Championship
	v S. Davis	16-18	Final	Embassy World Professional Championship
	v Knowles	3-5	Quarter-final	Winfield Australian Masters
	v Macleod	5-0	1st round	Langs Supreme Scottish Masters
	v Knowles	6-5	Semi-final	Langs Supreme Scottish Masters
	v S. Davis	4-9	Final	Langs Supreme Scottish Masters
	v Stevens	5-0	1st round	Carlsberg Challenge

	v Knowles	**9-7**	**Final**	**Carlsberg Challenge**
	v Williams	5-3	1st round	Jameson International
	v Meo	5-1	2nd round	Jameson International
	v Knowles	4-5	Quarter-final	Jameson International
	v Oliver	5-1	1st round	Rothmans Grand Prix
	v S. Francisco	1-5	2nd round	Rothmans Grand Prix
	v Campbell	9-7	1st round	Coral UK Open
	v Mountjoy	9-2	2nd round	Coral UK Open
	v S. Davis	4-9	Quarter-final	Coral UK Open
1985	v Browne	5-2	1st round	Mercantile Credit Classic
	v King	2-5	2nd round	Mercantile Credit Classic
	v Thorne	5-2	1st round	Benson & Hedges Masters
	v Spencer	5-2	Quarter-final	Benson & Hedges Masters
	v Thorburn	4-6	Semi-final	Benson & Hedges Masters
	v Chalmers	9-5	1st round	Tolly Cobbold English Professional Championship
	v N. Foulds	9-7	2nd round	Tolly Cobbold English Professional Championship
	v Longworth	5-9	Quarter-final	Tolly Cobbold English Professional Championship
	v T. Jones	6-5	1st round	Dulux British Open
	v S. Francisco	4-5	2nd round	Dulux British Open
	v Meo	5-1	1st round	Benson & Hedges Irish Masters
	v Thorburn	5-3	Quarter-final	Benson & Hedges Irish Masters
	v Knowles	6-4	Semi-final	Benson & Hedges Irish Masters
	v Higgins	**9-5**	**Final**	**Benson & Hedges Irish Masters**
	v W. Jones	10-4	1st round	Embassy World Professional Championship
	v Meo	13-11	2nd round	Embassy World Professional Championship
	v Knowles	10-13	Quarter-final	Embassy World Professional Championship
	v Johnson	5-4	Quarter-final	Winfield Australian Masters
	v Meo	3-6	Semi-final	Winfield Australian Masters
	v Higgins	5-0	1st round	Langs Scottish Masters
	v Thorne	2-6	Semi-final	Langs Scottish Masters
	v Parrott	5-3	Semi-final	Carlsberg Challenge
	v Higgins	**8-3**	**Final**	**Carlsberg Challenge**
	v Fagan	5-2	3rd round	Goya Matchroom Trophy
	v King	5-2	4th round	Goya Matchroom Trophy
	v Reynolds	5-1	5th round	Goya Matchroom Trophy
	v S. Davis	5-3	Quarter-final	Goya Matchroom Trophy
	v N. Foulds	9-5	Semi-final	Goya Matchroom Trophy
	v Thorburn	10-12	Final	Goya Matchroom Trophy
	v Fitzmaurice	5-0	3rd round	Rothmans Grand Prix
	v O'Boye	5-4	4th round	Rothmans Grand Prix
	v S. Francisco	4-5	5th round	Rothmans Grand Prix
	v Thorburn	3-5	1st round	BCE Canadian Masters
	v Bradley	9-4	3rd round	Coral UK Open
	v Chappel	9-5	4th round	Coral UK Open
	v Higgins	9-6	5th round	Coral UK Open
	v Knowles	9-4	Quarter-final	Coral UK Open
	v S. Davis	5-9	Semi-final	Coral UK Open

Jimmy White

1986	v Fowler	5-1	3rd round	Mercantile Credit Classic
	v Virgo	5-2	4th round	Mercantile Credit Classic
	v Gauvreau	5-2	5th round	Mercantile Credit Classic
	v S. Davis	5-2	Quarter-final	Mercantile Credit Classic
	v Williams	9-7	Semi-final	Mercantile Credit Classic
	v Thorburn	**13-12**	**Final**	**Mercantile Credit Classic**
	v Knowles	3-5	1st round	BCE Belgian Classic
	v Meo	5-4	1st round	Benson & Hedges Masters
	v Dennis Taylor	5-3	Quarter-final	Benson & Hedges Masters
	v S. Davis	6-3	Semi-final	Benson & Hedges Masters
	v Thorburn	5-9	Final	Benson & Hedges Masters
	v Williamson	9-1	3rd round	Tolly Cobbold English Professional Championship
	v Williams	9-5	4th round	Tolly Cobbold English Professional Championship
	v N. Foulds	4-9	Quarter-final	Tolly Cobbold English Professional Championship
	v P. Francisco	4-5	3rd round	Dulux British Open
	v Meo	5-2	Quarter-final	Benson & Hedges Irish Masters
	v Fagan	6-0	Semi-final	Benson & Hedges Irish Masters
	v Thorne	**9-5**	**Final**	**Benson & Hedges Irish Masters**
	v Virgo	10-7	1st round	Embassy World Professional Championship
	v Parrott	13-8	2nd round	Embassy World Professional Championship
	v S. Davis	5-13	Quarter-final	Embassy World Professional Championship

MARK WILDMAN (England)

Born 25.1.36
Turned professional 1979
World ranking 43 (25)

Although he has made most impact as a billiards player, once winning and twice being runner-up for the world professional title, Wildman proved his quality as a snooker player by reaching the semi-finals of the 1984 Lada Classic with wins over John Virgo, Silvino Francisco and Eddie Charlton. He is a member of ITV's commentary team.

1980	v Jonik	7-9	Qualifying	Embassy World Professional Championship
	v Wilson	9-8	Qualifying	Coral UK Championship
	v Spencer	9-7	1st round	Coral UK Championship
	v F. Davis	6-9	2nd round	Coral UK Championship
1981	v Bennett	9-3	Qualifying	John Courage English Professional
	v Thorne	2-9	1st round	John Courage English Professional
	v Edmonds	3-9	Qualifying	Embassy World Professional Championship
	v Morra	5-3	Qualifying	Jameson International
	v E.McLaughlin	3-5	Qualifying	Jameson International
	v Sinclair	8-9	Qualifying	Coral UK Championship
1982	v G. Foulds	9-8	Qualifying	Embassy World Professional Championship
	v White	4-9	Qualifying	Embassy World Professional Championship

	v Gibson	5-1	Qualifying	Jameson International
	v Hallett	5-2	Qualifying	Jameson International
	v Dennis Taylor	2-5	1st round	Jameson International
	v Dunning	5-4	1st round	Professional Players Tournament
	v Mans	5-4	2nd round	Professional Players Tournament
	v Johnson	4-5	3rd round	Professional Players Tournament
	v Roscoe	9-4	Qualifying	Coral UK Championship
	v Reardon	5-9	1st round	Coral UK Championship
1983	v S. Davis	2-5	1st round	Benson & Hedges Masters
	v B. Harris	10-7	Qualifying	Embassy World Professional Championship
	v Griffiths	8-10	1st round	Embassy World Professional Championship
	v B. Harris	5-2	Qualifying	Jameson International
	v Mountjoy	4-5	1st round	Jameson International
	v Jonik	5-4	1st round	Professional Players Tournament
	v David Taylor	5-3	2nd round	Professional Players Tournament
	v Stevens	0-5	3rd round	Professional Players Tournament
	v Greaves	9-5	Qualifying	Coral UK Championship
	v Thorne	5-9	1st round	Coral UK Championship
1984	v Virgo	5-2	Qualifying	Lada Classic
	v S. Francisco	5-1	1st round	Lada Classic
	v Charlton	5-4	Quarter-final	Lada Classic
	v Meo	3-5	Semi-final	Lada Classic
	v Andrewartha	9-10	Qualifying	Embassy World Professional Championship
	v W. Jones	0-5	Qualifying	Jameson International
	v J. McLaughlin	5-3	1st round	Rothmans Grand Prix
	v Mountjoy	0-5	2nd round	Rothmans Grand Prix
	v T. Jones	2-9	Qualifying	Coral UK Open
1985	v Fagan	3-5	Qualifying	Mercantile Credit Classic
	v Longworth	3-9	1st round	Tolly Cobbold English Professional Championship
	v Gibson	6-1	1st round	Dulux British Open
	v Stevens	2-5	2nd round	Dulux British Open
	v Edmonds	7-10	Qualifying	Embassy World Professional Championship
	v Scott	1-5	3rd round	Goya Matchroom Trophy
	v Duggan	5-4	3rd round	Rothmans Grand Prix
	v Thorburn	2-5	4th round	Rothmans Grand Prix
	v Drago	5-9	3rd round	Coral UK Open
1986	v West	2-5	3rd round	Mercantile Credit Classic
	v Cripsey	9-5	3rd round	Tolly Cobbold English Professional Championship
	v Meo	3-9	4th round	Tolly Cobbold English Professional Championship
	v Jenkins	5-4	3rd round	Dulux British Open
	v Thorburn	1-5	4th round	Dulux British Open
	v Edmonds	9-10	Qualifying	Embassy World Professional Championship

GLEN WILKINSON (Australia)

Born –
Turned professional 1985
World ranking 102

1985	v Jenkins	6-2	1st round	Australian Professional Championship
	v Heywood	7-3	2nd round	Australian Professional Championship
	v Charlton	2-8	Quarter-final	Australian Professional Championship
	v Demarco	5-2	1st round	Goya Matchroom Trophy
	v Longworth	0-5	2nd round	Goya Matchroom Trophy
	v Gilbert	4-5	1st round	Rothmans Grand Prix
	v Smith	9-4	1st round	Coral UK Open
	v Fowler	6-9	2nd round	Coral UK Open
1986	v O'Boye	1-5	1st round	Mercantile Credit Classic
	v Watchorn	5-4	1st round	Dulux British Open
	v Donnelly	4-5	2nd round	Dulux British Open
	v Kearney	5-10	Qualifying	Embassy World Professional Championship

REX WILLIAMS (England)

Born 20.7.33
Turned professional 1951
World ranking 16 (27)

Chairman of the World Professional Billiards and Snooker Association and an ITV commentator, Williams was world professional billiards champion on a challenge basis from 1968 until 1980 and twice won the event after it had been restored to a tournament format in 1982 and 1983.

By reaching the semi-finals of the Mercantile Credit Classic with wins over Tony Knowles and Alex Higgins and through consistent performances in other ranking tournaments, Williams improved from 27th in the world rankings to 16th last season.

1969	v Bennett	38-11	Quarter-final	World Professional Championship
	v Spencer	18-55	Semi-final	World Professional Championship
1970	v G. Owen	11-31	Quarter-final	World Professional Championship (Apr)
1972	v Reardon	25-23	Quarter-final	World Professional Championship
	v Higgins	30-31	Semi-final	World Professional Championship
1973	v Thorburn	16-15	2nd round	World Professional Championship
	v Spencer	7-16	Quarter-final	World Professional Championship
1974	v Pulman	15-12	2nd round	World Professional Championship
	v Mans	15-4	Quarter-final	World Professional Championship
	v Miles	7-15	Semi-final	World Professional Championship
	v M. Owen	5-3	1st round	Norwich Union Open
	v Reardon	2-5	Quarter-final	Norwich Union Open
1975	v Higgins	5-3	Quarter-final	Benson & Hedges Masters
	v Reardon	4-5	Semi-final	Benson & Hedges Masters
	v Anderson	15-4	2nd round	World Professional Championship
	v Higgins	12-19	Quarter-final	World Professional Championship

1976	v Meadowcroft	7-15	1st round	Embassy World Professional Championship
1977	v Thorburn	6-13	1st round	Embassy World Professional Championship
1978	v Thorne	3-9	Qualifying	Embassy World Professional Championship
	v Griffiths	9-8	Qualifying	Coral UK Championship
	v Miles	8-9	1st round	Coral UK Championship
1979	v Spencer	2-6	Semi-final	Holsten Lager International
	v Greaves	9-2	Prelim	Embassy World Professional Championship
	v Miles	5-9	Qualifying	Embassy World Professional Championship
1980	v Wych	7-9	Qualifying	Embassy World Professional Championship
	v Barrie	9-1	Qualifying	Coral UK Championship
	v Mountjoy	9-8	1st round	Coral UK Championship
	v David Taylor	9-7	2nd round	Coral UK Championship
	v Reardon	4-9	Quarter-final	Coral UK Championship
1981	v Hood	9-4	Qualifying	Embassy World Professional Championship
	v Edmonds	7-9	Qualifying	Embassy World Professional Championship
	v French	5-0	Qualifying	Jameson International
	v White	5-1	1st round	Jameson International
	v F. Davis	5-0	2nd round	Jameson International
	v Dennis Taylor	1-5	3rd round	Jameson International
	v French	9-3	Qualifying	Coral UK Championship
	v Roscoe	9-4	Qualifying	Coral UK Championship
	v Dunning	9-4	Qualifying	Coral UK Championship
	v Meo	8-9	2nd round	Coral UK Championship
1982	v Black	9-2	Qualifying	Embassy World Professional Championship
	v Mountjoy	3-10	1st round	Embassy World Professional Championship
	v Medati	5-3	Qualifying	Jameson International
	v E. McLaughlin	5-1	Qualifying	Jameson International
	v Griffiths	2-5	1st round	Jameson International
	v Ross	5-0	1st round	Professional Players Tournament
	v Charlton	2-5	2nd round	Professional Players Tournament
	v G. Foulds	9-7	Qualifying	Coral UK Championship
	v S. Davis	6-9	1st round	Coral UK Championship
	v Darrington	10-0	Qualifying	Embassy World Professional Championship
	v F. Davis	10-1	Qualifying	Embassy World Professional Championship
	v S. Davis	4-10	1st round	Embassy World Professional Championship
1983	v French	5-1	Qualifying	Jameson International
	v Reynolds	3-5	Qualifying	Jameson International
	v Sheehan	5-1	1st round	Professional Players Tournament
	v Knowles	4-5	2nd round	Professional Players Tournament
	v V. Harris	9-6	Qualifying	Coral UK Championship
	v Wilson	4-9	1st round	Coral UK Championship
1984	v Reardon	5-4	Qualifying	Lada Classic
	v Meo	3-5	1st round	Lada Classic
	v Oliver	10-8	Qualifying	Embassy World Professional Championship
	v White	6-10	1st round	Embassy World Professional Championship
	v Meadowcroft	5-4	Qualifying	Jameson International
	v White	3-5	Qualifying	Jameson International
	v Chalmers	5-0	1st round	Rothmans Grand Prix
	v Stevens	3-5	2nd round	Rothmans Grand Prix
	v Fisher	9-8	Qualifying	Coral UK Open

Rex Williams

	v Werbeniuk	9-1	1st round	Coral UK Open
	v Higgins	7-9	2nd round	Coral UK Open
1985	v Donnelly	5-3	Qualifying	Mercantile Credit Classic
	v Dennis Taylor	5-3	1st round	Mercantile Credit Classic
	v Griffiths	3-5	2nd round	Mercantile Credit Classic
	v T. Jones	9-6	1st round	Tolly Cobbold English Professional Championship
	v S. Davis	2-9	2nd round	Tolly Cobbold English Professional Championship
	v Fowler	4-6	1st round	Dulux British Open
	v F. Davis	10-6	Qualifying	Embassy World Professional Championship
	v Griffiths	3-10	1st round	Embassy World Professional Championship
	v King	3-5	3rd round	Goya Matchroom Trophy
	v Watterson	5-2	3rd round	Rothmans Grand Prix
	v Dennis Taylor	2-5	4th round	Rothmans Grand Prix
	v King	9-5	3rd round	Coral UK Open
	v P. Francisco	9-7	4th round	Coral UK Open
	v Stevens	7-9	5th round	Coral UK Open
1986	v Watterson	5-0	3rd round	Mercantile Credit Classic
	v V. Harris	5-1	4th round	Mercantile Credit Classic
	v Knowles	5-2	5th round	Mercantile Credit Classic
	v Higgins	5-2	Quarter-final	Mercantile Credit Classic
	v White	7-9	Semi-final	Mercantile Credit Classic
	v Miles	9-6	3rd round	Tolly Cobbold English Professional Championship
	v White	5-9	4th round	Tolly Cobbold English Professional Championship
	v Drago	5-1	3rd round	Dulux British Open
	v Bales	5-4	4th round	Dulux British Open
	v Werbeniuk	3-5	5th round	Dulux British Open
	v S. Francisco	4-10	1st round	Embassy World Professional Championship

IAN WILLIAMSON (England)

Born 1.12.58
Turned professional 1982
World ranking 67 (47)

1982	v Donnelly	5-3	Qualifying	Jameson International
	v Kelly	1-5	Qualifying	Jameson International
	v Dodd	1-9	Qualifying	Coral UK Championship
1983	v French	10-8	Qualifying	Embassy World Professional Championship
	v Dodd	9-10	Qualifying	Embassy World Professional Championship
	v Darrington	3-5	Qualifying	Jameson International
	v White	2-5	1st round	Professional Players Tournament
	v Hargreaves	9-4	Qualifying	Coral UK Championship
	v Black	6-9	Qualifying	Coral UK Championship
1984	v Houlihan	10-5	Qualifying	Embassy World Professional Championship
	v Hines	10-6	Qualifying	Embassy World Professional Championship

	v Miles	6-10	Qualifying	Embassy World Professional Championship
	v V. Harris	5-0	Qualifying	Jameson International
	v G. Foulds	4-5	Qualifying	Jameson International
	v Thornley	5-2	Qualifying	Rothmans Grand Prix
	v Werbeniuk	5-2	1st round	Rothmans Grand Prix
	v Johnson	5-4	2nd round	Rothmans Grand Prix
	v Knowles	2-5	3rd round	Rothmans Grand Prix
	v P. Francisco	2-9	Qualifying	Coral UK Open
1985	v Kearney	5-3	Qualifying	Mercantile Credit Classic
	v Fagan	1-5	Qualifying	Mercantile Credit Classic
	v Bradley	8-9	Qualifying	Tolly Cobbold English Professional Championship
	v Chappel	5-6	Qualifying	Dulux British Open
	v Medati	8-10	Qualifying	Embassy World Professional Championship
	v J. McLaughlin	5-3	2nd round	Goya Matchroom Trophy
	v Werbeniuk	2-5	3rd round	Goya Matchroom Trophy
	v Gilbert	4-5	2nd round	Rothmans Grand Prix
	v Mikkelsen	3-9	2nd round	Coral UK Championship
1986	v John Rea	4-5	2nd round	Mercantile Credit Classic
	v Parkin	9-4	2nd round	Tolly Cobbold English Professional Championship
	v White	1-9	3rd round	Tolly Cobbold English Professional Championship
	v Cripsey	5-4	2nd round	Dulux British Open
	v Knowles	1-5	3rd round	Dulux British Open
	v Van Rensberg	9-10	Qualifying	Embassy World Professional Championship

CLIFF WILSON (Wales)

Born 10.5.34
Turned professional 1979
World ranking 23 (22)

Severe problems with his eyesight were the predominant cause of a 15-year retirement between the first phase of Wilson's career, in which he was a close and intense rival of Ray Reardon's in their native Tredegar, and the second, in which he recaptured the Welsh amateur title 21 years after he first won it and went on to win the World Amateur Championship in 1978. His professional career has been a thing of fits and starts but has included wins over three fellow Welshmen, Doug Mountjoy, Terry Griffiths and Reardon, and also over Jimmy White, Tony Knowles and Willie Thorne.

1979	v Pulman	9-7	2nd round	Coral UK Championship
	v Griffiths	4-9	3rd round	Coral UK Championship
1980	v Jonik	9-6	Qualifying	Embassy World Professional Championship
	v Mountjoy	6-10	1st round	Embassy World Professional Championship
	v Wildman	8-9	Qualifying	Coral UK Championship

1981	v Andrewartha	6-5	Prelim	Woodpecker Welsh Professional Championship
	v Mountjoy	9-6	Semi-final	Woodpecker Welsh Professional Championship
	v Reardon	6-9	Final	Woodpecker Welsh Professional Championship
	v Andrewartha	9-4	Qualifying	Embassy World Professional Championship
	v Sinclair	9-4	Qualifying	Embassy World Professional Championship
	v David Taylor	6-10	1st round	Embassy World Professional Championship
	v Meadowcroft	4-5	1st round	Jameson International
	v Johnson	5-9	Qualifying	Coral UK Championship
1982	v M. Owen	6-0	1st round	Welsh Professional Championship
	v Griffiths	6-9	Semi-final	Welsh Professional Championship
	v Medati	9-5	Qualifying	Embassy World Professional Championship
	v Charlton	5-10	1st round	Embassy World Professional Championship
	v Johnson	5-4	Qualifying	Jameson International
	v Mountjoy	5-4	1st round	Jameson International
	v White	5-2	2nd round	Jameson International
	v Knowles	4-5	Quarter-final	Jameson International
	v Morra	5-2	1st round	Professional Players Tournament
	v Knowles	5-4	2nd round	Professional Players Tournament
	v Reynolds	1-5	3rd round	Professional Players Tournament
	v E. McLaughlin	9-6	Qualifying	Coral UK Championship
	v Thorne	9-7	1st round	Coral UK Championship
	v White	5-9	2nd round	Coral UK Championship
1983	v Thorburn	3-5	1st round	Lada Classic
	v Roscoe	6-4	Quarter-final	Woodpecker Welsh Professional Championship
	v Mountjoy	3-9	Semi-final	Woodpecker Welsh Professional Championship
	v Everton	10-1	Qualifying	Embassy World Professional Championship
	v Johnson	10-8	Qualifying	Embassy World Professional Championship
	v Mountjoy	2-10	1st round	Embassy World Professional Championship
	v Donnelly	1-5	Qualifying	Jameson International
	v Bennett	5-1	1st round	Professional Players Tournament
	v Virgo	5-2	2nd round	Professional Players Tournament
	v Thorburn	3-5	3rd round	Professional Players Tournament
	v Williams	9-4	1st round	Coral UK Championship
	v Reardon	4-9	2nd round	Coral UK Championship
1984	v Charlton	0-5	Qualifying	Lada Classic
	v Roscoe	6-2	1st round	Strongbow Welsh Professional Championship
	v Reardon	9-4	Semi-final	Strongbow Welsh Professional Championship
	v Mountjoy	3-9	Final	Strongbow Welsh Professional Championship
	v Mifsud	8-10	Qualifying	Embassy World Professional Championship
	v Dodd	1-5	Qualifying	Jameson International
	v Donnelly	5-2	1st round	Rothmans Grand Prix
	v Reardon	4-5	2nd round	Rothmans Grand Prix

	v Dodd	9-8	Qualifying	Coral UK Open
	v Griffiths	9-6	1st round	Coral UK Open
	v Thorburn	3-9	2nd round	Coral UK Open
1985	v Fowler	5-4	Qualifying	Mercantile Credit Classic
	v Mountjoy	5-4	1st round	Mercantile Credit Classic
	v Johnson	0-5	2nd round	Mercantile Credit Classic
	v Longworth	3-6	1st round	Dulux British Open
	v Fagan	9-10	Qualifying	Embassy World Professional Championship
	v Roscoe	6-3	Quarter-final	BCE Welsh Professional Championship
	v Mountjoy	2-9	Semi-final	BCE Welsh Professional Championship
	v Roscoe	5-1	3rd round	Goya Matchroom Trophy
	v Chappel	5-0	4th round	Goya Matchroom Trophy
	v Johnson	1-5	5th round	Goya Matchroom Trophy
	v Bales	5-1	3rd round	Rothmans Grand Prix
	v Scott	5-3	4th round	Rothmans Grand Prix
	v Drago	5-2	5th round	Rothmans Grand Prix
	v Dennis Taylor	2-5	Quarter-final	Rothmans Grand Prix
	v Cripsey	7-9	3rd round	Coral UK Open
1986	v Browne	3-5	3rd round	Mercantile Credit Classic
	v Newbury	6-4	Quarter-final	Zetters Welsh Professional Championship
	v Griffiths	1-9	Semi-final	Zetters Welsh Professional Championship
	v Chaperon	5-3	3rd round	Dulux British Open
	v Stevens	0-5	4th round	Dulux British Open
	v Charlton	6-10	1st round	Embassy World Professional Championship

JIM WYCH (Canada)

Born 11.1.55
Turned professional 1979
World ranking 32 (52)

After reaching the quarter-finals of the Embassy World Championship at his first attempt in 1980, Wych did not compete regularly on the circuit until last season.

Largely through reaching the quarter-finals of the Dulux British Open with wins over Tony Knowles and John Parrott, he rose 20 places in the rankings, to 32nd.

1980	v John Bear	9-5	Qualifying	Embassy World Professional Championship
	v Williams	9-7	Qualifying	Embassy World Professional Championship
	v Pulman	10-5	1st round	Embassy World Professional Championship
	v Dennis Taylor	13-10	2nd round	Embassy World Professional Championship
	v Thorburn	6-13	Quarter-final	Embassy World Professional Championship
1981	v Knowles	3-9	Qualifying	Embassy World Professional Championship
	v Johnson	2-5	1st round	Jameson International
1982	v Higgins	3-5	1st round	Benson & Hedges Irish Masters
	v John Bear	4-9	Qualifying	Embassy World Professional Championship
	v Bennett	5-0	Qualifying	Jameson International
	v Werbeniuk	3-5	1st round	Jameson International
	v Kelly	5-0	1st round	Professional Players Tournament

	v White	0-5	2nd round	Professional Players Tournament
1984	v Ganim	10-1	Qualifying	Embassy World Professional Championship
	v Scott	10-6	Qualifying	Embassy World Professional Championship
	v Fagan	10-3	Qualifying	Embassy World Professional Championship
	v Reardon	7-10	1st round	Embassy World Professional Championship
1985	v Bradley	10-7	Qualifying	Embassy World Professional Championship
	v Virgo	4-10	Qualifying	Embassy World Professional Championship
	v Sanderson	5-2	1st round	Canadian Professional Championship
	v John Bear	6-3	Quarter-final	Canadian Professional Championship
	v Thorburn	5-6	Semi-final	Canadian Professional Championship
	v Rempe	5-1	2nd round	Goya Matchroom Trophy
	v Mountjoy	1-5	3rd round	Goya Matchroom Trophy
	v V. Harris	3-5	2nd round	Rothmans Grand Prix
	v Duggan	9-5	2nd round	Coral UK Open
	v S. Francisco	8-9	3rd round	Coral UK Open
1986	v Demarco	5-0	2nd round	Mercantile Credit Classic
	v E. Hughes	2-5	3rd round	Mercantile Credit Classic
	v Van Rensberg	5-0	2nd round	Dulux British Open
	v Reynolds	5-3	3rd round	Dulux British Open
	v Knowles	5-4	4th round	Dulux British Open
	v Parrott	5-4	5th round	Dulux British Open
	v S. Davis	2-5	Quarter-final	Dulux British Open
	v Chappel	10-6	Qualifying	Embassy World Professional Championship
	v Duggan	10-5	Qualifying	Embassy World Professional Championship
	v Hallett	7-10	Qualifying	Embassy World Professional Championship

The following players have qualified, from a series of professional ticket tournaments, for membership of the World Billiards and Snooker Association and are therefore eligible to compete on the 1986–87 circuit.

Steve James (England), Jon Wright (England), David Roe (England), Nigel Gilbert (England), Paul Gibson (England), Ken Owers (England), Brian Rowswell (England), Terry Whitthread (England), Mark Bennett (Wales).

Figure in brackets denotes 1984–85 ranking.

Lou Condo (Australia), Mannie Francisco (South Africa), George Ganim (Australia), Steve Mizerak (USA) and Wayne Sanderson (Canada) are non-tournament playing members of the WPBSA.

SNOOKER GREATS

JOE DAVIS O.B.E. (1901–1978)
Although only one of the 'Big Four' at billiards, Joe Davis was undoubtedly the number one at snooker. With his friend Bill Camkin, a Birmingham billiard trader, he promoted and won the first World Professional Snooker Championship in 1927. He went on to win the title every year until 1940. The championship was suspended until 1946, at which point Davis beat Horace Lindrum 78-67 to take the title for the 15th time.

Davis then retired from Championship play. He continued to play in other tournaments and in the public's mind he was still the champion, whoever had won the World Championship in his absence.

His expertise at the three-ball game carried him to four World Professional Billiards titles but his name will always be synonymous with snooker. It was he who developed the modern break-making methods, using the black as the key colour, and it was he who brought the sport to the public's attention.

WALTER DONALDSON (1907–1973)
Consistent and steady, Walter Donaldson reached eight consecutive World Championship finals between 1948 and 1954. In 1947 and 1950 he beat Fred Davis to take the title.

As professional snooker's appeal dwindled in the mid-1950s, a disillusioned Donaldson turned his billiard room into a cowshed and broke up the slates of his table for crazy paving.

JOHN PULMAN (born 1926)
After winning the English Amateur Championship in 1946, John Pulman turned professional but was at his peak when the professional game was going through a period in the doldrums. He was never able to capitalise fully on his natural talent.

He won the world title in 1957 and then successfully withstood a series of challengers. When the influx of new professionals led to the Championship being restored to a tournament format, he once reached the final, losing to Ray Reardon.

An accident led to his retirement from playing in 1982 but he is still involved on the circuit as a member of ITV's commentary team.

THE CIRCUIT

WINFIELD AUSTRALIAN MASTERS

Having existed for four years as the Australian version of Pot Black, the Winfield Australian Masters was expanded in 1983 to an authentic tournament format although the final stages were still played in a television studio.

1983

First round: C. Thorburn beat W. King 3-1; J. White beat I. Anderson 3-2; K. Stevens beat D. Mountjoy 3-1; E. Charlton beat P. Morgan 3-2; A. Higgins beat J. Spencer 3-2; B. Werbeniuk beat Dennis Taylor 3-2; T. Meo beat David Taylor 3-0; A. Knowles beat J. Campbell 3-1

Quarter-finals: Thorburn beat White 4-2; Stevens beat Charlton 4-1; Werbeniuk beat Higgins 4-0; Knowles beat Meo 4-3

Semi-finals: Thorburn beat Stevens 5-2; Werbeniuk beat Knowles 5-0

Final: Thorburn beat Werbeniuk 7-3

1984

First round: W. Thorne beat C. Thorburn 4-1; J. Virgo beat D. Mountjoy 4-1; T. Meo beat B. Werbeniuk 4-0; K. Stevens beat P. Morgan 4-2; E. Charlton beat W. King 4-1; David Taylor beat I. Anderson 4-2; J. White beat J. Campbell 4-0; A. Knowles beat Dennis Taylor 4-2

Quarter-finals: Virgo beat Thorne 5-3; Charlton beat David Taylor 5-4; Meo beat Stevens 5-1; Knowles beat White 5-3

Semi-finals: Virgo beat Meo 6-2; Knowles beat Charlton 6-0

Final: Knowles beat Virgo 7-3

1985

First round: E. Charlton beat I. Anderson 4-2; J. Campbell beat A. Higgins 4-1; W. Thorne beat P. Morgan 4-2; J. Parrott beat S. Francisco 4-3; J. Johnson beat B. Werbeniuk 4-1; J. White beat David Taylor 4-0; T. Meo beat W. King 4-1; J. Virgo beat A. Knowles 4-1

Quarter-finals: Campbell beat Charlton 5-4; Parrott beat Thorne 5-0; White beat Johnson 5-4; Meo beat Virgo 5-3

Semi-finals: Campbell beat Parrott 6-4; Meo beat White 6-3

Final: Meo beat Campbell 7-2

CARLSBERG CHALLENGE

First staged in 1984, this four-man, studio-based event attracts large viewing figures on RTE and provides a pipeopener to the British circuit. In its first year it offered total prize-money of £20,000. Last year, this rose to £30,000.

1984

First round: A. Knowles beat A. Higgins 5-3; J. White beat K. Stevens 5-0

Final: White beat Knowles 9-7

1985

First round: J. White beat J. Parrott 5-3; A. Higgins beat C. Thorburn 5-4

Final: White beat Higgins 8-3

LANGS SCOTTISH MASTERS

The inaugural Langs Scottish Masters was staged in 1981 at the massive Kelvin Hall, Glasgow. It failed to attract large crowds and suffered other teething problems before redeeming itself the following season when it moved to the Holiday Inn, Glasgow. For the last two years it has been staged at another Glasgow hotel, the Hospitality Inn.

It is now firmly established as the first major event on the British circuit. Although it is restricted by invitation to eight players, it attracts most of the leading names and gives the Scottish public their only international tournament.

Jimmy White beat Cliff Thorburn to become the first titleholder but since then Steve Davis has completed a hat-trick of titles.

The event is televised by BBC Scotland and its prize-money has risen from £20,500 in 1981 to £31,000 with Cliff Thorburn taking the £10,500 first prize last season.

1981

Preliminary round: V. Harris beat I. Black 4-0

First round: J. White beat R. Reardon 5-4; S. Davis beat D. Mountjoy 5-0; C. Thorburn beat K. Stevens 5-1; A. Higgins beat V. Harris 5-3

Semi-finals: White beat Davis 6-5; Thorburn beat Higgins 6-2

Final: White beat Thorburn 9-4

1982
First round: Dennis Taylor beat J. White 5-4; S. Davis beat A. Knowles 5-4; T. Griffiths beat R. Reardon 5-3; A. Higgins beat E. Sinclair 5-1

Semi-finals: S. Davis beat Dennis Taylor 6-1; Higgins beat Griffiths 6-5

Final: S. Davis beat Higgins 9-4

1983
First round: C. Thorburn beat T. Griffiths 5-1; S. Davis beat M. Macleod 5-1; A. Knowles beat T. Meo 5-4; A. Higgins beat J. White 5-3

Semi-finals: Knowles beat Thorburn 6-2; S. Davis beat Higgins 6-2

Final: S. Davis beat Knowles 9-6

1984
First round: A. Knowles beat T. Griffiths 5-3; J. White beat M. Macleod 5-0; S. Davis beat C. Thorburn 5-2; A. Higgins beat K. Stevens 5-2

Semi-finals: White beat Knowles 6-5; S. Davis beat Higgins 6-4

Final: S. Davis beat White 9-4

1985
First round: J. White beat A. Higgins 5-0; C. Thorburn beat M. Macleod 5-1; S. Francisco beat A. Knowles 5-4; W. Thorne beat Dennis Taylor 5-2

Semi-finals: Thorne beat White 6-2; Thorburn beat Francisco 6-0

Final: Thorburn beat Thorne 9-7

GOYA MATCHROOM TROPHY

Instigated in 1981 as the Jameson International, this was the first tournament, apart from the World Championship, to carry world ranking points.

However, Jameson withdrew their sponsorship after the 1984 event and Goya, under their Matchroom range of men's toiletries, took over the event, changing its name and moving it to a new venue, Trentham Gardens, Stoke. Cliff Thorburn won his second consecutive tournament of the season when he overcame arrears of 0-7 to beat Jimmy White 12-10 in the final. Goya did not take up their option to sponsor the 1986 event.

1981 (*Jameson*)
Qualifying groups
1 M. Gibson beat S. Hood 5-3; Gibson beat M. Parkin 5-3; J. Dunning beat Gibson 5-3
2 C. Roscoe beat R. Andrewartha 5-2; D. Sheehan beat V. Harris 5-1; Roscoe beat Sheehan 5-1; J. Meadowcroft beat Roscoe 5-4
3 C. Everton beat K. Kennerley 5-4; M. Watterson beat P. Medati 5-3; Watterson beat Everton 5-4; P. Fagan beat Watterson 5-2
4 P. Houlihan *wo* J. Barrie *scr*; D. French beat G. Foulds 5-2; French beat Houlihan 5-3; R. Williams beat French 5-0
5 B. Demarco *wo* B. Mikkelsen *scr*; D. Hughes beat Jack Rea 5-4; Demarco beat Hughes 5-1; M. Hallett beat Demarco 5-4
6 E. Hughes beat M. Owen 5-1; J. Fitzmaurice beat B. Bennett 5-1; E. Hughes beat Fitzmaurice 5-3; E. Hughes beat E. Sinclair 5-2
7 E. McLaughlin beat I. Black 5-3; M. Wildman beat M. Morra 5-3; E. McLaughlin beat Wildman 5-3; E. McLaughlin beat D. Greaves 5-1
8 M. Macleod beat B. Kelly 5-1; J. Johnson beat J. Donnelly 5-4; Johnson beat Macleod 5-1; Johnson *wo* J. Pulman *scr*

First round: J. Johnson beat J. Wych 5-2; D. Martin beat J. Dunning 5-2; R. Williams beat J. White 5-1; A. Knowles beat M. Hallett 5-2; R. Edmonds beat E. Hughes 5-4; J. Meadowcroft beat C. Wilson 5-4; T. Meo beat E. McLaughlin 5-2

Second round: G. Miles beat Johnson 5-3; Martin beat B. Werbeniuk 5-2; Williams beat F. Davis 5-0; A. Higgins beat P. Fagan 5-3; J. Spencer beat Edmonds 5-3; J. Virgo beat Knowles 5-2; K. Stevens beat Meadowcroft 5-1; P. Mans beat Meo 5-3

Third round: Miles beat C. Thorburn 5-0; Martin beat E. Charlton 5-2; Virgo beat R. Reardon 5-3; David Taylor beat Stevens 5-0; Dennis Taylor beat Williams 5-1; Higgins beat D. Mountjoy 5-1; T. Griffiths beat Spencer 5-2; S. Davis beat Mans 5-3

Quarter-finals: Martin beat Miles 5-1; Higgins beat Griffiths 5-2; Dennis Taylor beat Virgo 5-2; S. Davis beat David Taylor 5-1

Semi-finals: Dennis Taylor beat Martin 9-1; S. Davis beat Higgins 9-8

Final: S. Davis beat Dennis Taylor 9-0

1982 (*Jameson*)
Qualifying groups
1 R. Edmonds beat D. Hughes 5-0; Edmonds beat G. Miles 5-1
2 V. Harris beat D. Sheehan 5-3; J. Virgo beat Harris 5-2
3 M. Fisher beat T. Murphy 5-1; Fisher beat F. Davis 5-3
4 B. Bennett beat M. Owen 5-2; J. Wych beat Bennett 5-0
5 M. Morra beat B. Demarco 5-2; D. Reynolds beat Morra 5-1
6 M. Watterson beat C. Everton 5-1; Watterson beat P. Fagan 5-1
7 E. Sinclair beat I. Anderson 5-2; Sinclair beat T. Meo 5-3
8 G. Scott beat B. Harris 5-4; Scott *wo* John Bear *scr*

9 J. Johnson *wo* J. Phillips *scr*; C. Wilson beat Johnson 5-4
10 E. Hughes beat M. Parkin 5-2; Hughes beat D. Martin 5-4
11 C. Ross *wo* D. Greaves *scr*; J. Meadowcroft beat Ross 5-0
12 I. Williamson beat J. Donnelly 5-3; B. Kelly beat G. Foulds 5-4; Kelly beat Williamson 5-1
13 C. Roscoe beat J. Dunning 5-2; D. French beat G. Cripsey 5-1; Roscoe beat French 5-2
14 M. Hallett beat F. Jonik 5-2; M. Wildman beat M. Gibson 5-1; Wildman beat Hallett 5-2
15 J. Fitzmaurice beat I. Black 5-3; L. Dodd beat M. Macleod 5-1; Dodd beat Fitzmaurice 5-3
16 R. Williams beat P. Medati 5-3; E. McLaughlin beat P. Houlihan 5-2; Williams beat McLaughlin 5-1

First round: A. Knowles beat Sinclair 5-2; Reynolds beat W. Thorne 5-3; S. Davis beat Roscoe 5-0; B. Werbeniuk beat Wych 5-3; David Taylor beat Fisher 5-1; K. Stevens beat Watterson 5-3; T. Griffiths beat Williams 5-2; J. Spencer beat Edmonds 5-2; Dennis Taylor beat Wildman 5-2; Virgo beat E. Charlton 5-4; P. Mans beat Dodd 5-3; J. White beat Meadowcroft 5-1; R. Reardon beat E. Hughes 5-3; C. Thorburn beat Scott 5-1; A. Higgins beat Kelly 5-3; Wilson beat D. Mountjoy 5-4

Second round: S. Davis beat Reynolds 5-0; David Taylor beat Werbeniuk 5-2; Stevens beat Mans 5-2; Griffiths beat Higgins 5-2; Dennis Taylor beat Thorburn 5-2; Wilson beat White 5-2; Virgo beat Spencer 5-4; Knowles beat Reardon 5-2

Quarter-finals: Virgo beat Dennis Taylor 5-3; David Taylor beat S. Davis 5-3; Knowles beat Wilson 5-4; Stevens beat Griffiths 5-3

Semi-finals: Knowles beat Stevens 9-3; David Taylor beat Virgo 9-5

Final: Knowles beat David Taylor 9-6

1983 (*Jameson*)
Qualifying groups
1 M. Watterson beat B. Demarco 5-3; Watterson beat P. Mans 5-4
2 T. Murphy beat D. Sheehan 5-2; W. Thorne beat Murphy 5-2
3 R. Williams beat D. French 5-1; D. Reynolds beat Williams 5-3
4 J. Donnelly beat B. Bennett 5-1; Donnelly beat C. Wilson 5-1
5 M. Darrington beat I. Williamson 5-3; S. Francisco beat Darrington 5-2
6 W. King beat I. Black 5-3; G. Miles beat King 5-3
7 D. Hughes beat M. Parkin 5-0; J. Johnson beat Hughes 5-1
8 B. Harris beat J. Dunning 5-3; M. Wildman beat Harris 5-2
9 D. Martin beat D. Greaves 5-1; Martin beat P. Fagan 5-0
10 R. Andrewartha beat C. Everton 5-1; E. Sinclair beat Andrewartha 5-4
11 P. Medati beat V. Harris 5-0; M. Macleod beat Medati 5-3
12 F. Davis beat B. Kelly 5-1; P. Morgan beat J. Fitzmaurice 5-4; Morgan beat Davis 5-3

13 M. Hallett beat C. Roscoe 5-2; M. Morra beat P. Watchorn 5-3; Morra beat Hallett 5-3
14 G. Foulds beat P. Burke 5-2; E. Hughes beat M. Fisher 5-4; Hughes beat Foulds 5-1
15 M. Gibson beat L. Dodd 5-1; G. Scott beat P. Houlihan 5-0; Scott beat Gibson 5-3
16 E. McLaughlin beat J. Campbell 5-2; R. Edmonds beat Jack Rea 5-1; Edmonds beat McLaughlin 5-1

First round: Dennis Taylor beat Reynolds 5-3; R. Reardon beat Macleod 5-2; Thorne beat J. Virgo 5-2; Morra beat J. White 5-3; D. Mountjoy beat Wildman 5-4; Martin beat A. Higgins 5-2; Watterson beat T. Meo 5-3; Scott beat B. Werbeniuk 5-3; T. Griffiths beat Miles 5-2; S. Davis beat Hughes 5-1; Donnelly beat David Taylor 5-3; Francisco *wo* K. Stevens *scr*; E. Charlton beat Johnson 5-2; C. Thorburn beat Sinclair 5-0; J. Spencer beat Morgan 5-1; A. Knowles beat Edmonds 5-1

Second round: Griffiths beat Scott 5-0; Spencer beat Knowles 5-4; Thorburn beat Dennis Taylor 5-3; Mountjoy beat Martin 5-0; Charlton beat Morra 5-3; Thorne beat Reardon 5-0; S. Francisco beat Donnelly 5-1; S. Davis beat Watterson 5-0

Quarter-finals: Griffiths beat Spencer 5-4; Thorburn beat Mountjoy 5-2; Charlton beat Thorne 5-0; S. Davis beat S. Francisco 5-1

Semi-finals: Thorburn beat Griffiths 9-8; S. Davis beat Charlton 9-2

Final: S. Davis beat Thorburn 9-4

1984 (*Jameson*)
Qualifying groups
1 G. Foulds beat P. Francisco 5-4; I. Williamson beat V. Harris 5-0; Foulds beat Williamson 5-4; Foulds beat J. Donnelly 5-3; J. Campbell beat Foulds 5-3
2 W. Jones beat P. Watchorn 5-0; M. Gibson beat P. Medati 5-3; Jones beat Gibson 5-2; Jones beat G. Scott 5-0; Jones beat M. Wildman 5-0
3 T. Jones beat D. French 5-1; S. Duggan beat Jones 5-2; E. Sinclair beat Duggan 5-0; Sinclair beat P. Mans 5-2
4 B. Bennett beat B. Demarco 5-1; Bennett *wo* P. Morgan *scr*; Bennett *wo* J. Wych *scr*; N. Foulds beat Bennett 5-0
5 R. Foldvari beat G. Rigitano 5-2; Foldvari beat R. Edmonds 5-1; L. Dodd beat Foldvari 5-3; Dodd beat C. Wilson 5-1
6 B. Mikkelsen beat T. Chappel 5-4; Mikkelsen beat C. Everton 5-0; C. Roscoe beat Mikkelsen 5-1; E. Hughes beat Roscoe 5-1
7 D. O'Kane beat M. Parkin 5-2; O'Kane beat E. McLaughlin 5-1; O'Kane beat J. Fitzmaurice 5-4; O'Kane beat M. Hallett 5-4
8 J. McLaughlin beat D. Greaves 5-3; F. Jonik beat McLaughlin 5-2; M. Gauvreau beat Jonik 5-1; Gauvreau beat J. Parrott 5-4
9 G. Cripsey beat P. Thornley 5-3; J. Dunning beat Cripsey 5-3; F. Davis beat Dunning 5-4; J. Virgo beat Davis 5-3

10 J. Hargreaves beat P. Houlihan 5-2; B. Kelly beat Hargreaves 5-2; Kelly beat W. King 5-4; S. Francisco beat Kelly 5-3
11 D. Fowler beat R. Chaperon 5-0; Fowler *wo* P. Mifsud *scr*; Fowler beat R. Andrewartha 5-0; Fowler beat D. Martin 5-0
12 M. Bradley beat M. Darrington 5-3; Bradley beat Jack Rea 5-2; M. Morra beat Bradley 5-3; J. Johnson beat Morra 5-0
13 D. Chalmers *wo* Condo *scr*; W. Oliver beat D. Hughes 5-4; Chalmers beat Oliver 5-4; J. Meadowcroft beat Chalmers 5-1; R. Williams beat Meadowcroft 5-4
14 P. Browne beat John Rea 5-2; I. Black beat Browne 5-4; Black beat M. Watterson 5-3; M. Macleod beat Black 5-3
15 S. Newbury beat S. Longworth 5-4; P. Burke beat A. Kearney 5-4; Newbury beat Burke 5-0; Newbury beat P. Fagan 5-0; Newbury beat G. Miles 5-1
16 R. Bales beat D. Sheehan 5-2; Bales beat T. Murphy 5-4; Bales beat M. Fisher 5-3; D. Reynolds beat Bales 5-4

First round: S. Davis beat Campbell 5-1; A. Higgins beat Sinclair 5-1; T. Griffiths beat N. Foulds 5-3; R. Reardon beat Dodd 5-4; E. Hughes beat D. Mountjoy 5-1; W. Thorne beat O'Kane 5-3; Gauvreau beat K. Stevens 5-1; Virgo beat C. Thorburn 5-0; S. Francisco beat J. Spencer 5-2; Dennis Taylor beat Fowler 5-0; Johnson beat E. Charlton 5-1; J. White beat Williams 5-3; T. Meo beat Macleod 5-1; Newbury beat B. Werbeniuk 5-2; A. Knowles beat Reynolds 5-1; David Taylor beat W. Jones 5-4

Second round: S. Davis beat David Taylor 5-1; Higgins beat Griffiths 5-4; E. Hughes beat Reardon 5-1; Thorne beat Gauvreau 5-3; S. Francisco beat Virgo 5-2; Dennis Taylor beat Johnson 5-2; White beat Meo 5-1; Knowles beat Newbury 5-4

Quarter-finals: S. Davis beat Higgins 5-1; E. Hughes beat Thorne 5-2; S. Francisco *wo* Dennis Taylor *scr*; Knowles beat White 5-4

Semi-finals: S. Davis beat E. Hughes 9-3; Knowles beat S. Francisco 9-6

Final: S. Davis beat Knowles 9-2

1985

First round: M. Darrington beat D. Gilbert 5-2; O. Agrawal beat P. Watchorn 5-2; M. Smith beat D. Sheehan 5-2; S. Simngam beat D. Greaves 5-2; G. Wilkinson beat B. Demarco 5-2; J. Rempe beat P. Burke 5-3; S. Hendry beat B. West 5-4; Jim Bear beat P. Houlihan 5-2; J. Caggianello beat J. Hargreaves 5-2; D. Mienie *wo* G. Watson *scr*; J. O'Boye beat M. Parkin 5-3; R. Bales beat T. Drago 5-2; D. Hughes beat A. Kearney 5-1; G. Cripsey beat B. Bennett 5-3

Second round: B. Mikkelsen beat M. Fisher 5-3; M. Gibson beat P. Francisco 5-4; P. Fagan beat Mienie 5-4; W. King beat Caggianello 5-0; R. Chaperon beat D. Chalmers 5-2; Bales beat R. Edmonds 5-0; G. Miles beat O'Boye 5-2; J. Fitzmaurice beat M. Watterson 5-2; T. Chappel beat J. Meadowcroft 5-2; C. Roscoe beat G. Foulds 5-3; E. McLaughlin beat Hendry 5-3; Jim Bear beat

J. Donnelly 5-2; T. Jones beat W. Kelly 5-3; M. Bradley beat John Rea 5-1; L. Dodd beat Simngam 5-4; Williamson beat J. McLaughlin 5-3; J. Dunning beat C. Everton 5-2; M. Morra beat B. Oliver 5-1; D. Fowler beat Agrawal 5-2; J. Wych beat Rempe 5-1; E. Sinclair beat Darrington 5-0; S. Longworth beat Wilkinson 5-0; Cripsey beat P. Medati 5-2; S. Newbury beat F. Jonik 5-4; S. Duggan beat F. Davis 5-1; I. Black beat G. Rigitano 5-4; R. Foldvari beat V. Harris 5-4; G. Scott beat J. Van Rensberg 5-4; T. Murphy beat Jack Rea 5-1; B. Harris beat P. Browne 5-3; W. Jones beat Smith 5-3; D. Hughes beat M. Gauvreau 5-4

Third round: S. Davis beat Bales 5-2; J. Virgo beat Miles 5-2; Chaperon beat S. Francisco 5-3; M. Macleod beat Fitzmaurice 5-1; Gibson beat E. Charlton 5-4; D. Reynolds beat Mikkelsen 5-0; J. White beat Fagan 5-2; King beat R. Williams 5-3; Chappel beat K. Stevens 5-3; C. Wilson beat Roscoe 5-1; J. Johnson beat Jim Bear 5-1; Bradley beat M. Hallett 5-4; David Taylor beat T. Jones 5-4; B. Werbeniuk beat Williamson 5-2; A. Knowles beat E. McLaughlin 5-1; N. Foulds beat Dodd 5-3; C. Thorburn beat Longworth 5-3; D. Martin beat Sinclair 5-1; D. Mountjoy beat Wych 5-1; J. Campbell beat Morra 5-2; W. Thorne beat Fowler 5-1; Scott beat M. Wildman 5-1; Duggan beat R. Reardon 5-4; Black beat P. Mans 5-4; T. Griffiths beat Newbury 5-2; J. Spencer beat Foldvari 5-4; T. Meo beat Dunning 5-0; J. Parrott beat W. Jones 5-3; A. Higgins beat D. Hughes 5-1; Murphy beat E. Hughes 5-3; Dennis Taylor beat Cripsey 5-1; B. Harris beat D. O'Kane 5-3

Fourth round: S. Davis beat Virgo 5-1; Macleod beat Chaperon 5-4; Reynolds beat Gibson 5-0; White beat King 5-2; Wilson beat Chappel 5-0; Johnson beat Bradley 5-2; David Taylor beat Werbeniuk 5-4; N. Foulds beat Knowles 5-3; Thorburn beat Martin 5-3; Campbell beat Mountjoy 5-1; Thorne beat Scott 5-1; Duggan beat Black 5-1; Griffiths beat Spencer 5-1; Parrott beat Meo 5-4; Higgins beat Murphy 5-2; Dennis Taylor beat B. Harris 5-3

Fifth round: S. Davis beat Macleod 5-1; White beat Reynolds 5-1; Johnson beat Wilson 5-1; N. Foulds beat David Taylor 5-4; Thorburn beat Campbell 5-0; Duggan beat Thorne 5-4; Parrott beat Griffiths 5-1; Dennis Taylor beat Higgins 5-1

Quarter-finals: White beat S. Davis 5-3; N. Foulds beat Johnson 5-2; Thorburn beat Duggan 5-2; Dennis Taylor beat Parrott 5-1

Semi-finals: White beat N. Foulds 9-5; Thorburn beat Dennis Taylor 9-5

Final: Thorburn beat White 12-10

ROTHMANS GRAND PRIX

Rothmans entered snooker sponsorship for the first time in the 1984–85 season by taking over the Professional Players Tournament and the television slot previously occupied by the State Express World Team

Classic. The Professional Players Tournament had been first staged by the World Professional Billiards and Snooker Association in 1982 with the aim of distributing some of its funds (accumulated from television fees and prize-money levies) to its own members.

It was consequently untelevised and not commercially sponsored but proved so successful that it attracted the BBC and Rothmans. Coincidentally, State Express announced its withdrawal from all sponsorship and snooker's team event was re-scheduled later in the season with reduced television coverage.

After preliminary rounds, the Rothmans Grand Prix, a world ranking tournament, was staged at Redwood Lodge, Bristol before moving to its final televised phase at the former home of the team event, The Hexagon, Reading.

The first Rothmans Grand Prix also gave Dennis Taylor his first major title of his 13-year professional career. The 1985 final, which saw Steve Davis avenge the 18-17 defeat he suffered at the Irishman's hands in the World Championship, was, at 2.14 a.m., the latest ever finish to a major final.

1982 (*Professional Players Tournament*)

First round: E. Sinclair beat F. Davis 5-2; J. Meadowcroft beat B. Bennett 5-4; M. Watterson beat J. Donnelly 5-4; T. Griffiths beat C. Roscoe 5-1; A. Higgins beat D. French 5-3; R. Reardon beat T. Murphy 5-0; B. Werbeniuk beat P. Morgan 5-3; C. Everton beat P. Fagan 5-2; C. Thorburn beat P. Medati 5-1; David Taylor beat I. Anderson 5-1; Dennis Taylor beat R. Edmonds 5-4; J. Wych beat B. Kelly 5-0; R. Williams beat C. Ross 5-0; P. Mans beat E. McLaughlin 5-2; W. Thorne beat B. Demarco 5-3; M. Wildman beat J. Dunning 5-4; J. Johnson beat G. Miles 5-1; E. Charlton beat D. Hughes 5-2; F. Jonik beat D. Mountjoy 5-3; K. Stevens beat E. Hughes 5-2; T. Meo beat M. Owen 5-4; C. Wilson beat M. Morra 5-2; A. Knowles beat P. Houlihan 5-4; J. Virgo beat I. Black 5-2; M. Hallett beat V. Harris 5-3; D. Martin beat M. Gibson 5-2; J. Fitzmaurice beat D. Sheehan 5-1; J. Spencer beat G. Foulds 5-1

Second round: Werbeniuk beat Jack Rea 5-2; Sinclair beat Meadowcroft 5-3; Thorburn beat Everton 5-2; Griffiths beat Watterson 5-2; Reardon beat Higgins 5-2; Dennis Taylor beat David Taylor 5-1; Wildman beat Mans 5-4; Charlton beat Williams 5-2; M. Macleod beat Thorne 5-4; White beat Wych 5-0; Johnson beat Stevens 5-1; Meo beat Jonik 5-0; Wilson beat Knowles 5-4; Virgo beat Hallett 5-2; Spencer beat Martin 5-3; Reynolds beat Fitzmaurice 5-0

Third round: Werbeniuk beat Thorburn 5-2; Johnson beat Wildman 5-4; Reynolds beat Wilson 5-1; Virgo beat Spencer 5-1; Charlton beat Meo 5-3; White beat Dennis Taylor 5-3; Griffiths beat Sinclair 5-3; Reardon beat Macleod 5-2

Quarter-finals: White beat Griffiths 5-2; Virgo beat Johnson 5-1; Reardon beat Werbeniuk 5-3; Charlton beat Reynolds 5-1

Semi-finals: White beat Virgo 10-4; Reardon beat Charlton 10-7

Final: Reardon beat White 10-5

1983 (*Professional Players Tournament*)
Qualifying: G. Ganim Jr beat G. Cripsey 5-4; S. Duggan beat M. Darrington 5-4; T. Jones beat W. Oliver 5-2; D. French beat N. Foulds 5-2; B. Bennett beat B. Demarco 5-4; P. Burke beat G. Foulds 5-4; V. Harris *wo* P. Mifsud *scr*; P. Medati beat D. Hughes 5-1; T. Murphy beat P. Browne 5-2; J. Parrott beat P. Watchorn 5-0; D. Sheehan beat P. Houlihan 5-2; M. Morra beat J. Hargreaves 5-0; D. Greaves beat R. Andrewartha 5-2; W. King beat B. Harris 5-3; P. Morgan beat M. Gibson 5-4

First round: R. Reardon beat Ganim 5-4; C. Thorburn beat V. Harris 5-1; J. Meadowcroft beat C. Roscoe 5-4; Duggan beat J. Dunning 5-2; J. Virgo beat French 5-4; J. Spencer beat I. Black 5-2; W. Thorne beat C. Everton 5-1; C. Wilson beat Bennett 5-1; T. Griffiths beat L. Dodd 5-3; J. White beat I. Williamson 5-2; Parrott beat P. Fagan 5-2; J. Johnson beat Burke 5-3; E. Hughes beat E. Sinclair 5-4; M. Fisher beat F. Davis 5-4; B. Werbeniuk beat T. Jones 5-4; E. Charlton beat E. McLaughlin 5-0; M. Watterson beat A. Higgins 5-2; K. Stevens beat R. Edmonds 5-1; D. Martin beat J. Fitzmaurice 5-0; T. Murphy beat M. Macleod 5-0; J. Campbell beat D. Mountjoy 5-3; David Taylor beat P. Morgan 5-3; G. Miles beat M. Gauvreau 5-3; M. Wildman beat F. Jonik 5-4; G. Scott beat Dennis Taylor 5-4; T. Meo beat W. King 5-2; S. Francisco beat M. Morra 5-3; D. Reynolds beat D. Greaves 5-1; R. Williams beat D. Sheehan 5-1; M. Hallett beat B. Kelly 5-0; A. Knowles beat P. Medati 5-1; S. Davis beat J. Donnelly 5-1

Second round: Reardon beat Duggan 5-2; Thorburn beat Meadowcroft 5-1; Thorne beat Spencer 5-1; Wilson beat Virgo 5-2; Griffiths beat Parrot 5-1; Johnson beat White 5-3; E. Hughes beat Werbeniuk 5-0; Charlton beat Fisher 5-4; Stevens beat Murphy 5-1; Martin beat Watterson 5-4; Wildman beat David Taylor 5-3; Campbell beat Miles 5-2; Meo beat Reynolds 5-0; S. Francisco beat Scott 5-1; Knowles beat Williams 5-4; Hallett beat S. Davis 5-2

Third round: Thorne beat Reardon 5-3; Thorburn beat Wilson 5-3; E. Hughes beat Griffiths 5-2; Johnson beat Charlton 5-0; Stevens beat Wildman 5-0; Campbell beat Martin 5-0; Knowles beat S. Francisco 5-0; Meo beat Hallett 5-3

Quarter-finals: Johnson beat Thorburn 5-1; Thorne beat E. Hughes 5-1; Meo beat Stevens 5-3; Knowles beat Campbell 5-3

Semi-finals: Knowles beat Thorne 9-7; Johnson beat Meo 9-6

Final: Knowles beat Johnson 9-8

1984
Qualifying: I. Williamson beat P. Thornley 5-2; J. Donnelly beat J. Hargreaves 5-4; B. Demarco *wo* P. Fagan *scr*; V. Harris beat F. Davis 5-1; J. Dunning beat D. Hughes 5-0; D. O'Kane beat B. Kelly 5-4; M. Gauvreau beat R. Foldvari

5-2; E. McLaughlin beat S. Longworth 5-2; M. Morra beat G. Cripsey 5-3; S. Duggan beat P. Browne 5-2; D. Sheehan *wo* L. Condo *scr*; Sheehan beat B. Mikkelsen 5-3; P. Burke beat M. Darrington 5-3; D. Chalmers beat R. Andrewartha 5-2; W. King beat D. Greaves 5-0; P. Medati beat L. Dodd 5-4; R. Chaperon beat A. Kearney 5-1; Chaperon beat M. Gibson 5-4; P. Francisco beat I. Black 5-4; G. Rigitano beat R. Edmonds 5-3; M. Bradley beat F. Jonik 5-1; W. Jones beat M. Watterson 5-3; John Rea beat J. Fitzmaurice 5-2; R. Bales *wo* J. Wych *scr*; S. Newbury beat M. Fisher 5-0; W. Oliver beat B. Bennett 5-3; C. Everton beat P. Houlihan 5-3; J. McLaughlin beat J. Meadowcroft 5-1; T. Chappel beat G. Scott 5-1; T. Murphy beat G. Foulds 5-1; T. Jones beat E. Sinclair 5-4; C. Roscoe beat D. French 5-0; P. Watchorn *wo* P. Morgan *scr*; D. Fowler *wo* P. Mifsud *scr*

First round: A. Knowles beat V. Harris 5-1; Dunning beat P. Mans 5-4; Williamson beat B. Werbeniuk 5-2; J. Johnson beat Medati 5-1; W. Thorne beat Newbury 5-2; M. Macleod beat King 5-4; N. Foulds beat Demarco 5-2; T. Jones beat T. Griffiths 5-3; R. Reardon beat Roscoe 5-1; C. Wilson beat Donnelly 5-2; Dennis Taylor beat Watchorn 5-1; J. Virgo beat Bradley 5-0; A. Higgins beat Bales 5-1; M. Hallett beat Sheehan 5-1; R. Williams beat Chalmers 5-0; K. Stevens beat Chappel 5-3; C. Thorburn beat Rigitano 5-4; J. Campbell beat W. Jones 5-4; T. Meo beat Burke 5-1; D. Martin beat Chaperon 5-4; D. Mountjoy beat E. McLaughlin 5-4; M. Wildman beat J. McLaughlin 5-3; J. Parrott beat Gauvreau 5-3; E. Charlton beat Everton 5-1; J. White beat Oliver 5-1; S. Francisco beat Duggan 5-3; P. Francisco beat J. Spencer 5-2; D. Reynolds beat Fowler 5-2; David Taylor beat O'Kane 5-1; John Rea beat E. Hughes 5-4; G. Miles beat Murphy 5-3; S. Davis beat Morra 5-2

Second round: Knowles beat Dunning 5-1; Williamson beat Johnson 5-4; Thorne beat Macleod 5-3; N. Foulds beat T. Jones 5-0; Reardon beat Wilson 5-4; Dennis Taylor beat Virgo 5-3; Hallett beat Higgins 5-3; Stevens beat Williams 5-3; Thorburn beat Campbell 5-1; Meo beat Martin 5-4; Mountjoy beat Wildman 5-0; Charlton beat Parrott 5-1; S. Francisco beat White 5-1; David Taylor beat John Rea 5-1; S. Davis beat Miles 5-0; Reynolds beat P. Francisco 5-4

Third round: Knowles beat Williamson 5-2; N. Foulds beat Thorne 5-1; Dennis Taylor beat Reardon 5-3; Stevens beat Hallett 5-3; Thorburn beat Meo 5-4; Mountjoy beat Charlton 5-4; Reynolds beat S. Francisco 5-1; S. Davis beat David Taylor 5-1

Quarter-finals: N. Foulds beat Knowles 5-2; Dennis Taylor beat Stevens 5-2; Thorburn beat Mountjoy 5-3; S. Davis beat Reynolds 5-0

Semi-finals: Dennis Taylor beat N. Foulds 9-3; Thorburn beat S. Davis 9-7

Final: Dennis Taylor beat Thorburn 10-2

1985

First round: B. West beat D. Demarco 5-2; P. Houlihan *wo* G. Robinson *scr*; S. Simngam beat D. Mienie 5-3; T. Drago beat P. Watchorn 5-2; R. Bales beat

M. Smith 5-1; G. Watson beat D. Sheehan 5-1; J. Hargreaves beat G. Cripsey 5-1; A. Kearney beat Jim Bear 5-3; D. Gilbert beat G. Wilkinson 5-4; J. O'Boye beat S. Hendry 5-4; D. Hughes beat B. Bennett 5-4; M. Darrington beat D. Greaves 5-2; O. Agrawal beat J. Rempe 5-2

Second round: West beat J. Meadowcroft 5-2; M. Watterson beat J. Caggianello 5-1; T. Jones beat Houlihan 5-4; Simngam beat F. Davis 5-3; G. Foulds beat Black 5-3; Drago beat W. King 5-4; G. Scott beat D. Chalmers 5-2; Bales beat M. Fisher 5-3; Watson beat C. Roscoe 5-2; G. Miles beat Rigitano 5-4; S. Newbury beat P. Burke 5-3; S. Longworth beat Hargreaves 5-2; T. Chappel beat L. Dodd 5-2; J. Van Rensberg beat E. McLaughlin 5-4; M. Gibson beat M. Bradley 5-4; R. Edmonds beat Kearney 5-2; B. Oliver beat P. Fagan 5-4; S. Duggan beat M. Gauvreau 5-4; Gilbert beat I. Williams 5-4; B. Mikkelsen beat T. Murphy 5-4; W. Jones beat John Rea 5-0; P. Francisco beat C. Everton 5-0; J. McLaughlin beat P. Medati 5-2; B. Harris beat P. Browne 5-3; J. Fitzmaurice beat E. Sinclair 5-3; O'Boye beat R. Chaperon 5-3; B. Kelly beat J. Donnelly 5-4; M. Morra beat D. Hughes 5-2; V. Harris beat J. Wych 5-3; Darrington beat R. Foldvari 5-3; Agrawal *wo* J. Dunning *scr*; D. Fowler beat F. Jonik 5-4

Third round: Dennis Taylor beat West 5-1; R. Williams beat Watterson 5-2; T. Meo beat T. Jones 5-2; E. Hughes beat Simngam 5-1; E. Charlton beat G. Foulds 5-1; Drago beat M. Macleod 5-3; Scott beat R. Reardon 5-4; C. Wilson beat Bales 5-1; K. Stevens beat Watson 5-0; Miles beat D. Reynolds 5-3; David Taylor beat Newbury 5-2; Longworth beat J. Parrott 5-2; D. Mountjoy beat Chappel 5-1; J. Campbell beat Van Rensberg 5-4; A. Knowles beat Gibson 5-1; Edmonds beat D. O'Kane 5-2; C. Thorburn beat Oliver 5-0; M. Wildman beat Duggan 5-4; J. Johnson beat Gilbert 5-2; M. Hallett beat Mikkelsen 5-3; W. Jones beat W. Thorne 5-0; P. Francisco beat J. Virgo 5-4; T. Griffiths beat J. McLaughlin 5-4; B. Harris beat J. Spencer 5-2; J. White beat Fitzmaurice 5-0; O'Boye beat P. Mans 5-3; S. Francisco beat Kelly 5-2; D. Martin beat Morra 5-2; A. Higgins beat V. Harris 5-1; N. Foulds beat Darrington 5-0; S. Davis beat Agrawal 5-0; Fowler beat B. Werbeniuk 5-1

Fourth round: Dennis Taylor beat Williams 5-2; Meo beat E. Hughes 5-3; Drago beat Charlton 5-3; Wilson beat Scott 5-3; Stevens beat Miles 5-2; Longworth beat David Taylor 5-1; Campbell beat Mountjoy 5-2; Knowles beat Edmonds 5-3; Thorburn beat Wildman 5-2; Johnson beat Hallett 5-4; P. Francisco beat W. Jones 5-3; Griffiths beat B. Harris 5-3; White beat O'Boye 5-4; S. Francisco beat Martin 5-3; Higgins beat N. Foulds 5-3; S. Davis beat Fowler 5-1

Fifth round: Dennis Taylor beat Meo 5-3; Wilson beat Drago 5-2; Stevens beat Longworth 5-3; Knowles beat Campbell 5-4; Thorburn beat Johnson 5-1; Griffiths beat P. Francisco 5-2; S. Francisco beat White 5-4; S. Davis beat Higgins 5-0

Quarter-finals: Dennis Taylor beat Wilson 5-2; Knowles beat Stevens 5-4; Thorburn beat Griffiths 5-1; S. Davis beat S. Francisco 5-2

Semi-finals: Dennis Taylor beat Knowles 9-6; S. Davis beat Thorburn 9-5

Final: S. Davis beat Dennis Taylor 10-9

Terry Griffiths, who reached the quarter-finals of the Rothmans Grand Prix

Rothmans Grand Prix finalists Dennis Taylor and Steve Davis with the Rothmans trophy

BCE CANADIAN MASTERS

In an attempt to emulate the success snooker has had in Britain, the WPBSA promoted an eight man event in Canada with, for the first time, British style same day television coverage. The tournament, sponsored by the equipment company Bristol Coin Equipment, was very successful and attracted large viewing figures for CBC in whose Toronto studios the matches were played.

First round: Dennis Taylor beat J. Parrott 5-1; R. Reardon beat A. Knowles 5-2; C. Thorburn beat J. White 5-3; S. Davis beat T. Griffiths 5-4

Semi-finals: Taylor beat Reardon 8-3; Davis beat Thorburn 8-1

Final: Taylor beat Davis 9-5

CORAL UK OPEN

Coral had sponsored this event since 1978 but, having established themselves as snooker's leading bookmaker, they declined to renew their contract. From the 1986–87 season, the event will be sponsored by Tennents, another company owned by Bass plc. The original sponsors in 1977 were Super Crystalate, the ball manufacturers.

Over the years the qualifications for entry to the event have varied. It was originally restricted to British passport-holders or permanent residents but is now open to all snooker-playing members of the World Professional Billiards and Snooker Association. Consequently, it is one of the six tournaments which carry ranking points.

Because of Coral's long-term contract, the event has not carried the same wealth of prize-money as more recently-sponsored ranking tournaments but has nevertheless gained prestige through its seniority and through being the only event, apart from the World Championship, in which no match is played over fewer than the best of 17 frames.

1977 (*Super Crystalate UK Championship*)
First round: J. Virgo *wo* J. Barrie *scr*; C. Ross beat J. Karnehm 5-4; P. Fagan beat Jack Rea 5-1; J. Meadowcroft beat P. Houlihan 5-1; D. Mountjoy beat R. Andrewartha 5-2; W. Thorne beat B. Bennett 5-1; J. Dunning beat M. Parkin 5-4; David Taylor beat D. Greaves 5-4

Second round: Virgo beat Dennis Taylor 5-2; G. Miles beat Ross 5-1; Fagan beat F. Davis 5-0; Meadowcroft beat R. Reardon 5-4; Mountjoy beat J. Spencer

5-3; Thorne beat R. Williams 5-4; Dunning *wo* J. Pulman *scr*; A. Higgins beat David Taylor 5-4

Quarter-finals: Virgo beat Miles 5-2; Fagan beat Meadowcroft 5-4; Mountjoy beat Thorne 5-4; Higgins beat Dunning 5-0

Semi-finals: Fagan beat Virgo 9-8; Mountjoy beat Higgins 9-2

Final: Fagan beat Mountjoy 12-9

1978

Qualifying: W. Thorne beat B. Bennett 9-4; R. Andrewartha beat P. Houlihan 9-3; D. Mountjoy beat J. Barrie 9-5; R. Williams beat T. Griffiths 9-8; J. Dunning beat D. Greaves 9-3; J. Virgo beat R. Edmonds 9-4; David Taylor beat M. Parkin 9-2; J. Meadowcroft beat Jack Rea 9-5

First round: David Taylor beat Fagan 9-7; Virgo beat J. Pulman 9-3; F. Davis beat Dunning 9-2; A. Higgins beat Meadowcroft 9-6; Thorne beat R. Reardon 9-6; G. Miles beat Williams 9-8; Mountjoy beat Dennis Taylor 9-4; Andrewartha beat J. Spencer 9-8

Quarter-finals: David Taylor beat Virgo 9-2; Higgins beat F. Davis 9-4; Miles beat Thorne 9-1; Mountjoy beat Andrewartha 9-4

Semi-finals: David Taylor beat Higgins 9-5; Mountjoy beat Miles 9-1

Final: Mountjoy beat David Taylor 15-9

1979

Qualifying: Jack Rea beat B. Bennett 9-8; M. Hallett beat M. Parkin 9-1; J. Dunning beat D. Greaves 9-8

First round: W. Thorne beat R. Andrewartha 9-4; P. Houlihan beat Jack Rea 9-3; S. Davis beat Dunning 9-3; P. Fagan beat Hallett 9-4; B. Werbeniuk beat J. Johnson 9-3; R. Edmonds beat J. Meadowcroft 9-3; T. Meo beat David Taylor 9-7; C. Wilson beat J. Pulman 9-7

Second round: S. Davis beat D. Mountjoy 9-5; T. Griffiths beat Wilson 9-4; A. Higgins beat Houlihan 9-3; Fagan beat G. Miles 9-5; Werbeniuk beat J. Spencer 9-8; Dennis Taylor beat Thorne 9-8; J. Virgo beat Meo 9-6; Edmonds beat F. Davis 9-6

Quarter-finals: Werbeniuk beat Edmonds 9-8; Dennis Taylor beat Fagan 9-6; Virgo beat S. Davis 9-7; Griffiths beat Higgins 9-7

Semi-finals: Virgo beat Dennis Taylor 9-4; Griffiths beat Werbeniuk 9-3

Final: Virgo beat Griffiths 14-13

1980

Preliminary round: M. Hallett beat B. Bennett 9-4; S. Hood beat C. Ross 9-3

Qualifying: Hallett beat R. Edmonds 9-8; E. Sinclair beat K. Kennerley 9-1; M. Wildman beat C. Wilson 9-8; J. Meadowcroft beat D. Greaves 9-1; R. Andrewartha beat A. Knowles 9-8; R. Williams beat J. Barrie 9-1; J. Johnson beat J. Dunning 9-6; T. Meo beat Hood 9-5

First round: Meo beat P. Houlihan 9-1; S. Davis beat Hallett 9-1; P. Fagan beat Johnson 9-4; Sinclair beat G. Miles 9-5; Thorne beat Meadowcroft 9-1; Wildman beat J. Spencer 9-7; Williams beat D. Mountjoy 9-8; Andrewartha beat J. Pulman 9-6

Second round: Meo beat J. Virgo 9-1; S. Davis beat B. Werbeniuk 9-3; Dennis Taylor beat Sinclair 9-6; T. Griffiths beat Fagan 9-8; A. Higgins beat Thorne 9-7; F. Davis beat Wildman 9-6; R. Reardon beat Andrewartha 9-3; Williams beat David Taylor 9-7

Quarter-finals: S. Davis beat Meo 9-5; Griffiths beat Dennis Taylor 9-2; Higgins beat F. Davis 9-6; Reardon beat Williams 9-4

Semi-finals: S. Davis beat Griffiths 9-0; Higgins beat Reardon 9-7

Final: S. Davis beat Higgins 16-6

1981

Qualifying groups

1 P. Medati beat E. McLaughlin 9-5; Medati beat J. Donnelly 9-7; W. Thorne beat Medati 9-6
2 M. Hallett beat V. Harris 9-4; Hallett beat D. Hughes 9-6; Hallett beat P. Fagan 9-5
3 M. Gibson beat J. Fitzmaurice 9-6; C. Everton beat Gibson 9-7; J. White beat Everton 9-4
4 J. Johnson beat T. Murphy 9-1; M. Watterson beat B. Bennett 9-4; Johnson beat Watterson 9-3; Johnson beat C. Wilson 9-5
5 P. Houlihan beat K. Kennerley 9-1; Houlihan beat I. Black 9-4; Houlihan beat J. Meadowcroft 9-4
6 G. Foulds beat B. Kelly 9-7; A. Knowles beat Foulds 9-1
7 E. Sinclair beat M. Wildman 9-8; Sinclair beat S. Hood 9-0; D. Martin beat Sinclair 9-7
8 R. Williams beat D. French 9-3; C. Roscoe beat M. Macleod 9-7; Williams beat Roscoe 9-4; Williams beat J. Dunning 9-4

First round: Thorne beat R. Edmonds 9-4; K. Stevens beat Hallett 9-4; White beat J. Virgo 9-6; Johnson beat J. Spencer 9-5; G. Miles beat Houlihan 9-5; Knowles beat F. Davis 9-6; A. Higgins beat Martin 9-7; T. Meo beat Williams 9-8

Second round: S. Davis beat Thorne 9-2; B. Werbeniuk beat Stevens 9-7; White beat Dennis Taylor 9-5; R. Reardon beat Johnson 9-7; T. Griffiths beat Miles

9-4; Knowles beat D. Mountjoy 9-6; Higgins beat David Taylor 9-5; Meo beat C. Thorburn 9-6

Quarter-finals: S. Davis beat Werbeniuk 9-5; White beat Reardon 9-8; Griffiths beat Knowles 9-5; Meo beat Higgins 9-4

Semi-finals: S. Davis beat White 9-0; Griffiths beat Meo 9-3

Final: S. Davis beat Griffiths 16-3

1982

Qualifying groups

1 T. Meo beat G. Scott 9-5
2 C. Wilson beat E. McLaughlin 9-6
3 D. Martin beat M. Macleod 9-6
4 J. Meadowcroft beat D. Hughes 9-8
5 J. Donnelly beat C. Ross 9-5
6 P. Houlihan *wo* J. Dunning *scr*
7 M. Hallett beat B. Demarco 9-1
8 B. Kelly beat J. Fitzmaurice 9-0
9 G. Foulds beat M. Gibson 9-2; R. Williams beat Foulds 9-7
10 V. Harris beat M. Owen 9-4; J. Johnson beat Harris 9-8
11 T. Murphy beat C. Everton 9-4; E. Sinclair beat Murphy 9-5
12 B. Harris beat G. Cripsey 9-6; Harris beat M. Watterson 9-3
13 M. Fisher beat I. Black 9-3; Fisher beat R. Edmonds 9-8
14 L. Dodd beat I. Williamson 9-1; Dodd beat D. French 9-7
15 B. Bennett *wo* J. Phillips *scr*; P. Medati beat Bennett 9-1
16 C. Roscoe beat Jack Rea 9-6; M. Wildman beat Roscoe 9-4

First round: S. Davis beat Williams 9-6; P. Fagan beat B. Harris 9-6; T. Griffiths beat Johnson 9-1; Dennis Taylor beat Meadowcroft 9-7; David Taylor beat Dodd 9-7; Meo beat G. Miles 9-4; J. Virgo beat Kelly 9-2; D. Mountjoy beat Houlihan 9-3; R. Reardon beat Wildman 9-5; Hallett beat F. Davis 9-7; Wilson beat W. Thorne 9-7; J. White beat Medati 9-7; J. Spencer beat Sinclair 9-8; A. Knowles beat Donnelly 9-6; D. Reynolds beat Fisher 9-6; A. Higgins beat Martin 9-7

Second round: S. Davis beat Fagan 9-3; Griffiths beat Dennis Taylor 9-7; Meo beat David Taylor 9-6; Virgo beat Mountjoy 9-5; Reardon beat Hallett 9-8; White beat Wilson 9-5; Spencer beat Knowles 9-6; Higgins beat Reynolds 9-8

Quarter-finals: Griffiths beat S. Davis 9-6; Meo beat Virgo 9-6; Reardon beat White 9-8; Higgins beat Spencer 9-5

Semi-finals: Griffiths beat Meo 9-7; Higgins beat Reardon 9-6

Final: Griffiths beat Higgins 16-15

1983

Qualifying groups

1 J. Johnson beat M. Gibson 9-6
2 T. Jones beat E. Sinclair 9-3

3 M. Wildman beat D. Greaves 9-5
4 M. Macleod beat B. Bennett 9-0
5 M. Watterson beat C. Everton 9-6; Watterson beat F. Davis 9-6
6 M. Darrington beat G. Cripsey 9-3; M. Hallett beat Darrington 9-1
7 N. Foulds beat C. Roscoe 9-2; Foulds beat J. Meadowcroft 9-2
8 V. Harris beat P. Houlihan 9-6; R. Williams beat Harris 9-6
9 D. French beat Jack Rea 9-5; D. Martin beat French 9-3
10 G. Foulds beat S. Duggan 9-8; Foulds beat L. Dodd 9-7
11 J. Parrott beat G. Scott 9-7; Parrott beat M. Fisher 9-0
12 R. Andrewartha beat W. Oliver 9-1; J. Dunning beat Andrewartha 9-2
13 T. Murphy beat B. Demarco 9-4; Murphy beat Donnelly 9-4
14 P. Medati beat D. Hughes 9-3; Medati beat R. Edmonds 9-7
15 B. Harris beat E. McLaughlin 9-8; Harris beat J. Fitzmaurice 9-3
16 I. Williamson beat J. Hargreaves 9-4; I. Black beat Williamson 9-6

First round: T. Griffiths beat Martin 9-4; Hallett beat G. Miles 9-4; Johnson beat J. Virgo 9-6; David Taylor beat N. Foulds 9-4; A. Knowles beat J. Jones 9-5; D. Mountjoy beat Watterson 9-2; A. Higgins beat Macleod 9-6; Medati beat D. Reynolds 9-3; C. Wilson beat Williams 9-4; R. Reardon beat B. Harris 9-7; Dennis Taylor beat Murphy 9-6; J. White beat Black 9-1; J. Spencer beat Dunning 9-7; T. Meo beat Parrott 9-7; W. Thorne beat Wildman 9-5; S. Davis beat G. Foulds 9-1

Second round: Griffiths beat Hallett 9-5; Johnson beat David Taylor 9-3; Knowles beat Mountjoy 9-5; Higgins beat Medati 9-1; Reardon beat Wilson 9-4; White beat Dennis Taylor 9-4; Meo beat Spencer 9-5; S. Davis beat Thorne 9-3

Quarter-finals: White beat Reardon 9-4; Griffiths beat Johnson 9-2; Higgins beat Knowles 9-5; S. Davis beat Meo 9-4

Semi-finals: Higgins beat Griffiths 9-4; S. Davis beat White 9-4

Final: Higgins beat S. Davis 16-15

1984

Qualifying rounds

1 T. Jones beat R. Chaperon 9-1; Jones beat P. Fagan 9-2; Jones beat M. Wildman 9-2
2 P. Watchorn beat B. Harris 9-7; Watchorn beat C. Everton 9-6; M. Fisher beat Watchorn 9-5; R. Williams beat Fisher 9-8
3 R. Foldvari beat D. Greaves 9-5; G. Cripsey beat Foldvari 9-7; J. Fitzmaurice beat Cripsey 9-8; J. Parrott beat Fitzmaurice 9-6
4 P. Francisco beat D. Sheehan 9-5; P. Francisco beat I. Williamson 9-2; E. Sinclair beat P. Francisco 9-8; S. Francisco beat Sinclair 9-4
5 D. Fowler beat B. Demarco 9-3; Fowler beat W. Oliver 9-3; Fowler beat F. Davis 9-4; Fowler beat N. Foulds 9-6
6 D. O'Kane beat W. Jones 9-7; O'Kane beat S. Duggan 9-6; G. Scott beat O'Kane 9-7; M. Macleod beat Scott 9-5

7 S. Newbury beat G. Rigitano 9-6; Newbury beat F. Jonik 9-3; L. Dodd beat Newbury 9-6; C. Wilson beat Dodd 9-8
8 J. McLaughlin beat D. French 9-3; McLaughlin *wo* P. Morgan *scr*; McLaughlin beat C. Roscoe 9-8; McLaughlin beat G. Miles 9-8
9 R. Bales beat D. Chalmers 9-2; Bales beat E. McLaughlin 9-4; M. Gauvreau beat Bales 9-8; Gauvreau beat P. Mans 9-6
10 G. Foulds beat D. Hughes 9-7; P. Browne beat Foulds 9-5; W. King beat Browne 9-5; King beat J. Virgo 9-4
11 John Rea beat B. Bennett 9-5; Rea beat F. Dunning 9-3; Rea beat R. Edmonds 9-6; J. Johnson beat Rea 9-6
12 T. Chappel beat P. Houlihan 9-3; Chappel beat I. Black 9-3; Chappel *wo* R. Andrewartha *scr*; Chappel beat D. Reynolds 9-6
13 J. Hargreaves beat P. Medati 9-6; M. Gibson beat Hargreaves 9-8; J. Donnelly beat Gibson 9-6; J. Campbell beat Donnelly 9-6
14 M. Bradley beat V. Harris 9-8; Bradley beat B. Kelly 9-6; Bradley beat J. Meadowcroft 9-7; M. Hallett beat Bradley 9-8
15 S. Longworth beat M. Darrington 9-5; Longworth beat P. Burke 9-4; M. Morra beat Longworth 9-1; E. Hughes beat Morra 9-8
16 T. Murphy beat A. Kearney 9-2; Murphy beat M. Watterson 9-4; Murphy beat D. Martin 9-8

First round: A. Higgins beat T. Jones 9-7; S. Davis beat Murphy 9-1; J. White beat Campbell 9-7; Williams beat B. Werbeniuk 9-1; W. Thorne beat Parrott 9-7; E. Charlton beat S. Francisco 9-4; D. Mountjoy beat Hallett 9-2; T. Meo beat E. Hughes 9-4; R. Reardon beat Fowler 9-2; K. Stevens beat Chappel 9-7; Dennis Taylor beat King 9-5; Wilson beat T. Griffiths 9-6; Johnson beat J. Spencer 9-6; David Taylor beat Macleod 9-6; A. Knowles beat Gauvreau 9-5; C. Thorburn beat J. McLaughlin 9-4

Second round: Thorne beat Charlton 9-7; White beat Mountjoy 9-2; Higgins beat Williams 9-7; Stevens beat Johnson 9-2; Reardon beat David Taylor 9-4; Thorburn beat Wilson 9-3; Knowles beat Dennis Taylor 9-2; S. Davis beat Meo 9-7

Quarter-finals: Higgins beat Thorne 9-5; S. Davis beat White 9-4; Thorburn beat Reardon 9-8; Stevens beat Knowles 9-7

Semi-finals: Higgins beat Thorburn 9-7; S. Davis beat Stevens 9-2

Final: S. Davis beat Higgins 16-8

1985

First round: D. Sheehan beat P. Watchorn 9-7; T. Drago beat D. Gilbert 9-5; G. Wilkinson beat M. Smith 9-4; O. B. Agrawal beat S. Hendry 9-2; B. West *wo* G. Robinson *scr*; G. Jenkins beat P. Burke 9-5; J. O'Boye beat B. Bennett 9-3; M. Darrington *wo* M. Parkin *scr*; P. Houlihan beat G. Watson 9-4; J. Hargreaves beat D. Mienie 9-7; D. Hughes beat A. Kearney 9-8; S. Simngam beat R. Bales 9-2; Jim Bear beat B. Demarco 9-1; G. Cripsey beat D. Greaves 9-4

Second round: Sheehan beat G. Scott 9-6; Drago beat J. Donnelly 9-8; S. Longworth beat M. Gibson 9-2; D. Fowler beat Wilkinson 9-6; M. Morra beat Agrawal 9-8; West beat C. Roscoe 9-5; G. Miles beat B. Oliver 9-4; T. Murphy beat C. Everton 9-4; M. Bradley beat Jenkins 9-3; T. Chappell *wo* J. McLaughlin *scr*; R. Edmonds beat J. Van Rensberg 9-5; F. Davis beat John Rea 9-8; B. Mikkelsen beat I. Williamson 9-3; P. Medati beat W. Kelly 9-1; O'Boye beat M. Gauvreau 9-5; V. Harris beat I. Black 9-3; L. Dodd *wo* Jack Rea *scr*; E. Sinclair beat G. Foulds 9-4; P. Browne beat D. Chalmers 9-4; W. Jones beat J. Fitzmaurice 9-3; J. Wych beat S. Duggan 9-5; Darrington beat R. Foldvari 9-6; T. Jones beat F. Jonik 9-4; J. McLaughlin beat R. Chaperon 9-5; S. Newbury beat Houlihan 9-3; J. Meadowcroft beat Hargreaves 9-8; P. Francisco *wo* G. Rigitano *scr*; W. King beat D. Hughes 9-0; Simngam beat M. Fisher 9-4; P. Fagan beat B. Harris 9-2; Jim Bear beat M. Watterson 9-0; Cripsey *wo* J. Dunning *scr*

Third round: S. Davis beat Sheehan 9-1; Drago beat M. Wildman 9-5; T. Meo beat Longworth 9-5; Fowler beat P. Mans 9-2; D. Mountjoy beat Morra 9-2; West beat E. Hughes 9-3; R. Reardon beat Miles 9-4; M. Macleod beat Murphy 9-7; J. White beat Bradley 9-4; Chappel beat D. O'Kane 9-5; A. Higgins beat Edmonds 9-8; F. Davis beat B. Werbeniuk 9-7; David Taylor beat Mikkelsen 9-6; J. Campbell beat Medati 9-7; A. Knowles beat O'Boye 9-5; J. Spencer beat V. Harris 9-5; C. Thorburn beat Dodd 9-4; J. Parrott beat Sinclair 9-2; W. Thorne beat Browne 9-6; J. Virgo beat W. Jones 9-7; S. Francisco beat Wych 9-8; D. Martin beat Darrington 9-3; T. Griffiths beat T. Jones 9-5; D. Reynolds beat J. McLaughlin 9-7; K. Stevens beat Newbury 9-7; M. Hallett beat Meadowcroft 9-1; P. Francisco beat E. Charlton 9-5; R. Williams beat King 9-5; J. Johnson beat Simngam 9-4; N. Foulds beat Fagan 9-5; Dennis Taylor beat Jim Bear 9-3; Cripsey beat C. Wilson 9-7

Fourth round: S. Davis beat Drago 9-2; Meo beat Fowler 9-2; West beat Mountjoy 9-4; Macleod beat Reardon 9-5; White beat Chappel 9-5; Higgins beat F. Davis 9-2; David Taylor beat Campbell 9-4; Knowles beat Spencer 9-7; Thorburn beat Parrott 9-6; Thorne beat Virgo 9-8; S. Francisco beat Martin 9-6; Griffiths beat Reynolds 9-7; Stevens beat Hallett 9-5; Williams beat P. Francisco 9-7; N. Foulds beat Johnson 9-8; Dennis Taylor beat Cripsey 9-2

Fifth round: S. Davis beat Meo 9-5; West beat Macleod 9-4; White beat Higgins 9-6; Knowles beat David Taylor 9-7; Thorne beat Thorburn 9-7; Griffiths beat S. Francisco 9-5; Stevens beat Williams 9-7; Dennis Taylor beat N. Foulds 9-5

Quarter-finals: S. Davis beat West 9-1; White beat Knowles 9-4; Thorne beat Griffiths 9-7; Dennis Taylor beat Stevens 9-1

Semi-finals: S. Davis beat White 9-5; Thorne beat Dennis Taylor 9-7

Final: S. Davis beat Thorne 16-14

HOFMEISTER WORLD DOUBLES CHAMPIONSHIP

Though pairs snooker had long been popular at grass roots amateur level, it was not until 1982 that professional snooker gained a World Doubles Championship when Hofmeister sponsored the inaugural event at Crystal Palace.

The venue was completely inappropriate to snooker's intimate, cosy ambience but the Championship proved popular with television audiences. The following season it moved to the better suited Derngate Centre in Northampton where it has since remained.

Last season, Steve Davis and Tony Meo took the title for the third time in four years. Their only defeat in the event came when Alex Higgins and Jimmy White beat them in the 1984 semi-finals *en route* to becoming champions. Last season, though, Higgins and White failed to survive as far as the televised stage, as they were beaten by Danny Fowler and Barry West in the third round.

ITV's coverage of the event was marred by an industrial dispute which disrupted various transmissions and blacked out the entire final.

1982

Qualifying groups

1 J. Johnson & C. Wilson *wo* M. Morra & F. Jonik *scr*; Johnson & Wilson beat R. Edmonds & J. Meadowcroft 6-4; R. Reardon & J. Spencer beat Johnson & Wilson 6-2
2 D. Martin & Dennis Taylor beat L. Dodd & D. French 6-2; T. Griffiths & D. Mountjoy beat Martin & Taylor 6-0
3 F. Davis & P. Medati beat J. Dunning & B. Demarco 6-0; A. Higgins & E. Charlton beat Davis & Medati 6-3
4 P. Houlihan & B. Bennett beat E. Sinclair & I. Black 6-2; D. Reynolds & M. Watterson beat Houlihan & Bennett 6-3; S. Davis & T. Meo beat Reynolds & Watterson 6-3
5 M. Hallett & G. Cripsey beat M. Macleod & E. McLaughlin 6-3; Hallett & Cripsey beat P. Fagan & G. Foulds 6-2; K. Stevens & J. Wych beat Hallett & Cripsey 6-4
6 V. Harris & I. Williamson beat T. Murphy & E. Hughes 6-1; R. Williams & J. Fitzmaurice beat Harris & Williamson 6-1; G. Miles & B. Werbeniuk beat Williams & Fitzmaurice 6-5
7 J. White & A. Knowles beat G. Scott & D. Hughes 6-2; White & Knowles beat David Taylor & W. Thorne 6-1
8 M. Fisher & M. Wildman beat C. Everton & C. Roscoe 6-3; Fisher & Wildman beat J. Donnelly & M. Gibson 6-5; C. Thorburn & J. Virgo beat Fisher & Wildman 6-2

First round: Griffiths & Mountjoy beat Stevens & Wych 6-1; S. Davis & Meo beat Thorburn & Virgo 6-2; White & Knowles beat Reardon & Spencer 6-2; Higgins & Charlton beat Miles & Werbeniuk 6-3

Semi-finals: Griffiths & Mountjoy beat Charlton & Higgins 10-7; S. Davis & Meo beat White & Knowles 10-5

Final: S. Davis & Meo beat Griffiths & Mountjoy 13-2

1983

Preliminary round: B. Bennett & P. Houlihan beat M. Gibson & M. Macleod 5-2; S. Duggan & J. Hargreaves beat W. Oliver & P. Browne 5-1; G. Scott & J. Parrott beat G. Foulds & N. Foulds 5-4; B. Harris & M. Morra beat D. Sheehan & E. McLaughlin 5-2

Qualifying: T. Murphy & P. Morgan beat P. Burke & D. Martin 5-4; J. Fitzmaurice & V. Harris beat Bennett & Houlihan 5-4; J. Donnelly & C. Roscoe beat W. King & J. Campbell 5-3; Duggan & Hargreaves beat D. Hughes & B. Kelly 5-0; J. Dunning & B. Demarco beat M. Hallett & G. Cripsey 5-4; R. Edmonds & J. Meadowcroft beat D. French & C. Everton 5-2; E. Hughes & L. Dodd beat Scott & Parrott 5-2; B. Harris & Morra beat M. Darrington & I. Williamson 5-1

First round: Murphy & Morgan beat I. Black & E. Sinclair 5-1; Dennis Taylor & R. Williams beat Fitzmaurice & V. Harris 5-1; T. Jones & S. Francisco beat Donnelly & Roscoe 5-2; G. Miles & G. Ganim beat Duggan & Hargreaves 5-3; F. Davis & M. Watterson beat Dunning & Demarco 5-3; D. Reynolds & P. Fagan beat Edmonds & Meadowcroft 5-0; E. Hughes & Dodd beat C. Wilson & J. Johnson 5-1; B. Harris & Morra beat M. Fisher & M. Wildman 5-2

Second round: S. Davis & T. Meo beat Murphy & Morgan 5-2; David Taylor & W. Thorne beat Dennis Taylor & Williams 5-4; E. Charlton & B. Werbeniuk beat T. Jones & S. Francisco 5-3; A. Higgins & K. Stevens *wo* Miles & Ganim *scr*; R. Reardon & J. Spencer beat F. Davis & Watterson 5-2; J. Virgo & C. Thorburn beat Reynolds & Fagan 5-2; T. Griffiths & D. Mountjoy beat E. Hughes & Dodd 5-3; A. Knowles & J. White beat B. Harris & Morra 5-4

Quarter-finals: S. Davis & Meo beat David Taylor & Thorne 5-3; Charlton & Werbeniuk beat Higgins & Stevens 5-1; Thorburn & Virgo beat Reardon & Spencer 5-0; Knowles & White beat Griffiths & Mountjoy 5-0

Semi-finals: S. Davis & Meo beat Charlton & Werbeniuk 9-1; Knowles & White beat Thorburn & Virgo 9-7

Final: S. Davis & Meo beat Knowles & White 10-2

1984

Qualifying: J. Donnelly & C. Roscoe beat S. Longworth & D. French 5-3; D. Chalmers & J. McLaughlin beat P. Fagan & B. Harris 5-0; M. Morra & M. Bradley beat I. Williamson & M. Darrington 5-1; G. Miles & P. Francisco beat J. Hargreaves & S. Duggan 5-1; T. Chappel & S. Newbury beat G. Rigitano & G. Scott 5-0; M. Gauvreau & D. Fowler beat B. Bennett & P. Houlihan 5-1; R. Bales & W. Oliver beat John Rea & E. McLaughlin 5-2;

J. Meadowcroft & R. Edmonds beat F. Jonik and R. Chaperon 5-4; V. Harris & J. Fitzmaurice beat P. Burke and B. Kelly 5-2; D. Sheehan & P. Watchorn beat M. Macleod & M. Gibson 5-0; F. Davis & M. Watterson beat C. Everton & R. Foldvari 5-3; P. Medati & P. Browne beat I. Black & E. Sinclair 5-1; D. Hughes & A. Kearney *wo* J. Dunning & B. Demarco *scr*

First round: D. Mountjoy & W. Jones beat Chappel & Newbury 5-1; S. Francisco & T. Jones beat J. Campbell & W. King 5-4; A. Higgins & J. White beat D. Martin & G. Cripsey 5-2; David Taylor & M. Hallett beat E. Hughes & L. Dodd 5-3; P. Francisco & Miles beat C. Wilson & J. Johnson 5-4; D. Reynolds & D. O'Kane beat Gauvreau & Fowler 5-4; Dennis Taylor & R. Williams beat Medati & Browne 5-0; Bales & Oliver beat G. Foulds & N. Foulds 5-2; S. Davis & T. Meo beat D. Hughes & Kearney 5-2; R. Reardon & T. Murphy beat F. Davis & Watterson 5-2; M. Fisher & M. Wildman beat Edmonds & Meadowcroft 5-3; E. Charlton & B. Werbeniuk beat Sheehan & Watchorn 5-2; T. Griffiths & J. Parrott beat Chalmers & J. McLaughlin 5-0; J. Virgo & K. Stevens beat Morra & Bradley 5-1; A. Knowles & J. Spencer beat V. Harris & Fitzmaurice 5-2

Second round: S. Davis & Meo beat Miles & P. Francisco 5-2; Virgo & Stevens beat Dennis Taylor & Williams 5-3; Higgins & White beat Reynolds & O'Kane 5-4; Thorburn & Thorne beat Mountjoy & W. Jones 5-3; Reardon & Murphy beat S. Francisco & T. Jones 5-3; Griffiths & Parrot beat Bales & Oliver 5-4; David Taylor & Hallett beat Charlton & Werbeniuk 5-4; Knowles & Spencer beat Fisher & Wildman 5-4

Quarter-finals: Knowles & Spencer beat Reardon & Murphy 5-4; Higgins & White beat Griffiths & Parrott 5-2; Thorburn & Thorne beat Virgo & Stevens 5-3; S. Davis & Meo beat Hallett & David Taylor 5-1

Semi-finals: Thorburn & Thorne beat Knowles & Spencer 9-1; Higgins & White beat S. Davis & Meo 9-6

Final: Higgins & White beat Thorburn & Thorne 10-2

1985

First round: P. Watchorn & D. Sheehan beat D. Greaves & G. Jenkins 5-4; G. Cripsey & G. Wilkinson beat P. Houlihan & B. Bennett 5-2; R. Bales & J. McLaughlin beat S. Simngam & O. Agrawal 5-3; J. Hargreaves & P. Burke beat T. Drago & J. O'Boye 5-3

Second round: D. Fowler & B. West beat R. Chaperon & M. Gauvreau 5-4; P. Mans & J. Campbell beat Watchorn & Sheehan 5-1; P. Medati & B. Browne beat R. Foldvari & M. Fisher 5-3; Cripsey & Wilkinson beat M. Gibson & D. O'Kane 5-4; T. Murphy & P. Fagan beat A. Kearney & D. Hughes 5-2; M. Bradley & D. Chalmers beat W. Oliver & M. Darrington 5-4; Bales & J. McLaughlin beat B. Mikkelsen & J. Meadowcroft 5-4; M. Wildman & R. Edmonds beat S. Hendry & G. Rigitano 5-3; T. Chappel & F. Jonik beat E. Sinclair & I. Black 5-1; I. Williamson & S. Duggan beat D. Gilbert & B. Harris 5-1; M. Watterson & F. Davis *wo* J. Fitzmaurice & V. Harris *scr*;

D. Reynolds & S. Longworth beat J. Van Rensberg & D. Mienie 5-4; Jim Bear & L. Dodd beat M. Morra & J. Wych 5-1; J. Donnelly & C. Roscoe beat Hargreaves & Burke 5-4; John Rea & E. McLaughlin beat G. Scott & G. Foulds 5-0; R. Williams & G. Miles *wo* J. Dunning & B. Demarco *scr*

Third round: Fowler & West beat A. Higgins & J. White 5-4; Mans & Campbell beat D. Martin & M. Macleod; M. Hallett & David Taylor beat Medati & Browne 5-4; T. Jones & R. Reardon beat Cripsey & Wilkinson 5-3; A. Knowles & J. Johnson beat Murphy & Fagan 5-2; W. Jones & D. Mountjoy beat Bradley & Chalmers 5-2; J. Spencer & S. Newbury beat Bales & J. McLaughlin 5-4; T. Griffiths & Dennis Taylor beat Wildman & Edmonds 5-4; C. Thorburn & W. Thorne beat Chappel & Jonik 5-1; W. King & C. Wilson beat Williamson & Duggan 5-3; P. Francisco & S. Francisco beat Watterson & F. Davis 5-0; J. Virgo & K. Stevens beat Reynolds & Longworth 5-0; E. Charlton & B. Werbeniuk beat Jim Bear & Dodd 5-4; N. Foulds & J. Parrott beat Donnelly & Roscoe 5-1; E. Hughes & M. Smith beat John Rea & E. McLaughlin 5-4; S. Davis & T. Meo beat Williams & Miles 5-2

Fourth round: Mans & Campbell beat Fowler & West 5-4; T. Jones & Reardon beat Hallett & David Taylor 5-0; W. Jones & Mountjoy beat Knowles & Johnson 5-4; Griffiths & Dennis Taylor beat Spencer & Newbury 5-0; Thorburn & Thorne beat King & Wilson 5-2; P. Francisco & S. Francisco beat Virgo & Stevens 5-3; N. Foulds & Parrott beat Charlton & Werbeniuk 5-4; S. Davis & Meo beat E. Hughes & Smith 5-1

Quarter-finals: T. Jones & Reardon beat Mans & Campbell 5-4; Griffiths & Dennis Taylor beat W. Jones & Mountjoy 5-2; Thorburn & Thorne beat P. Francisco & S. Francisco 5-3; S. Davis & Meo beat N. Foulds & Parrott 5-3

Semi-finals: T. Jones & Reardon beat Griffiths & Dennis Taylor 9-6; S. Davis & Meo beat Thorburn & Thorne 9-6

Final: S. Davis & Meo beat T. Jones & Reardon 12-5

KIT KAT BREAK FOR WORLD CHAMPIONS

This new event brought together the eight world champions who are still playing competitive snooker. Staged over four days, without television coverage, at the East Midlands Conference Centre, Nottingham, the tournament had a total prize fund of £30,000 with £10,000 going to the winner.

1985

First round: Dennis Taylor beat F. Davis 5-0; T. Griffiths beat R. Reardon 5-2; S. Davis beat J. Spencer 5-2; A. Higgins beat C. Thorburn 5-4

Semi-finals: Dennis Taylor beat Griffiths 6-4; S. Davis beat Higgins 6-1

Final: Dennis Taylor beat S. Davis 9-5

MERCANTILE CREDIT CLASSIC

The nature, status and sponsorship of this event has changed several times since 1980 when it was born as the Wilsons Classic, an invitation tournament recorded by Granada Television for later showing.

When the event was networked for the first time in 1982, it was still by invitation but it had a new sponsor, the Russian car company, Lada. Stepping in at the last moment, Lada by chance achieved an enormous bonus when, during his first round match at Oldham Civic Centre, Steve Davis compiled the first televised maximum break.

The event moved to its present home, the Spectrum Arena, Warrington, in 1983 and a year later earned the status of a world ranking tournament when it was thrown open to all professionals. 1984, though, was to be Lada's last year and in 1985 the city finance house, Mercantile Credit, stepped in with a total prize fund of £200,000.

Willie Thorne won his first major title and £40,000 by beating Steve Davis and Cliff Thorburn in the last two rounds. The 1986 final saw Jimmy White win his first ranking tournament with a 13-12 victory over Cliff Thorburn. White won the deciding frame on the black after needing a snooker with only the last two colours remaining.

1980 (Jan) (*Wilsons Classic*)
Final: J. Spencer beat A. Higgins 4-3

1980 (Dec) (*Wilsons Classic*)
Final: S. Davis beat Dennis Taylor 4-1

1982 (*Lada Classic*)
First round: T. Griffiths beat C. Thorburn 5-1; A. Higgins beat Dennis Taylor 5-1; R. Reardon beat David Taylor 5-1; S. Davis beat J. Spencer 5-2

Semi-finals: Griffiths beat Higgins 5-1; S. Davis beat Reardon 5-4

Final: Griffiths beat S. Davis 9-8

1983 (*Lada Classic*)
First round: E. Charlton beat J. Virgo 5-2; J. Spencer beat R. Reardon 5-3; C. Thorburn beat C. Wilson 5-3; D. Mountjoy beat T. Griffiths 5-1; David Taylor beat J. White 5-3; B. Werbeniuk beat A. Higgins 5-4; K. Stevens beat A. Knowles 5-0; S. Davis beat Dennis Taylor 5-2

Quarter-finals: Spencer beat David Taylor 5-2; Werbeniuk beat Mountjoy 5-2; Stevens beat Thorburn 5-3; S. Davis beat Charlton 5-4

Semi-finals: S. Davis beat Spencer 5-4; Werbeniuk beat Stevens 5-2

Final: S. Davis beat Werbeniuk 9-5

1984 (*Lada Classic*)
First qualifying round: G. Foulds beat M. Gauvreau 5-2; B. Demarco beat M. Gibson 5-2; N. Foulds beat P. Houlihan 5-3; M. Morra beat P. Burke 5-2; G. Ganim beat D. Hughes 5-2; I. Williamson beat D. French 5-1; J. Hargreaves beat W. King 5-3; W. Oliver beat D. Sheehan 5-3; T. Jones beat P. Mifsud 5-3; P. Morgan beat M. Darrington 5-3; G. Cripsey beat V. Harris 5-4; J. Parrott beat B. Bennett 5-0; P. Browne beat D. Greaves 5-2; P. Watchorn beat R. Andrewartha 5-2; S. Duggan beat B. Harris 5-2; P. Medati beat T. Murphy 5-4

Second qualifying round: E. McLaughlin beat G. Foulds 5-1; G. Scott beat Demarco 5-2; N. Foulds beat Jack Rea 5-1; Morra beat C. Everton 5-0; C. Roscoe beat Ganim 5-3; F. Jonik beat Williamson 5-1; Hargreaves beat B. Kelly 5-4; Oliver beat J. Donnelly 5-4; Morgan beat M. Watterson 5-3; T. Jones beat I. Black 5-0; J. Campbell beat Cripsey 5-3; Parrott beat J. Fitzmaurice 5-2; R. Edmonds beat Browne 5-1; M. Fisher beat Watchorn 5-4; L. Dodd beat Duggan 5-2; E. Hughes beat Medati 5-1

Third qualifying round: E. McLaughlin beat W. Thorne 5-3; D. Reynolds beat Scott 5-3; C. Wilson beat N. Foulds 5-4; S. Francisco beat Morra 5-1; Roscoe beat G. Miles 5-2; J. Johnson beat Jonik 5-2; M. Wildman beat Hargreaves 5-1; P. Fagan beat Oliver 5-1; E. Sinclair beat Morgan 5-2; M. Macleod beat T. Jones 5-2; Campbell beat F. Davis 5-0; Parrott beat D. Martin 5-1; R. Williams beat Edmonds 5-1; J. Meadowcroft beat Fisher 5-0; M. Hallett beat Dodd 5-1; E. Hughes beat J. Dunning 5-4

First round: K. Stevens beat E. McLaughlin 5-4; T. Griffiths beat Reynolds 5-2; E. Charlton beat Wilson 5-0; S. Francisco beat C. Thorburn 5-1; Roscoe beat B. Werbeniuk 5-4; J. Spencer beat Johnson 5-4; Wildman beat J. Virgo 5-2; A. Higgins beat Fagan 5-3; S. Davis beat Sinclair 5-2; Macleod beat David Taylor 5-4; J. White beat Campbell 5-1; Parrott beat D. Mountjoy 5-4; Williams beat R. Reardon 5-4; T. Meo beat Meadowcroft 5-1; Hallett beat Dennis Taylor 5-4; A. Knowles beat E. Hughes 5-1

Second round: S. Davis beat Spencer 5-1; Charlton beat White 5-2; Wildman beat S. Francisco 5-1; Knowles beat Hallett 5-3; Stevens beat Macleod 5-1; Griffiths beat Roscoe 5-2; Meo beat Williams 5-3; Parrot beat Higgins 5-2

Quarter-finals: Wildman beat Charlton 5-4; S. Davis beat Griffiths 5-4; Meo beat Stevens 5-2; Parrott beat Knowles 5-1

Semi-finals: Meo beat Wildman 5-3; S. Davis beat Parrott 5-4

Final: S. Davis beat Meo 9-8

1985

Preliminary round: P. Watchorn beat D. Hughes 5-0; B. Mikkelsen beat D. Chalmers 5-1

First qualifying round: T. Jones beat D. Greaves 5-2; J. Giannaros beat T. Chappel 5-2; S. Newbury beat V. Harris 5-3; G. Foulds beat R. Chaperon 5-3; D. Sheehan beat John Rea 5-2; R. Bales beat B. Bennett 5-1; R. Foldvari beat P. Houlihan 5-1; P. Medati beat G. Cripsey 5-4; J. McLaughlin beat B. Demarco 5-1; S. Longworth beat P. Francisco 5-4; A. Kearney beat D. French 5-1; P. Browne beat M. Bradley 5-3; W. Jones beat D. O'Kane 5-0; D. Fowler beat Rigitano 5-0; J. Hargreaves beat Darrington 5-2

Second qualifying round: T. Jones beat M. Gibson 5-0; Newbury beat P. Burke 5-1; G. Foulds beat F. Jonik 5-2; E. McLaughlin beat Sheehan 5-2; Bales beat B. Kelly 5-3; Foldvari beat Jack Rea 5-4; J. McLaughlin beat I. Black 5-0; Longworth beat B. Oliver 5-1; Watchorn beat Mikkelsen 5-1; I. Williamson beat Kearney 5-3; Browne beat C. Everton 5-0; S. Duggan beat W. Jones 5-0; Fowler beat T. Murphy 5-0; R. Edmonds beat Hargreaves 5-2

Third qualifying round: T. Jones beat L. Dodd 5-1; M. Gauvreau beat Giannaros 5-3; Newbury beat M. Morra 5-2; G. Foulds beat J. Fitzmaurice 5-1; E. McLaughlin beat F. Davis 5-1; Medati beat C. Roscoe 5-4; G. Scott beat J. McLaughlin 5-4; Longworth beat M. Fisher 5-1; J. Donnelly beat Watchorn 5-1; P. Fagan beat Williamson 5-1; W. King beat Duggan 5-4; Fowler beat J. Meadowcroft 5-2; Edmonds beat M. Watterson 5-2

Fourth qualifying round: S. Francisco beat T. Jones 5-1; Fagan beat M. Wildman 5-3; M. Hallett beat G. Foulds 5-4; M. Macleod beat E. McLaughlin 5-4; Medati beat J. Parrott 5-3; C. Wilson beat Fowler 5-4; Gauvreau beat E. Sinclair 5-1; J. Johnson beat Edmonds 5-4; Scott beat J. Campbell 5-4; E. Hughes beat Newbury 5-3; King beat D. Reynolds 5-2; R. Williams beat Donnelly 5-3; J. Virgo beat Bales 5-1; Longworth beat N. Foulds 5-3; Foldvari beat D. Martin 5-2; Browne beat G. Miles 5-3

First round: Longworth beat David Taylor 5-4; Johnson beat A. Knowles 5-1; C. Thorburn beat Scott 5-1; King beat J. Spencer 5-2; T. Griffiths beat Fagan 5-0; J. White beat Browne 5-2; E. Hughes beat T. Meo 5-4; Macleod beat Charlton 5-1; A. Higgins beat Gauvreau 5-3; Virgo beat B. Werbeniuk 5-2; Wilson beat D. Mountjoy 5-4; Williams beat Dennis Taylor 5-3; R. Reardon beat Hallett 5-3; S. Davis beat S. Francisco 5-0; W. Thorne beat Foldvari 5-2; K. Stevens beat Medati 5-4

Second round: Reardon beat E. Hughes 5-1; S. Davis beat Higgins 5-2; Virgo beat Macleod 5-0; Thorne beat Stevens 5-1; Thorburn beat Longworth 5-3; Griffiths beat Williams 5-3; Johnson beat Wilson 5-0; King beat White 5-2

Quarter-finals: S. Davis beat Reardon 5-1; Thorburn beat Griffiths 5-4; Johnson beat King 5-3; Thorne beat Virgo 5-1

Semi-finals: Thorne beat S. Davis 9-8; Thorburn beat Johnson 9-2

Final: Thorne beat Thorburn 13-8

1986

First round: D. Gilbert beat G. Watson 5-4; A. Kearney beat Jim Bear 5-0; S. Hendry beat D. Sheehan 5-2; B. Demarco beat O. Agrawal 5-4; M. Smith beat D. Mienie 5-1; J. O'Boye beat G. Wilkinson 5-1; B. West beat M. Darrington 5-0; P. Burke beat D. Hughes 5-3; S. Simngam beat J. Hargreaves 5-1; R. Bales beat M. Parkin 5-0; D. Greaves beat P. Watchorn 5-4; G. Jenkins *wo* G. Robinson *scr*; G. Cripsey beat T. Drago 5-4; P. Houlihan beat B. Bennett 5-0

Second round: T. Jones beat Gilbert 5-3; G. Foulds beat I. Black 5-2; W. King beat S. Duggan 5-2; P. Medati beat Kearney 5-2; Hendry beat G. Miles 5-1; M. Bradley beat B. Oliver 5-3; B. Mikkelsen beat G. Scott 5-1; J. Donnelly beat D. Chalmers 5-0; F. Davis beat B. Kelly 5-3; J. Wych beat Demarco 5-0; B. Harris beat M. Morra 5-3; Smith beat R. Edmonds 5-2; O'Boye beat S. Longworth 5-1; West beat J. Meadowcroft 5-0; J. McLaughlin beat E. McLaughlin 5-2; John Rea beat I. Williamson 5-4; R. Chaperon beat Burke 5-2; J. Van Rensberg beat W. Jones 5-4; P. Francisco beat F. Jonik 5-2; T. Murphy beat T. Chappel 5-4; M. Gauvreau beat Simngam 5-1; M. Gibson *wo* J. Dunning *scr*; P. Browne beat C. Everton 5-0; D. Fowler beat Bales 5-4; G. Rigitano beat L. Dodd 5-3; E. Sinclair beat Greaves 5-1; V. Harris beat C. Roscoe 5-1; M. Watterson beat Jenkins 5-2; M. Fisher beat Jack Rea 5-3; Cripsey beat S. Newbury 5-4; J. Fitzmaurice beat P. Fagan 5-3; Houlihan beat R. Foldvari 5-4

Third round: T. Jones beat W. Thorne 5-3; B. Werbeniuk beat G. Foulds 5-3; D. Mountjoy beat King 5-4; D. O'Kane beat Medati 5-0; Hendry beat S. Francisco 5-4; N. Foulds beat Bradley 5-3; Mikkelsen beat R. Reardon 5-3; J. Campbell beat Donnelly 5-2; F. Davis beat K. Stevens 5-2; E. Hughes beat Wych 5-2; J. Johnson beat B. Harris 5-4; P. Mans beat Smith 5-4; T. Meo beat O'Boye 5-3; West beat M. Wildman 5-2; C. Thorburn beat J. McLaughlin 5-1; M. Hallett beat John Rea 5-2; S. Davis beat Chaperon 5-1; Van Rensberg beat J. Parrott 5-3; P. Francisco beat E. Charlton 5-1; D. Martin beat Murphy 5-3; Gauvreau beat David Taylor 5-3; Browne beat C. Wilson 5-3; J. White beat Fowler 5-1; J. Virgo beat Gibson 5-3; A. Knowles beat Rigitano 5-4; M. Macleod beat Sinclair 5-2; V. Harris beat T. Griffiths 5-3; R. Williams beat Watterson 5-0; A. Higgins beat Fisher 5-0; Cripsey beat J. Spencer 5-1; Dennis Taylor beat Fitzmaurice 5-1; D. Reynolds beat Houlihan 5-1

Fourth round: Werbeniuk beat T. Jones 5-3; Mountjoy beat O'Kane 5-3; N. Foulds beat Hendry 5-4; Campbell beat Mikkelsen 5-2; E. Hughes beat F. Davis 5-3; Johnson beat Mans 5-2; Meo beat West 5-1; Thorburn beat Hallett 5-3; S. Davis beat Van Rensberg 5-1; P. Francisco beat Martin 5-2; Gauvreau beat Browne 5-3; White beat Virgo 5-2; Knowles beat Macleod 5-4; Williams beat V. Harris 5-1; Higgins beat Cripsey 5-2; Dennis Taylor beat Reynolds 5-4

Fifth round: Mountjoy beat Werbeniuk 5-3; N. Foulds beat Campbell 5-1; Johnson beat E. Hughes 5-1; Thorburn beat Meo 5-1; S. Davis beat

P. Francisco 5-0; White beat Gauvreau 5-2; Williams beat Knowles 5-2; Higgins beat Dennis Taylor 5-4

Quarter-finals: Mountjoy beat N. Foulds 5-3; Thorburn beat Johnson 5-4; White beat S. Davis 5-2; Williams beat Higgins 5-2

Semi-finals: Thorburn beat Mountjoy 9-6; White beat Williams 9-7

Final: White beat Thorburn 13-12

BCE BELGIAN CLASSIC

For the first time, a professional Snooker tournament was promoted on the continent of Europe. The game is already very popular in the countries that can receive British television and BCE, the leading equipment company, and the World Professional Billiards and Snooker Association successfully promoted this inaugural tournament in the Ostend Casino. The event was televised by the Belgian Television Service and attracted large viewing figures.

From the field of eight of the top nine players in the world (Cliff Thorburn declined the invitation due to a long-standing charity engagement in Canada) Terry Griffiths took the £12,000 first prize with a 9-7 victory over Kirk Stevens.

First round: A. Higgins beat Dennis Taylor 5-1; K. Stevens beat R. Reardon 5-1; A. Knowles beat J. White 5-3; T. Griffiths beat S. Davis 5-2

Semi-finals: Stevens beat Higgins 5-4; Griffiths beat Knowles 5-2

Final: Griffiths beat Stevens 9-7

BENSON AND HEDGES MASTERS

Inaugurated in 1975, the Benson and Hedges Masters is the oldest tournament on the circuit to have been continuously sponsored by the same company.

After only one year at the West Centre Hotel, it moved to the New London Theatre in Drury Lane thus establishing a link between snooker and theatre in the round. The event moved to its present home, Wembley Conference Centre, in 1979.

Initially, only the final was televised and only ten players were invited to compete. Now it is restricted to the top 16 players in the world rankings and is televised by the BBC for its full eight days.

Snooker's only London tournament, its prize fund has risen from £5,000 in 1975 to £150,000 in 1985.

In 1984, Kirk Stevens set a new break record when he compiled a 147 maximum in the semi-finals against Jimmy White.

Two years later, Cliff Thorburn was to set two tournament records when he became not only the first to retain the title, but also the first player to win it three times.

1975

First round: J. Pulman beat C. Thorburn 5-3; A. Higgins beat B. Werbeniuk 5-0

Quarter-finals: E. Charlton beat F. Davis 5-3; J. Spencer beat Pulman 5-3; R. Reardon beat G. Miles 5-3; R. Williams beat Higgins 5-3

Semi-finals: Spencer beat Charlton 5-2; Reardon beat Williams 5-4

Final: Spencer beat Reardon 9-8

1976

First round: F. Davis beat C. Thorburn 4-2; J. Pulman beat Dennis Taylor 4-2

Quarter-finals: G. Miles beat A. Higgins 4-1; R. Reardon beat Pulman 4-1; J. Spencer beat F. Davis 4-0; E. Charlton beat R. Williams 4-1

Semi-finals: Miles beat Spencer 5-4; Reardon beat Charlton 5-4

Final: Reardon beat Miles 7-3

1977

First round: D. Mountjoy beat J. Pulman 4-2; J. Spencer beat Dennis Taylor 4-2

Quarter-finals: R. Reardon beat R. Williams 4-1; G. Miles beat Spencer 4-1; A. Higgins beat P. Mans 4-2; Mountjoy beat F. Davis 4-2

Semi-finals: Mountjoy beat Higgins 5-3; Reardon beat Miles 5-2

Final: Mountjoy beat Reardon 7-6

1978

First round: J. Pulman beat P. Fagan 4-2; G. Miles beat F. Davis 4-3

Quarter-finals: J. Spencer beat Pulman 4-2; A. Higgins beat Dennis Taylor 4-3; C. Thorburn beat D. Mountjoy 4-2; R. Reardon beat Miles 4-1

Semi-finals: Higgins beat Reardon 5-1; Thorburn beat Spencer 5-3

Final: Higgins beat Thorburn 7-5

1979
First round: D. Mountjoy beat F. Davis 5-2; David Taylor beat P. Fagan 5-4

Quarter-finals: A. Higgins beat E. Charlton 5-2; P. Mans beat C. Thorburn 5-4; Mountjoy beat Spencer 5-0; R. Reardon beat Taylor 5-2

Semi-finals: Higgins beat Mountjoy 5-1; Mans beat Reardon 5-3

Final: Mans beat Higgins 8-4

1980
First round: C. Thorburn beat J. Virgo 5-3; A. Higgins beat F. Davis 5-1

Quarter-finals: R. Reardon beat Dennis Taylor 5-3; T. Griffiths beat Thorburn 5-3; J. Spencer beat E. Charlton 5-2; Higgins beat P. Mans 5-1

Semi-finals: Griffiths beat Spencer 5-0; Higgins beat Reardon 5-2

Final: Griffiths beat Higgins 9-5

1981
First round: P. Mans beat S. Davis 5-3; D. Mountjoy beat E. Charlton 5-0; F. Davis beat K. Stevens 5-4; J. Spencer beat Dennis Taylor 5-2

Quarter-finals: A. Higgins beat Mountjoy 5-1; C. Thorburn beat Mans 5-4; Spencer beat R. Reardon 5-1; T. Griffiths beat F. Davis 5-2

Semi-finals: Higgins beat Thorburn 6-5; Griffiths beat Spencer 6-5

Final: Higgins beat Griffiths 9-6

1982
First round: R. Reardon beat Dennis Taylor 5-3; D. Mountjoy beat J. Spencer 5-4; T. Meo beat David Taylor 5-2; E. Charlton beat J. White 5-4

Quarter-finals: Meo beat C. Thorburn 5-0; S. Davis beat Mountjoy 5-2; A. Higgins beat Charlton 5-1; T. Griffiths beat Reardon 5-3

Semi-finals: S. Davis beat Meo 6-4; Griffiths beat Higgins 6-5

Final: S. Davis beat Griffiths 9-5

1983
First round: B. Werbeniuk beat A. Higgins 5-4; E. Charlton beat T. Meo 5-3; T. Griffiths beat K. Stevens 5-3; C. Thorburn beat J. Johnson 5-2; R. Reardon beat D. Reynolds 5-1; D. Mountjoy beat J. Virgo 5-1; S. Davis beat M. Wildman 5-2; J. White beat David Taylor 5-2

Quarter-finals: Charlton beat Werbeniuk 5-3; Thorburn beat Griffiths 5-3; Reardon beat White 5-2; Mountjoy beat S. Davis 5-4

Semi-finals: Thorburn beat Charlton 6-5; Reardon beat Mountjoy 6-3

Final: Thorburn beat Reardon 9-7

1984

First round: A. Knowles beat Dennis Taylor 5-2; R. Reardon beat J. Virgo 5-3; J. Spencer beat C. Thorburn 5-4; T. Griffiths beat B. Werbeniuk 5-1; J. White beat E. Charlton 5-2; A. Higgins beat D. Mountjoy 5-2; K. Stevens beat David Taylor 5-1; S. Davis beat T. Meo 5-0

Quarter-finals: Griffiths beat Spencer 5-4; Knowles beat Higgins 5-1; White beat Reardon 5-3; Stevens beat S. Davis 5-3

Semi-finals: Griffiths beat Knowles 6-4; White beat Stevens 6-4

Final: White beat Griffiths 9-5

1985

First round: J. White beat W. Thorne 5-2; J. Spencer beat E. Charlton 5-3; R. Reardon beat David Taylor 5-1; C. Thorburn beat Dennis Taylor 5-3; D. Mountjoy beat Knowles 5-3; T. Meo beat K. Stevens 5-2; T. Griffiths beat B. Werbeniuk 5-2; A. Higgins beat S. Davis 5-4

Quarter-finals: White beat Spencer 5-2; Thorburn beat Reardon 5-0; Mountjoy beat Meo 5-4; Griffiths beat Higgins 5-1

Semi-finals: Thorburn beat White 6-4; Mountjoy beat Griffiths 6-2

Final: Thorburn beat Mountjoy 9-6

1986

First round: C. Thorburn beat J. Johnson 5-3; T. Griffiths beat A. Higgins 5-4; E. Charlton beat K. Stevens 5-4; A. Knowles beat S. Francisco 5-1; S. Davis beat David Taylor 5-4; W. Thorne beat R. Reardon 5-4; J. White beat T. Meo 5-4; Dennis Taylor beat D. Mountjoy 5-2

Quarter-finals: Thorburn beat Griffiths 5-2; Knowles beat Charlton 5-4; S. Davis beat Thorne 5-4; White beat Dennis Taylor 5-3

Semi-finals: Thorburn beat Knowles 6-4; White beat S. Davis 6-3

Final: Thorburn beat White 9-5

DULUX BRITISH OPEN

When Yamaha withdrew from sponsorship of a televised non-ranking tournament, the WPBSA had the opportunity to stage another ranking event and the Dulux British Open was created, in 1985, to fill the late February/early March slot.

The first final saw Silvino Francisco beat Kirk Stevens 12-9 and was the first in a major tournament not to feature a British player.

The following year, Steve Davis won his third ranking tournament of the season with a 12-7 victory over Willie Thorne.

1985

Qualifying: T. Chappel beat I. Williamson 6-5; D. Chalmers beat P. Burke 6-5; John Rea beat M. Fisher 6-0; W. King beat P. Medati 6-4; D. Fowler beat C. Everton 6-1; T. Murphy beat D. Sheehan 6-3; R. Foldvari beat S. Duggan 6-4; V. Harris beat L. Dodd 6-1; T. Jones beat G. Foulds 6-0; P. Francisco beat B. Kelly 6-3; D. O'Kane beat G. Cripsey 6-4; S. Newbury beat P. Browne 6-0; M. Bradley beat M. Morra 6-2; A. Kearney beat M. Watterson 6-4; D. French beat E. McLaughlin 6-0; R. Chaperon beat P. Fagan 6-5; B. Harris beat J. Meadowcroft 6-1; S. Longworth beat F. Davis 6-1; B. Mikkelsen beat D. Hughes 6-0; G. Scott beat M. Darrington 6-3; J. Giannaros beat C. Roscoe 6-1; F. Jonik beat J. McLaughlin 6-2; W. Jones beat J. Donnelly 6-1; P. Watchorn beat J. Fitzmaurice 6-1; R. Bales beat I. Black 6-4; M. Gauvreau beat D. Greaves 6-3; M. Gibson beat B. Demarco 6-1; R. Edmonds beat D. Mienie 6-1

First round: D. Reynolds beat Giannaros 6-3; M. Macleod beat Murphy 6-5; E. Hughes beat Watchorn 6-4; Longworth beat C. Wilson 6-3; W. Jones beat J. Johnson 6-5; M. Hallett *wo* Mikkelsen *scr*; C. Thorburn beat G. Rigitano 6-3; A. Higgins beat Bales 6-3; Chaperon beat B. Werbeniuk 6-1; S. Francisco beat Kearney 6-4; T. Meo beat Foldvari 6-0; W. Thorne beat W. Oliver 6-3; B. Harris beat E. Charlton 6-3; J. White beat T. Jones 6-5; A. Knowles beat French 6-2; N. Foulds beat J. Hargreaves 6-1; Newbury beat E. Sinclair 6-3; M. Wildman beat Gibson 6-1; J. Spencer beat Jonik 6-0; V. Harris beat D. Mountjoy 6-5; O'Kane beat J. Campbell 6-4; G. Miles beat Edmonds 6-1; T. Griffiths beat Chalmers 6-0; R. Reardon beat King 6-5; J. Parrott beat John Rea 6-4; Bradley beat David Taylor 6-3; K. Stevens beat Gauvreau 6-3; J. Virgo beat P. Francisco 6-2; Fowler beat R. Williams 6-4; D. Martin beat B. Bennett 6-0; S. Davis beat Chappel 6-5; Dennis Taylor beat Scott 6-2

Second round: Newbury beat Griffiths 5-3; Bradley beat Fowler 5-4; S. Davis beat Virgo 5-2; Knowles beat Longworth 5-2; O'Kane beat V. Harris 5-3; Thorburn beat Reynolds 5-3; Higgins beat N. Foulds 5-1; Dennis Taylor beat Parrott 5-2; Macleod beat Thorne 5-0; Martin beat Reardon 5-4; Miles beat Spencer 5-3; S. Francisco beat White 5-4; Meo beat Hallett 5-4; E. Hughes beat B. Harris 5-4; Stevens beat Wildman 5-2; Chaperon beat W. Jones 5-2

Third round: Meo beat Knowles 5-2; S. Davis beat Bradley 5-2; O'Kane beat Martin 5-4; S. Francisco beat Chaperon 5-2; Dennis Taylor beat Newbury 5-3; E. Hughes beat Macleod 5-2; Stevens beat Miles 5-2; Higgins beat Thorburn 5-2

Quarter-finals: Stevens beat Dennis Taylor 5-2; S. Davis beat O'Kane 5-1; S. Francisco beat Meo 5-4; Higgins beat E. Hughes 5-2

Semi-finals: Stevens beat S. Davis 9-7; S. Francisco beat Higgins 9-6

Final: S. Francisco beat Stevens 12-9

1986

First round: J. O'Boye beat Jim Bear 5-1; J. Hargreaves *wo* G. Watson *scr*; O. B. Agrawal beat D. Greaves 5-3; D. Gilbert beat P. Burke 5-1; S. Hendry beat D. Hughes 5-1; G. Wilkinson beat P. Watchorn 5-4; D. Sheehan beat S. Simngam 5-2; G. Jenkins beat B. Demarco 5-1; B. West beat B. Bennett 5-1; G. Cripsey beat M. Darrington 5-4; P. Houlihan *wo* G. Robinson *scr*; A. Kearney beat M. Smith 5-2; R. Bales beat M. Parkin 5-1; T. Drago *wo* D. Mienie *scr*

Second round: T. Jones beat O'Boye 5-2; F. Davis beat W. Kelly 5-4; G. Scott beat D. Chalmers 5-1; Hargreaves beat R. Edmonds 5-3; L. Dodd beat F. Jonik 5-4; W. Jones beat G. Rigitano 5-1; G. Miles beat Agrawal 5-4; R. Chaperon beat V. Harris 5-0; John Rea beat W. King 5-1; D. Fowler beat T. Chappel 5-4; Gilbert beat M. Morra 5-4; P. Browne beat Hendry 5-0; J. Donnelly beat Wilkinson 5-4; S. Newbury beat W. Oliver 5-2; Sheehan *wo* M. Watterson *scr*; Jenkins beat J. Meadowcroft 5-2; I. Black beat M. Gibson 5-0; B. Harris beat E. Sinclair 5-3; P. Medati beat C. Everton 5-1; West beat E. McLaughlin 5-3; P. Fagan beat J. Fitzmaurice 5-4; C. Roscoe beat B. Mikkelsen 5-4; I. Williamson beat Cripsey 5-4; J. Wych beat J. Van Rensberg 5-0; P. Francisco beat G. Foulds 5-2; S. Longworth beat Houlihan 5-3; M. Bradley beat Jack Rea 5-1; S. Duggan beat T. Murphy 5-1; J. McLaughlin beat M. Fisher 5-3; R. Foldvari beat Kearney 5-2; Bales *wo* J. Dunning *scr*; Drago beat M. Gauvreau 5-3

Third round: S. Francisco beat T. Jones 5-2; M. Macleod beat F. Davis 5-4; T. Griffiths beat Scott 5-3; N. Foulds beat Hargreaves 5-4; W. Thorne beat Dodd 5-2; P. Mans beat W. Jones 5-2; K. Stevens beat Miles 5-3; C. Wilson beat Chaperon 5-3; John Rea beat R. Reardon 5-3; J. Virgo beat Fowler 5-1; E. Charlton beat Gilbert 5-2; Browne beat J. Spencer 5-0; T. Meo beat Donnelly 5-3; Newbury beat D. O'Kane 5-3; C. Thorburn beat Sheehan 5-0; M. Wildman beat Jenkins 5-4; S. Davis beat Black 5-2; D. Martin beat B. Harris 5-1; Medati beat David Taylor 5-1; J. Campbell beat West 5-4; Fagan beat D. Mountjoy 5-1; J. Parrott beat Roscoe 5-2; A. Knowles beat Williamson 5-1; Wych beat D. Reynolds 5-3; P. Francisco beat J. White 5-4; Longworth beat E. Hughes 5-4; A. Higgins beat Bradley 5-3; M. Hallett beat Duggan 5-3; J. Johnson beat J. McLaughlin 5-2; B. Werbeniuk beat Foldvari 5-4; Bales beat Dennis Taylor 5-4; R. Williams beat Drago 5-1

Fourth round: Macleod beat S. Francisco 5-1; Griffiths beat N. Foulds 5-3; Thorne beat Mans 5-1; Stevens beat Wilson 5-0; Virgo beat John Rea 5-0; Charlton beat Browne 5-1; Meo beat Newbury 5-0; Thorne beat Wildman 5-1; S. Davis beat Martin 5-1; Campbell beat Medati 5-4; Parrott beat Fagan 5-0; Wych beat Knowles 5-4; P. Francisco beat Longworth 5-2; Higgins beat Hallett 5-1; Werbeniuk beat Johnson 5-3; Williams beat Bales 5-4

Fifth round: Griffiths beat Macleod 5-2; Thorne beat Stevens 5-4; Virgo beat Charlton 5-4; Meo beat Thorburn 5-3; S. Davis beat Campbell 5-0; Wych beat Parrott 5-4; Higgins beat P. Francisco 5-2; Werbeniuk beat Williams 5-3

Quarter-finals: Thorne beat Griffiths 5-4; Virgo beat Meo 5-3; S. Davis beat Wych 5-2; Higgins beat Werbeniuk 5-1

Semi-finals: Thorne beat Virgo 9-4; S. Davis beat Higgins 9-3

Final: S. Davis beat Thorne 12-7

CAR CARE PLAN WORLD CUP

When State Express withdrew from their five-year sponsorship of the team championship, their slot in the television schedules was taken over by the Rothmans Grand Prix, as was their venue, The Hexagon, Reading.

However, a new sponsor, venue, format and date were found and the Guinness World Cup was played on a knock-out basis at the Conference Centre, Bournemouth in March with all four days' play being televised by the BBC.

But after only one year Guinness withdrew from the sponsorship and, with only nine days before the start of the event, the WPBSA secured a £50,000 contribution towards the £100,000 prize fund for the 1986 event from Car Care Plan.

The remainder of the prize money was from the WPBSA but the event nevertheless saw its total prize money drop from £125,000 in 1985 to £100,000 in 1986.

1979 (*State Express World Team Classic*)
Group A
England (F. Davis, G. Miles, J. Spencer) beat Rest of World (P. Mans, J. van Rensberg, P. Fagan) 8-7; England beat Northern Ireland (Jack Rea, A. Higgins, Dennis Taylor) 8-7; Northern Ireland beat Rest of World 8-7

Group B
Wales (R. Reardon, T. Griffiths, D. Mountjoy) beat Canada (C. Thorburn, K. Stevens, B. Werbeniuk) 9-6; Australia (E. Charlton, G. Owen, P. Morgan) beat Canada 8-7; Wales beat Australia 9-6

Final: Wales beat England 14-3

1980 (*State Express World Team Classic*)
Group A
Wales (R. Reardon, T. Griffiths, D. Mountjoy) beat Canada (C. Thorburn, K. Stevens, B. Werbeniuk) 10-5; Canada beat Rest of World (J. Rempe, E. Sinclair, P. Mans) 9-6; Wales beat Rest of World 13-2

Group B
England (F. Davis, J. Virgo, David Taylor) beat Ireland (A. Higgins, Dennis Taylor, P. Fagan) 11-4; Australia (E. Charlton, I. Anderson, P. Morgan) beat England 8-7; Ireland beat Australia 10-5

Semi-finals: Wales beat Ireland 8-7; Canada beat England 8-5

Final: Wales beat Canada 8-5

1981 (*State Express World Team Classic*)
Preliminary match: Republic of Ireland (E. Hughes, P. Fagan, D. Sheehan) beat Scotland (I. Black, M. Macleod, E. Sinclair) 4-2

Group A
England (S. Davis, J. Spencer, David Taylor) beat Australia (I. Anderson, E. Charlton, P. Morgan) 4-3; Northern Ireland (T. Murphy, Dennis Taylor, A. Higgins) beat Australia 4-1; England beat Northern Ireland 4-3

Group B
Wales (R. Reardon, D. Mountjoy, T. Griffiths) beat Canada (K. Stevens, C. Thorburn, B. Werbeniuk) 4-2; Wales beat Republic of Ireland 4-0; Canada beat Republic of Ireland 4-2

Semi-finals: England beat Canada 4-2; Wales beat Northern Ireland 4-3

Final: England beat Wales 4-3

1982 (*State Express World Team Classic*)
Preliminary match: Scotland (E. Sinclair, J. Donnelly, I. Black) beat Republic of Ireland (E. Hughes, P. Fagan, D. Sheehan) 4-2

Group A
England (A. Knowles, S. Davis, J. White) beat Northern Ireland (A. Higgins, T. Murphy, Dennis Taylor) 4-3; Scotland beat Northern Ireland 4-1; England beat Scotland 4-1

Group B
Canada (C. Thorburn, B. Werbeniuk, K. Stevens) beat Wales (T. Griffiths, D. Mountjoy, R. Reardon) 4-3; Canada beat Australia (E. Charlton, P. Morgan, I. Anderson) 4-0; Wales beat Australia 4-1

Semi-finals: England beat Wales 4-2; Canada beat Scotland 4-0

Final: Canada beat England 4-2

1983 (*State Express World Team Classic*)
Preliminary match: Scotland (E. Sinclair, M. Macleod, I. Black) beat Republic of Ireland (B. Kelly, E. Hughes, P. Fagan) 4-2

Group A
Wales (D. Mountjoy, R. Reardon, T. Griffiths) beat Canada (C. Thorburn, B. Werbeniuk, K. Stevens) 4-3; Canada beat Australia (E. Charlton, W. King, J. Campbell) 4-2; Wales beat Australia 4-0

Group B
England (S. Davis, A. Knowles, T. Meo) beat Northern Ireland (A. Higgins, T. Murphy, Dennis Taylor) 4-1; Northern Ireland beat Scotland (E. Sinclair, I. Black, M. Macleod) 4-3; England beat Scotland 4-0

Semi-finals: Wales beat Northern Ireland 4-1; England beat Canada 4-2

Final: England beat Wales 4-2

1985 (*Guinness World Cup*)
First round: Wales beat Australia 5-4 (T. Griffiths drew with E. Charlton 1-1; D. Mountjoy beat J. Campbell 2-0; R. Reardon lost to W. King 0-2; Mountjoy drew with Charlton 1-1; Griffiths beat King 1-0); England A beat Scotland 5-4 (S. Davis lost to E. Sinclair 0-2; A. Knowles drew with M. Macleod 1-1; T. Meo beat J. Donnelly 2-0; S. Davis drew with Sinclair 1-1; Knowles beat Macleod 1-0); England B beat Rest of World 5-2 (J. White beat S. Francisco 2-0; W. Thorne drew with J. Rempe 1-1; J. Spencer drew with D. O'Kane 1-1; White beat Francisco 1-0); Ireland beat Canada 5-2 (Dennis Taylor beat K. Stevens 2-0; E. Hughes drew with C. Thorburn 1-1; A. Higgins drew with B. Werbeniuk 1-1; Higgins beat Thorburn 1-0)

Semi-finals: Ireland beat Wales 5-3 (Dennis Taylor drew with Mountjoy 1-1; E. Hughes lost to Griffiths 0-2; Higgins beat Reardon 2-0; Higgins beat Mountjoy 2-0); England A beat England B 5-2 (S. Davis beat Spencer 2-0; Knowles drew with Thorne 1-1; Meo drew with White 1-1; S. Davis beat White 1-0)

Final: Ireland beat England A 9-7 (Dennis Taylor drew with Knowles 1-1; E. Hughes lost to S. Davis 0-2; Higgins drew with Meo 1-1; Dennis Taylor drew with Knowles 1-1; Dennis Taylor drew with S. Davis 1-1; E. Hughes drew with Knowles 1-1; Higgins beat Meo 2-0; Higgins beat S. Davis 2-0)

1986
First round: Ireland A beat Ireland B 5-0 (A. Higgins beat P. Fagan 2-0; E. Hughes beat T. Murphy 2-0; Dennis Taylor beat P. Browne 1-0); Wales beat Scotland 5-1 (D. Mountjoy beat M. Macleod 2-0; R. Reardon drew with E. Sinclair 1-1; T. Griffiths beat J. Donnelly 2-0); Canada beat Rest of World 5-0 (C. Thorburn beat T. Drago 2-0; K. Stevens beat O. B. Agrawal 2-0; B. Werbeniuk beat S. Simngam 1-0); England beat Australia 5-2 (A. Knowles drew with J. Campbell 1-1; J. White drew with E. Charlton 1-1; S. Davis beat W. King 2-0; S. Davis beat Campbell 1-0)

Semi-finals: Ireland A beat Wales 5-2 (Higgins beat Mountjoy 2-0; Hughes lost to Reardon 0-2; Dennis Taylor beat Griffiths 2-0; Taylor beat Griffiths 1-0); Canada beat England 5-3 (Thorburn drew with Knowles 1-1; Stevens beat White 2-0; Werbeniuk drew with S. Davis 1-1; Thorburn drew with S. Davis 1-1)

Final: Ireland A beat Canada 9-7 (Dennis Taylor drew with Thorburn 1-1; Hughes lost to Stevens 0-2; Higgins beat Werbeniuk 2-0; Higgins drew with Stevens 1-1; Higgins drew with Thorburn 1-1; Hughes drew with Stevens 1-1; Taylor beat Werbeniuk 2-0; Taylor drew with Thorburn 1-1)

BENSON AND HEDGES IRISH MASTERS

In 1978 the Benson and Hedges Irish Masters began as a low-key tournament with round robin groups and play-off semi-finals and final. It was not until 1981, when it changed to a straight knock-out formula, that it became established as a major event.

Although restricted to 12 players, its importance on the circuit really lies in its timing – it is the last tournament before the World Championship. Its mixture of serious competitiveness and Irish hospitality makes this tournament the ideal pre-championship warm-up for the leading players.

1978
Final: J. Spencer beat D. Mountjoy 5-3

1979
Final: D. Mountjoy beat R. Reardon 6-5

1980
Final: T. Griffiths beat D. Mountjoy 9-8

1981
First round: Dennis Taylor beat J. Spencer 4-2; S. Davis beat J. Virgo 4-3

Quarter-finals: T. Griffiths beat K. Stevens 4-0; C. Thorburn beat D. Mountjoy 4-0; R. Reardon beat S. Davis 4-2; A. Higgins beat Dennis Taylor 4-2

Semi-finals: Griffiths beat Thorburn 6-5; Reardon beat Higgins 6-5

Final: Griffiths beat Reardon 9-7

1982
First round: Dennis Taylor beat D. Sheehan 5-3; T. Meo beat J. Spencer 5-3; A. Higgins beat J. Wych 5-3; D. Mountjoy beat E. Hughes 5-4

Quarter-finals: T. Griffiths beat Meo 5-3; R. Reardon beat Dennis Taylor 5-4; S. Davis beat Mountjoy 5-2; Higgins beat C. Thorburn 5-4

Semi-finals: Griffiths beat Reardon 6-3; S. Davis beat Higgins 6-2

Final: Griffiths beat S. Davis 9-5

1983
First round: J. White beat Dennis Taylor 5-4; T. Meo beat P. Burke 5-0; D. Mountjoy beat A. Knowles 5-1; E. Charlton beat David Taylor 5-4

Quarter-finals: R. Reardon beat Meo 5-4; A. Higgins beat White 5-2; S. Davis beat Charlton 5-1; T. Griffiths beat Mountjoy 5-4

Semi-finals: Reardon beat Higgins 6-3; S. Davis beat Griffiths 6-2

Final: S. Davis beat Reardon 9-2

1984
First round: T. Griffiths beat B. Werbeniuk 5-2; Dennis Taylor beat E. Hughes 5-1; T. Meo beat J. White 5-4; A. Higgins beat E. Charlton 5-2

Quarter-finals: Dennis Taylor beat C. Thorburn 5-2; Griffiths beat A. Knowles 5-0; Higgins beat R. Reardon 5-2; S. Davis beat Meo 5-4

Semi-finals: Griffiths beat Dennis Taylor 6-5; S. Davis beat Higgins 6-4

Final: S. Davis beat Griffiths 9-1

1985
First round: E. Charlton beat Dennis Taylor 5-4; J. White beat T. Meo 5-1; E. Hughes beat R. Reardon 5-0; A. Higgins beat T. Griffiths 5-2

Quarter-finals: A. Knowles beat Charlton 5-3; White beat C. Thorburn 5-3; S. Davis beat Hughes 5-4; Higgins beat K. Stevens 5-3

Semi-finals: White beat Knowles 6-4; Higgins beat S. Davis 6-2

Final: White beat Higgins 9-5

1986
First round: E. Hughes beat R. Reardon 5-2; W. Thorne beat T. Griffiths 5-2; T. Meo beat A. Higgins 5-4; P. Fagan *wo* K. Stevens *scr*

Quarter-finals: C. Thorburn beat Hughes 5-1; Thorne beat Dennis Taylor 5-2; J. White beat Meo 5-2; Fagan beat A. Knowles 5-4

Semi-finals: Thorne beat Thorburn 6-4; White beat Fagan 6-0

Final: White beat Thorne 9-5

EMBASSY WORLD PROFESSIONAL CHAMPIONSHIP

The World Professional Championship was first organised by – and won by – Joe Davis in 1927 when Joe and a Birmingham billiard trader, Bill Camkin, persuaded the then governing body, the Billiards Association and Control Council, to sanction it. That first final was played, inauspiciously, in one of Camkin's billiard halls in John Bright Street, Birmingham, and it was not until the mid-1930s that the Championship began to parallel and then overtake billiards as the main attraction at the game's 'holy of holies', Thurstons in Leicester Square.

Davis dominated the Championships before the war and won it again in 1946 – his 14th title – before retiring from championship play. The Championship, still played over the entire season with the final often scheduled to last a fortnight, was dominated for the next decade by Joe's younger brother, Fred, with eight wins, and a dour Scot, Walter Donaldson, with two.

But the cumbersome nature of the format and the advent of other forms of entertainment – especially television – caused the popularity of the event to decline and Fred did not enter the 1957 Championship, when for the first time it was won by John Pulman. With apathy now reigning, there was no Championship at all for the next six years. Through the efforts of Rex Williams it was revived in 1964 on a challenge basis, a system which continued until 1968, by which time Pulman had successfully countered seven challenges.

Commercial sponsorship was forthcoming for the first time in the 1968–69 season, so ending the era of challenge matches, and Players No. 6 also sponsored the 1970 event. In late 1970, the tournament was staged in Australia for the first time – without a sponsor. There was no sponsorship in 1972 either, although another tobacco company, Park Drive, filled the breach in 1973 and 1974.

Those two years saw the end of the Championship being staged throughout the season at a variety of venues. Eight tables were installed in one venue and the event was compressed into a fortnight. Although the set-up was found to be unwieldy with so many tables the pattern of the modern tournament format began to emerge.

After another sojourn in Australia in 1975, the event came back to Britain the following year and acquired its present sponsors, Embassy. A year later, it found its present home, the Crucible Theatre, Sheffield.

Now, the top 16 players on the world ranking list are exempted until the last 32 at Sheffield and the other players come through a qualifying section which in 1985 and 1986 was played at Preston Guild Hall on six tables. Until the semi-finals, two tables are used at Sheffield with a screen being lowered before play to separate the playing areas.

The Crucible Theatre and the Embassy World Championship have now attained such a special relationship that it is difficult to imagine the world champion being crowned anywhere else.

1927
First round: M. Inman beat T. Newman 8-5; T. Carpenter beat N. Butler 8-3

Second round: T. A. Dennis beat F. Lawrence 8-7; A. Cope beat A. Mann 8-6; J. Davis beat J. Brady 10-5; Carpenter beat Inman 8-3

Semi-finals: J. Davis beat Cope 16-7; Dennis beat Carpenter 12-10

Final: J. Davis beat Dennis 20-11

1928
First round: T. Newman beat F. Smith 12-6; A. Mann beat A. Cope 14-9

Second round: Newman beat T. A. Dennis 12-5; F. Lawrence beat Mann 12-11

Third round: Lawrence beat Newman 12-7

Final: J. Davis beat Lawrence 16-13

1929
First round: F. Lawrence beat A. Mann 13-12

Semi-finals: J. Davis beat Lawrence 13-10; T. A. Dennis beat K. Prince 14-6

Final: J. Davis beat Dennis 19-14

1930
First round: F. Lawrence beat A. Mann 13-11; N. Butler beat T. Newman 13-11

Semi-finals: J. Davis beat Lawrence 13-2; T. A. Dennis beat Butler 13-11

Final: J. Davis beat Dennis 25-12

1931
Final: J. Davis beat T. A. Dennis 25-21

1932
First round: C. McConachy beat T. A. Dennis 13-11

Final: J. Davis beat McConachy 30-19

1933
First round: W. Donaldson beat W. Leigh 13-11

Semi-finals: J. Davis beat Donaldson 13-1; W. Smith beat T. A. Dennis 16-9

Final: J. Davis beat Smith 25-18

1934
Final: J. Davis beat T. Newman 25-23

1935
First round: W. Smith beat C. Stanbury 13-12

Semi-finals: Smith beat A. Mann 13-4; J. Davis beat T. Newman 15-10

Final: J. Davis beat Smith 25-20

1936
First round: C. O'Donnell beat S. Lee 16-15; H. Lindrum beat H. Terry 20-11; J. Davis beat T. Newman 29-2; W. Smith beat S. Smith 16-15; C. Stanbury beat A. Mann 22-9

Second round: Alec Brown beat Stanbury 16-15; Lindrum beat O'Donnell 19-6 (*retd*); J. Davis beat W. Smith 22-9; S. Newman *wo*

Semi-finals: J. Davis beat Alec Brown 21-10; Lindrum beat S. Newman 29-2

Final: J. Davis beat Lindrum 34-27

1937
First round: W. A. Withers beat F. Davis 17-14

Second round: J. Davis beat Withers 30-1; H. Lindrum beat S. Lee 20-11; W. Smith beat T. Newman 16-15; S. Smith beat Alec Brown 18-13

Semi-finals: Lindrum beat W. Smith 20-11; J. Davis beat S. Smith 18-13

Final: J. Davis beat Lindrum 32-29

1938
First qualifying round: H. Holt beat C. W. Read 21-10

Second qualifying round: F. Davis beat Holt 23-8

First round: F. Davis beat Alec Brown 14-6 (*retd ill*); S. Smith beat C. Stanbury 27-4; J. Davis beat S. Lee 24-7; W. Smith beat T. Newman 16-15

Semi-finals: J. Davis beat W. Smith (*nrs*); S. Smith beat F. Davis (*nrs*)

Final: J. Davis beat S. Smith 37-24

1939
First qualifying round: W. Donaldson beat H. Holt 18-13; H. W. Laws beat S. Newman 19-12

Second qualifying round: Donaldson beat Laws 18-13

First round: S. Smith beat S. Lee 21-10; W. Donaldson beat C. Falkiner 21-10; T. Newman beat A. Mann 19-12; F. Davis beat C. Stanbury 19-12

Second round: J. Davis beat W. Smith 19-12; F. Davis beat T. Newman 20-11; Alec Brown beat H. Lindrum 17-14; S. Smith beat Donaldson 16-15

Semi-finals: J. Davis beat F. Davis 17-14; S. Smith beat Alec Brown 20-11

Final: J. Davis beat S. Smith 43-30

1940
Qualifying round: H. Holt beat C. Stanbury 18-13

First round: W. Donaldson beat Holt 24-7; J. Davis beat Alec Brown 20-11; F. Davis beat S. Lee 20-11; S. Smith beat T. Newman 22-9

Semi-finals: J. Davis beat Donaldson 22-9; F. Davis beat S. Smith 17-14

Final: J. Davis beat F. Davis 37-36

1946
First qualifying round: K. Kennerley beat F. Lawrence 22-9; C. Stanbury beat J. Barrie 18-13; S. Newman beat W. Leigh 16-15

Second qualifying round: Kennerley beat T. Reece 8-2 (*retd*); S. Newman beat Stanbury 17-14

Third qualifying round: S. Newman beat Kennerley 21-10

First round: J. Davis beat W. Donaldson 21-10; S. Newman beat S. Lee 19-12; F. Davis beat Alec Brown 24-7; H. Lindrum beat H. Holt 17-14

Semi-finals: J. Davis beat S. Newman 21-10; Lindrum beat F. Davis 16-12

Final: J. Davis beat Lindrum 78-67

1947
First qualifying round: Albert Brown beat J. Pulman 21-14; W. Leigh beat H. F. Francis 19-16; S. Lee beat J. Lees 19-16; K. Kennerley beat C. Stanbury 23-12; E. Newman *wo* H. Holt *scr*

Second qualifying round: J. Barrie beat F. Lawrence 25-10; Albert Brown beat Newman 28-7; Kennerley beat A. Mann 23-12; Leigh beat Lee 25-10

Third qualifying round: Albert Brown beat Barrie 24-11; Kennerley beat Leigh 21-14

Fourth qualifying round: Albert Brown beat Kennerley 21-14

First round: H. Lindrum beat Albert Brown 39-34; S. Smith beat Alec Brown 43-28; W. Donaldson beat S. Newman 46-25; F. Davis beat C. McConachy 53-20

Semi-finals: Donaldson beat Lindrum 39-32; F. Davis beat Smith 39-32

Final: Donaldson beat F. Davis 82-63

1948
First qualifying round: C. Stanbury beat E. Newman 26-9; W. Leigh beat H. Holt 18-17; J. Barrie beat H. F. Francis 19-16; J. Pulman *wo* S. Lee *scr*

Second qualifying round: Leigh beat Barrie 21-14; Pulman beat Stanbury 19-16

Third qualifying round: Pulman beat Leigh 18-17

First round: F. Davis beat Alec Brown 43-28; C. McConachy beat J. Pulman 42-29; Albert Brown beat S. Smith 36-35; W. Donaldson beat K. Kennerley 46-25

Semi-finals: F. Davis beat McConachy 43-28; Donaldson beat Alec Brown 40-31

Final: F. Davis beat Donaldson 84-61

1949
First qualifying round: C. Stanbury beat H. F. Francis 18-17

Second qualifying round: Stanbury beat Jack Rea 18-17

Third qualifying round: Stanbury beat H. Holt 18-17

First round: W. Donaldson beat Stanbury 58-13; J. Pulman beat Albert Brown 42-29; S. Smith beat Alec Brown 41-30; F. Davis beat K. Kennerley 50-21

Semi-finals: Donaldson beat Pulman 49-22; F. Davis beat Smith 42-29

Final: F. Davis beat Donaldson 80-65

1950
First qualifying round: W. Smith beat W. A. Withers 28-7; H. Holt beat H. W. Laws 26-9; S. Lee beat C. Stanbury 20-15; K. Kennerley beat J. Barrie 21-14

Second qualifying round: Kennerley beat Smith 22-13; Lee beat Holt 16-8 (*retd ill*)

Third qualifying round: Kennerley beat Lee 21-14

First round: Albert Brown beat J. Pulman 37-34; W. Donaldson beat K. Kennerley 42-29; G. Chenier beat P. Mans 37-34; F. Davis beat Alec Brown 44-27

Semi-finals: Donaldson beat Albert Brown 37-34; F. Davis beat Chenier 43-28

Final: Donaldson beat F. Davis 51-46

1951
First qualifying round: J. Barrie beat S. Lee 23-12

Second qualifying round: Barrie beat H. W. Laws 28-7

First round: F. Davis beat Barrie 42-29; H. Lindrum beat Albert Brown 43-28; W. Donaldson beat K. Kennerley 41-30; J. Pulman beat S. Smith 38-33

Semi-finals: Donaldson beat Lindrum 41-30; F. Davis beat Pulman 22-14 (*retd ill*)

Final: F. Davis beat Donaldson 58-39

1952
First round: Alec Brown beat R. Williams 39-22; Jack Rea beat J. Lees 38-32; Albert Brown beat J. Pulman 32-27 (*records incomplete*)

Semi-finals: W. Donaldson beat Albert Brown 31-30

Final: F. Davis beat Donaldson 38-35

1953
First qualifying round: W. Smith beat J. Lees 21-14; K. Kennerley beat R. Williams 25-12

Second qualifying round: Kennerley beat Smith 42-29

First round: Albert Brown beat Alec Brown 35-26; J. Pulman beat Jack Rea 36-25; W. Donaldson beat Kennerley 42-19; F. Davis beat J. Barrie 32-29

Semi-finals: Donaldson beat Brown (*nrs*); F. Davis beat Pulman 36-25

Final: F. Davis beat Donaldson 37-34

1954
First round: J. Pulman beat Jack Rea 31-30

Semi-finals: W. Donaldson beat Alec Brown 36-25; F. Davis beat Pulman 32-29

Final: F. Davis beat Donaldson 39-21

1955
First round: J. Pulman beat R. Williams 22-15; Jack Rea beat H. Stokes (*nrs*)

Semi-finals: F. Davis beat Rea 36-25; Pulman beat Alec Brown (*nrs*)

Final: F. Davis beat Pulman 37-34

1956
Semi-finals: J. Pulman beat Jack Rea 36-25; F. Davis beat R. Williams 35-26

Final: F. Davis beat Pulman 38-35

1957
Semi-finals: J. Pulman beat R. Williams 21-16; Jack Rea beat K. Kennerley 25-12

Final: Pulman beat Rea 39-34

Through lack of public support no Championship was organised between 1957 and 1964. After a truce with the BA and CC a new system was adopted whereby the champion defended his title against a series of single challengers. These matches resulted as follows:

1964
J. Pulman beat F. Davis 19-16; J. Pulman beat R. Williams 40-33

1965
J. Pulman beat F. Davis 37-36; J. Pulman beat R. Williams 25-22 (*matches*); J. Pulman beat F. Van Rensberg 39-12

1966
J. Pulman beat F. Davis 5-2 (*matches*)

1968
J. Pulman beat E. Charlton 39-34

1969 (*Players No. 6*)
First round: J. Spencer beat J. Pulman 25-18; R. Williams beat B. Bennett 25-4; G. Owen beat Jack Rea 25-17; F. Davis beat R. Reardon 25-24

Semi-finals: Spencer beat Williams 37-12; G. Owen beat Davis 37-24

Final: Spencer beat Owen 37-24

1970 (April) (*Players No. 6*)
First round: David Taylor beat B. Bennett 11-8

Quarter-finals: J. Pulman beat David Taylor 31-20; G. Owen beat R. Williams 31-11; R. Reardon beat F. Davis 31-26; J. Spencer beat Jack Rea 31-15

Semi-finals: Pulman beat G. Owen 37-12; Reardon beat Spencer 37-33

Final: Reardon beat Pulman 37-33

1970 (November)
Round robin
J. Spencer beat P. Mans 20-17; beat N. Squire 27-10; beat J. Pulman 23-14
R. Reardon beat Mans 22-15; beat E. Charlton 21-16; beat Spencer 21-16
W. Simpson beat G. Owen 19-18; beat Pulman 21-16; beat Mans 19-18
Charlton beat Squire 27-10; beat Mans 26-11; beat Owen 23-14
Owen beat P. Morgan 26-11; beat Squire 26-11; Morgan beat Simpson 21-16

Semi-finals: Spencer beat Reardon 34-15; Simpson beat Charlton 27-22

Final: Spencer beat Simpson 37-29

1972
First qualifying round: A. Higgins beat R. Gross 15-6; M. Parkin beat G. Thompson 11-10; G. Miles beat B. Bennett 15-6; J. Dunning beat P. Houlihan 11-10

Second qualifying round: Higgins beat Parkin 11-3; Dunning beat Miles 11-5

First round: J. Pulman beat Dunning 19-7; Higgins beat Jack Rea 19-11

Quarter-finals: J. Spencer beat F. Davis 31-21; E. Charlton beat David Taylor 31-25; Higgins beat Pulman 31-23; R. Williams beat R. Reardon 25-23

Semi-finals: Higgins beat Williams 31-30; Spencer beat Charlton 37-32

Final: Higgins beat Spencer 37-32

1973 (*Park Drive*)
First round: P. Houlihan beat Jack Rea 9-2; D. Greaves beat B. Bennett 9-8; G. Miles beat G. Thompson 9-5; P. Mans beat R. Gross 9-2; W. Simpson beat M. Parkin 9-3; C. Thorburn beat Dennis Taylor 9-8; David Taylor beat J. Dunning 9-4; J. Meadowcroft *wo* K. Kennerley *scr*

Second round: F. Davis beat Greaves 16-1; Miles beat J. Pulman 16-10; E. Charlton beat Mans 16-8; G. Owen beat Simpson 16-14; R. Reardon beat Meadowcroft 16-10; R. Williams beat Thorburn 16-15; J. Spencer beat David Taylor 16-5; A. Higgins beat Houlihan 16-3

Quarter-finals: Higgins beat F. Davis 16-14; Spencer beat Williams 16-7; Charlton beat Miles 16-6; Reardon beat G. Owen 16-6

Semi-finals: Charlton beat Higgins 23-9; Reardon beat Spencer 23-22

Final: Reardon beat Charlton 38-32

1974 (*Park Drive*)
Qualifying: J. Dunning beat D. Greaves 8-2; W. Simpson beat Jack Rea 8-3; J. Meadowcroft beat P. Houlihan 8-5; C. Thorburn beat A. McDonald 8-3; J. Pulman beat J. Karnehm 8-0; David Taylor beat R. Gross 8-7; M. Owen beat Dennis Taylor 8-1

First round: B. Bennett beat Simpson 8-2; B. Werbeniuk beat G. Thompson 8-3; Meadowcroft beat K. Kennerley 8-5; M. Owen beat M. Parkin 8-5; P. Mans beat I. Anderson 8-1; Pulman beat S. Lee 8-0; Dunning beat David Taylor 8-6; P. Morgan beat Thorburn 8-4

Second round: Mans beat J. Spencer 15-13; Dunning beat E. Charlton 15-13; M. Owen beat G. Owen 15-8; A. Higgins beat Bennett 15-4; G. Miles beat Morgan 15-7; R. Williams beat Pulman 15-12; F. Davis beat Werbeniuk 15-5; R. Reardon beat Meadowcroft 15-3

Quarter-finals: Williams beat Mans 15-4; Reardon beat M. Owen 15-11; Miles beat Dunning 15-13; F. Davis beat Higgins 15-14

Semi-finals: Miles beat Williams 15-7; Reardon beat F. Davis 15-3

Final: Reardon beat Miles 22-12

1975
Qualifying: P. Tarrant beat B. Bennett 15-8; L. Condo beat M. Parkin 15-8; D. Greaves beat J. Charlton 15-14

First round: W. Simpson beat R. Mares 15-5; J. Pulman beat Tarrant 15-5; David Taylor beat R. King 15-8; I. Anderson beat Condo 15-8; Dennis Taylor beat P. Mans 15-12; G. Owen beat Greaves 15-3; B. Werbeniuk beat J. Meadowcroft 15-9; C. Thorburn beat P. Morgan 15-6

Second round: R. Reardon beat Simpson 15-11; J. Spencer beat Pulman 15-10; A. Higgins beat David Taylor 15-2; R. Williams beat Anderson 15-4; Dennis Taylor beat F. Davis 15-14; G. Owen beat J. Dunning 15-8; E. Charlton beat Werbeniuk 15-11; Thorburn beat G. Miles 15-2

Quarter-finals: Reardon beat Spencer 19-17; Higgins beat Williams 19-12; Dennis Taylor beat G. Owen 19-9; Charlton beat Thorburn 19-12

Semi-finals: Charlton beat Dennis Taylor 19-12; Reardon beat Higgins 19-14

Final: Reardon beat Charlton 31-30

1976
First qualifying round: Jack Rea beat I. Anderson 8-5; D. Greaves beat J. Charlton 8-5; J. Meadowcroft beat D. Wheelwright 8-1; R. Gross beat M. Parkin 8-5; L. Condo beat M. Owen 8-6

Second qualifying round: Jack Rea beat B. Bennett 8-5; David Taylor beat Greaves 8-1; Meadowcroft beat Gross 8-4; W. Thorne beat Condo 8-3

First round: R. Reardon beat J. Dunning 15-7; Dennis Taylor beat G. Owen 15-9; P. Mans beat G. Miles 15-10; Meadowcroft beat R. Williams 15-7; E. Charlton beat J. Pulman 15-9; F. Davis beat B. Werbeniuk 15-12; A. Higgins beat C. Thorburn 15-14; J. Spencer beat David Taylor 15-5

Quarter-finals: Reardon beat Dennis Taylor 15-2; Mans beat Meadowcroft 15-8; Charlton beat F. Davis 15-13; Higgins beat Spencer 15-14

Semi-finals: Reardon beat Mans 20-10; Higgins beat Charlton 20-18

Final: Reardon beat Higgins 27-16

1977

First qualifying round: J. Virgo beat R. Andrewartha 11-1

Second qualifying round: P. Fagan beat J. Meadowcroft 11-9; Virgo beat J. Dunning 11-6; W. Thorne beat B. Bennett 11-4; J. Pulman *wo*; David Taylor beat D. Greaves 11-0; C. Thorburn beat C. Ross 11-0; Dennis Taylor beat J. Karnehm 11-0; D. Mountjoy beat Jack Rea 11-9

First round: R. Reardon beat Fagan 13-7; J. Spencer beat Virgo 13-9; G. Miles beat Thorne 13-4; Pulman beat F. Davis 13-12; E. Charlton beat David Taylor 13-5; Thorburn beat R. Williams 13-6; Dennis Taylor beat P. Mans 13-11; Mountjoy beat A. Higgins 13-12

Quarter-finals: Spencer beat Reardon 13-6; Pulman beat Miles 13-10; Thorburn beat Charlton 13-12; Dennis Taylor beat Mountjoy 13-11

Semi-finals: Spencer beat Pulman 18-16; Thorburn beat Dennis Taylor 18-16

Final: Spencer beat Thorburn 25-21

1978

First qualifying round: M. Parkin beat B. Bennett 9-4; R. Andrewartha beat J. Karnehm 9-0; J. Barrie beat D. Greaves 9-3; P. Houlihan beat C. Ross 9-1

Second qualifying round: D. Mountjoy beat Andrewartha 9-3; P. Fagan beat J. Dunning 9-5; W. Thorne beat R. Williams 9-3; B. Werbeniuk beat M. Parkin 9-2; P. Mans beat Barrie 9-6; David Taylor beat P. Morgan 9-7; Houlihan beat J. Meadowcroft 9-6; F. Davis beat J. Virgo 9-8

First round: Mans beat J. Spencer 13-8; G. Miles beat David Taylor 13-10; Fagan beat A. Higgins 13-12; F. Davis beat Dennis Taylor 13-9; E. Charlton beat Thorne 13-12; C. Thorburn beat Houlihan 13-8; Werbeniuk beat J. Pulman 13-4; R. Reardon beat Mountjoy 13-9

Quarter-finals: Mans beat Miles 13-7; F. Davis beat Fagan 13-10; Charlton beat Thorburn 13-12; Reardon beat Werbeniuk 13-6

Semi-finals: Mans beat F. Davis 18-16; Reardon beat Charlton 18-14

Final: Reardon beat Mans 25-18

1979

First qualifying round: D. Mountjoy beat D. Mienie 9-1; T. Griffiths beat B. Bennett 9-2; P. Houlihan beat J. Barrie 9-5; W. Thorne beat J. Charlton 9-3; J. Virgo beat M. Parkin 9-0; J. Dunning beat Jack Rea 9-5; R. Williams beat D. Greaves 9-2; J. Meadowcroft beat J. Van Rensberg 9-7; R. Andrewartha beat R. Edmonds 9-8; S. Davis beat I. Anderson 9-1; K. Stevens beat R. Amdor 9-1

Second qualifying round: Virgo beat Thorne 9-8; B. Werbeniuk beat Andrewartha 9-2; David Taylor beat Dunning 9-8; Mountjoy beat Houlihan 9-6; S. Davis beat P. Fagan 9-2; Griffiths beat Meadowcroft 9-6; Stevens beat J. Pulman 9-0; G. Miles beat Williams 9-5

First round: E. Charlton beat Mountjoy 13-6; Werbeniuk beat J. Spencer 13-11; Virgo beat C. Thorburn 13-10; F. Davis beat Stevens 13-8; Dennis Taylor beat S. Davis 13-11; A. Higgins beat David Taylor 13-5; Griffiths beat P. Mans 13-8; R. Reardon beat Miles 13-8

Quarter-finals: Charlton beat F. Davis 13-4; Dennis Taylor beat Reardon 13-8; Virgo beat Werbeniuk 13-9; Griffiths beat Higgins 13-12

Semi-finals: Griffiths beat Charlton 19-17; Dennis Taylor beat Virgo 19-12

Final: Griffiths beat Dennis Taylor 24-16

1980

Qualifying groups

1 Jack Rea beat B. Bennett 9-1; W. Thorne beat K. Robitaille 9-4; Thorne beat Rea 9-1
2 S. Davis beat C. Ross 9-3; P. Morgan beat P. Thornely 9-4; Davis beat Morgan 9-0
3 M. Hallett beat K. Kennerley 9-2; K. Stevens beat D. Greaves 9-3; Stevens beat Hallett 9-3
4 J. Johnson beat R. Andrewartha 9-5; P. Houlihan beat Johnson 9-6; T. Meo beat J. Van Rensberg 9-1; Meo beat Houlihan 9-1
5 R. Amdor beat B. Mikkelsen 9-7; R. Williams beat Amdor 9-4; J. Wych beat John Bear 9-5; Wych beat Williams 9-7
6 F. Jonik beat M. Wildman 9-7; C. Wilson beat Jonik 9-6
7 R. Edmonds beat M. Parkin 9-2; S. Hood beat J. Dunning 16-7; Edmonds beat Hood 9-6
8 E. Sinclair beat M. Morra 9-5; Sinclair beat D. Mienie 9-7; J. Meadowcroft beat Sinclair 9-1

First round: S. Davis beat P. Fagan 10-6; A. Higgins beat Meo 10-9; D. Mountjoy beat Wilson 10-6; Wych beat J. Pulman 10-5; J. Virgo beat Meadowcroft 10-2; Stevens beat G. Miles 10-3; David Taylor beat Edmonds 10-3; B. Werbeniuk beat Thorne 10-9

Second round: S. Davis beat T. Griffiths 13-10; Higgins beat P. Mans 13-6; Stevens beat J. Spencer 13-8; E. Charlton beat Virgo 13-12; C. Thorburn beat

Mountjoy 13-10; Wych beat Dennis Taylor 13-10; R. Reardon beat Werbeniuk 13-6; David Taylor beat F. Davis 13-5

Quarter-finals: David Taylor beat Reardon 13-11; Thorburn beat Wych 13-6; Stevens beat Charlton 13-7; Higgins beat S. Davis 13-9

Semi-finals: Thorburn beat David Taylor 16-7; Higgins beat Stevens 16-13

Final: Thorburn beat Higgins 18-16

1981

Qualifying groups

1 W. Thorne beat M. Morra 9-5; D. Greaves beat M. Parkin 9-5; Thorne beat Greaves 9-3
2 J. White beat B. Mikkelsen 9-4; White beat J. Meadowcroft 9-8
3 R. Edmonds beat M. Wildman 9-3; R. Williams beat S. Hood 9-4; Edmonds beat Williams 9-7
4 T. Meo beat J. Johnson 9-8; M. Hallett beat F. Jonik 9-1; Meo beat Hallett 9-4
5 J. Dunning beat B. Bennett 9-6; Dunning beat P. Fagan 9-7
6 D. Martin beat I. Anderson 9-3; Martin beat J. Pulman 9-2
7 C. Wilson beat R. Andrewartha 9-4; E. Sinclair beat P. Morgan 9-8; Wilson beat Sinclair 9-4
8 A. Knowles beat C. Ross 7-0 (*retd*); Knowles beat J. Wych 9-3

First round: G. Miles beat Knowles 10-8; David Taylor beat Wilson 10-6; D. Mountjoy beat Thorne 10-6; K. Stevens beat Dunning 10-4; Meo beat J. Virgo 10-6; S. Davis beat White 10-8; B. Werbeniuk beat Martin 10-4; J. Spencer beat Edmonds 10-9

Second round: C. Thorburn beat Miles 13-2; David Taylor beat F. Davis 13-3; T. Griffiths beat Meo 13-6; S. Davis beat Alex Higgins 13-8; Mountjoy beat E. Charlton 13-7; Dennis Taylor beat Stevens 13-11; Werbeniuk beat P. Mans 13-5; R. Reardon beat Spencer 13-11

Quarter-finals: Thorburn beat David Taylor 13-6; S. Davis beat Griffiths 13-9; Mountjoy beat Dennis Taylor 13-8; Reardon beat Werbeniuk 13-10

Semi-finals: S. Davis beat Thorburn 16-10; Mountjoy beat Reardon 16-10

Final: S. Davis beat Mountjoy 18-12

1982

Qualifying groups

1 John Bear beat F. Jonik 9-4; Bear beat J. Wych 9-4
2 D. Hughes beat C. Everton 9-4; T. Meo beat Hughes 9-4
3 D. Reynolds beat D. Sheehan 9-5; Reynolds beat R. Edmonds 9-6
4 E. Hughes *wo* D. Mienie *scr*; A. Knowles beat Hughes 9-7
5 M. Wildman beat G. Foulds 9-8; J. White beat Wildman 9-4
6 C. Roscoe beat B. Mikkelsen 9-6; W. Thorne beat Roscoe 9-1

7 P. Medati beat J. Phillips 9-3; C. Wilson beat Medati 9-5
8 P. Houlihan beat I. Anderson 9-5; D. Martin beat Houlihan 9-3
9 M. Macleod beat E. McLaughlin 9-8; J. Dunning beat Macleod 9-4
10 M. Watterson beat B. Demarco 9-6; J. Meadowcroft beat Watterson 9-7
11 D. French beat B. Bennett 9-3; P. Fagan beat French 9-6
12 I. Black beat M. Parkin 9-6; R. Williams beat Black 9-2
13 J. Johnson beat V. Harris 9-4; M. Hallett beat Johnson 9-8
14 J. Donnelly beat M. Gibson 9-8; E. Sinclair beat B. Kelly 9-8; Donnelly beat Sinclair 9-8
15 P. Morgan beat D. Greaves 9-2; S. Francisco beat C. Ross 9-0; Francisco beat Morgan 9-1
16 M. Morra beat T. Murphy 9-5; J. Fitzmaurice *wo* J. Pulman *scr*; Fitzmaurice beat Morra 9-7

First round: Knowles beat S. Davis 10-1; G. Miles beat Martin 10-5; B. Werbeniuk beat Bear 10-7; E. Charlton beat Wilson 10-5; S. Francisco beat Dennis Taylor 10-7; Reynolds beat F. Davis 10-7; J. Virgo beat Hallett 10-4; R. Reardon beat Donnelly 10-5; A. Higgins beat Meadowcroft 10-5; D. Mountjoy beat Williams 10-3; Fagan beat David Taylor 10-9; K. Stevens beat Fitzmaurice 10-4; P. Mans beat Meo 10-8; White beat C. Thorburn 10-4

Second round: Knowles beat Miles 13-7; Charlton beat Werbeniuk 13-5; S. Francisco beat Reynolds 13-8; Reardon beat Virgo 13-8; Thorne beat Spencer 13-5; Higgins beat Mountjoy 13-12; Stevens beat Fagan 13-7; White beat Mans 13-6

Quarter-finals: Charlton beat Knowles 13-11; Reardon beat S. Francisco 13-8; Higgins beat Thorne 13-10; White beat Stevens 13-9

Semi-finals: Reardon beat Charlton 16-11; Higgins beat White 16-15

Final: Higgins beat Reardon 18-15

1983
Qualifying groups
1 B. Kelly beat B. Demarco 10-4; S. Francisco beat Kelly 10-5
2 P. Morgan beat P. Burke 10-9; G. Miles beat Morgan 10-6
3 T. Murphy beat P. Houlihan 10-9; J. Virgo beat Murphy 10-8
4 R. Williams beat M. Darrington 10-0; Williams beat F. Davis 10-1
5 M. Wildman beat B. Harris 10-7; Wildman *wo* J. Wych *scr*
6 R. Edmonds beat F. Jonik 10-4; D. Reynolds beat Edmonds 10-6
7 M. Fisher beat P. Fagan 10-8; E. McLaughlin beat D. Greaves 10-7; Fisher beat McLaughlin 10-9
8 T. Meo beat V. Harris 10-0; G. Foulds beat M. Gibson 10-6; Meo beat Foulds 10-4
9 I. Black beat M. Morra 10-9; P. Medati beat John Bear 10-7; Black beat Medati 10-4
10 C. Wilson beat C. Everton 10-1; J. Johnson beat P. Watchorn 10-0; Wilson beat Johnson 10-8

11 M. Macleod beat M. Owen 10-5; D. Martin beat M. Parkin 10-1; Martin beat Macleod 10-7
12 J. Meadowcroft beat B. Bennett 10-3; G. Cripsey beat D. Hughes 10-2; Meadowcroft beat Cripsey 10-6
13 J. Donnelly beat D. Sheehan 10-6; J. Campbell beat M. Watterson 10-6; Campbell beat Donnelly 10-2
14 L. Dodd *wo* J. Dunning *scr*; I. Williamson beat D. French 10-8; Dodd beat Williamson 10-9
15 M. Hallett beat R. Andrewartha 10-7; W. King beat I. Anderson 10-6; Hallett beat King 10-6
16 E. Hughes beat J. Fitzmaurice 10-7; E. Sinclair beat C. Roscoe 10-2; Hughes beat Sinclair 10-8

First round: A. Higgins beat Reynolds 10-4; W. Thorne beat Virgo 10-3; B. Werbeniuk beat Martin 10-4; David Taylor beat Meadowcroft 10-2; E. Charlton beat Dodd 10-7; J. Spencer beat Hallett 10-7; Dennis Taylor beat S. Francisco 10-9; S. Davis beat Williams 10-4; C. Thorburn beat Campbell 10-5; T. Griffiths beat Wildman 10-8; P. Mans beat Black 10-3; K. Stevens beat Fisher 10-2; D. Mountjoy beat Wilson 10-2; Meo beat J. White 10-8; A. Knowles beat Miles 10-3; R. Reardon beat E. Hughes 10-7

Second round: Higgins beat Thorne 13-8; Werbeniuk beat David Taylor 13-10; Charlton beat Spencer 13-11; S. Davis beat Dennis Taylor 13-11; Thorburn beat Griffiths 13-12; Meo beat Mountjoy 13-11; Knowles beat Reardon 13-12; Stevens beat Mans 13-3

Quarter-finals: Higgins beat Werbeniuk 13-11; S. Davis beat Charlton 13-5; Thorburn beat Stevens 13-12; Knowles beat Meo 13-9

Semi-finals: Thorburn beat Knowles 16-15; S. Davis beat Higgins 16-5

Final: S. Davis beat Thorburn 18-6

1984

Qualifying groups

1 J. Parrott beat D. Hughes 10-3; Parrott beat C. Everton 10-2; Parrott beat P. Mans 10-0
2 B. Mikkelsen beat P. Medati 10-8; Mikkelsen beat F. Jonik 10-9; W. Thorne beat Mikkelsen 10-3
3 M. Morra beat G. Foulds 10-2; T. Murphy beat J. Fitzmaurice 10-8; Morra beat Murphy 10-5; Morra beat D. Reynolds 10-7
4 W. Sanderson beat P. Morgan 10-8; P. Mifsud beat E. Hughes 10-5; Mifsud beat Sanderson 10-5; Mifsud beat C. Wilson 10-8
5 J. Van Rensberg beat V. Harris 10-7; R. Edmonds beat D. Greaves 10-0; Van Rensberg beat Edmonds 10-9; S. Francisco beat Van Rensberg 10-3
6 I. Williamson beat P. Houlihan 10-5; M. Hines beat I. Black 10-5; Williamson beat Hines 10-6; G. Miles beat Williamson 10-6
7 M. Gibson beat G. Rigitano 10-7; M. Fisher beat P. Thornley 10-8; Gibson beat Fisher 10-7; J. Johnson beat Gibson 10-3

8 E. McLaughlin beat J. Hargreaves 10-5; R. Andrewartha *wo* John Bear *scr*; Andrewartha beat McLaughlin 10-8; Andrewartha beat M. Wildman 10-9
9 J. Wych beat G. Ganim Jr 10-1; G. Scott beat L. Heywood 10-7; Wych beat Scott 10-6; Wych beat P. Fagan 10-3
10 P. Browne beat S. Duggan 10-9; C. Roscoe beat B. Demarco 10-7; Browne beat Roscoe 10-4; E. Sinclair beat Browne 10-1
11 M. Gauvreau beat J. Campbell 10-7; G. Cripsey beat M. Parkin 10-4; Gauvreau beat Cripsey 10-1; Gauvreau beat M. Macleod 10-6
12 I. Anderson beat G. Watson 10-4; J. Donnelly beat P. Watchorn 10-7; Donnelly beat Anderson 10-6; F. Davis beat Donnelly 10-5
13 W. King beat T. Jones 10-9; M. Watterson beat B. Bennett 10-5; King beat Watterson 10-8; King beat Dave Martin 10-8
14 J. Caggianello beat M. Darrington 10-7; W. Oliver beat J. Dunning 10-3; Oliver beat Caggianello 10-7; R. Williams beat Oliver 10-8
15 N. Foulds beat D. French 10-5; L. Dodd beat J. Giannaros 10-1; Foulds beat Dodd 10-4; Foulds beat J. Meadowcroft 10-2
16 B. Harris beat D. Sheehan 10-3; P. Burke beat B. Kelly 10-7; Burke beat Harris 10-4; M. Hallett beat Burke 10-5

First round: S. Davis beat King 10-3; J. Spencer beat Miles 10-3; T. Griffiths beat Mifsud 10-2; B. Werbeniuk beat F. Davis 10-4; N. Foulds beat A. Higgins 10-9; D. Mountjoy beat Hallett 10-4; Dennis Taylor beat Johnson 10-1; Parrott beat A. Knowles 10-7; C. Thorburn beat Morra 10-3; Thorne beat J. Virgo 10-9; J. White beat Williams 10-6; E. Charlton beat Andrewartha 10-4; K. Stevens beat Sinclair 10-1; David Taylor beat Gauvreau 10-5; S. Francisco beat T. Meo 10-5; R. Reardon beat Wych 10-7

Second round: S. Davis beat Spencer 13-5; Griffiths beat Werbeniuk 13-5; Mountjoy beat N. Foulds 13-6; Dennis Taylor beat Parrott 13-11; Thorburn beat Thorne 13-11; White beat Charlton 13-7; Stevens beat David Taylor 13-10; Reardon beat S. Francisco 13-8

Quarter-finals: S. Davis beat Griffiths 13-10; Dennis Taylor beat Mountjoy 13-8; White beat Thorburn 13-8; Stevens beat Reardon 13-2

Semi-finals: S. Davis beat Dennis Taylor 16-9; White beat Stevens 16-14

Final: S. Davis beat White 18-16

1985

Qualifying groups

1 G. Rigitano beat D. Sheehan 10-9; Rigitano beat B. Harris 10-4; Rigitano beat B. Kelly 10-6; Rigitano beat M. Fisher 10-2; N. Foulds beat Rigitano 10-8
2 D. O'Kane *wo* J. McLaughlin *scr*; O'Kane beat V. Harris 10-5; O'Kane beat F. Jonik 10-5; O'Kane beat L. Dodd 10-7; O'Kane beat D. Martin 10-8
3 S. Longworth beat J. Giannaros 10-1; Longworth beat G. Cripsey 10-8; J. Van Rensberg beat Longworth 10-7; M. Gauvreau beat Van Rensberg 10-9; D. Reynolds beat Gauvreau 10-1

4 R. Chaperon beat R. Bales 10-7; Chaperon beat L. Heywood 10-1; Chaperon beat P. Morgan 10-3; F. Davis beat Chaperon 10-9; R. Williams beat F. Davis 10-6
5 D. Hughes beat D. French 10-5; S. Newbury beat Hughes 10-9; Newbury beat P. Burke 10-3; Newbury beat G. Scott 10-2; E. Hughes beat Newbury 10-6
6 M. Hines beat T. Chappel 10-8; Hines beat P. Watchorn 10-4; M. Gibson beat Hines 10-7; P. Fagan beat Gibson 10-8; Fagan beat C. Wilson 10-9
7 D. Fowler beat J. Hargreaves 10-0; Fowler *wo* G. Watson *scr*; Fowler *wo* J. Caggianello *scr*; Fowler beat J. Donnelly 10-0; J. Parrott beat Fowler 10-2
8 R. Foldvari *wo* P. Thornley *scr*; Foldvari beat B. Oliver 10-3; R. Edmonds beat Foldvari 10-3; Edmonds beat M. Wildman 10-7
9 D. Chalmers beat D. Greaves 10-3; Chalmers beat E. McLaughlin 10-9; Chalmers beat I. Black 10-4; M. Hallett beat Chalmers 10-1
10 G. Foulds beat M. Parkin 10-6; Foulds beat C. Everton 10-2; Foulds beat C. Roscoe 10-7; J. Johnson beat Foulds 10-6
11 P. Medati beat B. Bennett 10-4; Medati beat I. Williamson 10-8; Medati beat W. King 10-9; S. Francisco beat Medati 10-7
12 I. Anderson beat A. Kearney 10-8; P. Browne beat Anderson 10-5; M. Morra beat Browne 10-6; J. Campbell beat Morra 10-9
13 W. Jones beat John Rea 10-3; Jones beat J. Dunning 10-6; Jones beat M. Watterson 10-5; Jones beat G. Miles 10-8
14 M. Bradley beat D. Mienie 10-4; Bradley beat B. Mikkelsen 10-9; J. Wych beat Bradley 10-7; J. Virgo beat Wych 10-4
15 P. Francisco beat B. Demarco 10-4; Francisco beat T. Murphy 10-4; Francisco beat J. Meadowcroft 10-5; M. Macleod beat Francisco 10-7
16 T. Jones beat M. Darrington 10-2; Jones beat S. Duggan 10-8; Jones beat J. Fitzmaurice 10-4; Jones beat E. Sinclair 10-2

First round: S. Davis beat N. Foulds 10-8; David Taylor beat O'Kane 10-4; A. Higgins beat Reynolds 10-4; T. Griffiths beat Williams 10-3; R. Reardon beat E. Hughes 10-9; Fagan beat W. Thorne 10-6; Parrott beat J. Spencer 10-3; K. Stevens beat Edmonds 10-8; C. Thorburn beat Hallett 10-8; B. Werbeniuk beat Johnson 10-8; Dennis Taylor beat S. Francisco 10-2; E. Charlton beat Campbell 10-3; J. White beat W. Jones 10-4; T. Meo beat Virgo 10-6; D. Mountjoy beat Macleod 10-5; A. Knowles beat T. Jones 10-8

Second round: S. Davis beat David Taylor 13-4; Griffiths beat Higgins 13-7; Reardon beat Fagan 13-9; Parrott beat Stevens 13-6; Thorburn beat Werbeniuk 13-3; Dennis Taylor beat Charlton 13-6; White beat Meo 13-11; Knowles beat Mountjoy 13-6

Quarter-finals: S. Davis beat Griffiths 13-6; Reardon beat Parrott 13-12; Dennis Taylor beat Thorburn 13-5; Knowles beat White 13-10

Semi-finals: S. Davis beat Reardon 16-5; Dennis Taylor beat Knowles 16-5

Final: Dennis Taylor beat S. Davis 18-17

Joe Johnson and his wife Terryll celebrate his Embassy World Championship victory

1986

First qualifying round: D. Gilbert beat R. Bales 10-7; O. Agrawal beat D. Hughes 10-6; A. Kearney beat G. Wilkinson 10-5; B. Oliver beat J. O'Boye 10-8; D. Sheehan beat P. Houlihan 10-7; M. Gibson beat G. Jenkins 10-4; S. Simngam beat B. Bennett 10-0; Jim Bear beat P. Burke 10-8; T. Drago beat G. Cripsey 10-4; M. Smith beat D. Greaves 10-4; B. West *wo* J. Giannaros *scr*; P. Thornley beat D. Mienie 10-3; R. Grace beat M. Parkin 10-8; S. Hendry beat B. Demarco 10-7; P. Watchorn *wo* J. Rempe *scr*; B. Mikkelsen beat J. Hargreaves 10-7; M. Darrington *wo* W. Sanderson *scr*

Second qualifying round: J. Wych beat T. Chappel 10-6; S. Duggan beat M. Fisher 10-3; T. Jones beat V. Harris 10-7; Gilbert beat M. Bradley 10-7; S. Newbury beat Agrawal 10-5; I. Black beat B. Harris 10-8; G. Scott beat Kearney 10-8; D. Fowler beat Oliver 10-8; C. Roscoe beat G. Foulds 10-3; W. King beat Sheehan 10-4; Gibson beat M. Morra 10-9; P. Medati beat Simngam 10-9; R. Chaperon beat F. Jonik 10-8; M. Gauvreau beat Jim Bear 10-5; F. Davis beat D. Chalmers 10-6; P. Francisco beat Drago 10-4; J. Donnelly beat Smith 10-6; West beat J. Dunning 10-3; T. Murphy beat J. McLaughlin 10-7; Thornley beat P. Fagan 10-7; W. Jones beat Grave 10-3; Hendry beat P. Browne 10-9; E. Sinclair beat P. Morgan 10-8; J. Van Rensberg beat I. Williamson 10-9; John Rea beat E. McLaughlin 10-6; S. Longworth beat Watchorn 10-7; G. Miles beat C. Everton 10-3; R. Foldvari beat G. Rigitano 10-6; M. Watterson beat Mikkelsen 10-2; L. Dodd beat J. Fitzmaurice 10-6; Darrington beat J. Meadowcroft 10-6; R. Edmonds beat B. Kelly 10-0

Third qualifying round: Wych beat Duggan 10-5; Gilbert beat T. Jones 10-7; Newbury beat Black 10-2; Fowler beat Scott 10-7; King beat Roscoe 10-5; Medati beat Gibson 10-6; Gauvreau beat Chaperon 10-8; P. Francisco beat F. Davis 10-1; West beat Donnelly 10-5; Murphy beat Thornley 10-3; Hendry beat W. Jones 10-8; Van Rensberg beat Sinclair 10-2; Longworth beat John Rea 10-4; Foldvari beat Miles 10-7; Dodd beat Watterson 10-1; Edmonds beat Darrington 10-5

Fourth qualifying round: M. Hallett beat Wych 10-7; D. Martin beat Gilbert 10-5; J. Spencer beat Newbury 10-7; Fowler beat M. Macleod 10-6; D. Reynolds beat King 10-7; C. Wilson beat Medati 10-6; R. Williams beat Gauvreau 10-3; N. Foulds beat P. Francisco 10-9; B. Werbeniuk beat West 10-8; E. Hughes beat Murphy 10-7; Hendry beat O'Kane 10-9; J. Campbell beat Van Rensberg 10-6; J. Virgo beat Longworth 10-8; J. Parrott beat Foldvari 10-6; P. Mans beat Dodd 10-7; Edmonds beat M. Wildman 10-9

First round: Hallett beat Dennis Taylor 10-6; J. Johnson beat Martin 10-3; A. Higgins beat J. Spencer 10-7; T. Griffiths beat Fowler 10-2; K. Stevens beat Reynolds 10-6; E. Charlton beat Wilson 10-6; S. Francisco beat Williams 10-4; A. Knowles beat N. Foulds 10-9; C. Thorburn beat Werbeniuk 10-5; E. Hughes beat David Taylor 10-7; W. Thorne beat Hendry 10-8; Campbell beat R. Reardon 10-8; J. White beat Virgo 10-7; Parrott beat T. Meo 10-4; D. Mountjoy beat Mans 10-3; S. Davis beat Edmonds 10-4

Second round: Johnson beat Hallet 13-6; Griffiths beat Higgins 13-12; Stevens beat Charlton 13-12; Knowles beat S. Francisco 13-10; Thorburn beat

E. Hughes 13-6; Thorne beat Campbell 13-9; White beat Parrott 13-8; S. Davis beat Mountjoy 13-5

Quarter-finals: Johnson beat Griffiths 13-12; Knowles beat Stevens 13-9; Thorburn beat Thorne 13-6; S. Davis beat White 13-5

Semi-finals: Johnson beat Knowles 16-8; S. Davis beat Thorburn 16-12

Final: Johnson beat S. Davis 18-12

NATIONAL PROFESSIONAL CHAMPIONSHIPS

ENGLISH PROFESSIONAL CHAMPIONSHIP

John Courage sponsored the first English Professional Championship in 1981 but the event was not held again until 1985 when Tolly Cobbold, another brewer, switched its support from an invitation tournament. The Tolly Cobbold Classic had been recorded by Anglia Television for showing later in the year and their coverage too was switched to the Championship.

From the 1984–85 season, the staging of all the national professional championships became easier when the WPBSA decided to inject cash to the tune of £1,000 per entrant into both domestic and other national championships. The Welsh and Scottish Professional Championships are the only other events to be televised.

1981 (*John Courage*)
Qualifying: R. Edmonds beat M. Hallett 9-3; J. Johnson beat A. Knowles 9-2; M. Wildman beat B. Bennett 9-3; J. Dunning beat D. Greaves 9-4; J. Meadowcroft beat J. Barrie 9-3

First round: Edmonds beat F. Davis 9-6; T. Meo beat J. Virgo 9-6; G. Miles beat S. Hood 9-1; S. Davis beat Meadowcroft 9-2; J. Spencer beat P. Houlihan 9-1; W. Thorne beat Wildman 9-2; Johnson *wo*; Dunning beat David Taylor 9-8

Quarter-finals: S. Davis beat Spencer 9-7; Meo beat Miles 9-7; Thorne beat Dunning 9-0; Edmonds beat Johnson 9-5

Semi-finals: S. Davis beat Edmonds 9-0; Meo beat Thorne 9-8

Final: S. Davis beat Meo 9-3

1985 (*Tolly Cobbold*)
Qualifying: D. Fowler beat W. Oliver 9-7; M. Bradley beat I. Williamson 9-8; T. Jones beat P. Houlihan 9-1; L. Dodd beat R. Bales 9-5; J. Fitzmaurice beat D. Greaves 9-3; M. Fisher beat D. French 9-8; S. Duggan beat B. Harris 9-8; D. Hughes beat M. Watterson 9-5; D. Chalmers beat J. Meadowcroft 9-3; S. Longworth beat R. Edmonds 9-4; P. Medati beat J. Hargreaves 9-8; G. Foulds beat F. Davis 9-2; G. Cripsey beat B. Bennett 9-0; G. Scott beat V. Harris 9-7

First round: S. Davis beat Fowler 9-3; M. Hallett beat Duggan 9-4; J. Johnson beat Scott 9-1; T. Meo beat Fisher 9-3; J. Virgo beat M. Darrington 9-0; D. Reynolds beat Fitzmaurice 9-2; R. Williams beat T. Jones 9-6; W. Thorne beat Dodd 9-1; Longworth beat M. Wildman 9-3; J. White beat Chalmers 9-5; Medati beat J. Spencer 9-4; N. Foulds beat D. Hughes 9-3; David Taylor beat Cripsey 9-5; J. Parrott beat G. Foulds 9-4; D. Martin beat G. Miles 9-7; A. Knowles beat Bradley 9-8

Second round: Virgo beat Johnson 9-4; Reynolds beat Thorne 9-6; S. Davis beat Williams 9-2; Meo beat Hallett 9-4; Knowles beat Martin 9-3; David Taylor beat Parrott 9-7; White beat N. Foulds 9-7; Longworth beat Medati 9-7

Quarter-finals: Meo beat Reynolds 9-4; Longworth beat White 9-5; Knowles beat David Taylor 9-2; S. Davis beat Virgo 9-2

Semi-finals: Knowles beat Longworth 9-6; S. Davis beat Meo 9-8

Final: S. Davis beat Knowles 9-2

1986 (*Tolly Cobbold*)
First round: D. Gilbert beat B. West 9-8; P. Houlihan beat J. Hargreaves 9-5

Second round: M. Bradley beat Gilbert 9-5; F. Davis beat D. Hughes 9-6; T. Jones beat B. Harris 9-5; W. Oliver beat L. Dodd 9-5; P. Medati beat D. Greaves 9-4; S. Longworth beat S. Duggan 9-4; G. Cripsey beat J. Meadowcroft 9-1; G. Scott beat B. Bennett 9-1; I. Williamson beat M. Watterson 9-1; R. Edmonds beat M. Smith 9-8; D. Fowler beat M. Darrington 9-3; Houlihan *wo* J. Dunning *scr*; D. Chalmers beat Fisher 9-2; R. Bales beat V. Harris 9-7

Third round: S. Davis beat Bradley 9-3; D. Martin beat F. Davis 9-8; J. Virgo beat T. Jones 9-7; J. Parrott beat Oliver 9-0; W. Thorne beat Medati 9-2; D. Reynolds beat Longworth 9-5; M. Wildman beat Cripsey 9-5; T. Meo beat Scott 9-1; J. White beat Williamson 9-1; R. Williams beat Miles 9-6; N. Foulds beat G. Foulds 9-4; Edmonds beat David Taylor 9-6; J. Johnson beat Fowler 9-7; J. Spencer beat Houlihan 9-5; M. Hallett beat Chalmers 9-1; A. Knowles beat Bales 9-4

Fourth round: S. Davis beat Martin 9-4; Virgo beat Parrott 9-6; Reynolds beat Thorne 9-8; Meo beat Wildman 9-3; White beat Williams 9-5; N. Foulds beat Edmonds 9-4; Johnson beat Spencer 9-7; Hallett beat Knowles 9-5

Quarter-finals: S. Davis beat Virgo 9-2; Meo beat Reynolds 9-4; N. Foulds beat White 9-4; Hallett beat Johnson 9-6

Semi-finals: Meo beat S. Davis 9-7; N. Foulds beat Hallett 9-8

Final: Meo beat Foulds 9-7

IRISH PROFESSIONAL CHAMPIONSHIP

1972
Challenge: A. Higgins beat Jack Rea 28-12

1978
Challenge: A. Higgins beat Dennis Taylor 21-7

1979
Challenge: A. Higgins beat P. Fagan 21-13

1980
Challenge: Dennis Taylor beat A. Higgins 21-15

1981
Challenge: Dennis Taylor beat P. Fagan 22-21

1982
First round: E. Hughes beat D. Sheehan 6-1

Quarter-finals: E. Hughes beat Jack Rea 6-0; T. Murphy beat P. Fagan 6-2

Semi-finals: Dennis Taylor beat Murphy 6-0; A. Higgins beat E. Hughes 6-2

Final: Taylor beat Higgins 16-13

1983
First round: Dennis Taylor beat B. Kelly 6-0; P. Fagan beat T. Murphy 6-4; A. Higgins beat Jack Rea 6-3; E. Hughes beat P. Burke 6-2

Semi-finals: Higgins beat E. Hughes 6-2; Taylor beat Fagan 6-1

Final: Higgins beat Taylor 16-11

1985 (*Strongbow*)
Preliminary: J. McLaughlin beat D. Sheehan 6-3

Qualifying: P. Burke beat A. Kearney 6-4; T. Murphy beat P. Browne 6-3; B. Kelly beat P. Watchorn 6-2; Jack Rea beat McLaughlin 6-5

Quarter-finals: P. Fagan beat Murphy 6-2; Dennis Taylor beat Jack Rea 6-0; A. Higgins beat Burke 6-0; E. Hughes beat Kelly 6-2

Semi-finals: Taylor beat Hughes 6-5; Higgins beat Fagan 6-3

Final: Taylor beat Higgins 10-5

1986 (*Strongbow*)
First round: B. Kelly beat Jack Rea 5-0; T. Murphy beat J. O'Boye 5-0; E. Hughes beat D. Sheehan 5-0; A. Kearney beat P. Fagan 5-0; J. McLaughlin beat P. Watchorn 5-0; P. Burke beat P. Browne 5-4

Quarter-finals: Dennis Taylor beat Kelly 6-1; Murphy beat Kearney 6-2; A. Higgins beat McLaughlin 6-2; Hughes beat Burke 6-3

Semi-finals: Taylor beat Murphy 6-3; Higgins beat Hughes 6-2

Final: Taylor beat Higgins 10-7

SCOTTISH PROFESSIONAL CHAMPIONSHIP

1980
Challenge: E. Sinclair beat C. Ross 11-6

1981
First round: M. Gibson beat B. Demarco 5-3; J. Donnelly beat E. Sinclair 5-0; E. McLaughlin beat C. Ross 5-3; I. Black beat M. Macleod 5-4

Semi-finals: Gibson beat Donnelly 6-4; Black beat E. McLaughlin 6-3

Final: Black beat Gibson 11-7

1982
First round: M. Macleod beat J. Donnelly 6-5

Quarter-finals: C. Ross beat B. Demarco 6-5; M. Gibson beat E. McLaughlin 6-3; I. Black beat Macleod 6-0; E. Sinclair beat J. Phillips 6-3

Semi-finals: Black beat Ross 6-4; Sinclair beat Gibson 6-2

Final: Sinclair beat Black 11-7

1983
First round: J. Donnelly beat B. Demarco 6-4; I. Black beat E. McLaughlin 6-4; M. Macleod beat M. Gibson 6-5

Semi-finals: E. Sinclair beat Donnelly 6-5; Macleod beat Black 6-2

Final: Macleod beat Sinclair 11-9

1985
First round: M. Macleod beat E. McLaughlin 6-4; M. Gibson beat I. Black 6-2; John Rea beat J. Donnelly 6-2; E. Sinclair beat B. Demarco 6-3

Semi-final: Macleod beat Gibson 6-4; Sinclair beat John Rea 6-2

Final: Macleod beat Sinclair 10-2

1986 (*Canada Dry*)
First round: S. Hendry beat B. Demarco 6-1

Quarter-finals: Hendry beat M. Macleod 6-5; I. Black beat E. McLaughlin 6-4; John Rea beat J. Donnelly 6-1; M. Gibson beat E. Sinclair 6-4

Semi-finals: Hendry beat Black 6-2; Gibson beat John Rea 6-0

Final: Hendry beat Gibson 10-5

WELSH PROFESSIONAL CHAMPIONSHIP

1977 (*William Hill*)
Challenge: R. Reardon beat D. Mountjoy 12-8

1980 (*Woodpecker*)
First round: D. Mountjoy beat T. Griffiths 9-6; R. Reardon beat C. Wilson 9-3

Final: Mountjoy beat Reardon 9-6

1981 (*Woodpecker*)
Qualifying: C. Wilson beat R. Andrewartha 6-5

First round: Wilson beat D. Mountjoy 9-6; R. Reardon beat T. Griffiths 9-6

Final: Reardon beat Wilson 9-6

1982 (*Woodpecker*)
First round: C. Wilson beat M. Owen 6-0; T. Griffiths beat C. Roscoe 6-2; R. Reardon beat C. Everton 6-1; D. Mountjoy beat R. Andrewartha 6-3

Semi-finals: Griffiths beat Wilson 9-6; Mountjoy beat Reardon 9-7

Final: Mountjoy beat Griffiths 9-8

1983 (*Woodpecker*)
First round: T. Griffiths beat C. Everton 6-1; R. Reardon beat R. Andrewartha 6-2; C. Wilson beat C. Roscoe 6-4; D. Mountjoy beat M. Owen 6-0

Semi-finals: Reardon beat Griffiths 9-4; Mountjoy beat Wilson 9-3

Final: Reardon beat Mountjoy 9-1

1984 (*Strongbow*)
First round: D. Mountjoy beat C. Everton 6-1; T. Griffiths beat R. Andrewartha 6-1; R. Reardon beat M. Owen 6-1; C. Wilson beat C. Roscoe 6-2

Semi-finals: Mountjoy beat Griffiths 9-5; Wilson beat Reardon 9-4

Final: Mountjoy beat Wilson 9-3

1985 (*BCE*)
First round: S. Newbury beat W. Jones 6-2; T. Chappel beat M. Owen 6-0

Quarter-finals: R. Reardon beat C. Everton 6-2; D. Mountjoy beat Newbury 6-5; C. Wilson beat C. Roscoe 6-3; T. Griffiths beat Chappel 6-0

Semi-finals: Griffiths beat Reardon 9-3; Mountjoy beat Wilson 9-2

Final: Griffiths beat Mountjoy 9-4

1986 (*Zetters*)
First round: T. Chappel *wo* M. Owen *scr*; W. Jones beat Everton 6-2

Quarter-finals: T. Griffiths beat Chappel 6-4; C. Wilson beat S. Newbury 6-4; D. Mountjoy beat C. Roscoe 6-4; W. Jones beat Reardon 6-4

Semi-finals: Griffiths beat Wilson 9-1; Mountjoy beat W. Jones 9-7

Final: Griffiths beat Mountjoy 9-3

The WPBSA's prize fund subsidy to national domestic championships of £1,000 per player from 1985 onwards enabled these events to be staged annually and scheduled properly.

There had previously been Australian and Canadian Professional Championships but these had been played in an haphazard way. Eddie Charlton won the Australian title for the first time in 1964 and was beaten only in 1968 until last season when John Campbell beat him 10-7 in the final.

AUSTRALIAN PROFESSIONAL CHAMPIONSHIP

First round: G. Wilkinson beat G. Jenkins 6-2; G. Robinson beat J. Charlton* 6-0; L. Condo beat E. Charlton* 6-2

Second round: Wilkinson beat L. Heywood 7-3; R. Foldvari beat Robinson 7-2; J. Giannaros beat Condo 7-2; I. Anderson *wo* G. Ganim *scr*

Quarter-finals: E. Charlton beat Wilkinson 8-2; P. Morgan beat Giannaros 8-4; W. King beat Anderson 8-2; J. Campbell beat Foldvari 8-5

Semi-finals: Charlton beat Morgan 9-3; Campbell beat King 9-6

Final: Campbell beat Charlton 10-7

* Members of the Australian Professional Association but not the WPBSA

CANADIAN PROFESSIONAL CHAMPIONSHIP

First round: J. Caggianello beat Jim Bear 5-4; R. Chaperon beat P. Thornley 5-1; B. Mikkelsen beat G. Watson 5-3; John Bear beat M. Morra 5-4; J. Wych beat W. Sanderson 5-2

Quarter-finals: Chaperon beat K. Stevens 6-4; F. Jonik beat Mikkelsen 6-4; C. Thorburn beat Caggianello 6-2; Wych beat John Bear 6-3

Semi-finals: Chaperon beat Jonik 6-3; Thorburn beat Wych 6-5

Final: Thorburn beat Chaperon 6-4

PROFESSIONAL BILLIARDS

THE WORLD PROFESSIONAL BILLIARDS CHAMPIONSHIP

Founded in 1870, the World Professional Billiards Championship is the oldest of all the game's events but since snooker has become by far the most popular of the billiard table games it has declined steadily in public appeal.

The problems started in the 1930s when the four best players in the world, Walter Lindrum, Joe Davis, Tom Newman and Clark McConachy, mastered all aspects of the game so completely that they effectively killed it as a public entertainment. They did such a thorough job that there was only one Championship between 1934 and 1968 that they did not claim – when Rex Williams travelled to New Zealand and beat McConachy, then 73 and suffering from Parkinson's disease.

Williams successfully defended the title three times against various challengers but lost it in June 1980 to Joe's younger brother Fred, who thus became only the second player to have held world titles at both billiards and snooker – the first, of course, was Joe.

In November 1980, the event reverted to a tournament format and a variety of playing systems was tried: time-limit games, points-up games and, for the first time last season, the best of five games of 400-up. This formula gave frequent climaxes, as in frames of snooker, and also eliminated the possibility of very large breaks.

1985 also saw Channel 4 attempt a 'Pot Black'-style billiards event, the Blue Arrow Masters. Viewing figures for this were encouraging and the BBC agreed to televise the final of the 1986 World Professional Championship which was again played over the best of five games of 400 up. It is anticipated that, in 1987, they will televise the semi-finals and final.

World Professional Billiards Championship (1870–1920)

1870 (Feb)	W. Cook	J. Roberts Sr	1,200-1,083
(Apr)	J. Roberts Jr	W. Cook	1,000- 522
(June)	J. Roberts Jr	A. Bowles	1,000- 759
(Nov)	J. Bennett	J. Roberts Jr	1,000- 905
1871 (Jan)	J. Roberts Jr	J. Bennett	1,000- 637
(May)	W. Cook	J. Roberts Jr	1,000- 985
(Nov)	W. Cook	J. Bennett	1,000- 942
1872 (Mar)	W. Cook	J. Roberts Jr	1,000- 799
1874 (Feb)	W. Cook	J. Roberts Jr	1,000- 784

1875 (May)	J. Roberts Jr	W. Cook	1,000- 837
(Dec)	J. Roberts Jr	W. Cook	1,000- 865
1877 (May)	J. Roberts Jr	W. Cook	1,000- 779
1880 (Nov)	J. Bennett	W. Cook	1,000- 949
1881 (Jan)	J. Bennett	T. Taylor	1,000- 910
1885 (Apr)	J. Roberts Jr	W. Cook	3,000-2,908
(June)	J. Roberts Jr	J. Bennett	3,000-1,360
1899	C. Dawson	J. North	9,000-4,715
1900	C. Dawson	H. W. Stevenson	9,000-6,775
1901	H. W. Stevenson	C. Dawson	9,000-6,406
	C. Dawson	H. W. Stevenson	9,000-5,796
	H. W. Stevenson (*declared champion – no contest*)		
1903	C. Dawson	H. W. Stevenson	9,000-8,700
1908	M. Inman (*declared champion – no contest*)		
1909	M. Inman	A. Williams	9,000-7,662
Under Billiards Control Club Rules			
1909	H. W. Stevenson (*declared champion – no contest*)		
1910	H. W. Stevenson	M. Inman (*match abandoned*)	13,370-13,212
	H. W. Stevenson	M. Inman	18,000-16,907
1911	H. W. Stevenson	M. Inman	18,000-16,914
1912	M. Inman	T. Reece	18,000- 9,675
1913	M. Inman	T. Reece	18,000-16,627
1914	M. Inman	T. Reece	18,000-12,826
1919	M. Inman	H. W. Stevenson	16,000- 9,468
1920	W. Smith	C. Falkiner	16,000-14,500

World Professional Billiards Championship (1921–86)

Winner (breaks)	*Score (average)*	*Loser (breaks)*	*Score (average)*
1921			
First round			
C. Falkiner 560	7,334 (35.3)	H. W. Stevenson	5,084 (24.3)
T. Newman 467	8,000 (54.0)	T. Tothill	3,267 (22.0)
Semi-finals			
Newman 627, 531	8,000 (56.7)	Falkiner 587	6,627 (47.3)
T. Reece	*nr*	F. Lawrence	*nr*
Final			
Newman	16,000 (*nr*)	Reece	10,744 (*nr*)
1922			
First round			
T. Reece	8,000 (35.2)	C. McConachy	6,767 (29.9)
Semi-finals			
T. Newman 561, 512	8,000 (52.6)	J. Davis	5,181 (34.1)
C. Falkiner 391	8,000 (41.9)	Reece 455	7,289 (38.2)

Winner (breaks)	*Score (average)*	*Loser (breaks)*	*Score (average)*
Final			
Newman	16,000 (56.4)	Falkiner	15,167 (52.7)
1923			
First round			
M. Inman	16,000 (*nr*)	A. Peall	11,758 (*nr*)
C. Falkiner	16,000 (*nr*)	T. Reece	14,952 (*nr*)
Semi-finals			
T. Newman	16,000 (56.3)	Inman	14,506 (51.1)
850, 705, 500 × 4		701	
W. Smith	16,000 (71.7)	Falkiner	8,695 (29.2)
688		782, 620	
Final			
Smith	16,000 (46.4)	Newman	15,180 (44.0)
451, 446		638, 629, 575	
1924			
First round			
T. Newman	16,000 (71.4)	C. McConachy	8,703 (38.9)
875		349	
Final			
Newman	16,000 (43.5)	T. Reece	14,845 (40.3)
1,021			
1925			
T. Newman	16,000 (68.4)	T. Reece	10,092 (43.1)
957, 672		512	
1926			
T. Newman	16,000 (82.0)	J. Davis	9,505 (49.0)
637, 574, 588		414	
1927			
First round			
M. Inman	8,000 (*nr*)	T. Reece	5,527 (*nr*)
459		1,151	
Second round			
J. Davis	8,000 (*nr*)	Inman	6,895
504, 588			
Challenge round			
T. Newman	16,000 (73.0)	Davis	14,763 (68.0)
787, 1,073, 1,012, 891		2,501, 727	
1928			
First round			
T. Carpenter	8,000 (22.4)	T. Reece	7,283 (20.5)
Second round			
J. Davis	8,000 (66.4)	Carpenter	5,602 (41.8)
Challenge round			
Davis	16,000 (74.4)	T. Newman	14,874 (69.5)
529, 525, 501, 425, 408, 404, 403, 400		564, 489, 467, 455, 451, 427	

Winner (breaks)	*Score (average)*	*Loser (breaks)*	*Score (average)*
1929			
First round			
T. Newman	8,000 (74.1)	T. Carpenter	5,984 (55.4)
553		453	
Final			
J. Davis	18,000 (100.0)	Newman	17,219 (96.2)
838, 609, 599		723, 691, 672, 647, 576	
1930			
First round			
T. Newman	24,001 (85.1)	M. Inman	10,104 (35.8)
1,567, 1,047			
J. Davis	21,975 (82.0)	C. Falkiner	19,815 (74.0)
Final			
Davis	20,918 (113.1)	Newman	20,117 (109.9)
2,052, 500 × 9		500 × 12	
1932			
J. Davis	25,161 (112.0)	C. McConachy	19,259 (98.0)
1,058, 844, 774		1,432, 916, 889	
1933			
First round			
W. Lindrum	21,470 (*nr*)	T. Newman	20,252 (*nr*)
1,578, 984		877, 805	
J. Davis	20,136 (*nr*)	C. McConachy	16,110 (*nr*)
995		675	
Final			
Lindrum	21,815 (92.0)	Davis	21,121 (89.0)
1,492, 1,272, 1,013		792	
1934			
First round			
W. Lindrum	21,903 (*nr*)	C. McConachy	20,795 (*nr*)
1,065, 807		892, 829	
Final			
Lindrum	23,533 (*nr*)	J. Davis	22,678 (*nr*)
1,474, 1,353		824, 728	
1951			
C. McConachy	6,681 (60.0)	J. Barrie	5,057 (44.8)
481, 438, 425, 397, 376		367, 336	
1968			
R. Williams	5,499 (*nr*)	C. McConachy	5,234 (*nr*)
293		236, 200	
1971			
R. Williams	9,250 (*nr*)	B. Bennett	4,058 (*nr*)
480, 372, 353, 325, 302		132	
1973			
R. Williams	8,360 (50.7)	J. Karnehm	4,336 (26.1)
528, 363, 309		215	

Winner (breaks)	*Score (average)*	*Loser (breaks)*	*Score (average)*
1974			
R. Williams	7,017 (43.6)	E. Charlton	4,916 (30.4)
506, 365, 308, 307		488, 401	
1976			
R. Williams	9,105 (42.1)	E. Charlton	5,149 (23.9)
532, 349, 382, 306		333	
1980 (May)			
Challenge round			
F. Davis	5,978 (39.9)	R. Williams	4,452 (29.9)
403, 225, 234, 239, 275, 583		226, 202, 439, 229	
1980 (Nov)			
Qualifying			
P. Morgan	1,655 (21.5)	J. Dunning	1,107 (12.9)
M. Wildman	1,968 (26.2)	B. Bennett	678 (9.0)
S. Davis	1,809 (16.9)	K. Kennerley	965 (9.1)
Quarter-finals			
J. Barrie	2,186 (53.3)	S. Davis	870 (21.8)
335			
F. Davis	1,907 (43.3)	Morgan	978 (22.2)
309			
R. Edmonds	1,513 (19.4)	J. Karnehm	1,306 (17.0)
Wildman	1,476 (25.9)	R. Williams	1,415 (24.8)
Semi-finals			
F. Davis	1,253 (34.8)	Barrie	1,153 (32.0)
501			
Wildman	1,629 (21.4)	Edmonds	955 (12.6)
204			
Final			
F. Davis	3,037 (30.4)	Wildman	2,064 (20.6)
200, 361			
1982			
First round			
C. Everton	1,500 (23.4)	B. Bennett	556 (8.6)
Quarter-finals			
F. Davis	1,500 (30.6)	Everton	652 (13.6)
R. Williams	1,500 (31.9)	J. Karnehm	569 (11.9)
R. Edmonds	1,500 (16.5)	K. Kennerley	753 (8.2)
M. Wildman	1,500 (21.7)	J. Fitzmaurice	721 (10.5)
Semi-finals			
Williams	1,500 (20.3)	Davis	1,494 (19.9)
Wildman	1,500 (24.2)	Edmonds	765 (12.1)
203			
Final			
Williams	3,000 (26.1)	Wildman	1,785 (15.5)
207, 259, 217			

Winner (breaks)	*Score (average)*	*Loser (breaks)*	*Score (average)*
1983			
Qualifying			
I. Williamson	1,000 (12.5)	D. Martin	710 (8.8)
63, 79, 72, 81		52	
B. Bennett	1,000 (11.2)	G. Cripsey	683 (6.3)
63, 55, 58, 75		50	
First round			
J. Karnehm		M. Darrington	
I 122, 117, 53	752 (15.0)	54, 86, 67	679 (13.3)
II 59, 79	748 (12.1)	63	520 (8.4)
	1,500 (13.4)		1,199 (10.6)
B. Bennett		J. Fitzmaurice	
I 58	751 (10.0)		666 (8.8)
II 70, 80, 81, 50	749 (10.3)	61, 54	730 (10.1)
	1,500 (10.1)		1,396 (9.4)
C. Everton		I. Williamson	
I 153, 72, 84	752 (15.0)	60, 67, 52	591 (11.6)
II 105, 61, 59, 81	748 (17.8)	56, 68	494 (12.0)
	1,500 (16.3)		1,085 (11.8)
E. Charlton		T. Murphy	
I 85, 61, 53	751 (11.7)	61, 54, 51, 112	694 (10.8)
II 55, 102, 92	749 (18.3)	64, 56	411 (10.0)
	1,500 (14.3)		1,105 (10.5)
Quarter-finals			
R. Williams		Bennett	
I 87, 69, 63, 147, 107, 100 (*unf*)	751 (30.0)		225 (8.7)
II 105 (*full*), 233, 228, 50 (*unf*)	749 (30.6)		218 (9.5)
	1,500 (31.3)		443 (9.0)
F. Davis		Everton	
I 169, 113, 51, 147, 83 (*unf*)	751 (37.6)	51	236 (11.2)
II 121 (*full*), 66, 71, 427	749 (39.4)	94, 51	241 (12.7)
	1,500 (38.5)		477 (11.9)
R. Edmonds		Karnehm	
I 60, 75, 135, 61	559 (13.0)	83, 59, 71, 84, 68, 153	750 (17.4)
II 61, 358, 84, 64, 138, 92	941 (29.4)	91, 62	325 (9.8)
	1,500 (20.0)		1,075 (14.1)
Charlton		M. Wildman	
I 58, 116, 96, 59	750 (15.6)		408 (8.5)
II 53, 93, 65, 53, 81 (*unf*)	750 (15.0)	51, 58	370 (7.6)
	1,500 (15.3)		778 (8.0)

Winner (breaks)	*Score (average)*	*Loser (breaks)*	*Score (average)*
Semi-finals			
F. Davis		Charlton	
I 92, 88, 214, 93	750 (25.9)	86, 75	410 (14.1)
II 228, 166, 52, 125	750 (30.0)	80, 102, 76	546 (21.8)
	1,500 (27.8)		956 (17.7)
Williams		Edmonds	
I 56, 54, 194, 84, 161, 85 (*unf*)	750 (57.7)	50, 79	288 (22.2)
II 127 (*full*), 53, 316, 83 194 (*unf*)	750 (62.5)	70, 60, 100	383 (31.9)
	1,500 (60.0)		671 (26.8)
Final			
Williams		F. Davis	
I 50, 170, 54, 235, 132 (*unf*)	751 (32.7)	102	227 (9.5)
II 212 (*full*), 64, 192, 120, 67, 71	749 (46.8)	63, 103, 137	378 (23.6)
	1,500 (38.4)		605 (15.1)
1984			
Preliminary round			
T. Murphy		M. Darrington	
I 76	400 (12.5)		505 (15.8)
II 75	621 (17.7)	66	356 (10.2)
	1,021 (15.0)		861 (12.9)
First round			
P. Morgan		B. Bennett	
I 148, 54	508 (13.0)		306 (8.1)
II 79, 63	513 (17.7)	79, 65	333 (11.5)
	1,021 (15.0)		639 (9.5)
I. Williamson		C. Everton	
I 55, 112, 50	373 (12.4)		189 (6.5)
II 65	373 (14.3)		307 (11.4)
	746 (13.3)		496 (8.9)
J. Karnehm		G. Ganim Jr	
I 56, 62, 127, 52, 61	600 (23.1)	75, 91, 92	383 (14.2)
II 89, 106, 148	670 (23.1)	112 (*unf*)	350 (12.5)
	1,270 (23.1)		733 (13.3)
Murphy		J. Fitzmaurice	
I 52, 94 (*unf*)	425 (12.1)	53, 61	497 (14.2)
II 94 (*full*), 57, 138	625 (15.6)		371 (9.3)
	1,050 (14.2)		868 (11.6)
Quarter-finals			
F. Davis		Murphy	
I 66, 82, 61, 73	550 (21.1)	84, 61, 50	453 (17.4)
II 101, 114, 111, 110, 71	692 (26.6)	89, 81, 58	399 (16.0)
	1,242 (23.9)		852 (16.7)

Winner (breaks)	*Score (average)*	*Loser (breaks)*	*Score (average)*
E. Charlton		Karnehm	
I 130	343 (16.3)	75, 73, 93, 193	623 (28.5)
II 319, 64, 92 (*unf*)	601 (35.4)	62	308 (19.3)
	944 (24.8)		931 (24.5)
Williamson		R. Edmonds	
I 81, 96, 54	407 (22.6)	58, 65, 112, 65	432 (22.7)
II 124, 60, 72, 175	511 (31.9)	85, 57, 127	373 (23.3)
	918 (27.0)		805 (23.0)
M. Wildman		Morgan	
I 168, 97, 178, 107	749 (37.4)	65, 85	299 (14.2)
II 87 (*full*), 58, 50, 62, 71, 106	598 (15.8)	53, 53, 70, 50	460 (17.6)
	1,347 (28.7)		759 (15.8)
Semi-finals			
Charlton		F. Davis	
I 114, 94, 50, 81, 98, 121 (*unf*)	795 (29.4)	56, 55	268 (9.2)
II 144 (*full*), 61, 60, 65, 71, 62, 63	641 (27.9)	62, 135, 143, 124	561 (25.5)
	1,436 (28.7)		829 (16.6)
Wildman		Williamson	
I 226, 61	610 (23.5)	70	468 (17.3)
II 125, 188, 58, 91, 205	891 (35.6)	74, 103	381 (15.2)
	1,501 (29.4)		849 (16.4)
Final			
Wildman		Charlton	
I 111, 121, 241	599 (27.2)	100, 68, 50, 56	508 (23.1)
II 97, 115	446 (14.4)	101, 98, 54 (*unf*)	504 (16.3)
	1,045 (19.7)		1,012 (19.1)
1985			
First round			
P. Francisco 3		M. Darrington 0	
I 75, 125 (*unf*)	400 (22.2)	54	166 (9.2)
II 65	400 (12.6)		249 (7.5)
III 63, 55, 56	400 (16.1)		161 (6.7)
I. Williamson 3		B. Bennett 0	
I 96, 107	400 (17.0)	90	200 (8.6)
II 50, 164	400 (30.9)		89 (6.4)
III 50, 53, 65, 52	400 (15.4)	82	331 (12.7)
J. Karnehm 3		E. Charlton 0	
I 57, 56, 103, 89	400 (22.2)	154, 90	308 (16.2)
II 54, 184	400 (21.1)	77	217 (11.4)
III 98, 85	400 (14.8)	106	354 (12.6)
R. Edmonds 3		A. Higgins 0	
I 55, 68, 63, 111	400 (25.0)	69	188 (11.0)
II 51, 74, 147 (*unf*)	400 (26.7)	51, 89	221 (14.7)
III 81, 72, 121	400 (25.0)		110 (6.9)

Winner (breaks)	*Score (average)*	*Loser (breaks)*	*Score (average)*
M. Wildman 3		T. Jones 0	
I	400 (20.0)		237 (11.3)
II 188, 53, 55	400 (30.9)		144 (11.0)
III 98, 105, 103	400 (44.4)		125 (12.5)
N. Dagley 3		J. Fitzmaurice 0	
I 60, 63, 75 (*unf*)	400 (16.7)	60, 96	325 (13.5)
II 83, 94, 59, 67	400 (44.4)	103, 78	284 (28.4)
III 253	400 (33.5)		80 (6.7)
R. Foldvari *wo*		B. Oliver *scr*	
F. Davis 3		C. Everton 1	
I 84, 74, 82, 80	400 (16.2)	80	275 (11.4)
II 75, 78, 87	400 (28.6)		206 (13.7)
III 73, 100	293 (20.9)	70, 132 (*unf*)	400 (30.8)
IV 167, 150	400 (30.8)	54	156 (11.1)
Quarter-finals			
Dagley 3		Karnehm 0	
I 88, 270 (*unf*)	400 (80.0)		24 (4.8)
II 155, 56, 96, 60	400 (21.1)	102, 79	294 (14.7)
III 90, 104, 182 (*unf*)	400 (44.4)		59 (6.6)
Foldvari 3		F. Davis 0	
I 98, 80, 50 (*unf*)	400 (15.4)		130 (4.8)
II 107, 54, 114	400 (33.3)	84, 73, 50	316 (26.3)
III 161, 65, 88	400 (20.0)	71	342 (16.3)
Wildman 3		Francisco 0	
I 162, 102, 84 (*unf*)	400 (28.6)	55	186 (12.4)
II 184, 126 (*unf*)	400 (28.6)		106 (7.6)
III 245, 62, 50 (*unf*)	400 (66.7)		70 (10.0)
Edmonds 3		Williamson 1	
I 117	378 (15.0)	84, 73, 126 (*unf*)	400 (16.0)
II 159	400 (25.0)	65, 68	246 (15.4)
III 252, 102	400 (28.6)	79	212 (14.1)
IV 56, 54, 118	400 (23.5)	101, 67	248 (14.6)
Semi-finals			
Edmonds 3		Wildman 0	
I 69, 76, 97 (*unf*)	400 (28.6)	131	313 (22.3)
II 78, 73, 91	400 (22.3)	89	196 (10.3)
III 141, 60 (*unf*)	400 (22.3)	227	298 (16.6)
Dagley 3		Foldvari 0	
I 53, 52, 164	400 (22.2)	64, 146	352 (19.6)
II 104, 115	400 (25.0)	64, 88, 56	248 (14.6)
III 140	400 (15.4)	58, 50, 60	282 (11.0)
Final			
Edmonds 3		Dagley 1	
I 107, 150, 60	400 (33.3)	58, 201	395 (30.4)
II 159, 77	307 (28.0)	125, 126, 95	400 (40.0)
III 60, 140 (*unf*)	400 (26.6)	52, 106, 75	315 (19.6)
IV 188	400 (20.0)	60, 119, 52, 110	386 (19.3)

Winner (breaks)	*Score (average)*	*Loser (breaks)*	*Score (average)*
1986			
Qualifying			
R. Close 3		E. Hughes 1	
I 93	319 (12.8)	55, 122, 93 (*unf*)	400 (16.0)
II 77, 60, 98, 70 (*unf*)	400 (50.0)		105 (11.7)
III 64, 71	400 (15.4)	52	310 (11.5)
IV 142 (*unf*)	400 (19.1)	54, 75	338 (16.1)
G. Scott 3		B. Oliver 0	
I 75	400 (7.8)	52	344 (6.9)
II 54, 61	400 (12.9)		164 (5.3)
III	400 (9.3)	60	398 (9.5)
First round			
E. Charlton 3		T. Jones 0	
I 60, 73, 55	400 (10.3)		314 (8.1)
II 144, 59	400 (14.8)		180 (6.7)
III 110, 134 (*unf*)	400 (25.0)		73 (4.6)
I. Williamson 3		Scott 0	
I 53, 82	400 (14.3)	114, 56	372 (12.8)
II 56, 73, 63, 58	400 (13.8)		288 (10.3)
III 85, 60	400 (12.9)		251 (8.1)
R. Foldvari 3		J. Karnehm 1	
I 59, 65, 84 (*unf*)	400 (12.5)	68	282 (8.6)
II 154	273 (9.1)	54, 62, 81 (*unf*)	400 (13.3)
III 106, 69	400 (18.2)	50	268 (12.2)
IV 292	116 (10.6)		400 (36.4)
R. Edmonds 3		J. Fitzmaurice 0	
I 88, 86	400 (19.5)		131 (6.0)
II 129	400 (25.0)		104 (6.9)
III 64, 54	400 (12.1)		295 (8.9)
N. Dagley 3		B. Bennett 0	
I 59	400 (16.0)		148 (5.9)
II 59, 83, 94	400 (17.4)		190 (8.3)
III 95, 105, 154	400 (40.0)		107 (10.7)
Close 3		F. Davis 0	
I 130, 105, 109 (*unf*)	400 (50.0)		57 (6.3)
II 65, 55, 93, 58	400 (21.1)	63, 102	262 (13.8)
III 68, 94, 64, 66 (*unf*)	400 (40.0)	79, 88, 102	323 (29.3)
P. Francisco 3		C. Everton 0	
I 56	400 (11.4)		395 (11.3)
II 81, 85, 64	400 (11.5)	101, 70	397 (11.3)
III 52, 53	400 (10.8)	59	349 (9.4)
M. Wildman 3		G. Thompson 0	
I 85, 63, 65	400 (21.0)	52	240 (12.0)
II 63, 61, 131	400 (13.8)		203 (9.0)
III 70, 82	400 (14.8)		317 (11.3)

Robbie Foldvari – World Billiards Champion

Winner (breaks)	*Score (average)*	*Loser (breaks)*	*Score (average)*
Quarter-finals			
Edmonds 3		Francisco 0	
I	400 (12.9)	86	291 (9.1)
II 53	400 (15.4)		218 (8.4)
III 112, 55, 56	400 (12.9)	53	347 (10.8)
Dagley 3		Charlton 0	
I 57, 68	400 (16.7)	57	238 (10.0)
II 94, 116	400 (12.9)		130 (4.0)
III 62, 67	400 (13.7)	62	330 (11.3)
Foldvari 3		Close 0	
I 61, 119	400 (19.0)	55	231 (11.0)
II 174	400 (23.6)	94	358 (20.0)
III 133, 135	400 (21.5)	59, 56	241 (12.5)
Wildman 3		Williamson 2	
I 63, 55	400 (9.5)		272 (6.3)
II 121	400 (15.4)	99	355 (13.6)
III 78, 74	259 (16.2)	54, 107	400 (25.1)
IV 62, 96	282 (9.1)	69, 54, 50	400 (13.3)
V 51, 79	400 (12.5)	70	341 (10.3)
Semi-finals			
Dagley 3		Edmonds 1	
I 76	278 (9.3)	66, 97	400 (13.8)
II 55	400 (11.4)	54, 51	353 (9.9)
III 89, 60, 67	400 (16.7)	50	289 (12.0)
IV 74, 62, 64, 68	400 (18.7)	59	214 (9.7)
Foldvari 3		Wildman 1	
I 59, 72	400 (9.8)	75	394 (9.4)
II	191 (8.0)	93, 168 (*unf*)	400 (17.5)
III 65, 53, 67	400 (10.8)	58, 58	301 (7.9)
IV 99, 70, 87, 71 (*unf*)	400 (17.5)		138 (6.0)
Final			
Foldvari 3		Dagley 1	
I 64, 76	322 (11.1)	54, 54, 50, 66	400 (13.8)
II 117, 92, 73 (*unf*)	400 (30.8)	70	200 (15.4)
III 99, 182	400 (28.6)	73	178 (11.9)
IV 193, 73 (*unf*)	400 (30.7)	121	261 (20.0)

United Kingdom Professional Billiards Championship (1934–51)

1934			
J. Davis	18,745	T. Newman	18,301
537, 504		809, 693, 603, 547	
1935			
J. Davis	21,733	T. Newman	19,919
609, 1,264, 548, 564, 638, 1,002, 545		848, 677, 749, 732, 598	

Winner (breaks)	*Score (average)*	*Loser (breaks)*	*Score (average)*
1936			
First round			
W. Smith	10,373 (60.0)	S. Lee	7,212 (42.0)
Semi-finals			
T. Newman	9,561 (75.0)	S. Smith	7,792 (60.0)
J. Davis	10,965 (93.0)	W. Smith	9,566 (80.0)
Final			
J. Davis	21,710 (125.0)	T. Newman	19,790 (114.0)
1937			
First round			
S. Smith	8,135	S. Lee	4,209
(*match abandoned after nine sessions*)			
Semi-finals			
T. Newman	*wo*	W. Smith	*scr*
J. Davis	12,046	S. Smith	8,516
Final			
J. Davis	22,601 (146.0)	T. Newman	18,321 (118.0)
1,191, 1,179, 1,000, 997, 793, 592, 587, 580, 556, 550, 500		782, 774, 720, 671, 670, 603, 593, 588, 547	
1938			
Semi-finals			
T. Newman	8,959	S. Smith	7,227
556, 771, 602, 599		740	
J. Davis	15,238	S. Lee	6,048
1,013, 840, 988, 666			
Final			
J. Davis	20,933	T. Newman	19,542
1939–45 *No contests*			
1946			
J. Barrie	8,972	W. Leigh	6,782
1947			
S. Smith	7,002	J. Barrie	6,428
1948–49 *No contests*			
1950			
First round			
J. Barrie	7,645 (34.8)	S. Lee	5,593 (25.4)
Semi-finals			
J. Barrie	7,009 (46.7)	W. Smith	5,941 (39.6)
K. Kennerley	*wo*		
Final			
J. Barrie	9,046 (48.9)	K. Kennerley	5,069 (27.4)
1951			
F. Davis	8,120	K. Kennerley	6,011

United Kingdom Professional Billiards Championships (1979–83)

1979 (*Super Crystalate*)			
Quarter-finals			
J. Karnehm	2,041 (35.8)	J. Dunning	760 (13.1)
281, 286			
R. Williams	1,557 (31.8)	R. Edmonds	1,350 (27.0)
259, 309			
J. Barrie	2,292 (46.8)	S. Davis	629 (12.6)
238, 404, 206 (*unf*)			
F. Davis	1,953 (34.9)	B. Bennett	679 (12.1)
Semi-finals			
Williams	1,539 (32.7)	Karnehm	1,182 (24.6)
224, 372			
Barrie	1,548 (43.0)	F. Davis	1,031 (28.6)
227, 444		245	
Final			
Williams	2,952 (44.4)	Barrie	2,116 (32.0)
228, 388, 253		379	
1980			
First round			
S. Davis	1,670 (21.7)	S. Hood	1,029 (13.4)
B. Bennett	1,093 (12.0)	C. Ross	933 (10.1)
Quarter-finals			
J. Barrie	2,001 (32.8)	M. Wildman	815 (13.1)
J. Karnehm	1,990 (28.0)	K. Kennerley	842 (11.9)
322			
R. Edmonds	1,380 (17.7)	Bennett	914 (11.6)
R. Williams	1,871 (33.4)	S. Davis	862 (15.4)
205			
Semi-finals			
Karnehm	1,755 (35.1)	Barrie	1,085 (21.3)
225, 230		229	
Williams	2,159 (41.5)	Edmonds	789 (15.2)
230, 234 (*unf*)			
Final			
Karnehm	2,518 (28.0)	Williams	2,423 (26.6)
205, 208		256, 423	
1981			
Qualifying			
S. Davis	980	B. Bennett	770
R. Edmonds	1,881	G. Miles	473
206			
J. Pulman	1,078	K. Kennerley	879
Quarter-finals			
J. Karnehm	1,307 (22.2)	Edmonds	935 (15.8)
207			
J. Barrie	1,743 (41.5)	Pulman	509 (12.1)
381			

Winner (breaks)	*Score (average)*	*Loser (breaks)*	*Score (average)*
R. Williams	1,575 (50.8)	S. Davis	579 (18.1)
265, 385, 290			
F. Davis	1,304 (29.0)	M. Wildman	805 (17.9)
217			
Semi-finals			
Karnehm	1,338 (23.1)	Barrie	1,074 (18.5)
390			
Williams	2,003 (74.2)	F. Davis	999 (37.0)
217, 505, 231			
Final			
Williams	1,592 (45.5)	Karnehm	1,112 (31.8)
393, 385			
1983			
First round			
B. Bennett	750 (10.4)	D. Greaves	280 (3.7)
C. Everton	750 (28.9)	M. Darrington	177 (6.5)
I. Williamson	750 (14.4)	T. Murphy	625 (11.8)
R. Edmonds	750 (19.7)	J. Fitzmaurice	505 (13.3)
Quarter-finals			
Edmonds	1,500 (30.0)	J. Karnehm	1,194 (23.4)
M. Wildman	1,500 (41.7)	Everton	1,170 (33.4)
285, 217		393	
F. Davis	1,500 (42.9)	Williamson	604 (17.3)
292			
R. Williams	1,500 (46.9)	Bennett	230 (7.0)
246, 461 (*unf*)			
Semi-finals			
Wildman	1,500 (45.5)	Williams	1,272 (38.5)
495		225, 307	
F. Davis	1,500 (36.6)	Edmonds	936 (22.8)
208, 201			
Final			
Wildman	1,500 (21.4)	Davis	1,032 (14.5)

BILLIARDS PROFESSIONALS

NORMAN DAGLEY

Norman Dagley, from Earl Shilton, Leicestershire, won the World Amateur Billiards Championship twice, in 1971 and 1975, and the English Amateur Championship a record 15 times.

Prompted by the upturn in professional billiards, he turned professional comparatively late in his career and reached the final of the World Professional Championship at his first attempt in 1985 where he lost 3-1 to Ray Edmonds.

JACK KARNEHM

Although he has played snooker professionally, Jack Karnehm is predominantly a billiards player. He won the English Amateur Championship in 1969 and later that year also captured the World Amateur title when the event was staged in his home city, London.

He became a member of the World Professional Billiards and Snooker Association in 1971 and unsuccessfully challenged Rex Williams for the World Professional title in 1973. He did, however, beat Williams in the final of the Super Crystalate United Kingdom Championship in 1980.

BOB CLOSE

Bob Close, from Hartlepool, won the English Amateur Billiards Championship three times and was runner-up in the 1977 World Amateur Championship in Melbourne. He was granted billiards only membership of the World Professional Billiards and Snooker Association in 1985.

GEOFFREY THOMPSON

Geoffrey Thompson, from Leicester, was granted billiards only status by the World Professional Billiards and Snooker Association in 1985.

THE AMATEUR GAME

THE WORLD AMATEUR SNOOKER CHAMPIONSHIP

The English Amateur Billiards Championship is the oldest domestic amateur title. It was started in 1888 and was followed in 1916 by the English Amateur Snooker Championship. It was not until 1926 that the first World Amateur Billiards Championship, then called the British Empire Championship, was staged, and in 1963, the inaugural World Amateur Snooker Championship was held in Calcutta.

The two events then took place in alternate years until it was decided that from 1985 the snooker would become an annual event. For that first Championship in 1963 there were only five entries from four countries – England, Australia, India and Ceylon (now Sri Lanka). The 1984 Championship in Dublin boasted 41 players representing 22 countries – an indication of just how fast the game is developing all over the world.

Before India's Omprakesh Agrawal captured the title in Dublin, the event had been dominated by British players. Gary Owen (England) won it in 1963 and 1966 and another Englishman, David Taylor, in 1968. Jonathan Barron gave England their fourth title in 1970 and Ray Edmonds made it six in a row when he won both in 1972 and 1974.

Welshman Doug Mountjoy broke the stranglehold by taking the 1976 title and his fellow countryman Cliff Wilson won it in 1978 before England gave the Championship its youngest ever titleholder when Jimmy White won in 1980 at the age of 18. The title went back to Wales with Terry Parsons in 1982 and Parsons again reached the final in 1984 only to lose to Agrawal.

Each country affiliated to the International Billiards and Snooker Federation is entitled to send two competitors who are initially split into round robin groups with the quarter-finals onwards being knockout.

The biggest innovation in amateur snooker came in 1972 when the then world governing body, the Billiards and Snooker Control Council (now effectively the English body), lifted all restrictions on amateurs accepting prize-money or fees for exhibitions. This brought about a new breed of full-time amateur players who capitalise fully on a variety of privately organised tournaments which carry thousands of pounds in prize-money.

However, the money available in the 'amateur' game pales into insignificance when compared to the prosperity at the top of the professional game. Consequently, there is a high turnover of top amateurs who, as soon as they become eligible, join the professional ranks.

World Amateur Snooker Championships

	Wins	*For*	*Agst*	*Highest break*
1963 (*Calcutta*)				
G. Owen (England)	4	23	7	71
F. Harris (Australia)	3	21	17	52
M. J. M. Lafir (Ceylon)	2	19	18	67
T. Monteiro (India)	1	14	19	56
W. Jones (India)	0	7	24	36
1966 (*Karachi*)				
G. Owen (England)	5	30	7	118
J. Spencer (England)	4	26	14	101
W. Barrie (Australia)	3	23	22	73
M. J. M. Lafir (Ceylon)	2	22	20	45
L. U. Demarco (Scotland)	1	14	28	36
H. Karim (Pakistan)	0	6	30	60
1968 (*Sydney*)				
Group A				
David Taylor (England)	4	24	13	96
J. Van Rensberg (S. Africa)	3	22	14	–
H. Andrews (Australia)	2	17	16	–
T. Monteiro (India)	1	17	22	–
L. Napper (N. Zealand)	0	9	24	–
Group B				
M. Williams (Australia)	3	22	14	–
P. Morgan (Ireland)	3	19	14	88
M. J. M. Lafir (Ceylon)	2	19	16	–
S. Shroff (India)	2	20	19	–
R. Flutey (N. Zealand)	0	7	24	–

Play-offs
Semi-finals: Williams beat Van Rensberg 8-7; David Taylor beat Morgan 8-3
Final: David Taylor beat Williams 8-7

	Wins	*For*	*Agst*	*Highest break*
1970 (*Edinburgh*)				
Group A				
S. Hood (England)	5	20	9	50
P. Mifsud (Malta)	4	22	11	61
M. J. M. Lafir (Sri Lanka)	4	20	16	50
J. Phillips (Scotland)	4	19	18	62
D. Sneddon (Scotland)	2	17	17	38
L. Glozier (N. Zealand)	2	10	21	34
J. Clint (N. Ireland)	0	8	24	46
Group B				
J. Barron (England)	5	21	13	51
D. May (Wales)	4	22	18	64
S. Shroff (India)	3	18	14	47
E. Sinclair (Scotland)	3	16	16	49
J. Rogers (Ireland)	3	16	19	65
L. U. Demarco (Scotland)	2	15	19	32
H. Andrews (Australia)	1	13	22	35

Final: Barron beat Hood 11-7

	Wins	For	Agst	Highest break
1972 (*Cardiff*)				
Group A				
J. Van Rensberg (S. Africa)	3	12	6	45
K. Tristram (N. Zealand)	1	8	8	50
G. Thomas (Wales)	1	6	8	32
L. U. Demarco (Scotland)	1	6	10	41
Group B				
M. Francisco (S. Africa)	3	15	5	47
J. Barron (England)	3	15	10	50
A. Borg (Malta)	2	12	11	59
A. Lloyd (Wales)	2	11	14	41
T. Monteiro (India)	0	3	16	46
Group C				
P. Mifsud (Malta)	4	16	5	61
R. Edmonds (England)	3	14	7	101
J. Rogers (Ireland)	2	8	8	36
M. Berni (Wales)	1	7	12	47
B. Bennett (N. Zealand)	0	3	16	30
Group D				
A. Savur (India)	2	10	6	38
M. Williams (Australia)	2	9	7	48
D. Sneddon (Scotland)	2	9	9	34
D. May (Wales)	0	6	12	42
Semi-final groups				
Group A				
Barron	3	12	4	35
Savur	2	10	8	68
Tristram	1	6	8	29
Mifsud	0	6	12	50
Group B				
M. Francisco	2	11	9	70
Edmonds	2	11	9	39
Van Rensberg	1	8	10	51
Williams	1	9	11	78

Semi-finals: Edmonds beat Barron 8-6; M. Francisco beat Savur 8-7(51,72)
Final: Edmonds beat M. Francisco 11-10

	Wins	For	Agst	Highest break
1974 (*Dublin*)				
Group A				
R. Edmonds (England)	7	31	11	66
M. J. M. Lafir (Sri Lanka)	6	30	19	77
E. Sinclair (Scotland)	6	28	21	67
G. Thomas (Wales)	4	24	22	43
D. Sheehan (Ireland)	4	25	24	43
P. Donnelly (N. Ireland)	3	21	28	42
S. Shroff (India)	3	16	26	44
N. Stockman (N. Zealand)	2	18	29	51
J. Sklazeski (Canada)	1	18	31	79

	Wins	For	Agst	Highest break
Group B				
A. Lloyd (Wales)	8	32	14	104
W. Hill (N. Zealand)	5	26	21	58
P. Burke (Ireland)	4	26	20	71
L. Condo (Australia)	4	26	21	53
A. Borg (Malta)	4	27	23	37
D. Sneddon (Scotland)	4	23	21	54
A. Savur (India)	4	24	23	50
R. Cowley (Isle of Man)	3	16	27	50
N. J. Rahim (Sri Lanka)	0	2	32	25

Quarter-finals: Edmonds beat Condo 4(60)-3; Sinclair beat Hill 4-2; Burke beat Lafir 4-3; Thomas beat Lloyd 4-2
Semi-finals: Edmonds beat Sinclair 8(54)-4(79); Thomas beat Burke 8-2
Final: Edmonds beat Thomas 11-9

1976 (*Johannesburg*)

	Wins	For	Agst	Highest break
Group A				
D. Mountjoy (Wales)	7	28	9	107
J. Van Rensberg (S. Africa)	5	24	16	72
R. Edmonds (England)	4	20	18	77
N. Stockman (N. Zealand)	4	21	19	45
E. Sinclair (Scotland)	4	21	21	51
P. Burke (Ireland)	2	17	25	48
J. Van Niekerk (S. Africa)	1	17	27	35
P. Reynolds (Isle of Man)	1	14	27	46
Group B				
P. Mifsud (Malta)	6	25	9	47
S. Francisco (S. Africa)	6	27	12	68
T. Griffiths (Wales)	5	23	14	69
C. Ross (England)	4	19	17	58
R. Paquette (Canada)	4	22	22	72
E. Swaffield (N. Ireland)	1	16	26	59
L. Heywood (Australia)	1	13	27	46
L. Watson (Ireland)	1	9	27	45
Group C				
M. Francisco (S. Africa)	6	27	12	62
R. Atkins (Australia)	6	25	12	45
R. Andrewartha (England)	5	25	14	100
J. Clint (N. Ireland)	4	17	18	33
L. U. Demarco (Scotland)	3	21	21	75
B. Mikkelsen (Canada)	3	19	22	60
K. Tristram (N. Zealand)	1	9	27	46
R. Cowley (Isle of Man)	0	11	28	41

Elimination match: Griffiths beat Andrewartha 4(51)-0
Quarter-finals: Mountjoy beat Atkins 5(80)-1; Van Rensberg beat Griffiths 5-3(52); S. Francisco beat M. Francisco 5-1; Mifsud beat Edmonds 5-1
Semi-finals: Mountjoy beat S. Francisco 8(51)-2; Mifsud beat Van Rensberg 8(50)-4
Final: Mountjoy beat Mifsud 11(62, 79)-1

	Wins	*For*	*Agst*	*Highest break*
1978 (*Malta*)				
Group A				
K. Burles (Australia)	6	26	10	69
P. Mifsud (Malta)	6	26	10	62
J. Johnson (England)	5	23	9	101
J. Donnelly (Scotland)	5	20	13	78
D. McVeigh (N. Ireland)	2	15	20	56
P. Reynolds (Isle of Man)	2	10	22	45
V. Cremona (Malta)	2	9	25	–
M. Mohideen (Sri Lanka)	0	8	28	–
Group B				
A. Lloyd (Wales)	6	26	12	65
K. Stevens (Canada)	5	23	16	94
J. Grech (Malta)	4	23	16	63
E. Hughes (Ireland)	4	23	21	56
M. J. M. Lafir (Sri Lanka)	3	19	20	50
D. Meredith (N. Zealand)	3	18	20	81
S. Shroff (India)	2	14	23	39
L. McCann (N. Ireland)	1	10	27	40
Group C				
C. Wilson (Wales)	8	32	10	66
R. Paquette (Canada)	5	24	14	81
D. Kwok (N. Zealand)	5	23	20	49
A. Savur (India)	5	26	22	56
I. Williamson (England)	3	22	24	52
R. Atkins (Australia)	3	21	24	49
R. Miller (Scotland)	3	18	24	48
A. Borg (Malta)	2	15	27	44
C. Cooper (Isle of Man)	2	13	29	33

Elimination match: Grech beat Kwok 4-0
Quarter-finals: Burles beat Paquette 5-4; Stevens beat Mifsud 5-0; Johnson beat Lloyd 5(72)-0; Wilson beat Grech 5-4
Semi-finals: Johnson beat Burles 8(85)-4; Wilson beat Stevens 8(64)-2(81)
Final: Wilson beat Johnson 11(87)-5(66)

	Wins	*For*	*Agst*	*Highest break*
1980 (*Launceston*)				
Group A				
J. White (England)	6	24	9	99
A. Savur (India)	4	20	11	67
E. Hughes (Ireland)	4	21	13	127
J. Grech (Malta)	3	19	18	80
L. Adams (N. Zealand)	3	15	18	54
Loo Yap Long (Singapore)	1	6	23	57
R. Burke (N. Ireland)	0	11	24	50
Group B				
J. Giannaros (Australia)	6	24	11	54
S. Newbury (Wales)	4	20	14	100
R. Paquette (Canada)	4	20	15	90
D. Meredith (N. Zealand)	4	20	16	67

	Wins	*For*	*Agst*	*Highest break*
G. Parikh (India)	2	17	18	46
S. Clarke (N. Ireland)	1	10	22	44
Lau Weng Yew (Singapore)	0	8	24	36
Group C				
P. Mifsud (Malta)	6	24	3	77
R. Atkins (Australia)	4	19	15	67
J. Bonner (Australia)	4	17	17	53
W. King (Australia)	3	19	15	57
E. McLaughlin (Scotland)	3	16	16	67
J. O'Boye (England)	1	14	21	98
S. Padayachi (Fiji)	0	2	24	40
Group D				
A. Lloyd (Wales)	6	24	4	47
J. Campbell (Australia)	5	22	8	84
D. Sheehan (Ireland)	4	17	14	69
M. Gibson (Scotland)	3	16	20	80
H. Boteju (Sri Lanka)	2	16	20	45
P. Reynolds (Isle of Man)	1	11	23	35
W. Barrie (Australia)	0	7	24	39

Quarter-finals: Savur beat Lloyd 5(54)-3; Atkins beat Giannaros 5(53)-3(82); Mifsud beat Campbell 5(63)-3; White beat Newbury 5(70)-4
Semi-finals: Atkins beat Savur 8-6; White beat Mifsud 8(100)-6(83)
Final: White beat Atkins 11(80, 101)-2(60)

1982 (*Calgary*)

	Wins	*For*	*Agst*	*Highest break*
Group A				
J. Grech (Malta)	6	28	13	68
A. Kearney (Ireland)	6	26	15	57
D. O'Kane (N. Zealand)	6	28	18	68
B. McConnell (Canada)	5	26	19	43
P. Kippie (Scotland)	5	23	16	68
S. Habib (India)	4	22	21	52
V. Saengthong (Thailand)	3	20	28	73
Lui Yew Keong (Singapore)	1	13	30	60
J. A. Wahid (Sri Lanka)	0	6	32	26
Group B				
T. Parsons (Wales)	7	31	7	63
P. Browne (Ireland)	7	31	12	65
G. Kwok Kwan Shing (Hong Kong)	7	28	12	56
G. Parikh (India)	5	27	21	72
A. Thomson (Zimbabwe)	4	17	23	36
G. Kwok (N. Zealand)	3	17	26	62
H. Boteju (Sri Lanka)	2	15	28	31
W. Craig (Isle of Man)	1	14	29	35
T. Dada (Pakistan)	0	10	32	39
Group C				
J. Bear (Canada)	7	30	12	71
M. Bradley (England)	7	30	12	68

	Wins	*For*	*Agst*	*Highest break*
J. Jorgensen (Canada)	6	25	17	46
W. Mills (N. Ireland)	5	26	17	89
J. Giannaros (Australia)	5	25	21	68
P. Reynolds (Isle of Man)	3	23	23	36
Cheung Che-Ming (Hong Kong)	2	17	25	40
E. Amro (Egypt)	1	11	31	40
V. Yassa (Sudan)	0	3	32	22
Group D				
W. Jones (Wales)	6	27	13	70
P. Mifsud (Malta)	6	29	15	80
W. King (Australia)	6	29	17	83
R. Chaperon (Canada)	5	24	18	56
D. Chalmers (England)	5	25	24	57
R. Lane (Scotland)	3	23	23	44
S. Pavis (N. Ireland)	3	19	27	82
Lau Weng Yew (Singapore)	2	15	29	53
S. Sherif (Egypt)	0	7	32	27

Quarter-finals: W. Jones beat Kearney 5-1; Parsons beat Bradley 5(69, 54)-0; Grech beat Browne 5(55)-3; Bear beat Mifsud 5-2
Semi-finals: Parsons beat Jones 8(103, 87)-5(54); Bear beat Grech 8-7
Final: Parsons beat Bear 11(61, 58, 58)-8(57, 69)

1984 (*Dublin*)

Group A

	Wins	*For*	*Agst*	*Highest break*
A. Micallef (Malta)	9	38	16	75
T. Parsons (Wales)	8	37	11	102
P. Ennis (Ireland)	8	34	28	110
V. Saengthong (Thailand)	7	34	19	86
J. Sigurossonn (Iceland)	6	29	29	70
T. Finstad (Canada)	4	28	28	85
B. Bjorkman (Sweden)	4	26	27	52
A. Thomson (Zimbabwe)	3	24	34	36
D. Feeney (U.S.A.)	3	21	35	42
K. Sirisoma (Sri Lanka)	3	16	33	40
L. Talman (Belgium)	0	11	40	37
Group B				
D. John (Wales)	9	37	10	72
T. Drago (Malta)	8	35	15	132
A. Robidou (Canada)	8	36	20	107
S. Simngam (Thailand)	7	33	20	70
J. Long (Ireland)	6	30	24	62
M. G. Jayaram (India)	5	30	23	84
A. Campbell (Australia)	4	25	29	96
J. McIntyre (N. Ireland)	4	21	30	91
R. Cowley (Isle of Man)	3	20	30	52
M. Sedupathi (Sri Lanka)	1	6	36	37
C. D'Avoine (Mauritius)	0	3	40	38

	Wins	For	Agst	Highest break
Group C				
G. Wilkinson (Australia)	8	30	13	68
J. Wright (England)	7	27	14	68
H. Haenga (N. Zealand)	7	26	14	66
H. Bakahati (Egypt)	6	26	21	73
M. Colquitt (Isle of Man)	5	24	20	57
S. Hendry (Scotland)	5	23	22	118
T. Kollins (U.S.A.)	3	16	27	92
K. Friopjofssonn (Iceland)	3	15	28	28
H. Thwaites (Belgium)	1	3	32	21
Lui Yew Keong (Singapore)	*scr*			
Group D				
C. Archer (England)	9	32	15	80
O. Agrawal (India)	7	33	16	68
D. Kwok (N. Zealand)	5	27	21	64
G. Kwok Kwan Shing (Hong Kong)	5	26	23	129
H. Morgan (N. Ireland)	5	27	27	78
J. Selby (Wales)	4	24	23	72
L. Yew (Singapore)	3	25	28	55
G. Carnegie (Scotland)	3	22	32	69
M. Hallgren (Sweden)	2	17	32	43
M. Sadek (Egypt)	2	15	31	59

Quarter-finals: Agrawal beat John 5-4; Wright beat A. Micallef 5(69, 70)-1; Archer beat Drago 5-4; Parsons beat Wilkinson 5(66)-2
Semi-finals: Agrawal beat Wright 8(75)-5; Parsons beat Archer 8(58, 78, 52)-3
Final: Agrawal beat Parsons 11(69, 74, 62, 54)-7

1985

	Wins	For	Agst
Group A			
P. Mifsud (Malta)	8	37	16
R. Marshall (England)	7	33	21
G. Lackenby (Australia)	7	35	23
S. Robertson (N. Zealand)	7	33	24
J. Long (Ireland)	6	31	28
A. Essam (Egypt)	5	28	25
K. Erwin (Ireland)	5	28	27
J. Allan (Scotland)	5	27	29
M. Lemoy (Belgium)	3	22	35
M. Hallgren (Sweden)	2	23	32
I. Adam (Mauritius)	0	3	40
Group B			
J. McNellan (Scotland)	10	40	11
T. Whitthread (England)	8	34	11
T. Saelim (Thailand)	8	37	18
D. Kwok (N. Zealand)	6	28	22
S. Sawant (India)	6	28	22
L. K. Guan (Singapore)	5	25	27
T. Dada (Pakistan)	4	27	27
A. Thomson (Zimbabwe)	3	20	31

	Wins	*For*	*Agst*	*Highest break*
H. Boteju (Sri Lanka)	3	17	32	
P. Reynolds (Isle of Man)	2	18	35	
P. Rivet (Mauritius)	0	2	40	
Group C				
J.Grech (Malta)	9	39	12	
D. John (Wales)	8	37	14	
J. Bonner (Australia)	8	35	20	
G. Kwok Kwan Shing (Hong Kong)	7	35	22	
W. Pu-ob-Orm (Thailand)	6	29	23	
M. Sobala (Canada)	5	29	27	
L. A. Bux (Pakistan)	5	24	28	
H. Bakhaty (Egypt)	3	23	31	
K. Sirisoma (Sri Lanka)	2	14	33	
H. Ramj (Kenya)	1	13	37	
A. Agustsson (Iceland)	1	10	38	
Group D				
M. Bennett (Wales)	11	40	16	
G. Sethi (India)	9	34	15	
A. Robidoux (Canada)	8	34	22	
G. Burns (Ireland)	8	30	23	
J. Wright (England)	6	25	19	
S. Pavis (N. Ireland)	5	28	27	
B. Bjorkman (Sweden)	5	26	30	
M. Colquitt (Isle of Man)	5	25	30	
K. Fridthjofsson (Iceland)	3	14	32	
L. Nazarali (Kenya)	3	15	34	
D. Barron (Zimbabwe)	3	22	35	

Quarter-finals: Marshall beat McNellan 5(50)-1; John beat Bennett 5(44, 37)-2(30); Mifsud beat Whitthread 5(32, 39, 39)-2; Grech beat Sethi 5(42, 59, 50)-2(41, 30)
Semi-finals: John beat Marshall 8(37, 30, 40, 30, 46, 40, 32, 31)-4; Mifsud beat Grech 8(41, 58, 35)-4(56, 82, 40)
Final: Mifsud beat John 11(68, 32, 34, 59, 31, 39)-6(31, 47, 31, 48)

World Amateur Billiards Championships

	Won	*Score (average)*	*Highest break*	*No of centuries*
1926 (*London*)				
J. Earlham (England)	4	8,000 (25.6)	282	18
G. Shailer (Australia)	3	7,394 (16.8)	203	13
M. Smith (Scotland)	2	6,569 (12.7)	130	4
P. Rutledge (S. Africa)	1	5,902 (12.5)	142	2
T. McCluney (N. Ireland)	0	5,617 (11.9)	144	4
1927 (*London*)				
A. Prior (S. Africa)	3	6,000 (16.6)	184	9
H. F. Coles (Wales)	2	5,533 (12.2)	164	2
L. Steeples (England)	1	5,506 (14.8)	236	9
M. Smith (Scotland)	0	4,499 (12.6)	158	1

	Won	Score (average)	Highest break	No of centuries
1929 (*Johannesburg*)				
L. Hayes (Australia)	3	6,000 (15.5)	136	6
A. Prior (S. Africa)	2	5,512 (16.0)	226	7
H. F. Coles (England)	1	5,592 (14.7)	170	7
P. Rutledge (S. Africa)	0	2,882 (10.9)	164	1
1931 (*Sydney*)				
L. Steeples (England)	4	8,000 (37.3)	461	24
S. Lee (England)	3	7,126 (22.1)	433	18
L. Hayes (Australia)	2	6,113 (15.3)	167	6
H. Goldsmith (Australia)	1	4,995 (13.0)	179	4
W. Hackett (N. Zealand)	0	3,549 (7.7)	97	0
1933 (*London*)				
S. Lee (England)	4	12,402 (28.0)	394	31
T. Jones (Wales)	3	9,883 (18.7)	144	8
A. Prior (S. Africa)	2	9,113 (18.3)	235	13
M. Smith (Scotland)	1	8,292 (17.5)	166	5
J. Blackburn (N. Ireland)	0	6,362 (12.5)	94	0
1935 (*London*)				
H. F. Coles (England)	4	13,665 (28.4)	267	33
J. McGhie (Scotland)	3	9,359 (19.4)	207	11
I. Edwards (Wales)	2	9,814 (18.1)	196	11
S. Fenning (Ireland)	1	9,068 (17.4)	161	6
P. Deb (India)	0	7,461 (13.1)	123	5
1936 (*Johannesburg*)				
R. Marshall (Australia)	3	8,526 (22.0)	248	24
A. Prior (S. Africa)	2	7,014 (17.7)	197	11
J. Thompson (England)	1	7,705 (21.2)	245	15
A. Bowlly (S. Africa)	0	4,548 (9.0)	93	0
Three 2½ hour sessions				
1938 (*Melbourne*)				
R. Marshall (Australia)	6	17,626 (39.0)	427	59
K. Kennerley (England)	5	14,528 (30.1)	472	45
T. Cleary (Australia)	4	8,535 (19.7)	322	17
S. Moses (N. Zealand)	2	6,727 (13.1)	129	4
M. M. Begg (India)	2	6,685 (13.4)	111	2
A. Burke (S. Africa)	1	5,993 (12.0)	119	1
A. Albertson (N. Zealand)	1	5,805 (12.4)	107	1
1951 (*London*)				
R. Marshall (Australia)	6	14,735 (38.1)	423	42
F. Edwards (England)	5	13,459 (26.7)	345	36
T. Cleary (Australia)	4	12,373 (25.5)	330	31
W. Ramage (Scotland)	3	7,638 (19.1)	151	8
W. Pierce (Wales)	2	6,029 (13.6)	225	3
W. Jones (India)	1	7,202 (16.6)	138	10
E. Haslem (N. Ireland)	0	5,896 (14.1)	125	3
1952 (*Calcutta*)				
L. Driffield (England)	5	8,529 (34.5)	278	31
R. Marshall (Australia)	3	9,237 (37.3)	351	27

	Won	*Score (average)*	*Highest break*	*No of centuries*
C. Hirjee (India)	3	7,701 (22.7)	230	14
W. Ramage (Scotland)	3	6,525 (20.8)	211	10
W. Jones (India)	1	6,731 (23.3)	253	6
A. Yunoos (Burma)	0	3,768 (11.0)	79	0
1954 (*Sydney*)				
T. Cleary (Australia)	4	11,496 (33.5)	682	35
R. Marshall (Australia)	3	11,488 (36.0)	407	35
F. Edwards (England)	2	9,053 (24.7)	328	26
W. Jones (India)	1	8,523 (20.5)	209	17
T. G. Rees (S. Africa)	0	6,271 (16.9)	207	6
1958 (*Calcutta*)				
W. Jones (India)	5	16,493	501	56
L. Driffield (England)	4	14,370	499	48
T. Cleary (Australia)	3	13,626	431	52
C. Hirjee (India)	2	12,853	226	38
W. Asciak (Malta)	1	6,329	154	7
M. Hman (Burma)	0	5,633	215	8
1960 (*Edinburgh*)				
J. H. Beetham (England)	7	9,351	277	29
J. Long (Australia)	6	10,634	353	26
W. Jones (India)	5	12,397	589	30
M. Francisco (S. Africa)	4	7,773	148	11
W. Ramage (Scotland)	3	7,938	283	12
W. Asciak (Malta)	2	8,408	194	11
W. Dennison (N. Ireland)	1	6,231	155	4
A. Ramage (Scotland)	0	5,706	101	2
1962 (*Perth*)				
R. Marshall (Australia)	5	12,367 (35.6)	348	57
W. Jones (India)	5	10,805 (26.9)	489	34
T. Cleary (Australia)	4	9,808 (27.0)	315	27
J. H. Beetham (England)	3	7,626 (22.9)	283	18
S. Benajee (India)	3	8,332 (17.2)	219	9
R. A. Karim (Pakistan)	1	5,657 (11.9)	130	3
W. Harcourt (N. Zealand)	0	5,623 (14.3)	123	5
Play-off: Marshall beat Jones 3,623-2,891				
1964 (*Pukekohe*)				
W. Jones (India)	9	16,628 (24.5)	294	49
J. Karnehm (England)	8	12,953 (21.8)	390	28
M. Ferreira (India)	7	13,345 (19.0)	182	29
M. Francisco (S. Africa)	6	12,957 (22.0)	518	38
A. Nolan (England)	5	12,126 (19.9)	259	26
T. Cleary (Australia)	4	10,781 (13.9)	241	19
H. Robinson (N. Zealand)	3	7,643 (10.5)	85	0
T. Yesberg (N. Zealand)	2	7,528 (10.4)	80	0
M. Mavalwala (Pakistan)	1	8,404 (11.3)	174	1
A. E. Redmond (S. Africa)	0	6,914 (9.0)	107	1

	Won	Score (average)	Highest break	No of centuries
1967 (*Colombo*)				
L. Driffield (England)	8	13,556 (30.5)	421	53
M. J. M. Lafir (Ceylon)	7	12,562 (18.4)	218	31
M. Francisco (S. Africa)	6	12,477 (20.4)	301	32
M. Ferreira (India)	5	11,140 (19.5)	507	22
J. Long (Australia)	4	11,068 (17.5)	261	27
T. Cleary (Australia)	3	9,252 (11.6)	322	15
N. J. Rahim (Ceylon)	2	6,895 (8.8)	116	3
M. S. M. Marzuq (Ceylon)	1	7,153 (7.9)	88	0
F. Holz (N. Zealand)	0	5,350 (7.1)	68	0
1969 (*London*)				
J. Karnehm (England)	9	12,902	232	27
M. Ferreira (India)	7	14,115	629	34
M. Francisco (S. Africa)	7	13,760	335	35
M. J. M. Lafir (Ceylon)	7	12,934	296	28
R. Marshall (Australia)	6	13,033	216	33
M. Wildman (England)	6	11,739	274	22
R. Oriel (Wales)	5	13,306	297	30
S. Mohan (India)	5	13,407	219	24
P. Mifsud (Malta)	2	10,410	173	8
A. Twohill (N. Zealand)	1	10,016	146	12
F. Holz (N. Zealand)	0	6,061	65	0
1971 (*Malta*)				
Group A				
M. Francisco (S. Africa)	4	6,450	321	15
M. J. M. Lafir (Ceylon)	3	4,757	233	4
P. Mifsud (Malta)	2	4,142	134	2
D. Sneddon (Scotland)	1	3,160	121	2
L. Napper (N. Zealand)	0	3,798	87	0
Group B				
S. Mohan (India)	4	5,839	188	11
N. Dagley (England)	3	5,454	330	11
M. Ferreira (India)	2	4,423	227	4
C. Everton (Wales)	1	3,893	205	5
W. Asciak (Malta)	0	4,511	188	7
Play-offs:				
Dagley	3	6,041	348	17
M. Francisco	2	3,981	353	11
Mohan	1	3,822	327	11
Lafir	0	2,514	211	5
1973 (*Bombay*)				
M. J. M. Lafir (Sri Lanka)	9	16,956 (34.1)	859	43
S. Mohan (India)	7	17,016 (30.8)	468	53
M. Ferreira (India)	7	15,639 (25.4)	421	41
P. Tarrant (Australia)	6	13,200 (24.4)	373	36
C. Everton (Wales)	5	9,921 (18.2)	240	17
A. Nolan (England)	4	12,709 (20.8)	265	31
P. Mifsud (Malta)	4	12,253 (18.8)	203	23

	Won	Score (average)	Highest break	No of centuries
E. Simons (N. Zealand)	2	8,521 (12.4)	94	0
B. Kirkness (N. Zealand)	1	8,464 (13.5)	195	7
L. U. Demarco (Scotland)	0	7,488 (10.4)	87	0
1975 (*Auckland*)				
Group A				
N. Dagley (England)	5	9,257	477	24
D. Sneddon (Scotland)	4	6,272	124	4
G. Parikh (India)	3	6,471	197	16
J. Reece (Australia)	2	4,058	125	4
H. Robinson (N. Zealand)	1	4,529	123	2
M. Shaharwardi (Sri Lanka)	0	4,032	121	1
Group B				
M. Ferreira (India)	5	9,022	411	26
C. Everton (Wales)	4	6,043	272	13
R. Close (England)	3	5,449	164	10
T. Yesberg (N. Zealand)	2	4,373	131	3
J. Long (Australia)	1	4,598	157	5
B. Bennett (N. Zealand)	0	3,684	95	0

Play-offs
Semi-finals: Dagley beat Everton 1,293(222)-755; Ferreira beat Sneddon 2,470(211)-681
Final: Dagley beat Ferreira 3,385(200, 228, 202, 314)-2,268(281)

	Won	Score (average)	Highest break	No of centuries
1977 (*Melbourne*)				
Group A				
N. Dagley (England)	5	7,546	272	16
C. Everton (Wales)	4	4,962	170	7
S. Aleem (India)	3	7,028	263	11
G. Ganim Sr (Australia)	2	6,322	231	6
H. Robinson (N. Zealand)	1	4,133	93	0
J. Nugent (Scotland)	0	4,131	68	0
Group B				
M. Ferreira (India)	5	12,554	519	33
R. Close (England)	4	7,252	207	15
G. Ganim Jr (Australia)	3	6,424	192	9
T. Yesberg (N. Zealand)	2	4,349	109	1
W. Weerasinghe (Sri Lanka)	1	4,364	97	0
D. Pratt (Scotland)	0	4,316	108	1

Play-offs
Semi-finals: Ferreira beat Everton 2,155-1,310; Close beat Dagley 1,912(234)-1,781(236)
Final: Ferreira beat Close 2,683-2,564(231)

	Won	Score (average)	Highest break	No of centuries
1979 (*Colombo*)				
Group A				
M. Ferreira (India)	7	14,695	467	40
M. J. M. Lafir (Sri Lanka)	5	12,456	370	30
K. Shirley (England)	5	10,656	195	13
W. Barrie (Australia)	4	8,255	128	2
B. Kirkness (N. Zealand)	4	7,283	214	8
H. Nimmo (Scotland)	2	7,022	105	2

	Won	*Score (average)*	*Highest break*	*No of centuries*
M. S. U. Mohideen (Sri Lanka)	1	6,408	76	0
R. Lim Sin Foo (Singapore)	0	6,433	97	0
Group B				
N. Dagley (England)	6	12,539	466	39
P. Mifsud (Malta)	6	12,193	325	31
S. Agrawal (India)	6	11,924	355	30
G. Ganim Jr (Australia)	3	8,486	267	15
C. Everton (Wales)	3	6,905	211	11
W. A. J. Weerasinghe (Sri Lanka)	3	7,883	202	7
B. Bennett (N. Zealand)	1	6,083	101	1
E. Fisher (Canada)	0	4,198	88	0

Play-offs
Semi-finals: Mifsud beat Ferreira 2,489(338, 285)-1,856; Dagley beat Lafir 2,694(266, 444, 289)-1,692(240)
Final: Mifsud beat Dagley 2,943(361)-2,152

1981 (*New Delhi*)

Group A				
N. Dagley (England)	6	11,982	416	42
S. Agrawal (India)	5	12,967	384	39
G. Ganim Jr (Australia)	4	7,934	178	13
A. K. B. Giles (N. Zealand)	3	6,895	162	5
D. Sneddon (Scotland)	2	7,071	123	6
J. W. H. Boteju (Sri Lanka)	1	6,312	107	1
A. A. Essam (Egypt)	0	3,948	59	0
Group B				
M. Ferreira (India)	6	13,862	630	58
L. A. Bux (Pakistan)	5	8,712	257	21
R. Close (England)	3	7,161	217	15
J. Grech (Malta)	3	7,388	402	9
D. Meredith (N. Zealand)	3	6,507	154	7
H. Roberts-Thomson (Australia)	2	6,535	151	5
S. M. Shahawardi (Sri Lanka)	0	5,111	77	0

Semi-finals: Dagley beat Bux 2,890(229, 277, 218)-1,505(257); Ferreira beat Agrawal 3,272(213, 532, 327, 527, 630)-1,964(233, 253)
Final: Ferreira beat Dagley 2,725(208, 349, 245, 244)-2,631(223, 296, 281)

1983 (*Malta*)	*Won*	*Highest break*	*No of centuries*
Group A			
M. Ferreira (India)	6	463	31
R. Foldvari (Australia)	5	302	30
L. A. Bux (Pakistan)	4	177	9
H. Nimmo (Scotland)	3	224	6
D. Meredith (N. Zealand)	2	157	7
H. Griffiths (Wales)	1	112	1
A. Micallef (Malta)	0	122	6
Group B			
S. Agrawal (India)	5	635	42

	Won	*Highest break*	*No of centuries*
N. Dagley (England)	5	368	30
J. Grech (Malta)	5	286	31
V. Ellul (Malta)	2	145	2
R. Lim (Singapore)	2	96	–
W. Loughan (N. Ireland)	2	198	5
H. Boteju (Sri Lanka)	0	120	2

Semi-finals: Agrawal beat Foldvari 2,047(240, 503)-1,900(302, 225, 231); Ferreira beat Dagley 1,983(463)-1,919(258)

Final: Ferreira beat Agrawal 3,933(353, 398, 201, 254)-2,744(242, 212)

1985	*Won*	*Score (average)*	*Highest break*	*No of centuries*
Group A				
R. Marshall (Australia)	7		396*	
M. Ferreira (India)	6		341	
L. A. Bux (Pakistan)	5		229	
R. Robinson (N. Zealand)	4		100	
D. Sneddon (Scotland)	3		190	
T. Ward (England)	2		106	
Lau Weng Yew (Singapore)	1		92	
S. Clarke (N. Ireland)	0		101	
Group B				
G. Sethi (India)	7		604	
S. Agrawal (India)	6		599	
R. Close (England)	5		182	
H. Nimmo (Scotland)	3		146	
D. Meredith (N. Zealand)	3		263	
K. Sirisoma (Sri Lanka)	2		118	
F. Humphries (Australia)	1		131	
A. Micallef (Malta)	1		138	

**unfinished*

Semi-finals: Sethi beat Ferreira 2,513(201, 303)-2,379; Marshall beat Agrawal 2,782(300, 204)-1,872

Final: Sethi beat Marshall 3,809(546, 235, 348, 232, 257)-2,453(201)

World Amateur Championship Records

Snooker

E. Hughes (Ireland)	127	1980

Billiards

T. Cleary (Australia)	682 (2 pots)	1954
M. J. M. Lafir (Sri Lanka)	859 (5 pots)	1973
M. Ferreira (India)	467 (3 pots)	1979

NATIONAL AMATEUR CHAMPIONSHIPS

ENGLAND

Snooker

1916	C. N. Jacques
1917	C. N. Jacques
1918	T. N. Palmer
1919	S. H. Fry
1920	A. R. Wisdom
1921	M. J. Vaughan
1922	J. McGlynn
1923	W. Coupe
1924	W. Coupe
1925	J. McGlynn
1926	W. Nash
1927	O. T. Jackson
1928	P. H. Matthews
1929	L. Steeples
1930	L. Steeples
1931	P. H. Matthews
1932	W. E. Bach
1933	E. Bedford
1934	C. H. Beavis
1935	C. H. Beavis
1936	P. H. Matthews
1937	K. Kennerley
1938	P. H. Matthews
1939	P. Bendon
1940	K. Kennerley
1941–45	*No contests*
1946	H. J. Pulman
1947	H. Morris
1948	S. Battye
1949	T. C. Gordon
1950	A. Nolan
1951	R. Williams
1952	C. Downey
1953	T. C. Gordon
1954	G. Thompson
1955	M. Parkin
1956	T. C. Gordon
1957	R. Gross
1958	M. Owen
1959	M. Owen
1960	R. Gross
1961	A. Barnett
1962	R. Gross
1963	G. Owen
1964	R. Reardon
1965	P. Houlihan
1966	J. Spencer
1967	M. Owen
1968	David Taylor
1969	R. Edmonds
1970	J. Barron
1971	J. Barron
1972	J. Barron
1973	M. Owen
1974	R. Edmonds
1975	S. Hood
1976	C. Ross
1977	T. Griffiths
1978	T. Griffiths
1979	J. White
1980	J. O'Boye
1981	V. Harris
1982	D. Chalmers
1983	T. Jones
1984	S. Longworth
1985	T. Whitthread
1986	A. Harris

Billiards

1888	H. A. O. Lonsdale A. P. Gaskell
1889	A. P. Gaskell A. P. Gaskell
1890	A. P. Gaskell A. P. Gaskell W. D. Courtney
1891	W. D. Courtney A. P. Gaskell
1892	A. R. Wisdom S. S. Christey
1893	A. R. Wisdom S. H. Fry A. H. Vahid
1894	H. Mitchell W. T. Maughan
1895	*No contests*
1896	S. H. Fry
1897–98	*No contests*
1899	A. R. Wisdom
1900	S. H. Fry
1901	S. S. Christey
1902	A. W. T. Good A. W. T. Good
1903	A. R. Wisdom S. S. Christey
1904	W. A. Lovejoy
1905	A. W. T. Good
1906	E. C. Breed
1907	H. C. Virr
1908	H. C. Virr
1909	Major Fleming
1910	H. A. O. Lonsdale
1911	H. C. Virr
1912	H. C. Virr
1913	H. C. Virr
1914	H. C. Virr
1915	A. W. T. Good
1916	S. H. Fry
1917	J. Graham-Symes
1918	J. Graham-Symes
1919	S. H. Fry
1920	S. H. Fry
1921	S. H. Fry
1922	J. Graham-Symes
1923	W. P. McLeod
1924	W. P. McLeod
1925	S. H. Fry
1926	J. Earlam
1927	L. Steeples
1928	A. Wardle
1929	H. F. E. Coles
1930	L. Steeples
1931	S. Lee
1932	S. Lee
1933	S. Lee
1934	S. Lee
1935	H. F. E. Coles
1936	J. Thompson
1937	K. Kennerley
1938	K. Kennerley
1939	K. Kennerley
1940	K. Kennerley
1941–45	*No contests*
1946	M. Showman
1947	J. Thompson
1948	J. Thompson
1949	F. Edwards
1950	F. Edwards
1951	F. Edwards
1952	A. L. Driffield
1953	A. L. Driffield
1954	A. L. Driffield
1955	F. Edwards
1956	F. Edwards
1957	A. L. Driffield
1958	A. L. Driffield
1959	A. L. Driffield
1960	J. H. Beetham
1961	J. H. Beetham
1962	A. L. Driffield
1963	J. H. Beetham
1964	A. Nolan
1965	N. Dagley
1966	N. Dagley
1967	A. L. Driffield
1968	M. Wildman
1969	J. Karnehm
1970	N. Dagley
1971	N. Dagley
1972	N. Dagley
1973	N. Dagley
1974	N. Dagley
1975	N. Dagley
1976	R. Close
1977	R. Close
1978	N. Dagley
1979	N. Dagley
1980	N. Dagley
1981	N. Dagley
1982	N. Dagley
1983	N. Dagley
1984	N. Dagley
1985	R. Close
1986	K. Shirley

NORTHERN IRELAND

Snooker

1927 G. Barron
1928 J. Perry
1929 W. Lyttle
1930 J. Luney
1931 J. McNally
1932 Capt. J. Ross
1933 J. French
1934 Capt. J. Ross
1935 W. Agnew
1936 W. Lowe
1937 J. Chambers
1938 J. McNally
1939 J. McNally
1940 *No contest*
1941 J. McNally
1942–44 *No contests*
1945 J. McNally
1946 J. McNally
1947 J. Rea
1948 J. Bates
1949 J. Bates
1950 J. Bates
1951 J. Stevenson
1952 J. Stevenson
1953 J. Stevenson
1954 W. Seeds
1955 J. Stevenson
1956 S. Brooks
1957 M. Gill
1958 W. Agnew
1959 W. Hanna
1960 M. Gill
1961 D. Anderson
1962 S. McMahon
1963 D. Anderson
1964 P. Morgan
1965 M. Gill
1966 S. Crothers
1967 D. Anderson
1968 A. Higgins
1969 D. Anderson
1970 J. Clint
1971 S. Crothers
1972 P. Donnelly
1973 J. Clint
1974 P. Donnelly
1975 J. Clint
1976 E. Swaffield
1977 D. McVeigh
1978 D. McVeigh
1979 R. Burke
1980 S. Clarke
1981 T. Murphy
1982 S. Pavis
1983 J. McLaughlin Jr
1984 J. McLaughlin Jr
1985 S. Pavis
1986 C. Sewell

Billiards

1925 T. McCluney
1926 T. McCluney
1927 J. Sloan
1928 A. Davison
1929 J. Blackburn
1930 J. Blackburn
1931 J. Blackburn
1932 W. Lowe
1933 W. Mills
1934 W. Lowe
1935 W. Morrison
1936 J. Blackburn
1937 J. Blackburn
1938 W. Lowe
1939 W. Lowe
1940 *No contest*
1941 E. Haslem
1942–44 *No contests*
1945 E. Haslem
1946 J. Holness
1947 J. Bates
1948 J. Bates
1949 J. Bates
1950 J. Bates
1951 E. Haslem
1952 R. Taylor
1953 W. Scanlon
1954 W. Scanlon
1955 D. Turley
1956 J. Stevenson
1957 W. Scanlon
1958 W. Hanna
1959 W. Hanna
1960 W. Dennison
1961 R. Hanna
1962 N. McQuay
1963 W. Hanna
1964 { D. Anderson / D. Turley
1965 W. Ashe
1966 D. Anderson
1967 W. Loughan
1968 D. Anderson
1969 W. Loughan
1970 S. Crothers
1971 J. Bates
1972–73 *No contests*
1974 P. Donnelly
1975 P. Donnelly
1976 P. Donnelly
1977 T. Taylor
1978 W. Loughan
1979 J. Bates
1980 S. Clarke
1981 W. Loughan
1982 P. Donnelly
1985 F. Clarke
1986 D. Elliott

REPUBLIC OF IRELAND

Snooker

1931 J. Ayres
1932 *No contest*
1933 S. Fenning
1934 *No contest*
1935 S. Fenning
1936 *No contest*
1937 P. J. O'Connor
1938–39 *No contests*
1940 P. Merrigan
1941 *No contest*
1942 P. J. O'Connor
1943 *No contest*
1944 S. Fenning
1945–46 *No contests*
1947 C. Downey
1948 P. Merrigan
1949 S. Fenning
1950–51 *No contests*
1952 W. Brown
1953 S. Brooks
1954 S. Fenning
1955 S. Fenning
1956 W. Brown
1957 J. Connolly
1958 G. Gibson
1959–60 *No contests*
1961 W. Brown
1962 J. Weber
1963 J. Rogers
1964 J. Rogers
1965 W. Fields
1966 G. Hanway
1967 P. Morgan
1968 G. Hanway
1969 D. Dally
1970 D. Sheehan
1971 D. Sheehan
1972 J. Rogers
1973 F. Murphy
1974 P. Burke
1975 F. Nathan
1976 P. Burke
1977 J. Clusker
1978 E. Hughes
1979 E. Hughes
1980 D. Sheehan
1981 A. Kearney
1982 P. Browne
1983 J. Long
1984 P. Ennis
1985 G. Burns
1986 G. Burns

Billiards

1931 J. Ayres
1932 No contest
1933 J. Ayres
1934 S. Fenning
1935 S. Fenning
1936 S. Fenning
1937 T. O'Brien
1938–41 No contests
1942 S. Fenning
1943 No contest
1944 S. Fenning
1945–47 No contests
1948 W. Brown
1949 S. Fenning
1950–51 No contests
1952 M. Nolan
1953 D. Turley
1954 M. Nolan
1955 M. Nolan
1956 M. Nolan
1957 M. Nolan
1958 W. Dennison
1959–60 No contests
1961 K. Smyth
1962 K. Smyth
1963 J. Bates
1964 J. Bates
1965 L. Codd
1966 L. Codd
1967 P. Morgan
1968 P. Morgan
1969 J. Rogers
1970 L. Drennan
1971 L. Codd
1972 L. Codd
1973 T. Martin
1974 T. Doyle
1975 P. Fenelon
1976 J. Rogers
1977 E. Hughes
1978 E. Hughes
1979 L. Drennan
1980 P. Burke
1981 P. Burke
1982 D. Elliott
1984 A. Murphy
1985 A. Roche

SCOTLAND

Snooker

1931 G. Brown
1932–45 No contests
1946 J. Levey
1947 J. Levey
1948 I. Wexelstein
1949 W. Ramage
1950 W. Ramage
1951 A. Wilson
1952 D. Emerson
1953 P. Spence
1954 D. Edmond
1955 L. U. Demarco
1956 W. Barrie
1957 T. Paul
1958 J. Phillips
1959 J. Phillips
1960 E. Sinclair
1961 J. Phillips
1962 A. Kennedy
1963 E. Sinclair
1964 J. Phillips
1965 L. U. Demarco
1966 L. U. Demarco
1967 E. Sinclair
1968 E. Sinclair
1969 A. Kennedy
1970 D. Sneddon
1971 J. Phillips
1972 D. Sneddon
1973 E. Sinclair
1974 D. Sneddon
1975 E. Sinclair
1976 E. Sinclair
1977 R. Miller
1978 J. Donnelly
1979 S. Nivison
1980 M. Gibson
1981 R. Lane
1982 P. Kippie
1983 G. Carnegie
1984 S. Hendry
1985 S. Hendry
1986 S. Muir

Billiards

1913 Capt. Croneen
1914–21 No contests
1922 H. L. Fleming
1923 M. Smith
1924 No contest
1925 W. D. Greenlees
1926 M. Smith
1927 M. Smith
1928 M. Smith
1929 J. McGhee
1930 M. Smith
1933 A. Ramage
1934 N. Canney
1935 H. King
1936 N. Canney
1937 J. McGhee
1938 J. McGhee
1939 No contest
1940 W. McCann
1941–45 No contests
1946 J. Levey
1947 A. Ramage
1948 W. Ramage
1949 W. Ramage
1950 A. Ramage
1951 W. Ramage
1952 J. Murray
1953 J. Bates
1954 J. Bates
1955 W. Ramage
1956 W. Ramage
1957 W. Ramage
1958 W. Ramage
1959 W. Ramage
1960 A. Ramage
1961 P. Spence
1962 W. Ramage
1963 W. Ramage
1964 W. Ramage
1965 W. Ramage
1966 W. Ramage
1967 W. Ramage
1968 A. Kennedy
1969 A. Kennedy
1970 D. Sneddon
1971 D. Sneddon
1972 L. U. Demarco
1973 D. Sneddon
1974 D. Sneddon
1975 D. Sneddon
1976 D. Sneddon
1977 J. Nugent
1978 D. Sneddon
1979 H. Nimmo
1980 D. Sneddon
1981 D. Sneddon
1982 W. Kelly
1983 H. Nimmo
1985 D. Sneddon

WALES

Snooker

1930 T. Jones
1931 T. Jones
1932 T. Jones
1933 T. Jones
1934 T. Jones
1935 T. Jones

1936 T. Jones
1937 G. Howells
1938 B. Gravenor
1939 W. E. James
1940–46 No contests
1947 T. Jones
1948 R. Smith
1949 A. J. Ford
1950 R. Reardon
1951 R. Reardon
1952 R. Reardon
1953 R. Reardon
1954 R. Reardon
1955 R. Reardon
1956 C. Wilson
1957 R. D. Meredith
1958 A. Kemp
1959 J. R. Price
1960 L. Luker
1961 T. Parsons
1962 A. J. Ford
1963 R. D. Meredith
1964 M. L. Berni
1965 T. Parsons
1966 L. L. O'Neill
1967 L. L. O'Neill
1968 D. Mountjoy
1969 T. Parsons
1970 D. T. May
1971 D. T. May
1972 G. Thomas
1973 A. Lloyd
1974 A. Lloyd
1975 T. Griffiths
1976 D. Mountjoy
1977 C. Wilson
1978 A. Lloyd
1979 C. Wilson
1980 S. Newbury
1981 C. Roscoe
1982 T. Parsons
1983 W. Jones
1984 T. Parsons
1985 M. Bennett
1986 K. Jones

Billiards

1920 H. F. E. Coles
1921 H. F. E. Coles
1922 H. F. E. Coles
1923 H. F. E. Coles
1924 H. F. E. Coles
1925 Unknown
1926 Unknown
1927 Unknown
1928 G. Moore
1929 J. Tregoning
1930 Unknown
1931 L. Prosser
1932 T. Jones
1933 T. Jones
1934 Unknown
1935 I. Edwards
1936 J. Tregoning
1937 B. Gravenor
1938 J. Tregoning
1939 B. Gravenor
1940–45 No contests
1946 T. G. Rees
1947 T. C. Morse
1948 J. Tregoning
1949 I. Edwards
1950 W. Pierce
1951 W. Pierce
1952 J. Tregoning
1953 B. Sainsbury
1954 R. Smith
1955 J. Tregoning
1956 A. J. Ford
1957 R. Smith
1958 R. W. Oriel
1959 A. J. Ford
1960 C. Everton
1961 R. W. Oriel
1962 R. W. Oriel
1963 R. W. Oriel
1964 R. W. Oriel
1965 R. W. Oriel
1966 R. W. Oriel
1967 R. W. Oriel
1968 D. E. Edwards
1969 R. W. Oriel
1970 R. W. Oriel
1971 R. W. Oriel
1972 C. Everton
1973 C. Everton
1974 R. W. Oriel
1975 R. W. Oriel
1976 C. Everton
1977 C. Everton
1978 R. W. Oriel
1979 R. W. Oriel
No further contests

AUSTRALIA

Snooker

1953 W. Simpson
1954 W. Simpson
1955 E. Pickett
1956 R. Marshall
1957 W. Simpson
1958 F. Harris
1959 K. Burles
1960 K. Burles
1961 M. Williams
1962 W. Barrie
1963 F. Harris
1964 W. Barrie
1965 W. Barrie
1966 M. Williams
1967 M. Williams
1968 M. Williams
1969 W. Barrie
1970 M. Williams
1971 M. Williams
1972 M. Williams
1973 M. Williams
1974 L. Condo
1975 R. Atkins
1976 R. Atkins
1977 R. Atkins
1978 K. Burles
1979 J. Campbell
1980 W. King
1981 W. King
1982 J. Giannaros
1983 G. Lackenby
1984 G. Wilkinson
1985 J. Bonner

Billiards

1913 G. B. Shailer
1914–19 No contests
1920 J. R. Hooper
1921 G. B. Shailer
1922 G. B. Shailer
1923 G. B. Shailer
1924 E. Eccles
1925 G. B. Shailer
1926 L. W. Hayes
1927 L. W. Hayes
1928 L. W. Hayes
1929 A. H. Hearndon
1930 S. Ryan
1931 H. L. Goldsmith
1932 A. Sakzewski
1933 L. W. Hayes
1934 L. W. Hayes
1935 L. W. Hayes
1936 R. Marshall
1937 R. Marshall
1938 R. Marshall
1939 R. Marshall
1940–45 No contests
1946 R. Marshall
1947 T. Cleary
1948 R. Marshall
1949 R. Marshall
1950 T. Cleary
1951 R. Marshall
1952 R. Marshall
1953 R. Marshall
1954 R. Marshall
1955 R. Marshall
1956 J. Long
1957 R. Marshall
1958 T. Cleary
1959 R. Marshall
1960 J. Long
1961 R. Marshall

1962 R. Marshall
1963 R. Marshall
1964 J. Long
1965 T. Cleary
1966 T. Cleary
1967 J. Long
1968 J. Long
1969 R. Marshall
1970 R. Marshall
1971 M. Williams
1972 P. Tarrant
1973 P. Tarrant
1974 J. Reece
1975 J. Long
1976 G. Ganim Jr
1977 G. Ganim Jr
1978 G. Ganim Jr
1979 G. Ganim Jr
1980 G. Ganim Jr
1981 G. Ganim Jr
1982 R. Foldvari
1983 R. Foldvari
1984 F. Humphreys
1985 R. Marshall

CANADA

Snooker

1979 J. Wych
1980 Jim Bear
1981 R. Chaperon
1983 A. Robidoux
1984 T. Finstad
1985 A. Robidoux

Billiards

1979 E. Fisher
1980 S. Holden
1981 R. Chaperon
1982 R. Chaperon

INDIA

Snooker

1939 P. K. Deb
1940 P. K. Deb
1941 V. R. Freer
1942 P. K. Deb
1943–45 *No contests*
1946 T. A. Selvaraj
1947 T. Sadler
1948 W. Jones
1949 T. A. Selvaraj
1950 F. Edwards (Eng)
1951 T. A. Selvaraj
1952 W. Jones
1953 A. L. Driffield (Eng)
1954 W. Jones
1955 T. A. Selvaraj
1956 M. J. M. Lafir
1957 M. J. M. Lafir
1958 W. Jones
1959 M. J. M. Lafir
1960 W. Jones
1961 M. J. M. Lafir
1962 R. Marshall (Aust)
1963 M. J. M. Lafir
1964 S. Shroff
1965 S. Shroff
1966 T. Monteiro
1967 S. Shroff
1968 S. Mohan
1969 S. Shroff
1970 S. Shroff
1971 T. Monteiro
1972 S. Shroff
1973 S. Shroff
1974 M. J. M. Lafir
1975 M. J. M. Lafir
1976 A. Savur
1977 M. J. M. Lafir
1978 A. Savur
1979 A. Savur
1980 J. White (Eng)
1981 G. Parikh
1984 G. Sethi
1985 G. Sethi

Billiards

1935 P. K. Deb
1936 P. K. Deb
1937 M. M. Begg
1938 P. K. Deb
1939 P. K. Deb
1940 S. H. Lyth
1941 V. R. Freer
1942 V. R. Freer
1943–45 *No contests*
1946 C. Hirjee
1947 C. Hirjee
1948 V. R. Freer
1949 T. A. Selvaraj
1950 W. Jones
1951 W. Jones
1952 W. Jones
1953 L. Driffield (Eng)
1954 W. Jones
1955 W. Jones
1956 C. Hirjee
1957 W. Jones
1958 C. Hirjee
1959 T. Cleary (Aust)
1960 W. Jones
1961 W. Jones
1962 R. Marshall (Aust)
1963 W. Jones
1964 W. Jones
1965 W. Jones
1966 W. Jones
1967 A. Savur
1968 S. Mohan
1969 M. Ferreira
1970 S. Mohan
1971 S. Mohan
1972 S. Mohan
1973 S. Mohan
1974 M. Ferreira
1975 G. C. Parikh
1976 M. Ferreira
1977 M. J. M. Lafir
1978 M. Ferreira
1979 M. Ferreira
1980 M. Ferreira
1981 G. Sethi
1982 M. Ferreira
1983 S. Agrawal
1984 G. Sethi
1985 M. Ferreira

MALTA

Snooker

1947 L. Galea
1948 T. B. Oliver
1949 L. Galea
1950 W. Asciak
1951 W. Asciak
1952 A. Borg

1953 A. Borg
1954 W. Asciak
1955 A. Borg
1956 W. Asciak
1957 W. Asciak
1958 W. Asciak
1959 A. Borg
1960 A. Borg
1961 A. Borg
1962 A. Borg
1963 M. Tonna
1964 A. Borg
1965 A. Borg
1966 A. Borg
1967 A. Borg
1968 P. Mifsud
1969 P. Mifsud
1970 P. Mifsud
1971 P. Mifsud
1972 P. Mifsud
1973 A. Borg
1974 A. Borg
1975 P. Mifsud
1976 P. Mifsud
1977 A. Borg
1978 P. Mifsud
1979 P. Mifsud
1980 J. Grech
1981 J. Grech
1982 P. Mifsud
1983 P. Mifsud
1984 T. Drago
1985 P. Mifsud

Billiards

1947 V. Micallef
1948 No contest
1949 E. Bartolo
1950 W. Asciak
1951 W. Asciak
1952 W. Asciak
1953 W. Asciak
1954 W. Asciak
1955 W. Asciak
1956 W. Asciak
1957 A. Asciak
1958 A. Asciak
1959 A. Asciak
1960 A. Asciak
1961 A. Borg
1962 J. Bartolo
1963 J. Bartolo
1964 W. Asciak
1965 A. Asciak
1966 A. Asciak
1967 A. Asciak
1969 P. Mifsud
1970 W. Asciak
1971 P. Mifsud
1972 W. Asciak
1973 P. Mifsud
1974 P. Mifsud
1975 P. Mifsud
1976 P. Mifsud
1977 P. Mifsud
1978 J. Grech
1979 P. Mifsud
1980 J. Grech
1981 No contest
1982 V. Ellul
1983 J. Grech

NEW ZEALAND

Snooker

1945 S. Moses
1946 J. Munro
1947 W. Thompson
1948 L. Stout
1949 L. Stout
1950 L. Stout
1951 N. Lewis
1952 L. Stout
1953 L. Stout
1954 R. Franks
1955 L. Stout
1956 L. Stout
1957 W. Harcourt
1958 W. Harcourt
1959 W. Thomas
1960 T. Yesberg
1961 F. Franks
1962 K. Murphy
1963 W. Harcourt
1964 T. Yesberg
1965 L. Napper
1966 L. Napper
1967 R. Flutey
1968 L. Napper
1969 L. Glozier
1970 K. Tristram
1971 B. J. Bennett
1972 N. Stockman
1973 W. Hill
1974 K. Tristram
1975 K. Tristram
1976 D. Kwok
1977 D. Meredith
1978 D. Meredith
1979 D. Meredith
1980 D. O'Kane
1981 D. Kwok
1982 D. Kwok
1983 D. Kwok
1984 D. Kwok
1985 P. de Groot

Billiards

1908 J. Ryan
1909 No contest
1910 F. Lovelock
1911 F. Lovelock
1912 H. Valentine
1913 H. Valentine
1914 N. Lynch
1915 W. E. Warren
1916 H. Siedeberg
1917 H. Siedeberg
1918 W. E. Warren
1919 H. Siedeberg
1920 W. E. Warren
1921 H. Siedeberg
1922 E. V. Roberts
1923 E. V. Roberts
1924 R. Fredotovich
1925 C. Mason
1926 E. V. Roberts
1927 E. V. Roberts
1928 A. Bowie
1929 L. Stout
1930 W. E. Hackett
1931 A. Duncan
1932 C. Mason
1933 A. Albertson
1934 H. McLean
1935 L. Holdsworth
1936 S. Moses
1937 S. Moses
1938 L. Holdsworth
1939 R. Carrick
1940 S. Moses
1941 R. Carrick
1942 R. Carrick
1943 A. Albertson
1944 S. Moses
1945 J. Shepherd
1946 R. Carrick
1947 C. Peek
1948 R. Carrick
1949 R. Carrick
1950 R. Carrick
1951 R. Carrick
1952 L. Stout
1953 A. Twohill
1954 A. Twohill
1955 A. Twohill
1956 A. Twohill
1957 A. Twohill
1958 A. Albertson
1959 A. Twohill
1960 W. Harcourt
1961 A. Albertson
1962 W. Harcourt
1963 H. C. Robinson
1964 T. Yesberg
1965 L. Napper
1966 A. Twohill
1967 A. Twohill
1968 A. Twohill
1969 E. Simmons
1970 L. Napper
1971 W. Harcourt
1972 B. Kirkness
1973 H. C. Robinson
1974 H. C. Robinson
1975 T. Yesberg
1976 H. C. Robinson
1977 B. Kirkness
1978 B. Kirkness
1979 R. Adams

1980 D. Meredith
1981 D. Meredith
1982 D. Meredith
1983 D. Meredith
1984 D. Meredith
1985 D. Meredith

SOUTH AFRICA

Snooker

1937 A. Prior
1938 A. H. Ashby
1939 A. Prior
1940–45 No contests
1946 F. Walker
1947 No contest
1948 F. Walker
1949 E. Kerr
1950 T. G. Rees
1951 T. G. Rees
1952 T. G. Rees
1953 J. Van Rensberg
1954 J. Van Rensberg
1955 J. Van Rensberg
1956 F. Walker
1957 J. van Rensburg
1958 R. Walker
1959 M. Francisco
1960 P. Mans Jr
1961 J. Van Rensberg
1962 J. Van Rensberg
1963 J. Van Rensberg
1964 M. Francisco
1965 M. Francisco
1966 M. Francisco
1967 J. Van Rensberg
1968 S. Francisco
1969 S. Francisco
1970 J. Van Rensberg
1971 M. Francisco
1972 J. Van Rensberg
1973 J. Van Rensberg
1974 S. Francisco
1975 M. Francisco
1976 No contest
1977 S. Francisco
1978 J. van Niekerk
1979 F. Ellis
1980 F. Ellis
1981 P. Francisco
1982 P. Francisco
1983 P. Francisco

Billiards

1920 Sgt Bruyns
1921 A. Prior
1922 A. Prior
1923 No contest
1924 A. Prior
1925 P. Rutledge
1926 A. Prior
1927 A. Percival
1928 P. Rutledge
1929–30 No contests
1931 A. Prior
1932–36 No contests
1937 A. M. Burke
1938 A. Prior
1939 A. Prior
1940–45 No contests
1946 P. G. Kempen
1947 No contest
1948 P. G. Kempen
1949 T. G. Rees
1950 T. G. Rees
1951 I. Drapin
1952 T. G. Rees
1953 T. G. Rees
1954 F. Walker
1955 F. Walker
1956 G. Povall
1957 F. Walker
1958 F. Walker
1959 M. Francisco
1960 R. Walker
1961 M. Francisco
1962 M. Francisco
1963 M. Francisco
1964 M. Francisco
1965 M. Francisco
1966 M. Francisco
1967 J. Van Rensberg
1968 M. Francisco
1969 M. Francisco
1970 M. Francisco
1971 M. Francisco
1972 S. Francisco
1973 S. Francisco
1974 M. Francisco
1975 S. Francisco
1976 No contest
1977 M. Francisco
1978 C. van Dijk
1979 C. van Dijk
1980 C. van Dijk
1981 P. Spence
1983 P. Francisco

SRI LANKA

Snooker

1951 M. S. A. Hassan
1952 M. J. M. Lafir
1953 M. J. M. Lafir
1954 M. J. M. Lafir
1955 M. J. M. Lafir
1956 M. J. M. Lafir
1957 M. J. M. Lafir
1958 M. J. M. Lafir
1959 M. J. M. Lafir
1960 M. J. M. Lafir
1961 M. J. M. Lafir
1962 M. J. M. Lafir
1963 M. J. M. Izzath
1964 M. J. M. Lafir
1965 M. J. M. Lafir
1966 M. J. M. Lafir
1967 N. J. Rahim
1968 No contest
1969 M. J. M. Lafir
1970 N. J. Rahim
1971 No contest
1972 N. J. Rahim
1973 M. J. M. Lafir
1974 *Abandoned*
1975 N. A. Rahim
1976 M. S. U. Mohideen
1977 M. S. U. Mohideen
1978 N. A. Rahim
1981 J. W. H. Boteju
1982 J. A. Wahid
1983 J. W. H. Boteju
1984 K. Scrisoma
1985 J. W. H. Boteju

Billiards

1951 M. J. M. Lafir
1952 M. J. M. Lafir
1953 M. J. M. Lafir
1954 A. C. Cambal
1955 T. A. Selvaraj
1956 T. A. Selvaraj
1957 M. J. M. Lafir
1959 M. J. M. Lafir
1960 M. J. M. Lafir
1961 M. J. M. Lafir
1962 M. J. M. Lafir
1963 M. H. M. Mujahid
1964 M. J. M. Lafir
1966 M. J. M. Lafir
1967 J. K. Bakshani
1969 M. J. M. Lafir
1970 M. J. M. Lafir
1972 M. J. M. Lafir
1973 M. J. M. Lafir
1974 S. Shaharwardi
1975 M. S. U. Mohideen
1976 W. Weerasinghe
1977 W. Weerasinghe
1978 J. W. H. Boteju
1979 W. Weerasinghe
1981 J. W. H. Boteju
1982 J. W. H. Boteju
1983 W. Weerasinghe
1984 J. W. H. Boteju
1985 K. Scrisoma

FIXTURES 1986–87

18–21 September	LANGS SCOTTISH MASTERS at Hospitality Inn, Glasgow Box office: 041 332 3311
26 September–5 October	First ranking tournament at Trentham Gardens, Stoke Box office: 0782 657341
18–26 October	ROTHMANS GRAND PRIX at The Hexagon, Reading Box office: 0734 591591
28 October–1 November	CANADIAN MASTERS in Toronto
14–30 November	TENNENTS UK OPEN at the Guild Hall, Preston Box office: 0772 21721
1–14 December	HOFMEISTER WORLD DOUBLES CHAMPIONSHIP at Derngate, Northampton Box office: 0604 24811
9–18 January	MERCANTILE CREDIT CLASSIC at venue to be announced
25 January–1 February	BENSON AND HEDGES MASTERS at Wembley Conference Centre Box office: 01 902 1234
20 February–1 March	DULUX BRITISH OPEN at Assembly Rooms, Derby Box office: 0332 369311
24–29 March	BENSON AND HEDGES IRISH MASTERS at Goffs, Kill, Co Kildare Box office: by post to venue
18 April–4 May	EMBASSY WORLD PROFESSIONAL CHAMPIONSHIP at Crucible Theatre, Sheffield By post to: Box Office, Crucible Theatre, 55 Norfolk Street, Sheffield S1 1DA

Although correct at time of going to press, all dates are subject to alteration.